THE MEXICAN REVOLUTION

A New Press People's History

ADOLFO GILLY

TRANSLATED BY PATRICK CAMILLER

THE NEW PRESS

NEW YORK
LONDON

First published as
La revolución interrumpida
By El Caballito, Mexico D.F. 1971

Expanded and revised editions, Verso Editions and NLB, London, 1983; and Ediciones Era,
Mexico, 1994

Requests for permission to reproduce selections from this book should be mailed to:
Permissions Department, The New Press, 38 Greene Street, New York, NY 10013

Published in the United States by The New Press, New York, 2005
Distributed by W. W. Norton & Company, Inc., New York

ISBN 1-56584-932-9 (hc.)
CIP data available

The New Press was established in 1990 as a not-for-profit alternative to the large,
commercial publishing houses currently dominating the book publishing industry. The
New Press operates in the public interest rather than for private gain, and is committed to
publishing, in innovative ways, works of educational, cultural, and community value that
are often deemed insufficiently profitable.

www.thenewpress.com

Composition by Westchester Book Composition

Printed in the United States of America

2 4 6 8 10 9 7 5 3 1

CONTENTS

Preface to the English-Language Edition

I wrote this book as a history and interpretation of the Mexican Revolution. Strictly speaking, it is not a work of investigation, but of reflection on what has been investigated and recounted and of synthesis of what remains scattered. Virtually all the factual material is drawn from the many writings of historians, witnesses, and protagonists of the 1910–20 revolution. My aim was to explain the logic of the revolutionary movement and the changes it brought to Mexican life, and at least to outline the conclusions for other countries and revolutions in Latin America, as well as in other parts of the contemporary world.

Many new studies have been published since the appearance in 1971 of the first Spanish-language edition of this book. I have also been able to consult other works that were not available to me in the restrictive conditions of Lecumberri, conducive though the prison calm may have been to study and reflection. However, all this new information does not alter the basic theses formulated in the text according to a certain expositive and interpretative method. Although the present edition incorporates new data and analysis, generally in endnotes but sometimes in the text itself, these do not modify the original conclusions in any fundamental way.

The first chapter, "Capitalist Development," is an exception in this respect. Without changing the basic view of the Porfirio Díaz era as one of headlong capitalist development in Mexico— a point now practically undisputed, though that was not the case when the first edition appeared—I have rewritten the whole chapter for this edition. Much of it has been thoroughly recast, but the main purpose has been to strengthen its framework of information and theoretical analysis.

Given my aim in writing this book, the endnotes are designed to throw further light on the main body of the text rather than to provide archival or bibliographic references in support of various assertions, or to facilitate later reading on the subject. This limitation has often been pointed out to me, especially in academic circles where such a backup is rightly considered almost obligatory. Nevertheless, if the author's limits or shortcomings as a historian are left aside, a series of complementary and, in my view, valid reasons may be given for the structure of the book.

Firstly, it is a work of political and cultural struggle, chosen at the time not only as a personal weapon with which to resist the oppression and arbitrariness of an absurd prison system like any other, but above all as a tool with which to prepare a continuation of the struggle for Marxism in Mexico and Latin America. My intention from the beginning was that it should be accessible, without any loss in scientific rigor, to a broad public stretching from academics to barely literate people; and that readers should be able to use it as an instrument of knowledge, understanding, and organization in their social revolutionary activity. This goal, which has, I hope, largely been realized, suffuses the style of the book and determines its structure.

Secondly, I could not have been successful in this task without the strictest attachment to historical truth. Every one of the factual points is based upon verifiable sources and has stood up to more than a decade of close examination and discussion. It is these data which underpin the character and sequence of the narrative. For although the selection of material inevitably involves an element of interpretation, I followed a basic rule throughout my work on the book: namely, to keep the presentation of facts strictly separate from an analysis of their significance, so that the reader may both register the historical information and, if necessary, dissent in part or in full from the given interpretation.

Perhaps the book's greatest innovation lies not in its assessment of the Mexican Revolution as a class war—a view held, to better or worse effect, by other writers—but in its *periodization of the whole cycle of the 1910–20 revolution* and its analysis of the process in interrelation with the broader world situation. Thus, it distinguishes the specific *curve of the revolution* and locates its peak at December 1914, whereas the school of history pragmatically impregnated with state ideology continues to see February 1917 as the culminating date.

Lastly, it is worth repeating the well-known point that a luxuriant apparatus of quotations and references is no guarantee of historical veracity or analytic rigor. The selection of data, sources, authors, and even quotations presupposes an interpretative criterion that is painfully lacking or deficient in more than one historical work: even if, from a formal point of view, the writer satisfies the most exacting academic requirements, a wealth of references cannot compensate for a dry text that lacks the understanding or imagination to choose and interrelate such material in faithful accordance with the movement of history.

Historical imagination is a loyal and indispensable servant of truth that has nothing in common with fantasy or caprice. It must be acquired in disciplines that allow us to grasp human beings, the subjects of history, as individuals, classes, and societies. These disciplines are none other than *rigor* of method and research, *love* of life, and practical *experience* of the social struggles in which the cloth of history is continually being woven and torn.

—Adolfo Gilly
Tepepan, Mexico D.F.
March 2005

FOREWORD

On October 2, 1968, several thousand Mexican students congregated in one of the oldest and most beautiful plazas of Mexico City, the Plaza de las Tres Culturas, to stage a peaceful protest against the policies of the Mexican government. The students demanded from the government the implementation of some of the main clauses of the constitution adopted by the victorious factions in Mexico's 1917 Revolution: freedom of the press, genuine elections, and freedom from police harassment. The speakers at the rally made sure to call on the students to carry out a policy of nonviolence and to demand peaceful changes in the country. As the meeting was nearing its end, a helicopter suddenly flew over the meeting and a flare lit up the square. At this point, troops arrived at the four corners of the historic square and began firing indiscriminately into the crowd. Hundreds were killed or wounded, hundreds if not thousands of others were imprisoned and some of them tortured in a military camp. This massacre was carried out by a government representing a political party, the *Partido Revolucionario Institucional*, which declared it was the legitimate heir of the Mexican Revolution. It is no wonder that many of Mexico's young people became completely disillusioned with the Mexican Revolution and sought inspiration and social models from outside the country.

Three years later in 1971, the first edition of the present book was published in Mexico. Its author, Adolfo Gilly, was a political prisoner being held since 1966 at the penitentiary of Lecumberri. The aim of the author was to return the revolution to the people. The book's success was phenomenal. Thousands of copies were sold in spite of the fact that the author was being held in jail. It was adopted as an official textbook by many faculties of history in Mexico. It was not only hailed by radical students who rediscovered the revolution through this book, but by people and intellectuals who had very different political opinions from those of the author. In an open letter to Adolfo Gilly, Mexico's Nobel Prize winning author, Octavio Paz, wrote: "Your contribution to the history of the Mexican Revolution is notable. In a few points you have said many new things, you have reminded us of others that we thought we had forgotten, and you have clarified things for us that seemed obscure."

Gilly's interest in the Mexican Revolution is definitely not a coincidence: since his early youth, Gilly had been either interested or directly involved in revolutionary movements. As a student of social sciences and law in Argentina, Gilly participated very actively in the political life of his country. He first joined the Socialist Party, but grew very critical of its policies and became a member of a revolutionary workers movement that was strongly inspired by the teaching of Russian revolutionary, Leon Trotsky. In 1955 he was an active participant in the general strike in Argentina that led to the resignation of Juan Domingo Perón. In subsequent years he was a socialist writer and organizer in the most diverse parts of Latin America and Europe. He lived in Bolivia from 1956 to 1960, where he cooperated with the Revolutionary Workers Party—a member of the Fourth International—in that country. In the sixties, he cooperated with the guerilla movement in Guatemala. He went to Colombia where he became friends with the revolutionary priest, Camilo Torres. In 1962 he went to Cuba, where he stayed through the missile crisis until he was expelled from the country in 1963 for no reason. This did not prevent a Cuban publishing house from publishing his book, *The Mexican Revolution* in 1998. In those years, Gilly constantly published articles and books throughout the world, but mainly in Latin America and the United States. His books *Inside the Cuban Revolution* and *The Guerilla Movement in Guatemala* were published by Monthly Review Press in the United States. In 1966 Gilly traveled to Mexico so he could enter Guatemala and establish contacts with the guerilla movement there. He was arrested by the Mexican police, charged with "subversion," and sentenced to six years in prison. That conviction was later reversed by the Mexican Supreme Court, a process that took six years while Gilly remained in prison. Fortunately, the penitentiary administration had segregated the political prisoners in a separate prison tract. The jail authorities obviously feared that these political prisoners might not only influence but organize other prisoners who were in the penitentiary.

The result was that the political wing of Lecumberri prison became a type of intellectual center. The prisoners discussed social, political, and economic problems, lectures were given, and manuscripts were scrutinized and criticized. Octavio Paz concurred with the opinion of U.S. historian, John Womack, when he called the prison of Lecumberri "our Institute of Political Science." Due to the help of friends inside and outside of the prison, Gilly was able to consult the most important works on the Mexican Revolution and other prisoners, many of them very knowledgeable about the revolution, who then discussed and criticized his manuscript.

Adolfo Gilly's exile from Mexico was not permanent. The prestige that his book had given him, as well as a series of articles that he had written on Mexico, and the help of prominent Mexican intellectuals—including Mexico's great writer, Carlos Fuentes—enabled Gilly to return to Mexico in 1976. He became a professor in the Department of Political Sciences at Mexico's National University and wrote a groundbreaking book on the administration of Lázaro Cárdenas, who carried out the most profound social reforms that Mexico underwent in the twentieth century. In 1982 Gilly was awarded Mexican citizenship and participated actively in the campaign of Cuauhtémoc Cárdenas against the regime of the *Partido Revolucionario Institucional*. When Cuauhtémoc Cárdenas became the first freely elected mayor of Mexico City, Gilly was one of the main collaborators in his reform-minded administration. These administrative activities did not prevent him from continuing to produce a spate of articles, essays, and books dealing with both contemporary and historical problems of Mexico, and to a lesser degree, of Latin America.

Gilly now had access to secondary and primary sources, which he could not study during the time that he spent in prison. His present book is not simply a translation of the book that he published in 1971. It is thoroughly revised, and greatly enriched. Do passion and historical accuracy contradict each other? At times this can be the case, but not in this book. Gilly is passionate about the popular classes of Mexico and their leaders, but equally objective about their weaknesses.

It is not surprising that Gilly's interest is concentrated on the popular movements that emerged during the revolution and which were led respectively by Emiliano Zapata and Francisco (Pancho) Villa. There is an enormous difference between the way these two movements and their leaders were portrayed—not only in the official historiography of the revolution in Mexico, but by many historians as well. Official historiography accepted Zapata into the pantheon of Mexican revolutionaries and very few historians, official or not, expressed any doubt as to the personal heroism and integrity of Zapata and his dedication to land reform. This attitude even extended to cold warriors in the United States. In the film *Viva Zapata,* director Elia Kazan, who had denounced many of his colleagues as communists and radicals before the House UN American Affairs Committee, eulogized the image of the revolutionary leader from Morelos.

This favorable attitude towards Zapata was not a coincidence. The victorious leaders from Sonora who ultimately assumed power at the end of the revolution in Mexico in 1920, hardly fought against Zapata, though they had earlier opposed his movement. It was thus not too difficult for them to co-opt his image. Their main battles had been fought against Pancho Villa. It was their rivals for national power, Venustiano Carranza and Pablo Gonzalez who had directed the fight against Zapata and were responsible for his assassination. For the cold warriors in the United States, Zapata was the one leader of a revolution in Latin America who had never attacked American interests. This had nothing to do with Zapata's personal attitude or that of his movement—he definitely was a Mexican nationalist—but with the fact that there were no American interests in Morelos and adjoining areas and very few Americans lived there. By embracing Zapata, official historiography had put him in a strait-jacket. In official parlance he was described as an agrarian reformer whose aims did not go beyond land reform. This is a view that Gilly does not accept. Gilly calls the embryonic state that Zapata and his movement created in Morelos, the Morelos Commune. The precedent for this, Gilly believes, was the Paris Commune that was established for several months in Paris after the war between Prussia and France in 1870. Both workers and artisans in Paris attempted to create a model for a new kind of state. What could the urban population of Paris have in common with the peasant population of Morelos? Gilly sees three kinds of similarities between the two states: both attempted to create direct democracy from below, both advocated and practiced egalitarianism, and both established public ownership of some of the main means of production (although the sugar factories of Morelos were owned and controlled by the state). The egalitarianism of Morelos was based in the village communities and direct democracy meant that it was these communities that elected representatives to regional power centers. By portraying Zapatismo in this way, Gilly not only contradicted official historiography but the views of a man who strongly influenced his ideas: Trotsky. The latter had stated: "The peasantry left to itself can only produce local detachments of guerrillas where a primitive democracy is only a cover for the personal dictatorship of the atamans."

The differences between Gilly's portrayal of both Villa and his movement and official historiography were far greater than they were with respect to Zapata. For many years it had been far more difficult for official Mexico to digest Pancho Villa views or to absorb him into the Official Pantheon of Mexican Heroes. This was not only due to the fact that the victorious factions of the revolution had waged their main battles against Villa, but that they also had him assassinated. Finally, Villa had attacked the United States and his acceptance as a genuine revolutionary might have jeopardized their efforts to gain U.S. recognition. In the 1920s he was portrayed as a bandit—with an army of marginals—and no statue of his could be erected and no street could be named in his honor. The result of this official oblivion was that Villa lived on more strongly in the popular imagination. Finally in the 1960s the government of Gustavo Díaz Ordaz, one of the most conservative and bloodthirsty governments that Mexico has produced (it was Díaz Ordaz who ordered the massacre of students in 1968), facing declining popularity, attempted to co-opt Villa by inscribing his name in gold letters in the Chamber of Deputies. Nevertheless only one merit was conceded to Villa—that of having played a major role in the defeat of Victoriano Huerta's conservative military dictatorship.

Gilly considers Villa a peasant leader and his movement a heterogeneous array of people from the countryside—*hacienda* peons, tenants, peasants, some industrial workers, and others—whose goal was the destruction of the *hacienda* system and the division of *hacienda* lands among Mexico's peasants. The motley composition of Villa's movement might constitute an explanation as to why Villa, who clearly wanted the division of landed estates, did not formulate a clear land reform program as did Zapata, whose agrarian basis of village communities was far more homogenous. Instead of a program, Gilly feels that Villa's personality became a rallying point of his movement: "Within the Villa movement the great majority of peons and agricultural workers in the North as well as those who were steeped in poverty found a purpose, they felt incorporated into a new kind of life and that for the first time they could express themselves, fight to win, take decisions, and stop being repressed and vanquished."

What inspired them was that their leader "was also a peasant, the best warrior, the best rider and the best peasant among them. Villismo did not have a program, as Zapata did, but it had the personality of Villa: for lack of a program his personality was a symbol of the peasants and the poor who had risen up in arms."

Some of the most moving parts of this book refer to a man who has been largely forgotten and ignored in the historiography of the Mexican Revolution: General Felipe Angeles. He was the only general in the Federal Army who joined the revolutionaries. In every possible respect he was the antithesis of the traditional military man both in Mexico and Latin America. He was humane. At a time when every revolutionary faction shot their prisoners, Angeles freed them all. He was not arrogant. Although Angeles was an educated military man and Villa was not, he always reiterated how proud he was to have served under Villa. He was also honest. He left the revolution as he entered it, a poor man. What made him even more exceptional was the fact that he was an intellectual, a rarity among the military. He was not a democrat. His wide-ranging readings of Karl Marx and Kautsky had converted him into a socialist.

In the final account one has to ask, why did this book exercise such a profound influence? Is it only because of the passionate, and in many respects original, way in which Gilly portrayed the popular forces of the revolution and their leaders? Certainly this played a major role in the enormous echo that the first edition of this book had in Mexico. It was also Gilly's refusal to depict the revolutionary opponents in black and white terms and to have made sense of the enormous complexity of the Mexican Revolution. But there was more to it than that. There was, above all, Gilly's historical optimism. At first glance such a statement might seem out of place. Unlike other historians, Gilly is firmly convinced that the popular forces were doomed to defeat. In spite of Zapata's national vision the peasant leaders lacked a national program and thus the victory of the far more conservative faction led by Venustiano Carranza in the civil war that engulfed Mexico was all but inevitable. What Gilly insists on, however, was that the military defeat of the peasant revolutionaries that gave power to a new ruling class was by no means final. The new rulers of the country who emerged from the revolution could not rule in the same way that Porfirio Díaz and his supporters had done. They could not afford to ignore and repress the popular forces in the same way that Diaz had. The ten years of revolutionary warfare had left an indelible mark on Mexico's workers and peasants. Industrial workers, miners, and oil workers who had set up unions could not be ignored. A new consciousness had emerged among many peasants that did not end with their defeat. They had retained their arms and learned how to fight. They were a force to be reckoned with. In addition, Mexico's new rulers were extremely wary of the upper class that was seeking to regain its power. Thus, they were forced to make concessions to the popular classes and to tolerate one of the most radical regimes to ever emerge in Latin America, the government of President Lázaro Cárdenas, who carried out one of the greatest land reforms in the history of the continent. His land reform destroyed the political, and to a large degree, the economic power of the traditional *hacendado* class. In much of Latin America it was this class that played a major role in supporting and establishing military dictatorships. Its disappearance in Mexico had one radical consequence: Mexico was one of the very few Latin American countries not to have experienced any military dictatorship and not to have any government since 1920 overthrown by force and violence.

At first glance, Gilly's historical optimism might have seemed out of place for many readers of his first edition book in 1971–72. The massacre of students in 1968 was followed by what is now known as a "dirty war" against guerillas largely produced by the government's repressive policies with methods not dissimilar to those used by South American dictatorships. Yet Gilly's optimism was not unwarranted. Only a few years later a huge popular movement led by Lázaro Cárdenas' son, Cuauhtémoc Cárdenas, in which Gilly took a prominent part, emerged and played a decisive role in the democratization of Mexico.

Friedrich Katz
April 2005

Friedrich Katz is the Morton D. Hull Distinguished Service Professor of Latin American History, and Co-Director of the Mexican Studies Program, at Chicago University. He is the author of The Secret War in Mexico: Europe, the United States, and the Mexican Revolution (*1981*), *which won the Bolton Prize for best book on Latin American History, and* The Life and Times of Pancho Villa (*1998*).

THE MEXICAN REVOLUTION

1

CAPITALIST DEVELOPMENT

Much more than any other Latin American country, Mexico won its independence from Spain through a popular war whose principal leaders, clergymen Miguel Hidalgo and José María Morelos, were also representatives of the Jacobin wing of the revolution. As elsewhere in Latin America, however, it was not this wing that consummated victory or began the task of organizing the newly independent country, but rather the conservative tendencies that in the course of the struggle were able to eliminate the radical wing as a result of the decline of the people's intervention in the war.

"The Revolution of Independence was a class war, and its nature cannot be understood correctly unless we recognize the fact that unlike what happened in South America, it was an agrarian revolt in gestation. This is why the army (with its *criollos* like [Augustin de] Iturbide), the Church and the great landowners supported the Spanish crown, and these were the forces that defeated Hidalgo, Morelos and Javier Mina," wrote Octavio Paz in *The Labyrinth of Solitude*.

Mexico also bore the full brunt of the first expansive thrust by U.S. capitalism. In 1847, following a course begun years earlier with the Texas war, the United States invaded the country and took possession of half its territory—some two million square kilometers, comprising the present-day states of Texas, Nevada, Utah, Colorado, New Mexico, Arizona, and California. Although British domination was then growing in the world, and particularly in Latin America, youthful North American capitalism acquired its "living space" by seizing Mexican land in the manner of the old wars of conquest. This plunder, which left its mark in the memory of the Mexican people, was subsequently legalized by the Treaty of Guadalupe Hidalgo, signed in February 1848.

Some ten years passed before the rise of nationally conscious forces centered on Benito Juárez and his group of liberal politicians who were to organize the foundations of modern Mexico. Their social base was those sections of the emergent bourgeoisie who sought a new mode of entrance into world trade and a restructuring of the Mexican market and internal space.[1]

In 1855 the Ayutla Revolution carried the Liberal Party to power on a program involving the organization of capitalist development. Its main objective was to break the legal fetters on the extension of capitalist relations and on the expansion of the internal market, beginning with the capitalist land market itself.[2] In 1856 the Liberals passed a disentailment act that prohibited religious and civil bodies from owning more land than they needed to carry out their functions. Any excess was to be sold to the tenants (on the basis that the annual rental equalled 6 percent of the value) or, if they did not buy it, to anyone who made suitable application. In this way, the Liberals set out to create a class of agrarian smallholders, placing on the market not only the lands of the clergy, but also, through the liquidation of old communal property structures, the land of the Indian communities.

The liberal principles of the Reform were ratified in the 1857 Constitution. Throughout Latin America, with peculiarities determined by each country's prior development and incipient entrance into the new world market, the juridical bases of bourgeois national organization were beginning to take shape at a level generally much more advanced than the social forces or economic and cultural development of the country in question.[3] In a certain sense, then, the juridical principles of the 1857 Constitution were those of an imaginary country: a liberal utopia that fired and guided the imagination of its authors, but was only partially embodied in its methods and relationship to the real country.[4]

The clergy and the big *latifundistas* grouped in the Conservative Party rose up against the Reform legislation; they enjoyed the ideological support of Pope Pius IX, who declared null and void both these laws and the Mexican Constitution itself. The ensuing Reform war, continued in the war against French intervention, lasted until 1867. In 1862 and 1863, the Conservatives received help from invading French troops, who placed Maximilian of Habsburg on the throne as Emperor of Mexico.

Napoleon III's imperialist adventure in Mexico (in which the United States, following its own interests, supported the Mexican Liberals) ended with the withdrawal of the defeated French forces. In June 1867, on the Querétaro heights, Maximilian was shot alongside his two Mexican Army commanders, Miramón and Mejía.[5] The Liberal victory opened the road to capitalism in Mexico—a country which, at that time, had eight or nine million inhabitants to its two million square kilometers.

As in every struggle during the rise of the bourgeoisie, the barely nascent Mexican bourgeoisie had to rely upon popular support and Jacobin methods in order to sweep away the institutions and structures inherited from colonial times that now impeded its development. Karl Marx defined Jacobinism as the plebeian method of settling accounts with the feudal enemies of the bourgeoisie. In its struggle against the clergy, landowners, and invading French troops, Juárez's faction based itself upon a national war and decreed such sweeping measures as the 1859 nationalization of Church property. This same law prescribed the complete separation of church and state; the secularization of all religious orders; a ban on religious congregation; and the nationalization of the clergy's rural and urban property. The radical character of Juarist liberalism would leave a powerful imprint upon the formal structure of the Mexican juridical system, co-existing in a strange symbiosis with the deeply religious beliefs of the people. It would also mark the thinking of all left-wing currents rooted in the national reality, even though they were not always aware of it.

The main result of the Reform legislation, however, was not the rise of a new class of smallholders—which can never be created by laws—but the further concentration of agrarian property in latifundia. Thus, in the years after the legislation came into effect, not only Church property but also the lands of the Indian rural communities were divided into small individual plots, soon to be acquired at a ridiculous price, or else directly seized by big *latifundistas* in the region. For many decades, the latifundia would grow by devouring Indian communal land, particularly in the central, most populous region of the country, and turning the Indian peasants into peons of the big landowners.

The path was different in the less populated North—a region marginal to colonial development which had no fixed indigenous population. In these huge, arid, and mountainous stretches of land, above all in Sonora and Chihuahua, nomadic Indian tribes resisted the white and mestizo settlers until the middle of the 1880s. Captured land had to be continually protected from the Apaches, so that, apart from big latifundia like Luis Terraza's two-million-hectare holdings in Chihuahua, a rural middle class sprang up on relatively small and medium-size ranches or mini-haciendas. It should not be forgotten, however, that in 1870 the northern states of Sonora, Sinaloa, and Baja California held only 3 percent of Mexico's total population.

It was in this way that capitalist relations spread in the Mexican countryside throughout Porfirio Díaz decades. With only one four-year interval, when Manuel González, a trusted replacement, took the helm, this regime lasted thirty-five years, from 1876 until 1911.

During this period, the government passed a number of settlement acts, under which so-called surveying companies were set up to enclose common land and attract foreign settlers to work on it. As payment for their services, these companies were left with a third of the land in question. Belonging to a small, government-linked oligarchy, they had enclosed some forty-nine million hectares by 1906—a quarter of Mexico's territory. There was no such quantity of common land, and so these companies were really the organizational form through which land was violently seized from the peasant villages and communities. Thus, the huge latifundia of the central region swept up whole village populations as hacienda peons or laborers. But in the North, where the farmers and settlers were imbued with a strong tradition of municipal and regional autonomy from the distant central government, local communities began to clash openly with the haciendas after the end of the Apache Wars in 1885, and above all in the years before and after the end of the century.

This massive operation of dispossession, which continued under new methods and with a different scope the practice begun in colonial times, was designed not only to form big agrarian properties, but also to create a supply of free day laborers owning nothing other than their labor-power. In order to clear a path for itself, capitalism needed to liquidate the communal lands in Central Mexico, just as it needed to rob the Yaqui and Mayo Indians of their rich valley land in Sonora State and to integrate their men as a labor force into the newly formed units.[6]

Although the conditions were different, capitalism had operated a similar dispossession and enclosure of common land in its early stages in England and in continental Europe. As in these other countries, the peasants in Mexico did not peacefully give up their land. The Indian villages held fast to their traditions and communal forms of organization, and, where they still had them, to the land deeds issued by the Spanish Crown. They resisted, organized revolts, suffered massacres, and returned to their land only to be driven back into the mountains. "Just bandits" and peasant legends sprang up, so that even today, just outside the Sinaloa State capital, fresh flowers are laid every day at the cross marking the death of Heraclio Bernal, the "Thunderbolt of Sinaloa." Thus, modern latifundist property, the backward form of capitalist expansion in the Mexican countryside, had to advance through constant warfare with the peasant villages.

Just as, in the struggle to liquidate the feudal structures of Church property, it had been compelled to lean on the masses and employ the plebeian forms and methods of Jacobinism, so, in its struggle against the peasants, the bourgeoisie had to rely upon the methods of appropriation and plunder everywhere characteristic of primitive capitalist accumulation. In other words, it had to combine its own capitalist relations of production with precapitalist relations of peon-type dependence upon the hacienda; the local and regional domination of *hacendados* and *caciques* not unlike lords of the manor; the Indian rural communities which resisted to the end; and even slave forms of exploitation of the workforce. The Yaqui Indians and other tribes, having been robbed of their land after bitter armed resistance in Sonora, were sent in whole families and communities to work as slaves on the far-off Valle Nacional tobacco plantations. Joining petty criminals, vagrants, unemployed workers, and people lured by the promise of high wages after a night of drinking, they would lead the most wretched existence before succumbing to exhaustion, undernourishment, and diseases.[7]

Unlike the original period of capitalist formation in Europe, however, this process of accelerated accumulation at the expense of precapitalist economic forms took place during the period of worldwide expansion of capitalism. In some ways, then, it resembled the plunder of the U.S. and Canadian Indians, and in other ways the colonial wars conducted by the imperialist countries. But the colonial war was waged by the Mexican landowner-bourgeois government in its own country and against its own people.

The Yaqui War of the late 1870s and early 1880s, for example, was a genocidal campaign through which the army seized the so-called Yaqui Valley, one of the best agricultural regions in Sonora State. The Yaquis, headed by their chief, Cajeme (José María Leyva), and after his death by Tetabiate, fought a heroic yet hopeless war. The valley lands, wonderfully suited for growing cotton, sugar, and other crops, were then handed over to big Mexican and American landowners,[8] while all the Yaqui men, women, and children who could not escape to put up a decade-long resistance in the arid mountainous regions were either pacified as hacienda peons or sent to perish as slave laborers in the Valle Nacional or on the Yucatán henequen plantations.[9]

The federal army launched a similar war to turn the Yucatán

Maya lands into big, export-oriented henequen plantations, shipping off many of the dispossessed Mayas to work as slaves in the Cuban sugar fields. Such was the early "nationalism" of the Mexican bourgeoisie.[10]

These acts of appropriation and plunder transferred huge quantities of land throughout the country. In a host of local "mini-wars" of the haciendas against the peasant villages, centered on the land or the waters (a powerful instrument of domination in the landowner's hands), private militias or the armed bodies of the state served to break down the peasants' resistance. The repressive forces that conducted these operations were the federal army—*la Federación*, as the peasants still call it—and the rural police or Guardia Rural, acting for the landowners, *caciques*, and local political bosses. The "levy," a form of conscription into the army or special "contingents" destined for the army, was itself a further method of repression, mostly in the towns. Many conscripted soldiers died or disappeared in the Yucatán and other "pacification" campaigns, while the levy served as a punishment for anyone considered an agitator.

The Guardia Rural was composed of men trusted by, and effectively under the orders of, the big landowners. Many of these were, in fact, former *bandoleros*—often landless peasants forced to become bandits—whom the Díaz regime offered a place in the Guardia Rural as a means of filling its repressive apparatus and considerably reducing the level of banditry. As always, the forces used against the peasantry were themselves peasants, recruited willingly or unwillingly into the armed bodies of the state.

This internal war, resting on the liberal legislation of the Juárez era and the Porfirist army that both implemented and perverted it, called forth a constant stream of peasant revolts. Some of these were fought under the banner of socialist utopias,[11] the best known being the rebellion of Julio Chávez López in Chalco, Mexico State.

In 1861 a Greek utopian socialist, Plotino Rhodakanaty, had arrived in Mexico with the aim of translating his ideas into agrarian communes, and in 1865 he had founded the School of Thunderbolt .

and Socialism with the later support of the anarchist Francisco Zalacosta. Their ideas, as happened with other peasant ideologies in Mexico, were similar to those of the Russian populists: in 1861 Alexander Herzen had already coined the motto of every agrarian revolt: "Land and Liberty." Chávez López, one of Zalacosta's followers, rose up in early 1868 at the head of a group of peasants that soon numbered more than a thousand, occupying haciendas in Texcoco, San Martín Texmelucan, Tlalpan, and Morelos State.

The government unleashed a wave of repression, and whole villages accused of aiding the rebels—Chicoloapan, for example— were deported to Yucatán. At the beginning of 1869, Chávez López wrote to Zalacosta from Puebla: "I've now arrived here. There's a lot of discontent among the brothers because all the generals are trying to get their land. What would you think if we carried out the Socialist Revolution?" For its part, the Mexico City press demanded even more stringent measures. Insurgents were roaming the countryside, it reported, "proclaiming war on the rich and calling for redistribution of hacienda lands among the Indians."

In Chalco, on April 20, 1869, Chávez López gave the ever growing movement a programmatic banner in his *Manifesto to the Poor and Oppressed of Mexico and the World*. Although the peasant leader was influenced by Rhodakanaty's Fourierist ideology, his methods combined Zalacosta's anarchist doctrine of direct action with the older peasant tradition of armed uprising. He thereby distanced himself in practice from the pacifist Greek socialist. The *Manifesto* denounced the exploitation of the peasantry by the landowners, government, and Church, the plunder of village land (against which the Zapatist revolution would rally forty years later), the robbery in employers' shops, the debt slavery transmitted from father to son, and the wretched level of day-wages. His cry was the same as those launched a century or so earlier by Tupaj Amaru in Peru and Tupaj Katari in Bolivia: the landowners, "who ask us to resign ourselves," are the very ones who "have tirelessly exploited us and feasted on the sweat of our brows."

The aims of the movement were summarized as follows:

Brothers!
We want socialism, which is the most perfect form of living together in society. It is the philosophy of truth and justice, contained in the unshakeable triad: Liberty, Equality, Fraternity.

We seek to destroy at root the present evil of exploitation, which condemns some to be poor and others to enjoy riches and well-being; which turns some into wretches even though they work with all their might, and provides others with a life of bliss and leisure.

We want land to sow in peace and reap in tranquility, so that everyone is free to sow where it suits them best without having to pay any kind of tribute; so that everyone is free to unite as they think most fit, forming large or small agrarian societies that will jointly defend themselves without any need for a group of men to command and punish them.

We seek to abolish any trace of tyranny among equal men who will live in societies of brotherhood and mutual aid, establishing the Universal Republic of Harmony.

Mexicans! Such is our simple plan, which will triumph in some form after the true victory of freedom. We shall be persecuted, perhaps even riddled with bullets. But it does not matter, so long as hopes beat in our breast! What have we in life but to die rather than allow the burden of misery and suffering to continue for ever? We are scorned as liberals, branded as socialists and condemned as human beings. We must look beyond the present and raise our hearts around the sacred banner of the socialist revolution—the banner which proclaims from the heights of the Republic: *Abolish government and exploitation*! Let us look calmly towards our salvation, which lies in ourselves.

Shortly after issuing his *Manifesto*, Chávez López fell into the hands of government troops but managed to escape with the help of peasant sympathizers. He then continued his campaign, attacking haciendas, occupying villages, burning municipal records, and collecting fresh supplies of arms and money. In the end, federal troops under General Ramón Cuellar, who had already destroyed the villages in rebel areas, captured Chávez López and put his comrades to flight. The peasant leader was taken to Chalco, and on September 1, 1869, in the courtyard of the School of Thunderbolt and Socialism, he was shot on the direct instructions of the Juárez government.

Francisco Zarco analyzed this judicial murder in terms that, exactly a century later, would be used by less illustrious Mexican journalists to justify political repression against revolutionaries:

> Julio Lopez has ended his career on the scaffold. *He invoked communist principles, and was nothing but a common criminal.* The destruction of his gang makes property safe in many other parts of Mexico State. Here, as in many other states of the republic, it will eventually become an urgent task to deal with the question of landed property. But this must be done through carefully prepared legislative measures, in an atmosphere of calm and serenity, not through violent, revolutionary means.

Benito Juárez, like Porfirio Díaz somewhat later, mercilessly crushed this and all other peasant risings. In the heart of Mexico, too, capitalism thrust itself forward "dripping from head to toe, from every pore, with blood and dirt." Its methods were violence, murder, robbery, plunder, trickery, and constant bloodbaths.

However, it was also the world market context of 1870–1910 which made this the natural path of capitalist development in the conditions obtaining in Mexico at that time. Thus, the first impact of modern capitalism had involved the loss of half the national territory to an expansionist United States. Next came the internal growth of capitalist relations under the Porfirio Díaz regime—that is to say, the loss of Mexico's remaining territory by its age-old owners, the Indian peasantry; and the concentration of this property in the hands of a small number of Mexican and foreign landowners through methods in no way different from the colonial plunder analyzed by Rosa Luxemburg in *The Accumulation of Capital.*

The *army war* was just the surface of a more powerful and destructive *commodity war*, through which market relations expanded on the basis of the faster world extension of capitalism and its entry into the age of imperialism. This process involved determinate cycles of expansion, or wavelike pulsations of central capital corresponding to changes in Mexico and South America.

Thus, during the Porfirio Díaz regime, the separation of the producers from their means of production and the shift to generalized commodity regulation of labor-power (wages) and surplus-product extraction also proceeded through the multiform ruination of small agrarian and urban owner-producers and the resulting concentration of property without a display of armed violence. This aspect is obscured by bourgeois-liberal historians, the descendants of positivist thought, who paint the "dark history" of Porfirism by referring almost solely to agrarian spoliation. In reality, the transition from the Juarist era of the Reform and the Restored Republic to the Porfirio Díaz regime (particularly after the 1880–84 González interlude) coincides quite precisely with the world-market passage from free competition to the imperialist era.

In the sixteenth century, the wealth of New Spain had been one of the factors determining the world market that took shape under the impact of merchant capital. With the Wars of Independence, however, this whole region experienced a radical break in the late-colonial economic equilibrium and in a mode of insertion into the world market already shaken by the irresistible penetration of British and other contraband goods. The post-Independence "period of anarchy," as it is known in Mexico and other Latin American countries, then exhibited a breakdown in everything but the central government: the political order fragmented and whole regions fell under the sway of military *caudillos*; the economy shrank into local spheres and, to some extent, autarky; and trade either dried up or took a very hazardous course.

Only in the 1840s or thereabouts did a commercial bourgeoisie and its urban political representatives begin their slow and shaky ascent. This period of autonomous growth and gradual internal accumulation of capital was, of course, the time when free-market capitalism was conquering space in its heartlands—a process, symbolized by the spread of railways in Europe and the United States, that involved the loss of half of Mexico's original territory. Until about the mid-1860s, the lack of export capital entailed that, despite some limited investments, the direct production of surplus value in large-scale industry was almost entirely confined to Western Europe and the United States. The process of primitive accumulation continued to prevail over the logic of capital accumulation in the peripheral countries, only gradually dissipating the intricate web of small-scale urban and rural production. And since the industrial revolution advanced more slowly in transport than in manufacturing, the means of communication were in short supply on a world scale (above all in the less developed countries).

In the 1850s and 1860s, Mexico underwent its process of national formation under the aegis of the Juarist bourgeoisie. The state now created the juridico-political conditions for development of the relations of capitalist production and national consolidation of the internal market[12] (the Reform legislation, the 1857 Constitution, the strengthening of central government even beyond the framework of constitutional federalism). Liberal ideology reflected these conditions of development, while the Conservatives embodied, in broad outline, the staunch resistance of classes and client layers dominant in the old forms of production.

Another influence began to make itself felt in the 1870s: namely, the expansive thrust of a central capital that had now captured and consolidated its European and North American spheres, through the national unification of Germany and Italy and the American Civil War. By the 1880s the new expansion was having its full effect on Mexico, most evident in the dizzying spread of the railway network. Thus the total length of track soared from 666 kilometers in 1876 and 1,080 kilometers in 1880 to 5,891 kilometers in 1884, and then grew steadily if less sharply to reach some 20,000 kilometers in 1910.

The world was then entering the era of imperialism, which would determine the form of Mexico's emergence into the new world market and the process of material accumulation, as well as the new forms of labor exploitation. We should mention here the modern Porfirian hacienda and plantation economy; the industrial development in railways, textiles, foodstuffs, and then electricity; the new rise and modernization of the mining industry; the ruination of artisan and small peasant producers; and the tendency toward proletarianization and pauperization, involving a large and permanent industrial reserve army, with the resulting downward pressure on wages.[13]

The history of Porfirian Mexico revolves around the adjustment and headlong development of national capitalism in the conditions of world capital expansion marking the rise of imperialism; and hence around the accumulation of contradictions that brought the Mexican social formation to the outbreak of revolution in 1910. In more abstract terms, it is the history of a long period of dynamic equilibrium separating two revolutions: the Reform, which laid the basis for its existence, growth, and expansion; and the Mexican Revolution, engendered by the crisis in which the inherent contradictions of the process sought resolution.

As is well known, the real treasure found by the *conquistadores* in Mexico was the educated, disciplined workforce of the despotic-tributary societies, those vast masses who built the pyramids and irrigation canals, the precolonial "Thebes of the seven gates."[14]

From colonial times to the Republic, the Mexican economy may be seen as a succession of forms, changing in regard to both the system of domination and labor-power itself, in which this massive workforce was organized by the dominant classes for the extraction of the surplus product. The original *encomienda* system, involving the right to demand tribute and labor from the Indians of a particular area, directly articulated the Spanish Empire (and, through it, the emergent capitalism of Western Europe) with the agrarian communities that had been the base and source of surplus product for the dominant castes of the despotic-tributary regimes destroyed by the Conquest. This direct articulation, rather like a gearbox supposed to link the cogs of a huge iron wheel with a fragile wooden wheel, precipitated one of the greatest catastrophes in human history over little more than a century. About 90 percent of the pre-Conquest population[15] was annihilated as a result of overwork, disease, malnutrition, and systematic destruction of the equilibrium underlying its old conditions of existence, reproduction, and interchange with nature. Its bones, muscles, nerves, brain-matter, and life were almost literally transmitted into the mass of precious metal which, passing through Spain, enormously accelerated the initial impetus with which European capitalism was entering the world.

Used by the Spaniards as a cost-free labor tribute for the building of towns, palaces, and churches, this Indian labor-power went on reproducing itself in the agrarian community and providing the basic foodstuffs and domestic services for the Spanish dominant classes and assimilated remnants of the indigenous nobility. However, it was above all in the mines—the basic motor-force of the whole colonial enterprise—that such manpower was an indispensable asset. For not only did the *encomienda* system allow it to be forcibly employed on all these tasks; it placed no limits on its exploitation and swallowed up human lives with the same speed and intensity that the mines themselves displayed in devouring whole woodland areas. As disease added its effects to those of exploitation, the free fall in the supply of labor-power soon compelled a halt to the big construction works. A food system had to be found that did not rely exclusively on the indigenous community, and the provision of labor-power and mine supplies had to be organized on a new basis.[16]

The hacienda system that then emerged became, through successive transformations, the center of gravity of the Mexican economy for the next two and a half centuries. In other words, it became the main instrument for regulating the use of labor-power and extracting the surplus product, including that produced in the surviving indigenous communities, just as the extractive industry remained the principal channel along which a major part of that surplus product was transferred abroad.[17] This role explains the hacienda's vitality as an economic unit and its long-term ability to reproduce and stabilize the system.

The hacienda was the crucial gearbox that prevented the tough, fast-moving iron wheel of mining—bound up with the requirements of the world capitalist market and the formation of a wealthy dominant class in the colonial towns—from continuing to destroy the cogs of the slow, rudimentary wooden wheel of the indigenous community, then the main ground for the reproduction of labor-power and the extraction of the labor or product surplus. The Spanish hacienda institution was adapted to Mexico in the seventeenth century, and in the course of the eighteenth century it was consolidated as the main element regulating the use of labor-power. Since the plentiful supply of manpower had been squandered and exhausted in the previous period, the towns, mines, and haciendas developed various expedients for attracting and fixing their own workforce, including the gradual extension of wage labor and its subsidiary hybrid, debt-peonage.

In the evolving system, the hacienda acquired a fixed workforce in the shape of peons, servants, and artisans such as smiths, carpenters, masons, and even weavers. At the same time, according to the seasonal rhythm of field labor, it absorbed and repelled manpower from the indigenous communities. This labor-power continued to be mainly reproduced within the community: its surplus product was sucked out through the hacienda, which in turn produced food and other goods for the mines, the towns, and itself. Those who have seen the hacienda as an autarkic or closed economy cannot account for the fact that, right up to the time of Independence, it was the center of an economy directly linked to the world market through the export of precious metals.

Now, this colonial hacienda, where relations of servile dependence were already combined with imperfect forms of wage labor, was not the same as the later Porfirian hacienda, with its plantation system directly producing for both the internal and world markets. Between the two lie the Wars of Independence, the anarchic collapse of the colonial economy, the disintegration of the colonial hacienda itself, and the capitalist reconstruction of the hacienda system that began with the disentailment of Church property and communal lands and continued into the Porfirian era.

The colonial hacienda either took shape around good land whose occupants had been exterminated, or else directly seized the best communal land. Yet it also had to establish a metabolic relationship of coexistence with the agrarian community. In this way, the hacienda was remarkably elastic vis-à-vis the product and labor markets. It could withdraw into subsistence economy or expand its market output according to the cycle of the economy, so that it served both a regulatory and preserving role within the system.

For most of the peasant majority of the population, the hacienda also embodied and focused the power of the dominant classes, representing not the fragmented sovereignty of the feudal order, but the delegated fragmentation of the central power of the Viceroyship. The combined force of the Napoleonic wars in Europe and the revolutions of independence in Latin America destroyed the colonial state as an extension of the Spanish absolutist state. But the Revolution of Independence in Mexico did not succeed in creating another sufficiently cohesive central power able to exert its control over all the national territory. The fragmentation of power in the haciendas was prolonged under the Republic, while vast sectors of peasant society also escaped the control of the haciendas, folding themselves into the self-sufficient indigenous communities.

Together with his stewards and administrators, the figure of the *hacendado* personified the power of the dominant classes. The hacienda had a prison, a church, and a priest, distributing rewards and punishments for this life and the next. Indeed, as in the feudal system, the agrarian classes perceived no distinction between political and economic institutions, grounded as they were on the arbitrary, total power of the *hacendado*. This function then passed, suitably transformed, from the colonial to the Porfirian hacienda, so that the institution came to stand as the material form of the peasants' oppression and the principal object upon which their revolutionary fury would be vented after 1910. The same force that impelled the plebeian assault on the Bastille in 1789 drove the Mexican peasantry to capture the numerous Bastilles of the Porfirian haciendas. In the oral tradition of many peasant soldiers of the revolutionary armies, the revolution itself appeared as a series of hacienda seizures rather than an overthrow of the central state power.

Unlike the colonial hacienda, its Porfirian counterpart constituted itself in a direct link with the demands of an internal and world market whose norms were imposed by the dynamic of capitalist accumulation. This altered its relationship to the labor force, although tradition and the persistence of human memory transmitted many of the forms of domination and subordination.

In their constant disputes with the *hacendados* for land, water, woodland, pasture, and labor, the peasant communities had acquired a certain conflictual stability in their relationship with the colonial hacienda. But the new capitalist hacienda, developed on the basis of the disentailment acts, launched an ever more aggressive assault on these communities. Its greater land-hunger was determined not so much by the need to extend the surface under cultivation—huge areas devoured by the haciendas remained untilled—as by the need to release manpower by expropriating communal means of production and throwing the labor force onto the market. Nevertheless, the community largely retained its social role in reproducing labor-power, albeit in the surrogate forms of the peasant family and the landless or near-landless village.[18]

This land-hunger, actually a hunger for labor-power and the surplus value it produces, motivated the hacienda war on the villages and indigenous tribes and sparked, in turn, the countless revolts and lesser forms of resistance. The characteristic methods, ideologies, and motor-forces of peasant resistance brought up to date the old defensive war of the Mexican people against the agrarian, urban, and metropolitan exploiters.

At the same time, the Porfirian hacienda achieved a certain equilibrium in its utilization of labor-power, not only through state and private coercion of the workers, but also because this labor force accepted the framework of its relations with the hacienda and the development of various categories tied to the hacienda by diverse bonds of dependence and reciprocity. It was a complex system of agrarian social relations that constituted the rural basis of the *Pax Porfiriana*.

The hacienda workforce fell into four broad classes:

1. Permanently resident or cottage-dwelling peons, tillers, ranch hands, shepherds, and artisans living in the hacienda. Apart from their wage, they had the right to cultivate a small plot in the hacienda, to keep animals on hacienda land, and to draw a yearly ration of maize. Their job was to till the hacienda land or look after its livestock, but sometimes they also had to perform domestic tasks or even to go off and fight for the hacienda. This group was normally a minority of the workforce.

2. Seasonal workers, whether inhabitants of indigenous villages and agrarian communities or small landowners who had to supplement their income. The mode of payment was quite varied, but it included a wage component. The subcategory of so-called vagrant Indians migrated between various haciendas, mines, and towns in search of temporary waged employment.

3. Sharecroppers who lived in the hacienda and tilled a portion of its land. A part of their produce was paid to the hacienda as a lease, while the other part constituted their own income. Payment in kind was generally supplemented by labor duties.

4. Tenants who paid in cash or in kind to rent a certain amount of land, sometimes as much as a whole ranch. Like joint owners, they were able to hire their own workers.[19]

All these forms presented wide variations, readily combining with one another in different ways. Contradictions therefore appeared among the workforce and sometimes reached the point of open conflict—for example, between peons tied to the hacienda by their cottage, and seasonal workers resident in outlying villages and communities. This was naturally an obstacle to unity against the *hacendado*, and resulted in a highly complex mode of domination.

Already present in the colonial hacienda, such relations developed in various combined forms on its Porfirian counterpart. With the growing extension of wage and commodity relations, the dynamic haciendas were ever more directly linked to the raw materials and capital markets, yet continued to exist alongside traditional haciendas in a multiplicity of forms characteristic of any transitional period. Particularly after 1880, however, when Mexico witnessed the growth of cities, railways, manufacturing and extractive industries, a banking system, and money circulation, it was the haciendas producing sugar, livestock, cotton, henequen, coffee, and other primary products for the expanding world market that most clearly defined the capitalist features of the Porfirian hacienda. Precapitalist relations of dependence did still supplement the wage in tying down the labor force. But since the precise combination varied from one hacienda to the next, it is very difficult to draw any general picture.[20]

With these precautions in mind, we may now try to describe a typical hacienda in Central Mexico, where the supply of labor was quite plentiful and farmers mainly grew produce such as maize, wheat, and pulque for the internal market.

As a rule, the hacienda was comprised of the following: a central area, sometimes enclosed by high protective walls, in which were to be found the landowner's mansion along with all the comforts and trappings of the landed aristocracy; middle-grade housing for the steward and adminstrative staff; the hacienda offices, shop, church, jail, barns, and stables; a fruit and vegetable garden for the *señores* and their immediate family; and sometimes a small school for the employees' children.

The hacienda shop sold such items as coarse cloth, maize, beans, soap, and aguardiente, nearly always charging the peon more than the market price. These goods were advanced against his wage, which therefore sometimes involved only a minimal cash transaction. Not only did such payment in kind swell the employer's profits at the peon's expense; the accumulation of store debt, especially on occasions like a wedding, a birth, a funeral, or a period of sickness, further served to tie the laborer to the hacienda. Moreover, since the debt usually exceeded the means of payment, it was carefully recorded and transmitted from father to son. If an indebted peon tried to leave the hacienda, he would be hauled back by the *rurales* and become liable to punishment for theft.[21] For a long time, the lack of an alternative perspective bolstered the various forms of dependence on the *hacendado*. But when such a perspective seemed to emerge in the revolutionary movement, it blew apart the framework of submission and apparent consent.

Previous research and debate have yielded contradictory results concerning the role of debt-peonage in tying labor-power to the hacienda. Its significance seems to have varied with the region and period, as was the case with all kinds of forced labor. However, the widespread survival of more or less concealed forms of personal dependence heightened the conservative and retrograde character of the hacienda system in the eyes of the most dynamic social forces. Even for modern, typically capitalist landowners like the Madero family, the hacienda seemed to embody the backward, ossified social and political relations against which the revolutionary movement would focus its attack.

The railway became the very symbol of capitalist expansion in Mexico. In this rugged land, where the populous central plateau is surrounded by mountains and even the few navigable rivers can only be negotiated for limited stretches, a modern internal market absolutely required an answer to the problem of communication. The obvious solution—substitution of a railway network for the mule-tracks and cart- or coach-roads—could only be realized if it was in accord with the exigencies and capacities of capital in the central countries. The first railway concession was granted in 1837 to a rich Veracruz merchant, who was supposed to build the Mexico

City–Veracruz line. But it was only on January 1, 1873, after a number of fruitless transfers of construction rights, that the line was actually opened. Whereas a mere 205 kilometers had been completed by 1869, the remainder was finished in the space of four years. When Porfirio Díaz took over the presidency in 1876, Mexico had only 660 kilometers of track, on 114 of which mules were used as a traction force. By 1880 local companies operating regional state concessions had laid a further 226 kilometers.

The great change began in 1880. Foreign capital, which had not previously been compelled to expand, now responded to Mexican government offers and dramatically burst into the country's life.[22] In the years that followed, the railway network grew at dizzying speed: from a total of 1,086 kilometers at the end of 1880 to 1,661 in 1881, 3,583 in 1882, and 5,308 in 1883; or, to put it another way, at an annual rate of 21.6 percent, 52.9 percent, 115.7 percent, and 48.1 percent, respectively. The length of track then climbed to 7,680 kilometers in 1887 and 9,558 in 1890. By the turn of the century, it had nearly reached 14,000 kilometers. Mexico's railway network totalled 19,205 kilometers at the end of the Díaz era in 1910, and it has since grown only slightly to reach some 23,000 kilometers.

The railways were built and operated by British and North American companies, which, as in every other country save Britain itself, received huge grants in land and money. The state undertook to pay them a subsidy of six thousand pesos for every kilometer laid in flat regions, rising to twenty thousand pesos in the mountains; to supply them with free land "necessary" for railway construction; to authorize compulsory employment of the local population for a wage not exceeding fifty centavos a day; to exempt their capital from all taxation for a period of twenty years, and to waive customs duty on imported material; and, in some cases, to allow them to organize their own railway police, with the same attributions as those of the state police.

The network spread out from the center to the seaports (especially on the Gulf of Mexico) and to the northern frontier, covering the line of the historic trade routes drawn by geography and economics. In the emergent era of imperialism, however, exports were designed to meet the need for raw materials on a world market that was more dynamic and demanding than ever before. Thus, whereas the first railway, the Mexico City–Veracruz line, followed the most traditional foreign-trade route of New Spain, the great extensions that began in the 1880s directly linked the country to the U.S. network. Indeed, if one studies the genesis and structure of the two, they seem to merge into a single system; or, rather, the northward expansion of the Mexican railways seems to fuse with the southward spread of the North American network. The railway heralded a process of integration whereby the Mexican economy, in distinctive phases, yet with great depth and intensity, became subordinated to its North American counterpart.[23]

At its densest in the more populous and economically vital center of Mexico, the railway system changed the shape of the regions through which it passed: it radically altered local markets and price structures; it redrew the parameters of landed property by raising the value of land near the railway; it greatly increased the mobility of both goods and labor; it implanted the railway industry as a modern sector, free of artisan encumbrances, at the very heart of national economic activity; it proletarianized peasants and artisans for work on the construction and operation of the railways; and its progress through the country sharpened the regional inequality of Mexico's development.[24]

The railway transformed local life and hastened the disintegration of the old customs and norms of peasant existence. At the same time, of course, it spurred on the plunder of village land so characteristic of the Porfirian era, thereby provoking uprisings and resistance movements among the peasantry.[25]

The march of the railways also consolidated the political domination of the federal government, enabling it to speed troops to distant parts of the country and to crush local revolts like the Rio Blanco textile strike. Thus national unification acquired not only an economic character, but also the capitalist political content of centralized repression.

In 1905 the minister without portfolio Pablo Macedo wrote that the government could now rapidly use its troops to put down any revolt before it was able to spread. As opposed to the situation a few decades earlier, "the government of the Republic can now, thanks to the railway, make its power and authority felt in the remotest part of Mexico, quashing any sign of unrest or rebellion in fewer days than it used to take months." Not many years later, however, this wonderful "invention" turned into its opposite: the railway became the thruway of revolution.

Without arousing the slightest suspicion in the foreign owners and the Díaz regime, the railway system gave to the revolutionary armies their lines of movement and supply, acquiring such extraordinary importance that the image of the train became inextricably associated with the advances, battles, victories, and defeats of the revolution. The railway accentuated the highly mobile character of the armed struggle, already determined by the existence of huge uninhabited areas. Broadening the sweep of the struggle, it assisted those great transfers of military and human forces which, together with other factors, broke down the peasants' quietist isolation and forged the character of Mexico and its people.

The establishment of an internal market, the integration of the Mexican economy into the new world market, and the development of capitalist production under Porfirio Díaz should be seen as three aspects of a single movement. Its remarkably dynamic character is apparent from a large number of indicators.[26]

The railways expanded together with the whole communications system: the telegraph lines built alongside the track; the roads, on which banditry was reduced and sometimes even eliminated; the military and postal installations; and the first urban systems of electric lighting and drinking water.

Between 1895 and 1910, the number of towns with more than twenty thousand inhabitants rose from twenty-two to twenty-nine, and their combined population increased by some 44 percent. During the same period, town-dwellers grew from 9.2 to 11 percent of the total population, although these figures conceal a great unevenness of development. Thus, while old mining towns such as Zacatecas, San Luis Potosí, and Guanajuato were losing part of their population, other centers like Torreón (a new railway junction), Chihuahua, and Monterrey were rapidly growing in the North, Veracruz and Merida in the Gulf region, and, to a lesser extent, Mexico City, Guadalajara, Aguascalientes, and Toluca in central Mexico. The towns were ever more clearly becoming the centers of political decision making.

Monetary circulation grew at such a rate that it alone is enough to express the dynamic penetration of market relations. From little more than 25 million pesos in 1880–81, the mass of money in circulation had already climbed to 86 million in 1893–94 and stood at 310 million in 1910–11—*a twelvefold increase* in a thirty-year period during which wholesale prices only doubled. The number of pesos per capita rose, at a very uneven regional rate, from 2.46 in 1880–81 to 20.37 in 1910–11. Whereas metal coinage was the only medium of circulation at the beginning of the Díaz era, banknotes began to spread in the early 1880s in the major zones of economic activity, and bank deposits on call made their appearance in the 1890s. By 1910 metal coinage accounted for 38 percent of the money supply, banknotes for 38 percent, and deposits for the remaining 24 percent. The banking system underwent an important expansion. Although most of its capital was foreign-owned, a certain amount came from funds accumulated in the country by outside investors. In 1896 local customs barriers were finally abolished and the taxation system was modernized and centralized.

Foreign trade was another area of profound change. In the thirty-three years between 1877 and 1910, per capita exports quadrupled and imports very nearly tripled. The mass of exports increased six-fold at an average yearly rate of 6.1 percent, while imports grew three and a half times at an average of 4.7 percent.[27] As for the composition of foreign trade, exports began to shift away from the precious metals (above all silver) that made up 65 percent of the total at the start of the *Porfiriato*. Industrial metals took up a strong position, and traditional agricultural products such as henequen, pelts, and wood were joined by coffee, livestock, and chickpeas. In the import field, where manufactured consumer goods declined with the development of local industry, the share of raw materials and capital goods rose from 47 percent in 1889 to 57 percent in 1910. Machinery imports grew by some 170 percent between 1888 and 1910.

Industrial plants expanded at a sustained rate:

> The means of payment which the country could count on as a result of growing exports and the entry of foreign capital made it possible to acquire the requisite machinery, construction materials, equipment and other goods from abroad. These elements arrived together with more efficient labor systems, depending at first upon coal-fuelled steam-engines and later upon the motive force of electricity. The great technical innovations had their main impact in mining, metallurgy and the processing industries that developed in the large urban centers. Such activities were precisely those associated with the electrical industry, which appeared in the 1880s and was booming strongly in the first decade of the twentieth century.[28]

The geographical spread of the capacity installed in the electrical industry confirms the uneven character of industrial growth. In 1910, 80 percent was concentrated in the center of the country, 10.4 percent in the Gulf of Mexico region, 6.5 percent in the North, and only 3.5 percent in the northern and southern Pacific regions.

The influx of foreign capital played a decisive role in this process, above all when excess capital in the capitalist heartlands began to seek fresh fields. Foreign investment in Mexico totalled some 110 million pesos in 1884, rising dramatically to 3.4 million pesos in 1911. (The peso was on a par with the dollar at the beginning of the Porfirio Díaz regime, but in 1905, the year gold replaced silver as the base of the Mexican currency system, it was exchanging at the rate of two to one.)

In 1911 these investments were distributed as follows: railways, 33.2 percent; extraction industries, 27.1 percent (mining and metallurgy, 24 percent; oil, 3.1 percent); public debt, 14.6 percent; commerce and banking, 8.5 percent (banks, 4.9 percent; commerce, 3.6 percent); electricity and public services, 7 percent; agriculture, fishery, and forestry, 5.7 percent; processing industry, 3.9 percent. Sixty-two percent of foreign investment derived from European capital (of which 90 percent was British and French) and 38 percent from American capital. At that time, however, Mexico absorbed only 5.5 percent of U.S. foreign investment. European capital was diversifying its holdings in Mexico, while U.S. investment was concentrated in those branches—railways and extractive industries—that strictly complemented the North American economy.[29]

These proportions naturally fluctuated throughout the 1880–1910 period, and the involvement of national capital varied from one industry to the next. In textiles, the main processing industry of the time, the French capital stake derived partly from the metropolis and partly from on-the-spot reinvestment by French companies operating in Mexico. Another important branch, the steel industry, developed through a similar combination of new foreign investment, Mexican national capital, and reinvestment by foreign companies already present in the country. Mexican industrial capital was largely concentrated in the food and drink industry and— alongside Spaniards, Turks, Armenians, and Chinese—in the retail trade. Thus, the capital and economic power of the Mexican property-owning classes was still rooted in the big ranches, sugar, cotton, and coffee plantations, and the large or medium-size export farms. Even here, however, there was sizeable foreign investment in the latifundia of the North and in the cotton, india rubber, sugarcane, and coffee plantations.

The concentration of land ownership reached huge proportions. According to the 1910 Census, Mexico had a population of 15,160,400 for its 1,972,546 square kilometers. The rural population accounted for 80 percent, living in villages with fewer than five thousand inhabitants. The economically active population numbered 5,272,100, of which 3,592,100 or 68.1 percent worked in agriculture and fishing. In addition, the Census recorded 834 *hacendados* who, with 167,968,814 hectares in their hands, were the true masters of the national territory.

The years of the *Porfiriato* witnessed the consolidation of the youngest and most modern class in Mexico: the proletariat. It may, perhaps, be traced back to the textile workers of the post-Independence period; to the miners who, during colonial times, worked for a combination of a wage and a *partido* or share in output;[30] or the cigar workers who, after the viceroyship established a tobacco monopoly in 1764, were employed in huge concentrations like the Mexico City works (seven thousand in the year 1800).

Strictly speaking, however, all these sectors were part of the preparatory formation of a new proletarian class out of peasant and artisan layers. The real impetus came with the development of large-scale industry, around which a host of small workshops continued to revolve, and the generalization of wage labor as the sole means of subsistence for a class of workers owning nothing but their labor-power. This process took its final form in the Restored Republic and the early years of the Porfirian era, so that in the last two decades of the nineteenth century wage labor came to occupy the structurally, if not numerically, dominant position in the whole system of work relations.

From its origins in the Conquest and the colony, the Mexican labor force grew under the weight of a potent overdetermination. The bottomless pool of rural labor led, on the one hand, to a *constant squandering of manpower* and a depreciation of human life which, since the great fusion and wrenching of the Conquest, has spawned a distinctively Indo-Spanish ideology of death, recycled by capitalism to normalize the staggering disregard for safety at work; and, on the other hand, to a swollen industrial reserve army and a *constant downward pressure on wages.* This is one reason why whole generations of Mexican workers have found it so difficult to develop trade-union organization and to secure their gains, and why labor leaders have fairly easily eluded their control in order to become bureaucrats of a particularly despotic cast.

However, there is another side to the picture. Beginning in the 1870s, the disintegration of the old agrarian communities went hand in hand with the splitting of artisan layers into a few capitalist bosses at the top and a mass of wage laborers at the bottom. From its very origins, and even from its prehistory, the labor force never interrupted its efforts at organization marked by the ideologies of solidarity prevalent in both the peasant community and the artisan workshop.

These tendencies were initially most apparent in mining, the branch of the Mexican economy in which the world market had always played a determining role. It was here that the processes of technological innovation and capital accumulation were most strongly concentrated; here that a working class developed at a very early stage, with close links to the agrarian community through both family origin and the specific nature of the industry. From Independence until the 1910 Revolution, proletarian and proto-proletarian miners brought their distinctive skills and boldness to the ranks of the revolutionary fighting units.

The textile working class developed somewhat later, when the Banco de Avío began to sketch out a policy of industrialization in the 1830s. But the first factories, most of them spinning-mills, were linked to a large number of workshops in which the handicraft system of textile production still survived. In this sector too, one of the cornerstones of labor organization in Mexico, the decisive impetus for industrialization and the development of a modern working class came in the Díaz era.[31]

However, it was through the railway workers that the modern working class made its real entry into the arena of the Mexican class struggle. A large-scale capitalist industry without artisan relics, the railways were to revolutionize the organization of work and the country's economic and productive space. Their construction turned peasants into proletarians; and although their day-to-day running drew partly on labor trained in the crafts, it essentially developed a new and wholly industrial workforce, introducing a discipline, mentality, and rudimentary labor organization that were qualitatively different from the tradition of artisan struggle. We say *rudimentary* because the workers initially found it difficult to assimilate an awareness of the situation and to evolve corresponding methods of economic and trade-union struggle. They were faced with an eminently modern organization of work, new forms of the division of labor, a recomposition of the old crafts and skills acquired in the artisan or proto-capitalist workshops, a wave of forced migration connected with work and of voluntary displacement resulting from the structural and geographical extension of the labor market, and a whole new range of occupational diseases, accidents, and wage scales.

Nevertheless, within a fairly short space of time, the railway workers produced the first great industrial struggles of the Mexican proletariat, free of the artisan methods and ideologies that remained active and even necessary in other sectors.

Together with the mining industry, which underwent modernization in the 1890s after the new influx of foreign investment,[32] the railways also relayed the longer tradition of struggle and the greater experience of industrial life and union organization acquired by the American workers.

The U.S. technicians or specialist workers who came to Mexico received higher wages and various privileges as a result of their skills and union bargaining power. This led to a certain amount of friction with the Mexican labor force. But the U.S. workers also transmitted their ideology tinged with revolutionary syndicalism, establishing ties of class solidarity far closer than anything mentioned in official histories. They were among the first to go on strike against U.S. companies operating in Mexico, and their example was a fertile source for the experience and initiative of Mexican workers. It should also be noted that the many Mexicans who went to work in the United States brought back the organizational ideas and methods of struggle current in one of the most radical periods of the North American working class, particularly among the highly combative West Coast detachments.

The last decade of the Porfirian period witnessed the growth of new, up-to-date industries such as steel and electric power. The proletariat rooted in large-scale industry thereby increased its socio-occupational weight, although it still constituted a minority both in the overall labor force and in the category of factory and workshop wage earners.[33]

During the Díaz years, the wage curve varied from one branch of production to another. However, the statistics indicate a general decline between 1877 and 1892, followed by a rise until 1898 and then another fall which, by 1911, had brought wages below the level of 1877. The mining industry was a noteworthy exception, since it needed to attract labor to regions where it was in short sup- ply (northern Mexico, for example), and since skilled workers had to be found for the new extractive and processing techniques intro- duced after 1890.[34]

Wage disparities were also bound up with the uneven develop- ment of the labor market and the differential growth of regions and branches of the economy. Between 1895 and 1910, the labor force expanded at a faster rate than the general population in the Gulf states, the North, and the North Pacific, while an opposite trend was recorded in the Center and the depressed South Pacific region. In the North, high wages and the growth of mining, agriculture, and textiles attracted labor to the modern cotton industry of La Laguna, the mines of Chihuahua and Sonora, and the industrial town of Monterrey—to the regions whose capitalist bourgeoisie and petty bourgeoisie would head the victorious faction in the 1910 revolution.

The Mexican labor movement had its roots in the organizational forms and structures of the artisan layer. According to the specific character of the industry and region, it gradually moved away from this tradition during the Díaz era of capitalist growth. But the ideologies and methods of urban artisans had a power- ful influence on the industrial proletariat, not only before but even during and, in some cases, after the Revolution of 1910–20.

The first organizational forms, appearing especially after 1867, were based on ideas of cooperation and mutual aid. In this way, the artisans not only defended the product of their labor, but also organized cultural activity and elaborated an ideology—in meetings, newspapers, and other publications—that ran from Juarist liberalism through Christian humanism to utopian socialism. Later, at the interface with distinctively proletarian organization, they moved on to anarchist ideas.[35]

When they were still at quite an early stage, these movements underwent the influence of the 1871 Paris Commune. Although the revolution of the Paris workers was at first little known and subject to slander in the bourgeois press, its social impact was directly felt in Mexico and most other countries in Europe and the Americas, spread both by the propaganda of the First International and by the *communards* whom repression scattered throughout the world. The ideas and programs of the Commune were no longer confined to egalitarian utopias and dreams of a Republic of harmony founded upon cooperation and justice. Such ideologies, typical of small, independent producers, had given way to the first political project of the industrial proletariat that expressed the aim of conquering power and reorganizing society. In Mexico, however, although the sustained growth of the proletariat after 1880 combined with and prolonged the influence of the Paris Commune, it should not be forgotten that the constant stream of peasant and artisan labor into industry kept different ideological and organizational traditions alive in the incipient working-class consciousness.[36]

In 1871, a year before Juárez's death brought an era to a close, the journal *El Socialista* appeared with the words "for the defense of working-class rights and interests" in its logo. On September 10, 1871, *El Socialista* published the general statutes of the International Workingmen's Association: the declaration of the French Commune to the German workers had already been printed in the August issue, Number 6. In June 1884, *El Socialista* Number 39 published *The*

Communist Manifesto in a print-run of ten thousand, marking a historical point in the Mexican workers' movement. Its pages carried regular reports on the International, and on the European and North American workers' movement. Apart from the fact that *El Socialista* helped to pioneer the workers' press in Mexico, its publication of *The Communist Manifesto* is enough to assure it a place in the historical record. It disappeared in 1888, however, when Porfirist repression and the limitations of its artisan-based ideology made its further existence impossible.

In 1874, a new journal came out under the title *La Comuna*, later changed to *La Comuna Mexicana*, which altogether ran for forty-eight issues. *La Comuna* argued for redistribution of the land and embraced the slogan of the 1871 Paris Commune: abolition of the standing army and its replacement by a national guard. In other articles, including the series "Commune Letters," the journal defended the actions and demands of the Paris Commune.

Mexico's first labor federation, the Gran Círculo de Obreros, established its first leadership committee in September 1872, with a base mainly in the textile union and various craft sectors. When its first congress was held three and a half years later, the federation had thirty-five branches, the principal ones being in the textile centers of Puebla, Contreras, and Tialpan. *El Socialista* immediately became the official organ of the Gran Círculo, so that the new organization, though denying any interest in politics, combined the functions of a trade union with political concerns, actions, and teachings.

In March 1876 the Gran Círculo de Obreros organized the first Workers Congress of Mexico, which was attended by delegates from the thirty-five branches already in existence. *El Socialista* printed the initial congress appeal, as well as a weekly report on its proceedings. The main programmatic result of the congress was a manifesto in which artisan and working-class demands were mixed together according to the composition of the Gran Círculo and the ideological evolution of its members.

The manifesto took up the following points: (1) workers' education; (2) the creation of cooperative workshops; (3) political and social rights; (4) the freedom to elect public officials; (5) government appointment of "labor prosecutors" to defend the workers' interests; (6) regional state fixing of wages under workers' supervision; and (7) the holding of industrial craft exhibitions. The eighth point actually called for that basic measure, a sliding scale of wages, to be introduced: "Art. 8.—Modification of the wage-rate when the workers' needs so require, for just as the capitalists change the value of their commodities in suitable circumstances, so the worker has the right to increase the price of his labor in order to satisfy his individual and social needs."[37]

Throughout 1875, prior to the Workers Congress, a number of strikes had taken place among the industrial proletariat and workshop artisans. In January of that year, a strike movement in the textile factories of the Valley of Mexico called for wage-rises, a no-dismissal agreement, and, above all, "an end to the night-watch"—that is to say, a change from a fifteen-hour working day (6:00 A.M. to 9:00 P.M.) to one of twelve hours (6:00 A.M. to 6:00 P.M.), so that the last three night time hours would disappear. The workers appealed to the president of the Republic to act on their behalf, while the press invoked liberal principles against government intervention in this or any other conflict between labor and capital. In the end, the textile workers did not achieve victory—the Gran Círculo leadership decided to intervene not as spokesmen for the workers but as mediators between them and the employers.

In May 1875 the mutual society of artisan hatworkers called a strike against the employers' wage cut, receiving considerable support from other sectors. The Gran Círculo showed solidarity with the strikers and, according to an agreement printed in *El Socialista*, organized the collection of support funds among its affiliated bodies. At the end of July, the hatworkers finally won satisfaction and called off their strike.

In 1878 Francisco Zalacosta, the anarchist follower of Julio

Chávez López, founded the paper *La Internacional*. As well as publishing documents on the Paris Commune and reports from the European workers' movement, it featured a radical "Internationalist Programme" on the first page of each issue:

1. A Universal Social Republic, one and indivisible.
2. Dissolution of Government into a Social Contract.
3. Autonomous Municipal Administration.
4. Agrarian legislation for the surveying and demarcation of inalienable common land.
5. Liquidation of urban property interests.
6. Replacement of the Army by industrial phalanges.
7. Redemptory emancipation and all-round education of women.
8. Neutralization of capital's exploitative power over labor.
9. Gradual, balanced levelling of property.
10. Abolition of wages, and in the meantime strike action to raise daily industrial and agricultural pay.
11. Organization of the Social Phalanstery and formation of territorial banks for regulating labor and assuring the sale of goods.
12. A free zone, opening the market to all countries on earth.

In 1879 the Gran Círculo suffered a split when some of its founder-members accused the new leadership of being government agents. *El Socialista* ceased to be the organ of the federation and called a workers' congress for the end of the year. On December 13, a workers' and artisans' demonstration was held in the streets of Mexico City to inaugurate the congress. A red flag was carried at the head of the demonstration, many more mingling with national flags in the ranks of the marchers. There were also placards bearing such inscriptions as "Socialist Center of the Mexican Federation" and "Indian Alliance: Agrarian Law." Notwithstanding these banners, however, the Workers Congress approved an innocuous program and gave its backing to the bourgeois opposition candidate, Trinidad Garcia de la Cadena, for the presidential elections of 1880. For its part, the Gran Círculo decided to support the official candidate chosen by Porfirio Díaz. Both organizations subsequently languished and disappeared under the Díaz authoritarian regime, not only because of the repression directed against them, but because their confused and conciliatory policy totally disarmed them in the face of the regime. The disintegration of the Gran Círculo de Obreros marked the end of an epoch and coincided with the onset of headlong capitalist development. In the 1880s and 1890s, the growing industrial proletariat would evolve its own forms of union organization, above all through the railway, textile, and mining workers.

In 1887 the Society of Mexican Railwaymen was organized in Nuevo Laredo. In 1888 Nicasio Idar, a railwayman who had spent several years working in the United States, founded the Great Order of Mexican Railway Employees, whose organizational forms expressed the influence of the U.S. unions of the time. Within three years, however, the Order had been destroyed by government repression. In 1897 a new organization, the Confederation of Railway Societies of the Mexican Republic, received affiliations from the Puebla Union of Mexican Mechanics, the Aguascalientes Union of Mexican Boilermakers, the Union of Mexican Furnacemen, and the Union of Railway Carpenters and Painters. In 1904, not long before the great strikes that heralded the 1910 Revolution, all these unions came together in the Grand Mexican League of Railway Employees.

Once Porfirio Díaz had consolidated his regime with the reelection of 1884, it became the norm to repress any form of labor organization. However, the 250 or so strikes recorded between 1876 and 1911 testify to the continuity of working-class struggle against ascendant capitalism in the country's factories, mines, railways, haciendas, and other places of work, forming a kind of bridge between the early artisan or journeymen's associations and the workers' unions that developed in the first decade of the twentieth century.

One such movement was the 1881 strike of more than a thousand railway construction-workers in Toluca. Two years later, in January 1883, there was a workers' mutiny at the U.S.-owned and

U.S.-run mines in Pinos Altos, Chihuahua. The workers, who earned fifty centavos a day, demanded to be paid in cash once a week, while the company was determined to pay them once a fortnight, half in cash and half in company store coupons. For some reason, a worker and a company guard became involved in a fight in which both died. The company and the authorities organized white guards for the purposes of repression. The next day, the manager tried to calm down a protest march, but he was killed by a gunshot. In the days that followed, an officer in the army contingent sent to quash the rebellion set up a summary military court which, in a single day, sentenced five workers to death for "murder, malicious wounding, sedition, damage to property, and attempted arson." The five were shot forthwith and sixty others sentenced to forced labor.[38]

The highest number of strikes recorded during these years were called in textile factories—seventy-five in all. Next came the railways with sixty strikes and the cigar industry with thirty-five. There were about a dozen strikes in the mines and the same number in both the tram sector and the bakeries. Beneath the surface of the *Pax Porfiriana* and the positivist order and progress of rising capitalism, these struggles showed the tenacity of working-class and peasant struggle and the ripening of their ideas.

The forces that would later erupt in the revolution and shape its character matured and combined within the context of a nationally specific development of capitalism and mode of insertion into the modern world market. The most general historical feature that explains the forms of this process is uneven and combined development. Leon Trotsky sets it out in "Peculiarities of Russia's Development," chapter one of his *History of the Russian Revolution*:

> A backward country assimilates the material and intellectual conquests of the advanced countries. But this does not mean that it follows them slavishly, reproduces all the stages of their past. The theory of the repetition of historical cycles—Vico and his more recent followers—rests upon an observation of the orbits of old

pre-capitalistic cultures, and in part upon the first experiments of capitalist development. A certain repetition of cultural stages in ever new settlements was in fact bound up with the provincial and episodic character of that whole process. Capitalism means, however, an overcoming of those conditions. It prepares and in a certain sense realizes the universality and permanence of man's development. By this a repetition of the forms of development by different nations is ruled out. Although compelled to follow after the advanced countries, a backward country does not take things in the same order. The privilege of historic backwardness—and such a privilege exists—permits, or rather compels, the adoption of whatever is ready in advance of any specified date, skipping a whole series of intermediate stages. Savages throw away their bows and arrows for rifles all at once, without travelling the road which lay between those two weapons in the past. European colonists in America did not begin history all over again from the beginning. The fact that Germany and the United States have now economically outstripped England was made possible by the very backwardness of their capitalist development. On the other hand, the conservative anarchy in the British coal industry—as also in the heads of MacDonald and his friends—is a paying-up for the past when England played too long the role of capitalist pathfinder. The development of historically backward nations leads necessarily to a peculiar combination of different stages in the historic process. Their development as a whole acquires a planless, complex, combined character.

The possibility of skipping over intermediate steps is of course by no means absolute. Its degree is determined in the long run by the economic and cultural capacities of the country. The backward nation, moreover, not infrequently debases the achievements borrowed from outside in the process of adapting them to its own more primitive culture. In this the very process of assimilation acquires a self-contradictory character. Thus the introduction of certain elements of Western technique and training, above all military and industrial, under Peter I, led to a strengthening of serfdom as the fundamental form of labour organization. European armament and European loans—both indubitable products of a higher culture—led to a strengthening of czarism, which delayed in its turn the development of the country.

The laws of history have nothing in common with a pedantic schematism. Unevenness, the most general law of the historic process, reveals itself most sharply and complexly in the destiny of the backwardness. Under the whip of external necessity their backward culture is compelled to make leaps. From the universal law of unevenness thus derives another law which, for the lack of a better name, we may call the law of *combined development*—by which we mean a drawing together of the different stages of the journey, a combining of separate steps, an amalgam of archaic with more contemporary forms. Without this law, to be taken of course in its whole material content, it is impossible to understand the history of Russia, and indeed of any country of the second, third or tenth cultural class.[39]

As 1905 approached, marking the peak year of the Díaz era, "social peace" officially reigned in the country. Strikes and labor unions were outlawed, "agitators" punished by conscription, deportation to the plantations, or imprisonment. Peasant revolts had been drowned in blood, and the "pacification" of rebellious tribes seemed complete. Not having to face any organized opposition, apart from the harassed, imprisoned, or exiled groups of Magonistas, the federal government and its army held sway in every region. The peasant and urban population did maintain a silent resistance throughout the country, but without seeming to challenge the official appearance of things.

Mexico's economy, culture, and state administration had been modernized, and a class of landowners and industrialists had consolidated its rule and created its own political representation in the *científicos* around Porfirio Díaz.[40] Above all, from 1880 onward a steady rise in the crucial indicators of labor productivity and surplus creation had fueled the accumulation of capital and the general advance of the capitalist system. Whereas liberal ideas had been hegemonic in the 1860s and 1870s, a positivist ideology of continual, indefinite progress now held sway not only in the group of *científicos*, but in the new educational institutions (including the National University of Mexico and the National Preparatory School), the artistic and cultural centers, and even the institutions of repression. The Lecumberri panopticon prison, for example, a solid construction inspired on Jeremy Bentham's principles and projects, opened in the turn-of-the-century splendor of the regime.

Not only Mexico but the whole capitalist world was living through the Belle Époque, some of whose luster rubbed off onto the socialist movement through Bernstein's revisionist theses and the parliamentarism of European social democracy. It was quite natural, then, that Mexico's Congress, meeting in solemn session in December 1905, awarded Porfirio Díaz the Order of Military Merit, whose gold-and-jewel medallion bore the words, "He pacified and unified the nation."

It was natural, but was also rather late in the day. The apogee was nearing an end, and on the other side of the world the Russian workers and peasants had already begun to put out the festival lights. In this year of the first Russian revolution, the Petrograd general strike and the newly formed soviets were ushering in a century of great revolutions in the world. The period of bourgeois peace, opened by the defeat of the Paris Commune in 1871, was drawing to a close. It would not be long before the Díaz regime, which had sprung up and matured in the years between the Paris Commune and the Russian Revolution of 1905, began to feel the shock waves.

2
1910

Throughout the Porfirio Díaz regime, the haciendas had grown by swallowing up land together with the attached villages. By 1910 they encompassed 81 percent of all local communities in Mexico, the proportion varying considerably from region to region. In the central states, a relatively large number of Indian communities, though partly or wholly despoiled of their lands, waters, and woodland, had managed to survive outside the hacienda: 20.7 percent in Hidalgo, 23.7 percent in Morelos, 16.8 percent in Mexico State, 14.5 percent in Oaxaca, 20.1 percent in Puebla, 32.2 percent in Tlaxcala, and 24 percent in Veracruz. Altogether, some fifty-seven thousand communities lived within haciendas, while fewer than thirteen thousand remained independent.[1]

Capitalist development had tended toward the final destruction of the free villages and communal lands, as a culmination of a process initiated in colonial times and developed through the centuries-long conflict between villagers and *hacendados*. This process had speeded up with the rise of capitalist farming in Mexico, so that precapitalist forms of production and exploitation, though still present throughout the country and even quite vigorous in certain regions, became increasingly combined with, and subordinated to, capitalist wage-relations.

These contradictions were most apparent in Morelos State, then the center of a modern sugar industry, which since the 1890s had witnessed a fresh surge of capital investment, plant modernization, and irrigation renewal (often on the lines of the old precolonial systems) and a major development in trade and communications.

Now, the liquidation of free villages served not only an economic but also a political purpose. Whereas the Spanish Crown had co-existed with such rural, tributary communities, even defending some of their prerogatives against hacienda encirclement, the modern capitalist organization and individualist doctrines of the Restored Republic were hostile to any element of autonomous organization, any relation unmediated by money or unreceptive to direct or indirect market forms. The free villages, centered on their communal lands, therefore had to be eliminated.

As always, the villages resisted. For centuries they had fought back, clinging to their customs and their ancient communal traditions. Locked in interminable disputes with *hacendados* hungry for land and men, they flourished their land deeds from the time of the Viceroyship—almost magical documents which each village jealously guarded and handed down from generation to generation as material testimony to its social existence.

This defensive struggle, dispersed by its very nature, would eventually have been liquidated by the centralized powers of money and the state. However, while the development of capitalism ground down village resistance, it also created new forces and social contradictions that objectively stood on the side of the village in its clash with the state power that defended and represented the haciendas.

Empirically, without any conscious design or expectation, village resistance increasingly converged with other forms of peasant and working-class struggles against the Díaz regime. The urban petty bourgeoisie, too, swollen by the development of capitalism, was breaking from its former silence and attraction to Porfirian "peace and progress." By the turn of the century, the political ossification of the regime had so foreclosed upward social mobility that the petty bourgeoisie was driven into attitudes of discontent or even rebellion. This combined social pressure served, in turn, to produce symptoms of crisis and division among the capitalist and landowning bourgeoisie in whose name Porfirio Díaz and his party of *científicos* exercised power.

As we shall see, these contradictions were sharpened by the world economic crisis of 1907 and the series of social disorders, popular struggles, and revolutions that marked the first decade of the twentieth century (Russia, 1905; Iran, 1906–11, Portugal, 1909; China, 1909; the great U.S. strike movement culminating in the 1912 Paterson textile strike; the Chilean saltpeter strikes in Santa María de Iquique; the wave of strikes and the 1910 general strike in Argentina). Thus, although the forces in motion were not aware of the link, the changing world situation also had an influence on the political crisis that erupted in Mexico in 1910.

The peasants were less aware of this than any other social group. And yet, they had their own centuries-old form of organization, with characteristic internal relations that capitalism had been unable to eliminate. This social instrument, rudimentary as it was, allowed the peasantry to come together and find its collective bearings. In the life of society, moreover, in the antagonistic day-to-day relationship between free villages and the bourgeois society represented by *hacendados* and their stewards, the peasants could sense and sometimes even perceive the division of the bourgeoisie. Just as signs of rain in a clear sky are visible only to the peasant, so an instinct formed by a centuries-old social relation allowed them to see that something had changed in the look of the hacienda people and in the way they answered a greeting. The long-standing resistance was beginning to weigh up the new relationship of forces and to grow in audacity.

Communal organization enabled the peasants to take stock, discuss, and organize, eventually becoming the main political fulcrum for the Mexican peasant war of 1910–20. This organization, which essentially sought to uphold an idealized past, played a revolutionary role not in the long centuries of defensive resistance, but in the ten-year popular offensive against the state of landowners and bourgeoisie, at the very dawn of the era of revolutions heralded by the 1905 Russian Revolution. Although the peasant fighters had no such intention, nor, in most cases, any clear knowledge of what they were doing, the dynamic of their struggle involved not a return to the past, but an attack on the bases of the capitalist organization of state and society.

Here is the secret of the irresistible strength of the peasant war underpinning the Mexican Revolution; the basic kernel that explains the junction between precapitalist, communal forms of economic and social organization, and the socialistic or anarchist programs and utopias that, in the most radical components, continually passed through the ideologies of the revolution.

As in Ecuador, Bolivia, and Peru, as well as in many countries of Africa and Asia, the pre-Conquest civilization and social organization were based upon the internal relations, collective economy, and traditional customs of the old agrarian community. The Aztecs ruled over these communities or *calpulli* from their capital in Mexico, Tenochtitlan, just as the Incas in the Andes ruled over the *ayullus* from the imperial capital of Cuzco.

On a number of occasions, Marx focused his attention on the agrarian communities underlying the Asiatic dynasties and the forms in which their extraordinary capacity for survival combined with the expansion of modern colonial domination. Far from idealizing these communities, he brought out their characteristics of backwardness and immobility, their intrinsic resistance to change. At the same time, he tried to explain how, in the absence of differentiated landownership, the despots and dynasties that lived on tribute from these communities, and whose main social function was to carry out large-scale public works linked to the agrarian cycle (especially hydraulic construction), could rise and fall for centuries without altering the pattern of communal peasant life.

Thus, when British imperialism lay hold of India, it placed much of the existing social infrastructure at the service of its own colonial apparatus, while hardly touching the internal relations of the countryside. It merely substituted itself for the old powers at the top. To be sure, it thereby bound India to the world capitalist market, subjected the country to its own ends, brought it into the sweep of European history, developed an industrial and agricultural

working class, and sowed the seeds of anticolonialism and revolution. Yet it did not change the peasant depths of India. Although
capitalism exacted tributary payments, introducing some of its
products and partially dissolving the old relations, it was not able to
go beneath the surface. The Asiatic mode of production, as Marx
called it, therefore continued to exist. Unable to supplant it through
the generalization of capitalist relations, colonial domination sank
roots in this ancient mode and made it serve its own ends.[2]

Now, this mode of production is not merely Asiatic: it also appeared in Latin America, Africa, and, long ago, in parts of Europe.
In the Mediterranean, the development of trade and slavery
opened the way to classical antiquity and feudalism, in whose deep
soil West European capitalism later sank its roots. The barely emergent capitalist system spread through colonization to the rest of the
world, demolishing, dominating, or hemming in the various tribal
societies, agrarian despotisms, and other forms of social organization based upon blood ties and personal dependence. When the
Spaniards arrived in America, for example, the great Aztec, Maya,
and Inca civilizations of pre-Columbian Mexico, Central America,
and Andean America had a mode of social organization corresponding to Marx's "Asiatic mode of production," or, as other writers
prefer to call it, the despotic-tributary mode of production.

The Spanish Conquest—that is, the form of integration of
these lands into the nascent capitalist world market of the sixteenth
century—did not suppress the social relations of that mode of production (most notably, tribute-based forms of extracting the surplus product). It merely levelled the empires that rose atop those
relations. In Mexico and Peru, the two major centers of early
colonial expansion, the Spaniards liquidated the dominant priestly
and warrior caste and replaced it as the recipient of tribute in labor and in kind. Using the same manpower that had built the pyramids and dug the canals, the *conquistadores* raised new temples and
sanctuaries on the ruins of the old, in the manner of foreign con-
querors throughout the world.

The agrarian society that had sustained the old empires did not succumb in the same way, changing only at a snail's pace dictated by the slow development of metropolitan capitalism. Although part of it was physically exterminated, the other part went on reproducing the old pattern of communal agrarian life. The Spanish Crown, the pinnacle of a feudal-absolutist state, immediately set out to retain for its own advantage the old tributary relationship between the peasant communities and the central state power. It thereby came into continual conflict with the particular interests and jurisdiction of the local Spanish lords and *encomenderos*.

The Viceroyship authorities recognized village land claims and issued the deeds that would be carefully preserved in the centuries to come. Similarly, the Spaniards utilized such labor-service institutions as the Incan *mita*, through which the pre-Columbian empires had built roads, constructed pyramids, temples, and palaces, dug mines and canals, and realized the great public works of religion, war, and production. By imposing the logic of a new technology and mode of production, however, they shattered the old equilibrium both within the indigenous society and between that society and nature. In one of the most devastating social upheavals driven by the dynamic of primitive accumulation, they would eventually wipe out the greater part of the previously existing population.

As we have seen, the agrarian community persisted in combination with the haciendas after the establishment of a new equilibrium in the late seventeenth century and the eighteenth century. Among the Indian peasantry, its relations and customs preserved much greater strength than those of the Spaniards or the city and hacienda mestizos.

Porfirian capitalism hastened the decomposition of these communities, but it, too, failed to introduce a higher social relation into the countryside, even as it replaced the old artisan relation in the towns with the relations of solidarity stemming from proletarian cooperation in large-scale industry. Not only did some of the peasant communities survive, but the peasantry retained collective customs, egalitarian relations, and forms of production based upon cooperation,[3] mutual aid, and a language of community that were essentially alien to the capitalist relation. In the perpetual war that eventually ensued in the Mexican Revolution, these internal bonds therefore served the additional, higher function of solidarity. They may have been deformed, subordinated, and blunted through the growing distance and weakness of their material base, but still they survived.

The age-old cooperation is still alive in the customs, traditions, and language of the peasantry of Mexico and other such countries, which follows a quite specific social and cultural trajectory. Its opposition to the capitalist world involves a line of defense distinct from that of the European landowning peasantry. In an age of revolutions, its communal traditions may serve three functions: they may form part of the structure and basis of support for the organs of revolutionary struggle; they may fuse individual understanding with a collectivist perspective; and they may provide a basis for the transition to a higher organization of production and society.[4]

Marx and Engels always refused to idealize the old agrarian community or to imagine, in the manner of the Narodniks, that it could pass directly into socialist collective forms without undergoing the development of the productive forces fostered by capitalism. Nevertheless, they suggested that once capitalism had been overthrown in one or more countries, any remaining agrarian commune might then model itself on this socialist experience without passing through a capitalist stage. In the draft of a letter to Vera Zasulich dated March 8, 1881, Marx wrote:

As the latest phase in the primitive formation of society, the agrarian commune is at the same time a phase in the transition to the secondary formation, and therefore in the transition from a society based on communal property to one based on private property. The secondary formation does, of course, include the series of societies which rest upon slavery and serfdom. Does this mean, however, that the historical career of the agrarian commune is fated to end in this way? Not at all. Its innate dualism admits of an alternative: either its property element gains the upper hand over its collective element; or else the reverse will take place. Everything depends upon the historical context in which it is located.

In a second version of this letter he added:

> Its historical context—the *contemporaneity* of capitalist production, provides it with the ready-made material conditions for co-operative labour organized on a vast scale. It may therefore *incorporate the positive achievements* developed by the capitalist system, without having to pass under its harsh tribute. It may gradually replace small-plot agriculture with a combined, machine-assisted agriculture. After normal conditions have been created for the commune in its present form, it may become the *direct starting-point* of the economic system *towards which modern society is tending*; it may *open a new chapter* that does not begin with its own suicide.

In their 1882 preface to the Russian edition of *The Communist Manifesto*, Marx and Engels wrote:

> The *Communist Manifesto* set out to announce the inevitably approaching dissolution of modern bourgeois property. In Russia, however, we find that the fast-blossoming capitalist swindle and newly developing bourgeois landed property stand face to face with peasant communal ownership of the greater part of the land. This poses the question: Can the Russian commune, a form, albeit heavily eroded, of the primitive communal ownership of the land, pass directly into the higher, communist form of ownership? Or must it first go through the same process of dissolution which marks the West's historical development? Today there is only one possible answer. If the Russian revolution becomes the signal for proletarian revolution in the West, so that the two complement each other, then Russia's present communal land-ownership may serve as the point of departure for a communist development.[5]

To a greater or lesser degree, the components of the agrarian commune were still present in the Mexican peasantry at the outbreak of the revolution. This persistence helps to explain why the revolution acquired its various features and forms so specific in comparison with earlier revolution.

Nevertheless, the first great movements that heralded the revolution and gave expression to the national discontent stemmed from the proletariat rather than the peasantry. In developing urban industrial concentrations, a railway network, and a conscription-based national army (from which forcibly recruited peasants returned with the rudiments of modern military knowledge), capitalism provided the basis for the agrarian rebellion maturing in the countryside to culminate in a national-scale revolution rather than a mere peasant revolt. It was not local peasant risings, of the kind led by Julio Chávez López in the Juárez era, but great workers' strikes that most directly concentrated the country-wide ferment in centers of economic importance.

At least three major railway strikes took place in the first decade of the century—in 1903, 1906, and 1908. All had one of their main centers in San Luis Potosí, spreading to Nuevo León and, in 1906, also to Aguascalientes and Chihuahua. In an industrial branch that had been growing consistently for at least twenty years, the railworkers could already rely upon their own union organizations. But it was the miners and textile workers who, by meeting repression with strikes of an insurrectional form, pointed to the stormy times ahead.

On June 1, 1906, the Cananea copper miners in the north of Sonora State struck against the American company that owned the mine. They demanded the dismissal of a foreman; a minimum of five pesos for an eight-hour day; greater respect for the workforce; and a new rule that, where abilities were equal, the workers on every job should be 75 percent Mexican and 25 percent non-Mexican. These demands were incorporated into a manifesto that attacked the Díaz regime as an ally of foreign employers.

That very evening, three thousand strikers marched through

the streets of Cananea, waving Mexican flags and a few red flags and holding placards that proclaimed: "Five pesos for eight hours!" The demonstrators successfully called on those still at work to join the strike, so that a total of fifty-three hundred copper-miners were involved in the movement. When company guards attacked the demonstration and murdered one participant, the workers responded by killing several of the guards. The battle raged for two days, between, on the one hand, workers poorly armed with rifles and pistols they had seized, almost without ammunition, in an assault on the arsenal, and, on the other hand, well-armed state troops backed by a 275-strong battalion of U.S. "rangers" who crossed the border at the invitation of the Sonora governor.

After the strikers were defeated, their leaders received long prison sentences and were only freed by the revolution. Two of them would become officers in the revolutionary armies: Esteban Baca Calderón and the future divisional commander, Manuel M. Diéguez.

Seven months later, a second great strike brought still nearer the fall of the Díaz regime. In the middle of 1906, the Río Blanco textile workers in Veracruz State had set up a Gran Círculo de Obreros Libres, and it was not long before similar groups appeared in Puebla, Querétaro, Jalisco, Oaxaca, and the Distrito Federal. Employers' associations—headed by one of the most reactionary in the country, the Centro Industrial de Puebla—prohibited any form of labor organization on pain of dismissal, thereby provoking a number of work stoppages. On December 4, the strike began in Puebla and Oaxaca states. On December 14, the workers' leaders called on President Porfirio Díaz to arbitrate in the dispute, but on December 24 the textile employers decreed a lockout and left some thirty thousand workers without a job in the Center and South of the country.

On January 5, 1907, the president finally issued a ruling that denied the right of labor organization and ordered workers at the ninety-six textile factories then on strike to resume work on January 7. When the day came, the five thousand textile workers of Río Blanco did not go to work, but gathered in front of the gates to prevent anyone from entering. Company guards launched an attack and shot one of the workers to death. The crowd then ransacked and burned the company shop, and the workers, together with their wives and children, marched on Orizaba to demand the right to organize. The army lay in wait, however, and opened fire on the column as it reached a bend in the road. Hundreds were killed or wounded in this massacre. Next, the army went from street to street, house to house, in a hunt for workers. On January 8, Rafael Moreno and Manuel Juárez, chairman and secretary, respectively, of the Gran Círculo de Obreros Libres, were shot in front of the debris of the Río Blanco company shop.

The groups that helped to organize these strikes and took their leadership were linked to the Mexican Liberal Party headed by Ricardo Flores Magón. Since 1890, Flores Magón had begun publishing *Regeneración* as a weekly opposed to the government. Issue Number 20, dated December 31, 1900, already replaced the original heading, "Against the bad administration of justice!" with a new title, "An independent, fighting journal." Indeed, as it grew more radical and served to organize various struggles, *Regeneración* became one of the most influential forerunners of the Mexican Revolution.

In 1901 the *Regeneración* group founded the Mexican Liberal Party (PLM) around Ricardo Flores Magón, Camilo Arriaga, Antonio Díaz Soto y Gama, and Juan Sarabia. Both the party's name and its early ideology were descended from the radical wing of Juarism and the liberalism of the Reform years. In May 1901 Ricardo and his brother Jesús were arrested by the police, and repressive actions succeeded in breaking up the liberal clubs in Monterrey and San Luis Potosí. In October *Regeneración* suspended publication when faced with the threat that the two brothers would be killed in prison. In June 1903 the courts banned the circulation of any periodical that carried articles by Ricardo Flores Magón.

In January 1904 the inner core of the Liberal Party went into exile in the United States, where it resumed publication of *Regeneración* and mailed thousands of copies to Mexico. Flores Magón and his comrades established very close links with the Western Federation of Miners (WFM), the organizers of the Industrial Workers of the World (IWW), and anarchist leaders such as Emma Goldman. In 1905 Camilo Arriaga's moderate tendency broke with the radical group around Ricardo Flores Magón and left the organization. On October 2, police in the United States arrested the Flores Magón brothers and Juan Sarabia at the *Regeneración* offices, eventually releasing them in December. In fact, the whole period in the United States was marked by such incidents of repression, but also by the constant solidarity and support of the WFM, the IWW, and American radicals. In his 1908 presidential campaign, Eugene V. Debs energetically took up the defense of PLM leaders languishing in jail.

The new program of the Mexican Liberal Party, published at St. Louis, Missouri, in July 1906, constituted a major change of orientation that had been maturing at least since 1904. Calling for the overthrow of the dictatorship, it also argued for a number of political and social reforms: free elections and single-term presidency; the suppression of local political chieftains; compulsory lay education up to the age of fourteen, with better pay for schoolteachers; nationalization of church property placed in the name of various figureheads; a maximum eight-hour day and obligatory free Sundays; a minimum wage of one peso, or more in areas with a higher cost of living; regulation of home-based labor and domestic service; a ban on child labor before the age of fourteen; employer-funded improvement of hygiene and safety standards at work; compensation for work accidents; cancellation of all peon debts to the landowners, and abolition of employers' shops; establishment of an agricultural bank; restitution of village land and redistribution of unexploited farmland among the peasantry; and, lastly, protection of the Indian peoples.

This radical nationalist and democratic program, drawn up by what was then the extreme left wing of Mexican liberalism—and many of whose points would reemerge in the 1917 Constitution— was a milestone in Ricardo Flores Magón's evolution toward anarchism and an understanding of the need for an armed social revolution to expropriate the capitalists and big landowners.

The Magonists did not confine themselves to propaganda. They took an active part in the organization of struggles, which in turn speeded up their ideological evolution. The revolutionary-syndicalist positions of the Western Federation of Miners and the Industrial Workers of the World,[6] then in its best and most militant period, also had an influence on working-class components of the revolution and the Mexican labor movement, either directly through the Pacific coast ports and the cross-border flow of Mexican workers with experience in the United States, or through the ideological path of Magonism and the practical channel provided by certain U.S. labor organizers. Even today, the fighting banner of the Mexican unions is the red-and-black flag of anarcho-syndicalism.

In June 1908, Flores Magón and his Liberal Party comrades organized an uprising that prefigured the coming revolution and its characteristic methods. However, their plan for a nationwide insurrection on June 25 was discovered by the authorities, and a large number of party militants were arrested the day before. The small groups that went ahead in Viesca and Las Vacas, Coahuila, and Palomas, Chihuahua, were rapidly defeated.[7]

Up till then the constant peasant risings, dispersed in time and space and soon drowned in blood by the rural guards of the federal army, had lacked a national perspective and any program other than agrarian utopias or return to the past. Still, in their economic and political demands and their proletarian social base, the workers' struggles of the first decade of the twentieth century pointed toward a different future and tended to set themselves national goals. Thus Cananea demanded an eight-hour day and attacked the central government, while Río Blanco, which demanded the right of trade-union organization, was the culmination of a general textile strike. The working class did not yet have sufficient social weight in the country, and its main centers were widely dispersed and mostly far from the capital. Nevertheless, the workers' mobilizations would eventually link up with the peasant ferment beneath the surface of society, so that the vast peasant masses would find an answer and a road to the future in an alliance with urban revolutionary forces.

The evolution of the Magonist group from radical liberalism to insurrectionary anarchism was not merely an isolated phenomenon.

Cananea and Río Blanco drove forward the radicalization of the Magonist movement. They also sounded the alarm for the various factions of the bourgeoisie, which could feel the depth of the social crisis shaking the whole political structure of Mexican capitalism.[8]

The Mexican economy was hard hit by the 1907–08 world recession, one of the consequences of which was the collapse of the international copper market and the fall in other metal prices. Thousands of workers were laid off in the mines of Hidalgo, Sonora, Chihuahua, and Durango, as they were in many other industries. The 1907 crisis reduced still further Mexico's import capacity, already falling since the turn of the century. It also drove a number of banks into insolvency or, as in the case of the Banco de Londres y México, forced the government to mount a rescue operation. On the initiative of Finance Minister José Yves Limantour, head of the *científicos* group, the state further intervened to buy up the near-bankrupt railways. Nor did the harvests bring any relief: maize had to be imported to the value of 2 million pesos in 1907–08, 4,756,000 million pesos in 1908–09, and 15,497,000 million pesos in 1909–10. The general shortage of consumer goods, together with the rising unemployment, entailed a sharp decline in real wages and working-class incomes between 1908 and 1911.

This situation sharpened conflicts within the bourgeoisie and precipitated a struggle to replace Porfirio Díaz in the 1910 presidential elections. The bourgeois opposition, timidly roused since the turn of the century, stepped up its activity toward the end of the decade. The public head of one faction was a Porfirist politician, General Bernardo Reyes, who, though hostile to the *científicos* around the president, had been responsible as Nuevo León state governor for more than one act of savage repression in Monterrey. His "Reyist" tendency wished to see a certain change of political personnel, but only within the existing institutional framework. Although Reyes enjoyed support in sections of the army and among the Monterrey bourgeoisie, both of these feared the social consequences of a clash with Porfirio Díaz. It was Francisco I. Madero, a member of a rich family of landowners and industrialists from San Luis Potosí, who went beyond these limits and overcame Reyes's indecision. In the end, Reyes bowed to Porfirio Díaz's reelection drive and agreed to go into a gold-lined exile in November 1909. Madero's decision to stand against the dictator in the presidential elections therefore won him the support of many of the forces that had swung behind Reyes.

Madero had first planned a deal with the regime that would allow Porfirio Díaz to retire in a trouble-free manner. But when the old president proved intransigent, Madero began to call for free elections and a single-term presidency. His campaign not only attracted part of the Reyist movement, but more directly aroused the support and hopes of middle-class and popular layers of society. Like other politicians from the bourgeois opposition, Madero did not set out to head a revolution of the kind that eventually exploded in his hands. Rather, his aim was to contain and channel the popular revolutionary upsurge that everyone thought imminent, pushing aside the old dictator and assuring a peaceful succession through a number of political reforms.

The broad, heterogeneous movement around Madero brought together an important bourgeois sector whose axis of accumulation was shifting from agrarian property to industry (a sector typified by the Madero family itself); sections of the urban petty bourgeoisie styled by the dictatorship and anxious to secure democratic rights and political reforms; sections of the working class that hoped to win trade-union rights and better living conditions; and even sections of the peasantry that sought a release from the hacienda pressure on their little remaining village land, an improvement in the peons' oppressive lot, and above all some form of agrarian redistribution in favor of landless or expropriated peasants.

Díaz and the *científicos* feared that any political concession to Madero and his National Anti-Reelection Party would arouse the population and hasten the revolutionary explosion then maturing in the form of protests and mass discontent.

As often happens in such cases, both sides were right. The dispute within the bourgeoisie would inevitably, if temporarily, be won by whichever section turned the popular discontent to its own account, seeking to channel it by means of limited political concessions. This internecine conflict grew sharper under the impact of economic crisis, especially since, in the absence of independent popular organizations, the contending bourgeois factions did not feel directly threatened by an autonomous movement of the subaltern classes. Contrary to the wishes of all those factions, however, their division did eventually open the floodgates to the revolutionary intervention of the subaltern.[9]

Porfirio Díaz had himself reelected in June 1910, while the opposition candidate, Madero, was in prison. Madero was then conditionally released, and escaped to the United States in October. His San Luis Plan—dated October 5, San Luis Potosí—then declared the election results null and void, proclaimed Madero interim president, and affirmed the principle of a single-term presidency. According to point three of the plan, any land the courts and the authorities had expropriated through abuse of the Ley de Terrenos Baldíos would be restored to the original, mainly Indian, owners, and the relevant judgments and decrees would be subject to revision. This was the only point in the plan that, albeit in general terms, took up a social demand. And yet, it was enough to focus the peasants' attention throughout the country, encouraging them to follow the call to arms the plan issued for Sunday, November 20, 1910, "from 6.00 P.M. onwards."

Nothing seemed to happen at the appointed time. The Madero family, which had contributed money of its own and raised funds through contacts in the United States, fell into despondency and gave up the cause as lost. On November 18, the leader of the movement in Puebla, Aquiles Serdán, was hunted down by the federal army and killed alongside his family in a shoot-out at their home. But that was not the end: other forces were moving into action in other parts of the country.

The first risings took place in the northern state of Chihuahua, whose governor, Abraham González, was a Madero supporter. Francisco Villa, Pascual Orozco, and others, hitherto unknown except in their home district, led the small peasant units which inflicted successive defeats on the army detachments sent to put down the rebellion. At the same time, there were smaller-scale risings in Durango and Coahuila State. In these first guerrilla actions, the federal army already gave signs of that lack of initiative, timidity, and conservative leadership which would soon be amply demonstrated in the major battles. In fact, these were the precise opposite of the features beginning to emerge in the revolutionary guerrilla units.

The initial victories attracted, in ever greater number, splendid peasant riflemen and horse riders from the big cattle ranches. In January and February, the insurgency against the central government spread to other parts of the country. Already the peasants had the national focus for their previously scattered struggles: namely, the armed uprising itself. A new meaning of life swept the peasant masses, producing a flood to arms which, so long suppressed, was now becoming unstoppable. It was the goals of winning the land and taking revenge for injuries suffered generation after generation, rather than Madero's politics or personality, that drew ever more recruits to the peasant combat units.

In February 1911, Madero entered the country from the United States and set about regrouping his forces. On March 6 his attack on Casas Grandes was repulsed. However, Madero's military fortunes were not the decisive factor, and peasant uprisings continued throughout the month of March. In Morelos State, Emiliano Zapata and other local leaders organized the armed expropriation of several haciendas and began the struggle of what would soon be the Southern Liberation Army. Revolution was spreading from one state to the next, although Chihuahua in the North and Morelos in the South were already taking shape as the centers for the struggle as a whole.

Madero's representatives had never broken off talks with the regime in their search for a deal that would allow the peasant insurrection to be ended. In May, however, Madero assembled most of his Chihuahua forces, some three thousand men, in front of Ciudad Juárez. While he continued to hesitate, his military commanders, Villa and Orozco, decided by themselves to launch the assault. When the town fell on May 10, it was the first in the hands of the revolution. To the south, Zapata's forces established their headquarters in Cuautla after taking the town on May 20. The next day, they met no resistance as they entered the Morelos state capital, Cuernavaca.

Both Díaz and Madero understood this twin warning from north and south: an agreement had to be reached before the peasant war spun out of control. Thus, on May 21, Madero and government representatives signed the Ciudad Juárez Accords, by which Porfirio Díaz undertook to hand over interim presidential powers to Francisco León de la Barra, then secretary for external relations, who would proceed to organize general elections. The agreement also stipulated that fighting would cease between the governmental and revolutionary forces, and that in each state the latter would hand over their weapons to the federal army.

The accords were therefore designed to wind up the revolution, to disarm the masses, and to reestablish a bourgeois juridical order based on the federal army. Not a word was said about the land question or about any of the other issues mentioned in the San Luis Potosí Plan.

With his usual clarity, Luis Cabrera, the incisive critic of Porfirianism and the *Científicos* of the preceding years, published in those days an "Open Letter to Madero Concerning the Treaties of Ciudad Juárez," in which he invited him to "discern the economic and political needs of the country," and he told him:

> The responsibility that you hold at present is so serious that if you do not correctly perceive with the utmost clarity the political and economic reforms that the country demands, you will run the risk of having left alive the germs of future disturbances in the peace, or of not completely restoring calm to the country [...] If you do not

know how to fully satisfy the legitimate needs of the nation, you will leave planted the seeds of future revolutions, after having taught the people a dangerous form of rising in arms, putting our sovereignty in constant jeopardy.

Madero did not listen to this warning, which in due time became prophetic.

On May 25, 1911, Porfirio Díaz resigned, and on May 26 he boarded the steamboat *Ypiranga* to go into exile in France. An old connoisseur of the country and its people, in his resignation speech to Congress, the general summed up the meaning of his long government and intuited as no one else the profound character of the revolution that had begun:

"The Mexican people, who so generously heaped honors upon me, who proclaimed me their leader during the War of Intervention, who patriotically supported me in all endeavors undertaken to benfit the industry and the commerce of the Republic, this people, honorable congressmen, has risen up in millenarian armed bands, declaring my exercise of Supreme Executive Power as the cause of their insurrection.

Behind the program and leadership of Madero, Don Porfirio caught a glimpse of the uncontrollable peasant war and the Zapatista agrarian utopia.

Porfirio Díaz resigned on May 25 and left the next day on board the "Ypiranga" to take up exile in France. On June 7 Madero made a triumphal entry into Mexico City. As far as the bourgeoisie was concerned, the revolution had come to an end.[10] For the peasantry, however, the revolution was only just starting. In various parts of the country, small groups of armed Indians and peons seized large areas of land from the big haciendas, ploughing and sowing them under the protection of their own rifles. Many village communities thus reoccupied the land the haciendas had expropriated in previous years. The movement spread far and wide, while in Mexico City the top bourgeois politicians carried on with their deals and compromises. But although armed peasants took and cultivated the land in Chihuahua, Durango, Jalisco, Hidalgo, and Guerrero, it was above all in Morelos and Puebla that the movement became an irresistible statewide force.

It spelled ruin for the Ciudad Juárez Accords. With no national leaders and no overall plan, without waiting for laws or decrees, the peasantry was using its social strength to solve the land question through simple and direct methods of its own.

The Mexican Revolution was truly under way.

3

Zapatism

Zapatism was a concentrated expression of the nationwide peasant upsurge. After the fall of Díaz, armed redistribution of the haciendas took place in various parts of the country. The peasant units often refused to lay down arms. Where they disbanded or integrated into the army in conformity with the Ciudad Juárez Accords, it was not long before the returning guerrillas were denied work as peons and subjected to various forms of persecution. They therefore rose again in revolt, or prepared to do so.

Morelos State was a peasant stronghold for resistance to the Ciudad Juárez deal. Here, many free villages had remained outside the haciendas, either retaining or seeking to recover their lands, while a sizeable and concentrated agricultural proletariat had grown up on the sugar plantations. Zapatism had its roots in this dense population of peasants and agricultural workers, often one and the same people, living close to Mexico City; and in the old traditions of peasant struggle and organization, stretching back to the Wars of Independence and the Reform. "The uprising of the Morelos peasants took the shape of a social revolution, while the other revolutionary movements were mainly political," writes François Chevalier.

Now, although Morelos State was the front and operational base for Zapata's Southern Liberation Army, it was not an isolated area. Had it not been for the diffuse yet unstoppable nationwide uprising, there would have been no revolution in the South and no Emiliano Zapata. The South played a crucial role as the *nodal point* of a national situation. The Morelos villages created Zapatism and became Zapatist guerrillas, inventing a thousand forms of struggle to defeat the federal army, whether under Porfirio Díaz, Madero, Huerta, or Carranza. They held the bourgeois capital, Mexico City, in constant check and occupied it on two occasions. Through all the turns of the revolution, they formed a political center that never yielded or gave up the fight.

The sugar plantations had been the dominant economic reality in Morelos ever since the sixteenth century, and the region was traditionally the chief sugar producer in the Republic. In the late nineteenth century, the haciendas had swallowed up many of the communal lands, reducing the villages to islands surrounded by a sea of hacienda cane fields which formerly had been common lands. As 1910 approached, the plunder continued despite the stubborn resistance of the local population, many of whose leaders paid the price of imprisonment, deportation to Quintana Roo or Yucatán, and even death. This is what happened in 1904 to the Yautepec leaders when they tried to use the law against the Atlihuayan hacienda which, in a typical action the year before, had enclosed twelve hundred hectares of communal pastureland and sowed it with sugarcane.

In the first decade of the twentieth century, the Morelos plantation owners made big investments in machinery and turned the state into the most modern industrial region in the country. Twenty-four sugar mills produced more than a third of Mexico's output. This prosperity was also reflected in the homes of the *hacendados*: in their magnificent imported furniture, their sumptuous, European-style interior decoration, their multi-hectare gardens, their stables for polo and racehorses, and their kennels for hunting dogs.

At the beginning of 1909, an election was held for the Morelos State governorship. Echoing the national divisions within the ruling classes, Patricio Heyva, an oppositionist, stood as candidate with the support of future Zapatist leaders and possibly of Zapata himself. The police broke up meetings, jailing or outlawing opposition supporters, so that the regime's candidate, a rich local landowner called Pablo Escandón, emerged victorious with the help of the customary electoral fraud.

A few months later, a genuine election took place in the small village of Anenecuilco, which then had barely four hundred inhabitants. This time, the local population met in a general assembly, using the methods traditional in the preparation of peasant struggles and ensuring that the authorities would not discover and ban the meeting. The thirty-year-old man who was elected president of the Anenecuilco communal council on September 12, 1909, was Emiliano Zapata. All the peasants in the village agreed it had been a good election for the times of struggle ahead.[1]

Emiliano Zapata was born on August 8, 1879, into a peasant line that had long lived in the area comprising Anenecuilco and Villa de Ayala (a neighboring village with some seventeen hundred inhabitants). His ancestors had fought in the Independence and Reform wars. Emiliano inherited a certain amount of land and livestock, and was neither a poor nor a rich peasant according to the categories in local use. The small area and low yield of his land led Zapata to involve himself in the animal trade. He was also considered an equine expert, particularly in the field of horse-breaking, and his services were much in demand on the local haciendas. His elder brother, Eufemio, had moved to Veracruz and worked in commerce and various other occupations.

As he reached thirty years of age, Emiliano had a solid reputation among the local peasantry, and his family roots, as well as his own activity, had won him their trust. Alongside the other four members elected to the communal council at the same meeting, he became a depository of the communal land deeds dating back to colonial times and beyond. In fact, Anenecuilco was seven centuries old, and some of its papers were written in the Nahuatl language, which, by 1910, only 10 percent of the Morelos population could actually speak.

As in the rest of the country, these old communal deeds played an important role in the early stages of the revolution. The Mexican peasant revolution began without a prior theory or program.

The first objective of nationwide struggle was to recover communal lands. It appeared then as a natural continuation of the long struggle to enforce the legality of the peasants' historical claim.

The inner driving force of the revolution was much more powerful than that: it was a true insurrection against all the forms of oppression, repression, plunder, and exploitation intensified by capitalist development. At first, however, its lack of a distinctive programmatic core created the need for a basic, unexaggerated unifying demand—a demand acceptable to everyone, not as a subversion of the established order, but as a restoration of the rights and legality which the landowners, with government backing, had themselves violated and subverted. The communal land deeds were thus the material proof that legitimized recourse to armed insurrection, serving as a bridge in peasant consciousness between the age-old struggle to defend their lands and an all-round revolutionary offensive.

Basing itself on communal deeds, and profiting from the favorable situation in the country, the council over which Zapata presided kept up its legal struggle for the land. Unaware of the gathering storm, the new state governor, Escandón, redoubled the attack on village lands both through pro-landowner legislation and through protection of actual abuses.

In April 1910, while Zapata was away for several months, the Anenecuilco village leaders sent a petition to the governor. As he read their beseeching letter, Escandón could not have had the least suspicion that, a year later, these same men would take up arms, drive him from Morelos, and launch one of the greatest revolutions in history. "Since the rainy season is approaching," they wrote, "we poor laborers must begin to prepare the fields for our corn-sowing; we therefore . . . turn to the State Governor, imploring him to deign to be so kind as to grant us his support, so that we may sow these fields without fearing expropriation by the landowners of the Hacienda del Hospital. We are prepared to recognize whoever turns out to be the owner of this land, whether it is the village of San Miguel Anenecuilco or some other person. But we wish to sow this land

so that we do not suffer any harm. Sowing corn gives us our liveli-
hood; we have to support ourselves and our families on it."

The governor fobbed them off with bureaucratic procedures,
leaving the matter to die a rapid death. Meanwhile the Hacienda del
Hospital, using a time-honored method to divide the peasants against
one another, leased the land in dispute to people from Villa de Ayala,
who then began to sow it. For many of these months, Zapata had
been working as a horse-minder at the Mexico City residence of a
rich Morelos landowner. But when he returned in September 1910,
after the Independence Day festivities in the capital, the Anenecuilco
villagers began to change their methods. Gathering together eighty
armed men, Zapata went to the fields in question to address the Ayala peasants. He pleaded with them to leave, so that the conflict
would be with the hacienda rather than among the peasants; and in
this way the people of Anenecuilco remained in possession of their
land. Zapata then made an application to the central government,
which found in favor of Anenecuilco. After this victory, the people
of Villa de Ayala and other villages gave their support to Zapata. In
the closing months of the year, he followed the same approach in a
number of village-hacienda disputes: he would tear down the enclosure fences, distribute the land under the protection of his armed
men, and leave the peasants in possession of their plots. By this time,
however, the revolution had already begun in the North, and an insurrectional mood was also spreading in Morelos State.

In November 1910, Zapata organized conspiratorial meetings in
Villa de Ayala as a member of a group of Madero supporters. The
official leader of the group was Pablo Torres Burgos, but Zapata provided the real strength and authority. In December, Torres Burgos
went to meet Madero in the United States, agreeing on the details
for an uprising in the South to support the San Luis Postosí Plan.
Aquiles Serdán, in Puebla State, had been the urban center for the
Madero conspiracy in the South. But on November 18, two days
before the date set for an insurrection, the conspiracy had been discovered and Maderism beheaded in the region.

While the Villa de Ayala group waited for Torres Burgos to return, the peasantry began to show signs of impatience. The alarmed landowners and government rapidly set about arming themselves in the early part of 1911. But in February a number of local leaders came out in armed revolt with the support of their villagers, and formed units which, though rapidly spreading in Morelos State, lacked coordination or a clear political objective. In the middle of the month, Torres Burgos finally returned and confirmed that Madero recognized the group. He also showed them the documents by which he had been appointed Maderist leader in the state. Thus Madero's recognition linked the Villa de Ayala group to the broader national revolution. Although Zapata himself had been trying to contain his comrades' impatience, he had been preempted and drawn along by the initiative of other leaders—Genovevo de la O, for example, later one of his most distinguished commanders, had risen in revolt at the end of 1910 with just twenty-five men and a single rifle. But now that Zapata had Madero's political accreditation, he and Torres Burgos decided to launch the insurrection.

The two leaders met in Cuautla on March 10 to finalize their plans. The next day, they led the uprising in Villa de Ayala and successfully disarmed the police. Torres Burgos then read the San Luis Plan to the assembled population, calling on them all to join the revolution. He was greeted with cheers and loud applause, and most of the battle-fit males were recruited there and then. At the same rally, Otilio Montaño launched a slogan that already anticipated the split between Madero's plans and those of the southern peasantry. Instead of "Long Live Madero!" and "Death to Díaz!," he raised the cry: "Down with the haciendas! Long live the villages!"

The rebels' main objective was to seize the town of Cuautla. But first they had to acquire the necessary weapons, men, and battle experience. A few days after the revolution broke out in support of the San Luis Plan, the first military actions took place and the first disputes appeared in the leadership. At that very moment, however, Madero's designated leader, Torres Burgos, was surprised by federal troops and shot on the spot. The movement was left without a leader.

One of the strongest armed groups decided to elect Zapata commander-in-chief of the Southern Revolutionary Movement. In the ensuing process of selection, Zapata gradually imposed his authority as leader of the revolution in the South by the confidence his past reputation and current actions inspired.

Whereas Torres Burgos had been on the moderate wing of the original conspiratorial group, Zapata had been on the radical wing more closely linked with the peasantry. Nor was this the only difference: Torres Burgos's claim to the leadership had rested on his appointment by Madero, while Zapata's claim directly stemmed from rank-and-file recognition. But although this broke the tie of dependence with the exiled politician, it did not yet provide a new political legitimacy for Zapata's group. Indeed, Maderism was the main link with the national revolution for all the spontaneous peasant uprisings which, in the course of these months, were seeking a political center for their guerrilla activity.

The peasant revolution in the South took an ever more independent course. The fact that it initially rallied to Maderism, however, was neither an accident nor the result of a maneuver, but corresponded to a necessary phase in its development. Similarly, when Zapata waited for Madero's official recognition before he launched the uprising, even resisting the pressure of other groups that had already taken up arms, he was guided by political intuition rather than opportunist inclination. He could see that only a revolution, as opposed to a local peasant uprising, would secure the land. Thus, his insistence on the national affiliation of the southern movement had a deeply political significance. The Ayala group sought to link up with a national program, and the program at that time was the San Luis Potosí Plan. Zapata and his supporters entered the revolution as Maderists.

The people of the South rose up in the name of the San Luis Potosí Plan. In reality, however, they were only interested in that section of the plan which promised the return of their land. The faction that grasped the national political significance of the movement, Zapata's group in Villa de Ayala, united around itself all the other rebel groups in the region. Thus, despite the link with Madero, the southern movement had from the beginning a peasant leadership; and once Zapata took command, it displayed ever stronger signs of independence. The southern peasantry initially rose up in political support of a wing of the ruling elite. It then rapidly shifted to a de facto alliance, insofar as the revolution developed an independent leadership and an awareness of the conflict of class interests with Maderism. Finally, this alliance turned into an open break through the emergence of a distinct program. The Ayala Plan, which represented the birth of Zapatism, transformed the South into the national political center of the peasant revolution.

On March 29, 1911, in the kind of action that would often be repeated in the course of the war, revolutionary forces drove a locomotive through the gates of Chinameca hacienda. Zapata and his men burst into the precincts and made off with forty Savage rifles, the whole ammunition supply, and all the hacienda horses. As Zapata proudly recalled in later years, the revolution always armed itself with guns and bullets captured from the haciendas and the federal army.

Within a few weeks, Zapata's peasant column already numbered more than a thousand armed men. The campaign spread. And as Madero seemed to be nearing agreement with the government, Zapata brought forward the planned attack on Cuautla so as to establish his forces in a major regional town.

On May 20, Zapata captured Cuautla with some four thousand men, and then federal troops surrendered Cuernavaca, the state capital, without a fight. The Ciudad Juárez Accords were signed about the same time, and on May 25, Porfirio Díaz relinquished power.

The provisional government of León de la Barra tried to implement the main article of the agreement by disarming the peasant forces. But he was not successful in the South, where Zapata refused to lay down arms until the peasants' land had been returned.

Negotiations were continually started and broken off. In the end, the Zapatists did agree to disarm some of their forces, on the understanding that the government would give them financial compensation and pay for their weapons. To a large extent, however, this proved to be a maneuver by the peasants to gain time: they would hand in their unusable or antiquated rifles, hiding or collectively storing the rest.

Although many peasants also hid their guns in other parts of the country, the Morelos movement, with its largely independent leadership, was the only remaining focus of resistance. The interim government therefore sought to bring all its military pressure to bear on the South. The bourgeois press launched a campaign for the forcible disarming of the Zapatists and for the reappropriation of lands already seized by the peasantry. However, in Morelos, Oaxaca, Guerrero, and other parts of the South, the peasants continued to occupy haciendas and to cultivate their recently conquered land under the protection of their own guns.

So long as the agrarian revolution had an armed center, nothing could prevent it from maintaining its course through the peasantry's own initiative. The revolutionary peasants supported Zapata's intransigent refusal to hand in the weapons, understanding that any other position would entail federal army repression and loss of the occupied land.

The interim president wanted to send the army straight against Zapata's forces. But Madero hoped he could gain time, realizing that military repression would not end the revolt but spread it to the rest of the country. Madero tried on a number of occasions to win Zapata over. During their last personal meeting, which took place between August 18 and 25 at Zapata's Cuautla headquarters, he promised that his future government would legally endorse the return of the peasants' land. But the peasants themselves, with long experience of such matters, were not prepared to trade weapons for promises.

They were right: the federal army began its advance on Cuautla in an effort to defeat the Zapatistas. The talks broke down. Emiliano's brother, Eufemio, proposed that Madero should be shot there and then: "This little man has already betrayed the cause, and he's too delicate to be head of the revolution. It would be better to break with him: he's not going to keep any of his promises." But Emiliano refused, arguing that they should wait until he lost the people's trust: "When he breaks his promises, we'll soon find somewhere to string him up."

Madero was thus able to return to the capital, and the war against Zapatism resumed in all its fury. Zapata did not offer battle in Cuautla, but went through the state raising fresh troops and rearming his followers. On several occasions, he made incursions to the very gates of Mexico City. By September 1911 the whole of Morelos State was under arms.

On October 1 Madero emerged victorious from the elections, and on November 6 he assumed the presidency. His main concern was to put an end to the peasant revolution. But if he was to eliminate all the scattered pockets of resistance, he first had to do away with the only mass movement keeping alive the nationwide insurrection.

Emiliano Zapata drew the necessary political conclusion from Madero's rise to the presidency. Since Madero used his role as head of the revolution to call on the peasants to disarm and surrender, wielding the state power in support of this aim, the task was to form another organized pole of power that would stand against the continuity of the bourgeois-oligarchic state from Díaz to Madero. Of course, Zapata did not formulate or express his conclusion in these terms. But this is what he put into practice by issuing the Villa de Ayala Plan, just three weeks after Madero became president. It was to be the political expression of the nationwide peasant revolution, embodying Zapata's historical intransigence in the face of the bourgeois state and its three successive governments: Madero, Huerta, and Carranza.

★ ★ ★

Emiliano Zapata and Otilio E. Montaño, a local schoolteacher who had joined Zapata's forces at the beginning and was a member of his general staff, worked together on the draft in the mountains around Villa de Ayala. There is no room for doubt that, while Montaño was responsible for composing the final text, Zapata himself contributed the ideas. Montaño fulfilled a role that has often been played by country schoolteachers during and since the revolution: that is to say, he gave expression to the demands, feelings, and needs of the peasantry. Nevertheless, the peasantry itself "created" such teachers and conferred on them their role.[2]

The Ayala Plan comes, on the other hand, from a long Mexican lineage of revolutionary and agrarian-utopian plans that includes even José María Morelos's *Sentimientos de la Nación* (which is to say even the very foundations of the Mexican nation). They reiterate, under diverse forms, the persistent idea that the agrarian rent should be abolished, and they run through the entire nineteenth century and its peasant rebellions.[3]

The Ayala Plan was signed on November 28, 1911, by seven Zapatist generals, seventeen colonels, thirty-four captains, and one lieutenant, who together formed the Revolutionary Council of Morelos State. They were all peasants apart from Montaño and one other, and most of them were barely able to sign their name.[4] The plan bears the following title: "Liberation Plan of the sons of Morelos State who, fighting in the Insurgent Army, seek to fulfil the San Luis Potosí Plan, as well as further reforms considered beneficial to the Mexican Fatherland."

Madero, the document charged, had deserted the revolution, persecuted revolutionaries from his position of power, allied himself with elements from the Díaz dictatorship, broken the promises in the San Luis Potosí Plan in the name of the Ciudad Juárez Accords, and outlawed anyone who sought to uphold them. The Zapatist leaders therefore considered him a traitor: they no longer recognized him as head of the revolution or president of the republic, and openly called for him to be overthrown. After declaring that the revolutionary council would "accept no political deals or compromises until the dictatorial associates of Porfirio Díaz and Don Francisco I. Madero have been overthrown," the document adds the following basic points:

6. As a further component of our plan, we declare that the land, woodlands and waters usurped by the plantation-owners, *cientificos* or chieftains under cover of tyranny and venal justice shall become forthwith the property of the villages or citizens who have the appropriate deeds and have been dispossessed through the trickery of our oppressors. Such property will be resolutely defended with arms in hand. Any usurpers who claim the right to it must argue their case before special courts to be established at the victory of the revolution.

7. The vast majority of Mexican villages and citizens no longer own the land they tread: they must undergo the horrors of poverty, while the concentration of the land, woodlands and waters in a few hands makes it impossible for them to improve their social conditions in any way, or to devote themselves to industry or agriculture. Hence, the powerful landowners will be expropriated, and compensation paid for a third of these monopolies, so that the villages and citizens of Mexico may acquire common land and new settlements, legally obtaining funds for their village or for the tilling and sowing of the fields, and so that the Mexican people may in every way overcome their lack of prosperity and well-being.

8. *Hacendados, cientificos* and local chieftains who directly or indirectly oppose this plan will have their property nationalized. Their two-thirds will be used to provide war-compensation and pensions for the widows and orphans of those who die fighting for the plan.

9. Procedure with regard to the aforementioned property will be set forth in appropriate disentailment and nationalization acts. A norm and example may be the legislation on Church property introduced by the immortal Juárez, which dealt severely with the despots and conservatives who have forever sought to impose on us the ignominious yoke of oppression and reaction.

Although these key points of the plan only touch the land problem, the peasant movement thereby asserted its political independence of Madero's bourgeois-landowner leadership and subsequent bourgeois leaderships of the revolution.[5]

Many other plans appeared in the course of the civil war, the most advanced of which put forward workers' demands generally in line with the Liberal Party program of 1906. But two aspects basically determine the specific revolutionary character of the Ayala Plan. First, it proposes to nationalize all the property of enemies of the revolution—that is, all the landowners and capitalists of Mexico. Secondly, it goes beyond the Jacobin wing in stating that dispossessed peasants should *immediately* take over their land and that "such property will be resolutely defended with arms in hand."

All the other plans promised that, when the revolution had triumphed, various laws would be passed to redistribute the land in one way or another; or stated that peasants with the appropriate deeds would have to prove their validity in court before the landowners could be ousted. Zapata's plan, by contrast, called on the peasants to seize the land at once, arms in hand, and stipulated that the landowners would have to bring any claim before revolutionary courts. This transferred the burden of proof from the peasants to the landowners, turning the bourgeois legal regime upside down and establishing a revolutionary system of laws and courts.

Furthermore, the call for armed defense of the peasants' lands presupposed that the revolutionary regime would be grounded upon the armed people. The plan therefore contained the principle of military organization in territorial militias linked to the point of production: there would be no need for the barracks, professional army, and standing detachments which had traditionally substituted for such forms. Zapata consistently upheld this principle from the moment when he refused to hand over his arms to Madero.

This mode of functioning, which, as we shall see, was well described by Zapata's enemies, was one of his army's sources of indestructibility in periods of mass advance, but a source of weakness and fragmentation in times of retreat.

Emiliano Zapata did not set out to destroy the capitalist system: his ideas sprang from the peasantry, not from a socialist program. However, implementation of the Ayala Plan would have effectively smashed the living roots of capitalism. For it would have involved nationalization of all the property of the ruling classes. More important still—because actually applied by the peasantry—was the principle that the people themselves should decide, "arms in hand"; that, instead of waiting for the revolution to triumph and enact the necessary legislation, they would begin cultivating and defending the land.

The peasants of southern Mexico, however, were unable to carry this logic to its conclusion. The Ayala Plan, like the actions of the peasantry, only went so far as to counterpose popular initiative to capitalist power. It effectively created dual power, as the armed peasants themselves did throughout the revolution. But it did not raise the prospect of another state power. According to the plan itself, the duality established through revolution would issue in the reestablishment of bourgeois state power, albeit with the revolutionary-democratic guarantee that the weapons would remain in the hands of the peasantry.

The Ayala Plan did not, then, answer the crucial question of state power. Taken as a whole, it encapsulated the contradiction between peasant ideology and the revolutionary action of the armed peasantry. The methods were revolutionary, and posed a revolutionary challenge to capitalist power. But the peasantry could not rise to a nationwide social perspective or offer a revolutionary solution for the insurgent nation.

For any real answer had to rise above a local or particularist level to take up the national question of the state: the decisive factor, in the end, was not revolutionary land seizures, but control of the centralized state power. "If the peasantry does not follow the workers," Lenin once said, "it will march in the tow of the bourgeoisie. There is not, and cannot be, any middle way." The Zapatist peasantry confirmed this thesis. The final fate of the revolution would not be decided in the countryside, but in the cities. The mighty revolutionary impetus of the peasantry managed to reach the city, but once there it could do no more than leave power in the hands of a weak and terrified petty bourgeoisie which did, however, represent a viable option: that of the bourgeoisie.

Still, while the revolution was on the ascendancy, the Ayala Plan provided a political basis for the territorial power established by the Zapatists, and for the peasant government in Morelos, which adopted laws and other measures concerning health, education, communications, and supplies, as well as minting the Zapatist pesos.

This relative independence of the peasantry could only survive during the revolutionary rise of the masses. It expressed the dual nature not only of the peasantry in general, which tends toward the proletariat as an exploited class and toward the bourgeoisie as a class of property owners, but of the Morelos peasantry in particular, which comprised both peons or agricultural laborers and peasants tilling village land or aspiring to till their own. Once the peasant leaders had passed the first stage, however, and were faced with basic political choices, they could either follow a socialist course or bow to bourgeois legality. Indeed, the Zapatist peasant "party" did eventually split along those lines: whereas the reformist wing, mainly represented by intellectuals like Antonio Díaz Soto y Gama, joined up with Obregón, the revolutionary wing associated with Zapata and others confusedly sought a socialist perspective. We can see this, for example, in the views Zapata expressed in 1918 on the significance of the Russian Revolution. By then, however, revolutionary activity was already on the decline. The assassination of Emiliano Zapata itself closed the cycle of rise, peak, and decline that marked the revolutionary peasant war—a cycle already prefigured, for all its vicissitudes, in the internal contradiction of the Zapatist Ayala Plan.

The revolution spread in the South throughout December 1911, gripping the states of Morelos, Puebla, Guerrero, Tlaxcala, and Mexico early in the new year. In the most widely separated parts of the area, daily battles brought the Zapatist units, usually some three hundred to five hundred strong, into conflict with federal troops.

Where Zapatist forces were operating, the *hacendados* began to receive demands that they should pay their peons at least one peso a day or prepare to face the consequences. This is what happened, for example, to a Spanish hacienda owner in Chietla, Puebla State. Where the revolutionaries were already in firm control, however, they directly implemented the land distribution clauses of the Ayala Plan.

At the end of January 1912, Zapatist forces attacked Huajuapan de León in Oaxaca State. A journalist from a Mexico City daily commented: "I have become convinced that Zapatism has spread to an extraordinary degree. All the small villages are on the side of Emiliano Zapata. Major centers like Tepalcingo support his forces and greet them with abundant supplies, whereas they display a hostile attitude to government troops and refuse them everything."

In February 1912, armed peasant groups sprang up in support of Zapata in Michoacán and Hidalgo states. On February 3, the U.S. ambassador, Henry Lane Wilson, wrote to Washington that Zapata's troops effectively controlled all the territory between Cuernavaca, Morelos, and Chilpancingo, Guerrero. By March the Ayala banner held sway throughout the South, and the revolutionaries continually extended their power during the rest of the year.

As the struggle spread, so the Ayala Plan itself came into operation: villages took back their land from the haciendas, sometimes presenting a certificate but more often simply reaching a collective decision to cultivate the land and defend it with their guns. In some cases, the Zapatist high command issued decrees such as the following:

> Considering that Ixcamilpa village has presented the appropriate land-deeds, and that it has asked to take possession of its land from the chieftains who usurped it by brute force, we the undersigned, acting in the name of the Morelos Revolutionary Council and in conformity with the Ayala Plan, rule that they should take possession of the land which belongs to them and has belonged to them since the time of the Viceroyship, as is shown by the legal deeds

dating from the Viceroyship of New Spain, now Mexico. The inhabitants of the aforementioned village may immediately stake out their land up to the corresponding map-boundaries, being free to improve, cultivate or otherwise use the land in order to obtain its fruits. Freedom, Justice and Law!

Revolutionary Headquarters, 30 April 1912

General Eufemio Zapata, General O. E. Montaño, General Emiliano Zapata, General Francisco Mendoza, Divisional Commander, Jesús Morales, General Próculo Capistrán, [Zapata's deputy general] Jesús Navarro, Colonel Jesús Alcaide.

Right from the beginning until its peak in late 1914, the Zapatist army never departed from the form of territorial guerrilla militias. Whatever their size, these armed units operated under a common flag and recognized Zapata as commander-in-chief while retaining great independence of action under their own leader. When a major action was planned, several units would pool their forces, still maintaining their own leadership. The Zapatist troops had no barracks and received no pay, and they had no regular supplies apart from what the villages provided. Each soldier was also a peasant who worked his land. When a joint action was concluded, they would usually go back home to work. Although guerrillas would often travel a long distance to carry out an action, they could easily dissolve into the local working population at the approach of a superior federal force.

The shortage of money, weapons, and, above all, ammunition was always a limitation for the Zapatist army. It acquired nearly all its guns and ammunition in battle with the enemy—except for the very short periods in 1914 and 1915 when Zapata's troops occupied Mexico City. They had no funds to purchase bullets, nor, indeed, anyone from whom to buy them. Occasionally, workers at the National Cartridge Factory in the Federal District would smuggle them some supplies. But in 1918, the daily papers reported that a number of workers at the factory had been arrested and shot for such activity.

The peasant conception and structure of the war in the South did not permit a higher form of organization. Whereas the guerrilla form, driven by massive popular involvement, proved extraordinarily powerful during the rising tide of the movement, it displayed all its weakness when the masses began to retreat. For in this later stage, the guerrilla units had to bear the full brunt of the superior military organization of the Constitutionalist Army—a force which could base itself on the political and military centralization of the state apparatus, with its national, rather than localist, perspective.

From 1912 to 1914, the southern revolution continued its irresistible advance without having to fight any major battles. Even at its best moments, however, the fact that the class aims of the peasantry were limited to land ownership did not allow of more than a shadow of centralized power in areas controlled by the revolutionaries.

In general, the Zapatist forces did not hold on to towns, preferring to withdraw a few days or hours after they occupied them. They would constantly harry and ambush the federal army, retreat without offering a set battle, burn fields in enemy-held territory, and control or totally block the railway system. In other words, they applied a typical guerrilla tactic, basing it on the unqualified support of the entire population.[6]

The army met fire with fire, unleashing a war against the Morelos villages which set itself no bounds in time or content. For more than half of 1912, General Juvencio Robles sowed terror in the state and introduced a scorched-earth policy: there were mass shootings; whole villages were sacked or burned down; and any peasant suspected of helping the rebels was tortured along with his family. Although the name had not yet been invented, General Robles already applied a "strategic hamlet" policy, whose aim was to destroy Zapata's "nests" by herding village populations into larger centers and razing their homes. The peasantry responded to white terror and massive repression with an equally massive insurrection, in which every child and grandparent also had a part to play.

For the needs of the war, the Southern Liberation Army issued a whole series of decrees on supplies, troop conduct, communication, hygiene, and education. Together, these formed the "legislation" of the Morelos peasant power for the duration of the struggle. In fact, this "legislation" could only have been applied by the peasants, rather than a state bureaucracy. Its imprecision left ample scope for the class sense of the masses, for their fraternal, egalitarian conception of right and wrong as the best guarantee of justice. We may see this, for example, in a decree on supplies dating from the struggle against the Huerta government:

From General Emiliano Zapata, commander of the Southern and Central Revolution in the Republic, to the forces under his command, and to the villages and armed groups in the various military zones of the revolution.

1. It is strictly forbidden to slaughter livestock belonging to poor people or supporters of the cause. Except in cases prescribed below, anyone who contravenes this order is guilty of a serious crime and will be liable to punishment.

2. Food supplies for the liberation troops will come from livestock belonging to the revolution, formerly owned by the *hacendados* of Morelos State, or, more generally, by enemies of the cause. However, only forces acting under the command of the appropriate leaders may slaughter animals: isolated groups of two, three, five or eight revolutionaries, who, for no just reason, are without their designated leaders, are in no way allowed to do this.

3. If a revolutionary force is in an area where no livestock belongs to the revolution, and in lack of any other foodstuffs, it may avail itself of animals owned by supporters of the cause, always ensuring that they will not be gravely affected. Anyone who does not

respect this order is guilty of a serious offense and will be most severely punished without question of pardon.

4. *Non-members of the Revolutionary Army who, owing to poverty caused by depredations which the illegal Huerta mis-government*, through its treacherous supporters, *has committed in its own interests*, need to have access to livestock for their subsistence, *may slaughter animals belonging to the Revolution or to supporters of the cause. But whenever the livestock of supporters of the Revolution is to be used, it must belong to those who own many animals and will not be gravely affected.* In such cases, application should be made to the local authorities or to the nearest revolutionary commander, who will appoint a *commission* from the local inhabitants *and give it responsibility for slaughtering the required number of animals and distributing the meat among those most in need locally.* Anyone who disobeys this order is guilty of a serious offense and will be most severely punished.

5. Care must always be taken not to slaughter oxen, or cows which have recently given birth, except when the lack of sufficient livestock makes it necessary to use what is available. Those who breach this order will be severely punished.

6. It is strictly forbidden to brand animals which belong to the Revolution or are the property of other individuals. Anyone who does not respect this order will be severely punished.

Let this decree be printed, published, distributed and duly observed.

Morelos State Headquarters, 28 October 1913

Commander-in-chief of the Southern and Central Liberation Army, Emiliano Zapata.

In March 1912, Pascual Orozco led an antigovernment uprising in the North around a program of political and social reforms. It rapidly gained the Chihuahua State, but in May it suffered defeat at the hands of federal troops under Victoriano Huerta. During this campaign Francisco Villa, trained as a Maderist officer in Huerta's army, was nearly shot for insubordination—in the end, he was sent to prison in Mexico City, escaping before the fall of Madero. Within less than a year, fate had brought these three figures into total conflict: Huerta overthrew Madero with the support of Orozco and his men in the North; while Villa became the chief military leader of the revolution and eventually brought down the Huerta government in a series of victorious battles.

Although seemingly independent of each other, the Orozco revolt and Villa's imprisonment had closely related causes. Of the Chihuahua peasant leaders who supported Madero and his state governor, Abraham González, Orozco, and Vislla were the only ones to have strength, prestige, and authority of their own among the regional peasantry. It was they who together initiated the only successful battle of the Maderist revolution: the capture of Ciudad Juárez. In doing so, they violated Madero's express instruction that they should avoid combat and trust in his secret talks with the government. In fact, they had been forced to contrive various stratagems, sending advance units to draw the army's fire so that they could present the attack to Madero as a necessary riposte to enemy attack. This whole incident was one of the first serious manifestations of the clash between Madero and his peasant base.

When the Ciudad Juárez Accords were finally signed, Villa's and Orozco's officers went to see both leaders on behalf of their troops, expressing their disagreement with the deal and demanding an explanation of how the land problem would be solved. Under this intense pressure from below, Pancho Villa then arranged a talk with the governor and drew the reply: "We'll see what can be done to sell some national land to those who want to cultivate it. In the meantime, you must wait patiently until the new government is installed." The peasant leaders left in disgust. "Sell us national land?" they said. "Where are these national lands? Didn't the rich Chihuahua landowners build up their latifundia by purchasing national land, or by plundering the best of our land? Wasn't it for that reason that we took up arms and fought?"

The Orozco revolt would, in part, be a reflection of this discontent. Orozco became head of the Chihuahua rural guard, and Villa was brought into the army as an "honorary general." But whereas the rural guard had traditionally been used to "keep order" in the countryside and to defend the property of the *latifundistas,* Orozco did not try to prevent the spontaneous occupation and redistribution of the land which the peasantry launched in the region. When the Ayala Plan was issued in late November 1911, it explicitly designated Pascual Orozco as national leader of the anti-Madero revolution.

Orozco rose up a few months later against Madero's central government, relying upon support from the Chihuahua legislature and the senior and junior officers who had fought with him in the first phase of the Maderist revolution. It is said that he also received (covert) financial support from U.S. mining companies and the Terrazas family, which were disgruntled with the taxation policy of the Maderist governor, Abraham González. Orozco set forth the aims of his movement in the Empacadora Pact of March 25, 1912.

This program starts by acknowledging the principles of the San Luis Potosí Plan, the Ayala Plan, and the Tacubaya Plan.[7] It then denounces Madero's betrayal of the revolution, noting that he received $14 million for his movement and that "he made the revolution with the money of American millionaires and the indirect or covert support of the United States government." In return, "he placed the destiny of the fatherland in the hands of the American government." After enunciating plans for new elections and political reorganization of the country, the Empacadora Pact called for complete nationalization of the railways; a program of working-class measures to include abolition of employers' shops, payment of wages in cash, a maximum ten-hour day, prohibition of child labor below the age of ten (and a maximum six-hour day between ten and sixteen years of age), an increase in workers' wages and housing construction; and, finally, a land distribution program to include the return of plundered lands to their rightful owners, and the distribution of expropriated latifundia among the peasantry. Compensation for the latifundia should be in the form of government bonds, bearing 4 percent interest and repayable in part every ten years until final redemption.

When, as we have seen, General Huerta ordered Villa to be shot for "insubordination" during the campaign against Orozco, he was merely using a pretext to rid himself of the only other peasant leader with popular roots in Chihuahua. Villa was eventually saved by officers who could see that his execution would precipitate a violent reaction among the troops and the population. Under their pressure Madero had him sent to Mexico City, where he was held without trial first in Lecumberri Prison, and then in the military jail. Villa did not in fact realize that Madero's aim was to prevent him becoming leader of the whole northern peasantry, and he therefore retained his trust in the president. On December 26, however, when Madero's downfall seemed imminent, Villa escaped from Santiago Tlatelolco military prison and made his way to the United States.

Madero was overthrown and assassinated in February 1913. Pascual Orozco, already departing from the social concerns of the Empacadora Plan, then gave his backing to General Huerta, the military commander who had defeated him in Chihuahua the previous year. From this point Orozco, with his band of *Colorados*, was one of the fiercest defenders of the Huerta regime against Huerta's "insurbodinate" officer, General Francisco Villa. In furthering Huerta's ambitions of power, Orozco sent his own father to persuade Zapata that the struggle against Madero had triumphed, and that he should now lay down his arms and support the new government. In reply, Zapata erased Pascual Orozco's name from the Ayala Plan, and shot his father-cum-emissary in order to show beyond doubt that he would not negotiate with traitors.[8]

Throughout 1912 the main focus of the revolution remained in the South. The Mexico City press raised a hue and cry against Zapata, "the southern Attila," complaining that under his "barbaric socialism . . . hardly a single poor person in Morelos did not see his providence in the terrible rebel-leader." The papers denounced the incapability of the army and government; parliament called for the extermination of the Zapatistas; and the Madero government had to go begging in Europe and the United States for an additional $10 million loan with which to continue the war.

In a report to Congress on April 10, 1912, Madero tried to play down the spread of Zapatism: "Fortunately this amorphous agrarian socialism, which, given the rough intelligence of the Morelos peasantry, can only take the form of mindless vandalism, has not found an echo in other parts of the country." Despite this truculent language, however, the bourgeoisie did not believe in the assurances given by Madero.

The daily *El Imparcial*, organ of the old Díaz oligarchy, was one of the most violent in demanding implacable repression of the Zapatists. "Maybe Emiliano Zapata has some vague communist forebodings," we read in the issue of February 5, 1912, "and he may, in his stupidity, even believe that his banditry is nebulously linked to apostleship. Such a conviction perhaps explains his attractive power for the masses. Without realizing it, he may be intuitively preaching an apocalyptic doctrine of disintegration and extermination under the false banner of some vague egalitarianism." Another editorial in the same paper is headlined: "Zapatism: The Mortal Danger." The main argument is quite straightforward: "Either the government puts an end to Zapatism without delay, or Zapatism will eventually put an end to the government." It goes on to call for an "energetic purification" in Morelos, where "Zapatism is in the air people breathe, rooted in every inch they tread." "One does not require prodigious psychological insight," the editorial adds, "in order to discover who the Zapatists are and where they are to be found. . . . Everyone who inhabits Morelos and lives within the state boundaries is a Zapatist by sympathy, by fear, by convenience, by cowardice, by ignorance, by malice, by conviction, by subjugation, by weakness or by atavistic rebelliousness. These are the Zapatists; there they are."

The prose of the oligarchic newspaper reflects the fear of the property-owning classes in general—and more particularly, of the handful of big Morelos landowners, who fled without exception to Mexico City as the army was fighting it out with "Zapata and his troglodyte hosts" (*El Imparcial*). Nevertheless, the editorial gives a fair description of the popular war, which bogged down the skilled and well-armed federal troops.

> It comes to the notice of an army unit that a band of Zapatists has appeared in the vicinity, committing, as is their wont, all manner of outrages. The army immediately sets out for the place in question. What will it find? It finds a peaceful village: young men with spades in their hands; women bent over their grinding-stones; the authorities trying to discover the whereabouts of the men who attacked nearby haciendas, sad expressions, frightened looks. Where are the Zapatists? Who are the Zapatists? . . . The Zapatists have not moved: they are here, there they are! As in the old magic comedies, the stage-decoration and accessories have changed, but the characters are the same. Rifles have turned into spades, cartridge-belt into spindles, a den into a garden, a bandit into a navvy. Just one thing remains fixed, transparent, beyond dispute: the attack and the robbery.
>
> In the end, only these saturated surroundings can explain a revealing and typical fact: namely, the spontaneous generation of a large, tightly knit group of two thousand Zapatists near San Martín Texmelucan, who vanished overnight without leaving the slightest trace. How did they spring from nothing and return to nothing, these people whose exploits show them to be more real and tangible than nightmare phantoms? They had bodies and made some use of them. If they have disappeared so completely, it is because they could merge with the crowd who creates and hides them, like steam dissolving into the very water from which it originated.

The same kind of press accused Maderism of creating this situation with its promises of land contained in the San Luis Potosí Plan. President Madero answered these attacks through a letter to

El Imparcial published on June 27, 1912, in which he summarized his agrarian policy in power:

> I have always advocated the formation of smallholdings, but that does not mean that people should go and dispossess any landowner. . . . It is one thing to form smallholdings through constant effort, and another to divide up the big properties. I have never thought or suggested that in any of my speeches or proclamations. It would be utterly absurd to demand that the government should acquire all the big properties and divide them among smallhoders—which is what people usually understand by redistribution of the land. Quite simply, the government would not have enough money for such an operation, even if it were to contract such a huge loan that mere interest-payments would bankrupt the country.

He further maintained that the only unfulfilled promise was the one relating to the return of land to those arbitrarily dispossessed.

> Since the Ciudad Juárez Accords, so beneficial to the nation, involved a *modification* of the San Luis Potosí Plan, the new government had had to adapt all its actions to the law, recognizing the validity of court judgments and the legitimacy of every decree passed by the previous administration. It is therefore difficult to restore the land to those who have been unjustly dispossessed: the relevant judgments would have to be subject to review, in cases where the dispossession followed all the legal prescriptions.

If we compare his pettifogging arguments with the sense of egalitarian solidarity evident in every section of Zapata's decree on supplies, then we have an instant picture of the class forces locked in battle and of the simple and stubborn grandeur of Zapatism.

Under the Madero government, many different labor unions were able to operate openly. By mid-1912 there were the Longshoremen's

Guild of the Port of Tampico, the Mexican Mineworkers Union in the North, the Workers' Confederation in Torreón, the Confederation of Workers' Unions of the Mexican Republic in the port of Veracruz, the Union of Stonemasons and the Confederation of Mexican Typesetters in Mexico City, and various railway workers' organizations in different parts of the country. The workers' movement went through a phase of organization, and numerous strikes (by railway workers, longshoremen, textile workers, and miners, among others) won union demands. In January 1912, the government created the Department of Labor.

In July 1912, the *Casa del Obrero Mundial* (World Worker's House) was founded in Mexico City, organized by workers, artisans, and some unionist and anarchist intellectuals, among them several Spaniards, one of whom was quickly expelled from the country.

Anarchist ideas were also spread by the brothers Ricardo and Enrique Flores Magón of the Mexican Liberal Party (PLM) by way of their newspaper *Regeneración* (Regeneration), sent to Mexico from the United States. The Organizing Committee of the PLM, headed by Ricardo Flores Magón, had its base of operations in Los Angeles, California. The PLM had concentrated its forces in Baja California, and on January 29, 1911, a group of Magonists seized the border city of Mexicali to bring forward the "social revolution" that was the PLM's objective: "The revolt of Madero cannot call itself a Revolution," wrote Ricardo Flores Magón in March 1911. "Revolutions have to answer to social needs in order to be so considered. If not, they are only revolts."

The Magonists had the support of the members of the Industrial Workers of the World (IWW), known as the Wobblies, a revolutionary union organization based in the United States, and of anarchist, socialist, and unionist intellectuals and organizers like Emma Goldman, Jack London, and Joe Hill. However, they suffered the antagonism and repression of Porfirio Díaz, of the forces of Madero, and of the government in Washington: too many enemies at the same time. In late May, Joe Hill, a composer and singer of workers' songs (in November 1915 he would be shot during a wave of repression against the Wobblies), recruited IWW unionists in Los Angeles to join the Magonist rebellion, which in those days held the border city of Tijuana. This is how Hill described what he had seen on a trip to Tijuana: "As long as the red flag flew in Baja California, as much as I tried, I could not find a single 'important person' in the revolutionary ranks. I only found, in great numbers, ordinary, everyday workers."

On the other hand, groups of U.S. adventurers and soldiers of fortune also joined the movement. These were characters typical of the border region who were out for themselves and who created a climate as favorable to the disorganization of the movement as to provocations and ideas of annexing the territory of Baja California to the United States.

Porfirio Díaz, on April 1, 1911, declared that the movement of Baja California was composed of "bands of communists, among whom are many American pirates, with the fantastic idea of forming a socialist republic; such an ill-conceived proposal can do no less than provoke the greatest indignation of the country." From Los Angeles, the Organizing Committee of the PLM in a manifesto to Mexicans, responded as follows: "The Porfirists allege that those who are fighting in Baja California are foreigners, as though to fight for the liberty and welfare of the Mexican people, one had to be born on that very soil. . . . The Porfirists talk to you about patriotism, they, the traitors who have left in foreign hands the destiny of our race, they, the dogs who by giving our lands to foreigners forced us to leave the land in which we were born to seek our bread in this country."

On May 20, 1911, on the eve of the fall of Porfirio Díaz, Ricardo Flores Magón insisted in *Regeneration*: "Understand this well, lackeys of Díaz and Madero, the liberals have no intention of separating Baja California from the rest of Mexico. . . . Baja California constitutes . . . the principal base of our operations to extend the social revolution to all of Mexico."

However, it was not the Magonist social revolution, but the Maderist democratic revolution that was destined to triumph in those days. The Ciudad Juárez Accords and the resignation of Porfirio Díaz concentrated the diverse groups and factions in the struggle against Díaz around the Maderist course. Among these groups were many that had previously been attracted to the PLM, and hence the movement definitively took this Maderist direction. The Magonist rebellion remained isolated, and its weaknesses and contradictions sharpened. In June 1911, the rebellion was defeated in Baja California. On June 14, the Los Angeles police detained the leaders of the PLM, accusing them of organizing armed expeditions from U.S. territory against friendly governments.

In September 1911, the PLM issued a manifesto in which it called upon the people "to abolish the principle of private property," and for the working class, arms in hand, to expropriate the capitalist class and establish a system in which "land, housing, the machinery of production and the means of transportation were all used in common." The manifesto carried the words of the First International: "The emancipation of the workers should be the work of the workers themselves," and after approving the taking of land by the *campesinos*, it said: "[T]here is no need to limit ourselves to taking possession only of the land and agricultural implements: it is necessary for workers to resolutely take possession of their own industries, so that in this manner the lands, the mines, the factories, the workshops, the foundries, the carriers, the railroads, the ships, the warehouses of all kinds and housing remain in the power of each and every inhabitant of Mexico, without regard to sex."

The anarchism of Flores Magón, nevertheless, lacked any material instrument or organized forces in Mexico to bring its demands into practice. It could not, therefore, go beyond the field of general ideas and propaganda. Nor did it have the means of establishing contact and alliances with the peasants who later took up arms and seized lands, for whom the Ayala Plan would end up being much more real and accessible, and therefore more effective in the day-to-day practice of their own revolution.

★ ★ ★

The first attempted coup against Madero took place in the early days of his government, when Bernardo Reyes crossed the northern border on December 13, 1911 and called for a popular uprising. Though completely isolated and forced to surrender on December 25, Reyes retained some prestige and contacts among the officers of the federal army that Madero left totally unchanged. The next attempt, following the Orozco revolt, was headed by Porfirio Díaz's nephew, Félix Díaz, who brought out the Veracruz garrison on October 16, 1912, and tried to capitalize on the growing opposition to Madero within the army. But Félix Díaz did not have sufficient authority among the officers, and no one followed his lead. A week later, after his forces had been defeated, he was sent to Santiago Tlatelolco military prison. Thanks to the privileges and facilities the federal army granted its imprisoned officers, he was there able to meet with General Reyes and to establish a conspiratorial center against Madero's government.

As the year 1912 drew to an end, the Maderist government was paralyzed and in the throes of crisis. On its right, conservative currents representing hacienda interests were demanding still more vigorous repression against the peasant revolution; while on its left, petty-bourgeois currents within Maderism, including the so-called renewal deputies, were calling for reforms that would grant some land to the peasantry and thus tackle the roots of the insurgency.

The congressman Luis Cabrera, who two years later would become Carranza's ideologue and draft his agrarian legislation, most clearly expressed the viewpoint of such currents. In September 1912, he declared himself a Jacobin: "The Jacobin is a social type that appears when it is time to save nations from great catastrophes," he said. Speaking in the Chamber of Deputies in December 1912, he saw the need for legal measures to endow the villages with communal land (*ejidos*). Already in colonial times, he recalled, the peasants had come to depend upon three forms: the village property on which their houses stood; the land from which the local administration derived its resources; and the communal lands cultivated for the villagers' own subsistence. The disentailment acts then opened the floodgates for the haciendas to seize municipal and communal land by force or by corrupt court judgments, so that the peasants were left as prisoners in their stripped villages and forced to become casual hacienda laborers or to die of hunger.

Cabrera was seeking a very concrete way in which to defend private property. As things stood, the haciendas could no longer rely upon the armed forces to keep the peasantry subdued, and it would therefore be best to give it some land. For "either these people will pick up a rifle and go off to swell the Zapatist ranks, or they will find lawful ways of expending energy on their communal pastures, woodlands and farmland" for the six to eight months of the year in which they have no work on the hacienda.

Cabrera therefore proposed that, in conformity with the law and the Constitution, part of the hacienda land should be bought up and given to the villages as their communal property. Rejecting the demand for communal land contained in the Ayala Plan, he argued that the previous regime had legally recognized most of the hacienda land seized in one way or another from the peasantry, and that, whether they were fair or not, these land deeds should not be challenged by fresh legal proceedings. In other words, he defended the juridical continuity of the state—the very principle the Zapatist plan began by disavowing.[9]

As we have seen, Madero dismissed this reformist solution as utopian, but he was not able to put down Zapatism by force. The coup which would put an end to his government and his life was becoming a necessity for the ruling classes.

Since Porfirio Díaz leaned toward Britain in the imperialist rivalry for influence in Mexico, the U.S. government had initially been sympathetic to Madero. But now it looked with alarm on the spread of revolution on its southern border. President Taft moved a considerable number of troops to the frontier area, and even sent diplomatic notes threatening intervention "should the government of Mexico be incapable of protecting the lives and interests of Americans" in the country.

However, the Democratic Party candidate, Woodrow Wilson, won the U.S. presidential election in November 1912, defeating the incumbent president, William Howard Taft. The Democrats also won a majority in both houses of Congress. Thus, once the new administration came into office on March 4, 1913, the attitude of the White House toward Madero might change. The U.S. ambassador to Mexico, Henry Lane Wilson, deemed it necessary to strike first.

In February 1913, when everyone in Mexico was talking of the imminent overthrow of Madero, the U.S. ambassador wrote as follows to his government: "In my view, the general situation here has become very gloomy, not to say desperate." In Chihuahua, Durango, Coahuila, Nuevo León, and Zacatecas, "the hideous revolutionary ferment" was breaking out once again. "For two years now, more than a third of Mexico's states have been caught up in an ever-rising revolutionary movement. . . . This fact, as well as others which we do not have to mention here, has been greatly demoralizing and disturbing financial and banking circles in the country. Not only does it seriously damage commercial business and reduce credit; *above all* it is a threat to the very existence of these institutions."

A few days later, when the commander-in-chief of the operational army, General Huerta, overthrew the government, killed President Madero and Vice President José María Pino Suárez, and occupied the presidency, it was only natural that he should count on the support and approval of the U.S. ambassador, Henry Lane Wilson. However, Ambassador Wilson's opinion was not shared by other U.S. diplomats in various towns of the Republic.

The coup began on February 9. General Mondragón rose in revolt at the head of two thousand men, and with their help freed

Generals Bernardo Reyes and Félix Díaz. General Reyes then led his troops in an attack on the National Palace, falling at their head in the first exchange of fire. Félix Díaz took his place, and entrenched his forces in the sealed buildings of the Ciudadela, the barracks and the army depot of central Mexico City. Since the commander of the Maderist forces, General Lauro Villar, had been wounded in the attack on the palace, Madero appointed General Victoriano Huerta to take charge of operations. The Ciudadela was besieged, but in the next few days Huerta showed no interest in an assault and did not even prevent supplies from reaching the *golpistas*.

This peculiar siege ended after the "tragic ten days," which left many soldiers and civilians dead or wounded. Under the terms of an agreement signed on February 18, 1913, by Félix Díaz for the besieged and by Huerta for the besiegers, Madero was to be dismissed and provisionally replaced by Huerta himself, a new cabinet was to be formed, and Díaz was to be free to run as a candidate in the next presidential elections. Since, according to witnesses, the agreement was signed in the U.S. Embassy upon the personal intervention of Henry Lane Wilson, it has become known as the Ciudadela Pact or Embassy Pact.

Madero and Pino Suárez were arrested that day in the National Palace; they resigned their posts on February 19, and two days later they were murdered by their escort while being transferred to Lecumberri Prison "for their own safety."

In the last analysis Madero fell, as some of his own supporters predicted, because he had been powerless to stamp out Zapatism. But instead of stopping the revolution, the Huerta coup was the signal for the flames of peasant war to engulf the whole country.

The agrarian insurrection burst on all sides, following neither a plan nor a leadership. The strength of this peasant revolution greatly exceeded the capacity of ruling politicians to contain or repress it. Its elemental quest for land—expressed in such basic demands as immediate redistribution of the haciendas, restitution of village land, and armed protection of those working the land—attacked the very foundations of Mexican capitalism. For under the Porfirio Díaz regime, capitalist development had found its national center of gravity in the handful of big landowners who held most of the country and the state, so that agrarian property continued to be the essential basis of capitalist accumulation. The revolution, Zapata's "barbaric socialism," struck at precisely this point.

Thus, unlike earlier peasant wars, which opened the way for capitalism, the Zapatist revolution challenged the very foundations on which capitalism molded and sustained itself. In this sense, it prefigured the twentieth-century agrarian revolutions, rising from peasant war to an alliance with the urban subaltern classes, a whole reshaping of the state and, in many instances, national or socialist goals.

Although Emiliano Zapata could only glimpse this future, the breach he opened has never been sealed.

4

The Northern Division

The Northern Division was one of the greatest historical achievements of the Mexican subaltern classes, its emergence a turning-point in the peasant war and the revolution. They created this army out of nothing, sweeping everything in their path and hoisting one from their own ranks, Francisco Villa, the main military leader of the revolution.

Unlike the Zapatist forces, Villa's Northern Division was not politically independent during the period of its greatest military victories over the federal army. As it advanced on the center of the country in order to bring down the government, it appeared as one of the three armies supporting the bourgeois political leadership of the revolution.

Within this structure, it became ever more independent in its military activity, reflecting the need for political independence confusedly felt by its peasant base and leadership. But had it not been for the Zapatist army in the South, this need would never have found a form in which to express itself. The bourgeois and petty-bourgeois leaders of the revolution anticipated with dread a junction between Villa's peasant army swooping down from the North, and Zapata's peasant army closing on Mexico City from the South. For this would unite the strongest military and the strongest political talent acquired by the peasant leaders, drawing the insurrection together at a national level. These leaders realized that such a development would not only bring down their Huertist adversaries, but also expose their own perspective to the unpredictable dangers of an alien and hostile force: the revolutionary peasantry.

So long as the revolutionary upsurge continued, however, they did not have sufficient military, social, or political strength to oppose Zapatism and Villism or to prevent a linkup between the two.

The Ciudad Juárez Accords had sealed the political continuity between Porfirio Díaz and Madero on the clear basis of an end to the peasant insurrection. If Madero was assassinated by his own right wing, eventually headed by General Huerta, this was because he proved incapable of fulfilling this basic condition. The aim had been to contain the revolution in the rest of the country through Madero's remaining prestige, while isolating and militarily defeating it in its organized southern stronghold. With Madero's assassination, however, the last faint hope disappeared. The Huerta wing did not share this perspective, believing that prolonging of the Maderist regime would increase the attractive power of the South for the rest of the country. The U.S. ambassador's correspondence clearly reflected this feeling: "The situation has become very gloomy, not to say desperate."

In reality, the situation was not dependent upon what Madero did or failed to do: the revolution was already breaking throughout the whole country, and the Huertist coup merely sparked a generalized insurrection.

Huerta initially tried to vaunt his opposition to Madero as a way of neutralizing and attracting Orozco's forces in the North and, above all, Zapata in the South. Orozco did, indeed, rally to the Huertist counterrevolution. But although the new government, like Madero before it, offered Zapata safeguards, money, property, and posts in the Morelos administration, his response was to call for a struggle against Huerta in the name of the Ayala Plan, refusing to lay down arms to anyone until the principles in the plan had triumphed. By contrast, the governors of all but Coahuila and Sonora states recognized the Huerta regime.

As in the Maderist stage, Zapata's political attitude was crucial to the continuity of the revolution. The whole country was in revolt a few weeks after the fall of Maderism, and this time the focus was Zapata with his Ayala Plan and Southern Liberation Army.

Zapata's stand may have speeded up the anti-Huerta declaration of the fifty-three-year-old Venustiano Carranza, a big landowner who had been a senator under Porfirio Díaz, then a Madero supporter and governor of Coahuila State. It was not the only factor, however. Maderism had attracted support from the very broad section of the petty bourgeoisie which sought a democratic-nationalist way out from the Díaz dictatorship. It was among these layers that the tendency represented by the Maderist government had found a social base, also being able to count on much of the northern bourgeoisie and the Coahuila or Sonora *hacendados*. In confronting Huertism, then, Carranza assumed the continuity of a tendency which, on the one hand, saw concessions as the only way of containing the revolution, and on the other, aspired to become its national-bourgeois leadership with a political base in the nationalist petty bourgeoisie and, through their social connection, in the peasantry itself. Joined only by the Sonora State governor, José María Maytorena, Carranza refused to recognize Huerta as president, invoked the principle of constitutional continuity by referring to his own election in Coahuila, and called for the overthrow of "the usurper government."

This call was formalized in the Guadalupe Plan, a "manifesto to the nation," signed on March 26, 1913, over a month after the coup, in the hacienda of Guadalupe, Coahuila. Condemning the anti-Maderist coup, the plan rejected the Huerta government as well as every legislative or judicial authority and every state governor that recognized the federal government. It resolved to form a Constitutionalist Army, to support its declarations with arms, and to appoint Venustiano Carranza as commander-in-chief of the army. It further stipulated that the commander-in-chief, upon entering Mexico City, should assume charge of the executive power and call general elections for the presidency of the Republic.

When Carranza presented the draft plan to his young officer-supporters, a group including Captain Francisco J. Múgica argued for the inclusion of working-class demands, points referring to land distribution and the abolition of employers' shops, and a number of other social questions. In reply, Carranza stressed the need to unite the broadest possible forces and to neutralize the many enemies who would be turned against the revolution by such demands. First there had to be a military victory, and then could come the social reforms. By means of this old argument, typical of a leadership seeking to contain a revolutionary movement within its own horizons, Carranza forced acceptance of the Guadalupe Plan with its call for nothing more than a change in government.

This early discussion already pointed to one of the major contradictions of Carranzism, which persisted throughout the period of armed struggle and found new expression in the drafting of the Constitution—namely, the contradiction between Carranza's bourgeois leadership and the Jacobin wing rooted in the military and represented by Múgica and, to some extent, such figures as Lucio Blanco. Although Carranza permanently held this wing in check, he had to make concessions at crucial moments in order to retain it as his bridge to the masses. Obregón subsequently came to the fore as an arbiter in the dispute, as well as in the broader conflict between Carranzism and the revolutionary movement. But in order to carry this task to completion, he had to await a decline in the revolution, eliminating Carranza on the way. Conversely, in order to place its own stamp on the Constitution, the Jacobin wing had both to mature in the course of the struggle and to await a further extension and deepening of the revolution.

Despite the political poverty of the Guadalupe Plan, the Constitutionalist Army stood as a military pole of political legitimacy and material strength throughout the North for the uprising against Victoriano Huerta.

In March 1913, Francisco Villa crossed into Chihuahua from the United States, where he had taken refuge on escaping from prison. As an old Maderist, he joined the newly emerging Constitutionalist Army and used his prestige among the Chihuahua peasantry to organize a brigade. A few months later, this would become the Northern Division.

Under the Porfirio Díaz regime, a number of clashes with the landowners had forced Villa to go on the run, doing various jobs in the fields or living in the mountains from cattle-stealing.[1] His enemies would never cease to describe him as a bandit and an outlaw. But in this uneven struggle with the rural guards, he developed that natural capacity for combat and revolt which flourished in the brief Maderist campaign and earned him his authority as a military leader in Chihuahua. In addition, Villa very soon displayed a great talent as a military organizer: not only with the mass of peasant soldiers who made up his army, but also with the officers of his general staff, whether their origin was in the peasantry, the impoverished petty bourgeoisie, or the military academies. This side of his activity also proved fruitful among the working-class layers of the North, above all the miners and railway workers. The latter, in particular, the majority of whom were won over to Villism, played a decisive role in the organization of troop movements by train, and one of their number, General Rodolfo Fierro, occupied one of the highest positions on Villa's general staff. In this way, the Northern Division took shape and developed into an irresistible military machine.

The Constitutionalist Army also included other formations: the Northeast Army, under General Pablo González, which operated in the states of Tamaulipas and Nuevo León and throughout the Northeast of Mexico; and the Northwest Army, based in Sonora and commanded by Alvaro Obregón, which moved south through all the West Coast states.

While the Northeast Army conducted a hesitant and marginal compaign in its home region, the main battles of the civil war took place along Obregón's line of advance in the west and Villa's in the center. Both armies followed the course of the railway lines: the first the Pacific Railway, the second the Central Railway. And so, the tracks laid for the extraction of raw materials toward the north drew the northern revolution toward the center of Mexico.

Technically, Villa's division remained subordinate to the Northwest Army under Obregón. This was Carranza's personal decision, for although he had to rely on Villa's support, he displayed from the beginning an attitude of deep mistrust and hostility. In practice, Villa did not accept this hierarchical subordination, and the Northern Division acted as a formation equal to or higher in importance than the Northwest Army. However, since Carranza was never willing to call it an army, Villa's force has gone down in history as the Northern Division. In its heyday, it was much more feared by the enemy than any of the other military formations, armies or not.

The northern peasantry, roused by a revolution in which it saw the prospect of land, provided the soldiers for all three sections of the Constitutionalist Army. Most of the officers came from the provincial petty bourgeoisie (office workers, schoolteachers, well-off farmers), although some, like General Felipe Angeles, the Villist artillery commander and strategist, had previously been in the federal army. Alvaro Obregón was a well-to-do small farmer in Sonora State who soon distinguished himself both for his military flair and for his political talents and ambition. Plutarco Elías Calles, another future president and organizer of the post revolutionary Mexican state, had been a police superintendent in the small frontier town of Agua Prieta, Sonora. Manuel M. Diéguez, who won promotion as a divisional commander in Obregón's army, had led the 1906 strike in Cananea and was leader of the municipal council when Huerta launched his coup. The other Constitutionalist officers were of similar origin: some would die in the course of the war, while others rose to dizzying heights, becoming the millionaire pillars of the new national ruling class and its political and economic apparatus in the years after the 1910–20 revolution.

One group of officers, who later supported Obregonism in its political ascendance, developed as a revolutionary-nationalist, Jacobin, and even socialistic current within the Carranzist army. Its foremost exponent was undoubtedly Francisco J. Múgica, later head of the Jacobin wing at the Constituent Congress. This group fused revolutionary-nationalist ideology with the general influence of the insurgent peasantry, hoping to push through its ideas in the very development of the struggle. Victory, in its view, involved not merely a change in government, but a change in the basis of the Mexican state which would transfer land to the peasantry, expand working-class conquests, and open the way for a rather ill-defined socialist course.

Although there was a permanent conflict between Carranza and this group of officers, it did not always appear on the surface. For it was generally subordinate to the still deeper conflict with Villism in the army ranks, and to the open struggle with the government and the Zapatist movement. When General Lucio Blanco led his troops to capture the Tamaulipas border town of Matamoros on June 4, 1913, this provided one of the first occasions on which the conflict with Carranza openly expressed itself. After establishing firm control over the region, Blanco and his chief of staff, the then Major Múgica, decided that they should begin to apply the principles of the revolution by organizing land redistribution. In August, Múgica, as the driving force behind the project, expropriated a hacienda from a counterrevolutionary general and publicly distributed it among the peasants.

Carranza's reaction was swift and sharp: he ordered Blanco to call off any further land distribution, relieved him of his command, and transferred him to another zone. In his place he appointed General Pablo González, the future butcher of peasants and organizer of Zapata's murder, whose military incompetence was so great that he became known as "the general who never won a battle." In his talks with Carranza's emissaries, Múgica not only defended the expropriation in question but argued that the social reforms should be continued throughout the very course of the struggle, and that in Sonora State, where the Constitutionalist movement was initially strongest, property belonging to enemies of the revolution should be immediately nationalized.

However, Múgica came from Michoacán, and the social composition of the forces that led the revolutionary movement in Sonora and Coahuila was hardly propitious for his ideas. In both states, but particularly in Sonora, the modern *hacendados* and well-off small farmers who placed themselves at the forefront of the movement—typified by José María Maytorena and Alvaro Obregón, respectively—had no inclination toward measures of this kind. The Sonora-based army, and the Constitutionalist forces in general, assured regular pay for their soldiers. Unlike the Zapatists, then, these troops looked to army service as a means of subsistence for themselves and their families, in times when better-paid work was not available. If there were not enough funds to go around, Obregón would order the rank and file to be paid before the officers. (After all, higher grades had the hope, later confirmed in reality, that the victory of the revolution would bring them social advancement and much more substantial economic benefits.) Key to success was the uninterrupted control of Sonora since the beginning of the revolution—something Carranza could not match in Coahuila—which allowed the pre-existing state apparatus to maintain its well-organized administration, finances, economic resources, and local armed forces. This helps to explain the extraordinary weight of Sonorans within the Constitutionalist movement: they were, so to speak, the "Prussians" of Mexico's capitalist North, driving forward to conquer and unify the country during the first revolution and the successive governments of Huerta, Obregón, and Calles.[2]

On September 20, 1913 in Hermosillo, Sonora, the commander-in-chief, Venustiano Carranza, officially appointed General Alvaro Obregón to head the Northwest Army, with jurisdiction over Sonora, Chihuahua, and Sinaloa and the territory of Baja California. Obregón, whose forces controlled the whole of Sonora, had won two battles in March against the *federales*: one at Santa Rosa, the other at Santa María. Now, or shortly after, such leaders as Diéguez, Calles, and Iturbe, who had revolted on their own initiative at the time of the Huerta coup, integrated their military detachments into the Northwest Army.

Pancho Villa, whose brigade had already scored some victories, including the capture of San Andrés, therefore came under the jurisdiction of Obregón. On September 29, 1913, his own and other brigades united in the Northern Division, of which he was elected commander. On October 10, the brand-new division took the important railway junction of Torreón, capturing both military equipment and a sizeable quantity of rolling stock. Over the next year, Villa's division would increase its strength at breathtaking speed, rapidly surpassing in military importance the forces that operated under Obregón in the west of the country.

Until Torreón, Huerta had been strengthening his position in power with the help of internal and foreign credits. His first step was to shake off his allies from the February coup, Díaz and Mondragón, by attaching them to missions abroad, and to forge alliances with Catholic, Porfirist, and pro-Reyes politicians, as well as exercising an attractive power over the Orozco movement. In broad outline, he continued Madero's policy toward both capital and labor, as he also did on the land question. He tightened the links with British imperialism—the United States having inclined toward his ally and rival, General Félix Díaz—and asserted his own authority in the army. (Huerta's prestige as a capable officer and good organizer may well have been one of the reasons why Madero substituted him for Lauro Villar to crush the Ciudadela rising, since the president could not risk offending army opinion at that crucial juncture.) Huerta raised the strength of the army to eighty-five thousand, and a year later some two-hundred thousand *federales* were said to be under arms. It is possible, however, that a number of places were allocated and never actually filled, so that the money to pay and equip these "phantoms" went straight into the pockets of the correspondingly swollen officer corps. He also continued Madero's attempts to establish good relations with the trade-union leaders, seeking their active cooperation with his government or at least their neutrality in the civil war.

Official histories, picturing Huerta as an inept officer and a habitual drunkard, cast him as the villain of a piece in which all the other bourgeois leaders were fearless knights in shining armor. But although his fondness for drink is well established, this was not his defining characteristic, at least so long as he had some chance of success and was able to keep some control of the situation. He should be taken seriously, as he was by his enemies of the time. In essence, he was an army man who showed certain qualities on the battlefield and followed an energetic, skillful, and remorseless policy of reaction, both in organizing the counterrevolutionary repression and in resisting the pressures from Woodrow Wilson, which grew stronger and more menacing as he sought political support from Britain and other European powers.[3]

Huerta's career did not, of course, cover a wide span. Villa's triumph at Torreón dramatically cut it short by demonstrating the capacity for struggle and victory which the Constitutionalists had accumulated in this early period of the war. Huerta produced a coup within the regime in response to this military setback, the pressure from Washington, and the mounting opposition of the Mexican Congress. On October 10, 1913, he dissolved Congress and called presidential and parliamentary elections for October 27, which he naturally won. A few days before, however, on October 17, Carranza had counterattacked by declaring a provisional government in Sonora as the only legitimate authority for the whole national territory. On October 21, he produced his masterstroke: the federal army would be dissolved after the victory of the Constitutionalist forces. In this way, Carranza drew one of the key lessons from Madero's fate.

After the battle of Torreón, Villa returned to the North and prepared to take Chihuahua City in mid-November. But then, while still leading people to believe that he intended to capture the town, he carried out one of those maneuvers that greatly boosted his military reputation. He began by ordering a forced march to Ciudad Juárez in the North, and en route seized a train on its way down to Chihuahua. At the next station, he captured the telegraph operator and made him send a message to Ciudad Juárez in the name of the stationmaster, reporting that the track ahead had been cut by revolutionaries and asking for instruction. From Ciudad Juárez, the unsuspecting federal command ordered the train to return and to cable its position from every station along the route. Villa, with two thousand men, climbed onto the train, while the cavalry followed at a gallop. The operation was repeated at each station: he seized the telegraph operator, cut the line to the south, and cabled for instructions. In this way, the train full of Villists eventually reached Ciudad Juárez, all but announcing its arrival yet not arousing the least suspicion. Once in the town, Villa and his soldiers leapt from the train and quickly overcame the thunderstruck garrison. This bold stroke gave Villa crucial access to the frontier, from which he was able to receive military equipment and other supplies. The story of his feat also increased Villa's military prestige in the popular imagination, and made his Northern Division a recruiting agent for the revolutionary forces.

When the federal army sent troops from Chihuahua, Villa went out to defeat them on November 23, 1913, at the pitched battle of Tierra Blanca. On December 8, he occupied Chihuahua without a struggle, the *federales* already having abandoned the town; but the next day, fresh federal troops managed to retake Torreón. On January 11, 1914, he again defeated the Huertist army at the battle of Ojinaga. By early March, the Northern Division had secured the whole of Chihuahua State and completed preparations for a southward thrust to break the back of the federal forces in the center of the country.

Meanwhile, Obregón's army, having taken the Sinaloa capital, Culiacán, on November 20, 1913, had entered a period of military inactivity in which it mainly limited itself to controlling the northwestern coastal states of Sonora and Sinaloa. Everyone could see that the decisive battles were being prepared by Villa's advance on the center of the country. It was the Northern Division, not its two flanking armies, that had acquired sufficient impetus to beat the federal army in the central regions where its military strength was still intact. Villa's forces would break this strength by successively capturing Torreón and Zacatecas in April and June 1914: the key military engagements in this stage of the revolution. In March 1914, when the Northern Division left Chihuahua for Torreón with General Angeles already on its general staff, it was a strong and assured combat force at the height of its military capacities.

★   ★   ★

The golden period of the Northern Division lasted throughout 1914. It was a pole of attraction for the insurgent peasants, their women, their families. Its officers had all sprung from the same peasantry: audacity, bravery, and fighting capacity were the criteria for selection. With passion and love, John Reed describes in *Insurgent Mexico* how the Villists carried out their advance in the first half of this triumphal year. It was an armed mass that moved southward, engaging in battles big and small in its conquest of Mexico. On train or horse, accompanied by their women (who, if necessary, would also shoulder a rifle) and their children, the soldiers of the Northern Division embodied the irresistible force of the revolution.

Although the Villist advance had an appearance of great disorder, its actions displayed a higher order than that of any military regulations. It was imposed by the common will and the common objective guiding the peasant in arms. Victory meant land: there will be no more rich and poor after the revolution; we will all be equal and live in peace; we will have the land, and there will be no exploiters. Pancho Villa drew on this peasant wellspring to concentrate the universal will to victory under his own command. He could do this better than anyone, since he himself was a peasant, synthesizing all the qualities, desires, and aims of his men. By virtue of his organizational abilities, Villa was able to convert this armed mass into the best army of the Mexican Revolution.

The vast multitude of northern peons and landless peasants found life-purpose in Villism: for the first time they could express themselves, fighting to win and take control, not to suffer repression and defeat. Unlike the Zapatist movement in the South, Villism did not have a program. It was therefore Villa's own personality, as the best soldier, horseman, and countryman, that came to represent the insurgent peasantry.

The soldiers saw themselves in Villa, and he inspired them with absolute confidence. He raised to a heroic level the characteristic features of them all: courage, hatred and mistrust of the exploiters, implacability and cruelty in battle, astuteness and candor, tenderness

and solidarity toward the poor and oppressed, and also their instability. We can thus understand the many theatrical aspects of Villa's
actions as a means of communication with his base, an elementary
method of unifying the soldiers under his command.

Villa's personality was necessary to unite and give leadership to
those masses in motion, who in turn rallied and absorbed poor or
ambitious petty bourgeois, deserters, soldiers, and the armed units
spontaneously forming and then dissolving in northern villages before and after a battle. Most of the striking, energetic characteristics
the bourgeoisie deprecated in Villa—while concealing that thousands upon thousands of peasants were murdered in cold blood by
its own cruel commanders, from Carranza down—were in fact the
very features he needed to guide and command his army, in the
absence of the culture and education enjoyed by the federal army
officers who had attended military college. Since Villa, more than
any other figure in the revolution, spread terror among the ruling
classes, their denigration of him is merely an inverted reflection
of fear.

The terror, of course, originated not so much in Villa as in the
peasant revolution he represented. But he did know how to turn
it to advantage, nurturing and promoting the invincible reputation
of the Northern Division as an element in the military struggle.
For if the enemy can be filled with terror, the battle is already half
won. Many stories of Pancho Villa's cruelty were essentially no
more than basic instruments, sometimes instinctive, yet vital, with
which to sow revolutionary terror among the enemy class. On the
opposite side, Madero, Huerta, and Carranza all slaughtered the
Morelos peasantry en masse, burning, shooting, or deporting half
the population of the Zapatist zone.

"The [Napoleonic] army," Marx wrote, "was the small peasant
proprietors' *point d'honneur*, the peasant himself transformed into a
hero, defending his new possessions against external enemies, glori-
fying his recently won nationhood, and plundering and revolution-
izing the world. The uniform was the peasant's national costume,
the war was his poetry, the smallholding, extended and rounded off

in imagination, was his fatherland, and patriotism was the ideal form of his sense of property."[4] The Villist army was much more than this for the Mexican peasantry: it was its strength and "military party"; it was its human personality, which, denied for centuries by the oppressors, entered the world in fire and blood, cheerfully clearing its path of the bosses, the rich, and the privileged and leisure classes.

Partly through experience, partly through his own awareness and intelligence, Pancho Villa knew how to conduct his campaign. This explains the tremendous military impetus of the Northern Division. "When we win the Revolución," a Villist captain told John Reed, "it will be a government by the men (los hombres)—not by the rich. We are riding over the lands of the men. They used to belong to the rich, but now they belong to me and to the compañeros." An old peasant added: "The revolution is a good thing! When it's over, we'll never, ever be hungry, God willing."[5] With this concentrated charge of expectations, the Northern Division swept down to the capital, cutting the landowners' army to pieces on the way.

Victory does not come from hopes alone, but above all from organization of the fighting forces. In this Villa was a true master: he could make full use of the train to organize supplies, obtain funds and military equipment from the appropriate places, furnish thirty and even forty whitewashed hospital wagons with the latest surgical and other equipment, and ensure that wounded soldiers were speedily evacuated to the rear. He tried hard to introduce the norms of military regulation, productively integrating career officers into his army. He kept by his side General Angeles, the most outstanding of these officers, and used his artillery skills and knowledge of strategy in the main victories of the division.

As commander, Villa showed great vigor and audacity in the maneuvers of battle, for which the cavalry, his natural element and favorite weapon, was well suited. But he also had an inborn grasp of the economy of forces, and a concern for the fighting and living conditions of his troops. In complete contrast, federal officers looked on the simple soldier as cannon fodder for prodigal use on the battlefield. Not only did the Villist soldier have a revolutionary objective, but experience had taught him to believe that his leaders paid as much heed as possible to the men's lives. He therefore found it quite reasonable when an order required him to risk his life or even to go to his death.

Above all, however, the Northern Division was the army of the peasants, headed and mostly officered by peasants. Its trains were loaded with peasant men and women, who were becoming the masters of Mexico. Wherever it advanced, it would raise the peasants' hopes and focus their support. In every town or city it entered, prison doors were opened and pawnshops closed, giving back their belongings to the poor people. Its very lines of march encouraged them to rise in revolt, to seize the land, and to cultivate their own smallholdings on haciendas from which the big landowners had been expelled. Like the Zapatists and all people's armies, it had its own intelligence network: the peasants saw everything, and innumerable mouths kept it well informed about the enemy's plans for city defense, military operations, and so on. Thus, so long as the mass upsurge continued, the Northern Division was an invincible force. Through it, or under its protection, the peasant masses settled many big or small accounts that had built up over centuries of oppression and plunder—accounts with the rich, or their agents and allies, and with the *señores*, or their foremen, stewards, and rural guards. It was the revolution.

A magnificent fighter and organizer, Pancho Villa is a nightmarish memory for the Mexican ruling classes. He taught that the federal army was not invincible in civil war, leaving a tradition in Mexico that a peasant army, led by a peasant general, can win battle after battle until finally annihilating it as a military force. The bourgeoisie can tolerate and even forget this from one of its own, but it can never forgive it from an ex-peon born on its old haciendas. A peasant turned bandit who, though he received hardly any basic schooling, mastered to perfection all the arts of horsemanship, agriculture, and weaponry; who, though learning to write only in

Mexico City Prison, displayed a lightning organizational mind; who had unpredictable reactions and spread them among powerful enemy forces unknown to the bourgeoisie—such a man appeared to be the embodiment of absolute evil, of revolution. Most crucially, he showed that nothing the ruling classes considered vitally necessary was in fact indispensable; that since a peasant leader could organize what its own best administrators could never do, their rule as a class was not necessary. This is a nightmare for the rulers, but above all it is a further source of self-confidence for the people of Mexico. Thus, although official history denigrates Villa and extolls the figure of Carranza, Villa is still to be found in songs and *corridos*, in popular art and storytelling, and in the hopes of the poor and the oppressed.

The Northern Division was the military form of power of the peasants, just as Zapatism was essentially its social form. This was the irresistible force that in March 1914 swept down from Chihuahua to Torreón, and on April 2 overcame federal army resistance and seized the town.

Before Villa's twelve thousand men captured Torreón in several days of battle, they had taken the nearby towns of Sacramento, Ledo, and Gómez Palacios. A few days afterward, the Northern Division inflicted a fresh defeat on the federal army at San Pedro de las Colonias, destroying a rather tardy relief column swollen by remnants of the defeated Torreón garrison. These twin victories, the most devastating blow so far received by Huerta's army, left the Northern Division in control of a major city that was at once the center of an area rich in resources, an important railway junction, and an operational base for the attack on Mexico City. In fact, the town of Zacatecas was now the only remaining obstacle on the road to the capital.

The victories of Torreón and San Pedro de las Colonias increased the military prestige of Villa's army and shattered the fighting spirit of the government troops. Villa and Angeles decided that, after a brief halt to equip their men with the newly won Torreón supplies, the time would be ripe to mass on Zacatecas and resolve the war once and for all.

During the same month, April 1914, the Zapatists captured Iguala and Chilpancingo in Guerrero State; the Northeast Army took Monterrey, the capital and industrial city of Nuevo León; and the Americans intervened in Veracruz, effectively cutting off Huerta's supplies of European weapons through that port.

At this point, the second conflict in the Mexican Civil War came to the forefront: namely, the clash between Carranza's leadership and the peasant armies on which he relied to combat the Huerta faction.

Carranza needed to check the growing dominance earned by Villism through its military victories and its prestige among the peasantry. His first task, then, was to prevent the Northern Division from occupying Mexico City, as the previous course of the war would have logically suggested. Acting as commander-in-chief of the Constitutionalist Army, he sent Villa an order which, though absurd from a military point of view, was vital to his own political objectives. The order was to halt his advance, to refrain from attacking Zacatecas, and to swing his forces into an attack on Saltillo, the Coahuila State capital and official seat of the Carranza government, then in federal army hands.

Villa and Angeles objected to this illogical and diversionary maneuver, arguing that it left the enemy time to regroup and entrench itself in Zacatecas. But in the end they respected the order. Rounding off his political maneuver, Carranza sent emissaries to Obregón with instructions that his Northwest Army, inactive for several months, should profit from the weakening of federal resistance due to recent defeats and make a rapid advance on Mexico City.

For its part, the Northern Division duly marched on Saltillo, routed the enemy at Paredón on May 17, 1914, and, in the same process, captured a large quantity of arms and ammunition. Shortly afterward, it took the Coahuila State capital without a fight and left it in the hands of the Constitutionalists.

After the fall of Torreón the fate of the Huertist regime was sealed. Now began the next phase of the civil war in which the bourgeois Carranzist leadership struggled to hold the Villist and Zapatist armies in check. Although Carranza still needed Villa's backing as in the past, restraint was now becoming more important than support.

Carranza had to accept the power and methods of Villism, just as the bourgeoisie in the French Revolution had been compelled to accept the plebeian methods and revolutionary Terror of the Jacobins. Carranza also had both to contain the peasant forces within the structure and objectives of the Constitutionalist Army and to organize them in a militarily effective manner. The distant, hostile leadership of Carranza and his own officers had never been able to achieve these tasks, and success depended on the trust the armed peasants had in one of their own people, Pancho Villa.

Carranza's policy was the same as that of every weak national bourgeoisie: reliance upon active mass support, involving a mixture of concessions and restraints. But Carranza could not triumph through "classical" bourgeois forms and had to accept the revolutionary methods of Villism. All Carranza's stubborn efforts to save "the authority principle," as he liked to call it, showed both that he was aware of this emerging pattern and that he had no other choice.

For all its military strength, Villa's leadership could not by itself transcend the limitations of the Constitutionalist program. It did not comply with it—indeed, eventually the two came into conflict—but neither could it put anything else forward: it could only wring concessions for the peasantry and the "poor" within the confines of that program.

Furthermore, an army based on the military principles of the Northern Division was only possible within an alternative perspective of state power, which the peasants alone were incapable of providing. Without a state backbone, the peasantry could by itself attain only Zapatist-type forms of guerrilla army and guerrilla militia. And when Villa later had to fight against the Carranza-controlled state power, he was himself reduced to organizing—on a large scale, it is true—precisely this form of guerrilla warfare. His limitations were not at the abstract level of military-organizational capacity, but were concretely rooted in his peasant base.

After clearing the Saltillo region of enemy forces, Villa regrouped in Torreón with the aim of continuing his southward advance. Fresh orders then arrived, instructing him to wait and to commit part of his forces—three to five thousand men—in support of General Pánfilo Natera, whom Carranza had charged with the capture of Zacatecas. Villa was furious: he knew that Natera could not take Zacatecas; that the men he was supposed to send in support would not be enough to tip the struggle in favor of the attackers; and, above all, that the military victory the Northern Division could certainly secure was being snatched from their very hands. The conflict with Carranza now came right into the open. Villa refused to send his men as he had been ordered, and offered Carranza his resignation as commander of the Northern Division. The commander-in-chief immediately cabled his acceptance, at the same time summoning all the Northern Division generals to propose a successor at a special meeting. Villa was thanked for his services and ordered to take the military command in Chihuahua City.

In their reply to Carranza, the generals asked him to withdraw his acceptance of Villa's resignation. But he stood firm, invoking authority as a higher principle than military utility. There followed a violent exchange of telegrams: Carranza refused to give way; while the generals, continuing to recognize Villa, declared that they would no longer follow orders from the commander-in-chief. The whole Northern Division, together with its general staff, thereby came out in open insubordination against the Constitutionalist high command.

General Felipe Angeles was the political mind behind this military stand that saved from disintegration the commanding staff of the Northern Division. Venustiano Carranza would never forgive him. In the middle of June, Villa assembled all his military forces and began to follow the line of the railway down to the key town of Zacatecas. The early interruption in his advance, the absurd orders from Carranza, the political sabotage from above, the detour to Saltillo—none of these had taken the impetus from his mighty battle-machine. Indeed, Paredón and smaller combats had heightened the confidence and ardor of the Northern Division.

The "race" for Mexico City between the Northern Division and the Northwest Army now reached its climax. Villa still took on the major battles and minor flushing-out operations, while Obregón handled the minor battles and more extensive local engagements. There were two reasons for this division: first, although the federal army sought to contain both sections, it placed the greatest obstacles and the bulk of its troops in the way of Villa, seeing him as the inimical class threat; secondly, Carranza's headquarters tried to hinder the one, while impelling the other forward. Across the battle lines, then, a kind of bourgeois united front was tacitly established between Carranzism and Huertism, not to arrest the war, but to reduce the Villist danger. This "united front" also operated against Zapata, whom Carranza did not recognize and never ceased to describe as a bandit. And yet, the Zapatists played an important military role against the common Huertist enemy, constantly threatening the gates of Mexico City and tying down eight to ten thousand federal troops in the South while the Constitutionalist forces advanced from the North.

For their part, the Northern Division and the Southern Liberation Army increasingly formed a de facto peasant united front in which the Zapatist forces, militarily weaker but with a distinctive political program, exerted a powerful attraction over the Villists and gave them confidence for their inevitable break with Carranza. Their enemies, from Huerta to Carranza and Obregón, also saw them as closely related movements, and tried everything to prevent or delay a military linkup between the two.

Thus, although the war continued between the "reactionary" federal wing and the "progressive" Constitutionalist wing of the bourgeoisie, both were tacitly united in holding back the insurgent peasantry. The class division, obscured by the smoke of battle, now proved to be much deeper and longer-lasting than the thunderous clash of armies, eventually drawing up new battle lines that corresponded to the class struggle itself. This is, after all, the unyielding logic of every civil war.

It was therefore Obregón, benefiting from the tacit agreement of the bourgeois high command, who was destined to win the race for Mexico City ahead of Zapata and Villa. But since maneuvers are of much lesser historical importance than material class forces, Obregón's entry into the capital with the complicity of victorious friends and defeated enemies only served to put off the fateful hour. A few months later, at the highest point of the Mexican Revolution, the Villist and Zapatist armies triumphantly marched from north and south into Mexico City without firing a single shot.

On June 22, 1914, the Northern Division had begun its attack on Zacatecas, which had already been under fire from General Natera's troops for ten days. On June 23, in the largest armed action so far in the civil war, Villa captured Zacatecas and completely destroyed a twelve-thousand-strong federal army, with all its officers, trains, artillery, ammunition, and supplies. Only a few small detachments managed to escape annihilation. The road to Mexico City was open.

The next day, Villa decided to resume his advance, first despatching Angeles and a few Northern Division brigades to capture Aguascalientes in preparation for the entry into Mexico City. But now the high command of the Constitutionalist Army violently pulled in the reins. On June 24, after he had reported the Zacatecas victory to Carranza, thereby continuing to recognize him as supreme commander, Villa learned that he had just dismissed General Felipe Angeles as undersecretary of war responsible for the department in his cabinet. Carranza subsequently promoted Obregón and González as major generals, while keeping Villa at the lower rank of brigadier general. He also refused to recognize the Northern Division as an army, although it was militarily and numerically superior to those commanded by Obregón and González. Finally, Carranza held up the trains that delivered Monclova coal for Villa's locomotives, and impeded the delivery of arms and ammunition from the Northeast Army port of Tampico to the Northern Division. In effect, then, he took a series of civil war measures against Villa within the Constitutionalist camp itself.

With no coal for his trains and no ammunition for his troops, Villa had to end his advance and ordered Angeles to return to Chihuahua. He himself fell back on Torreón, leaving an advance guard in Zacatecas to keep control of the region and to maintain communications between this town and his permanent base in Chihuahua.

Carranza was in any case not yet seeking a break. He needed to gain time for the new and inevitable phase of the civil war that would pit him against Villa and Zapata. Moreover, some of his own officers, particularly the petty-bourgeois nationalist wing, were pressing for an agreement with Villa. For different reasons, both they and Carranza feared the consequences of a break on the rank-and-file soldiers, well aware that the Northern Division and its commander had unequal prestige among the Constitutionalist troops and the peasant towns and villages of the North.

Intermediaries for the Northeast Army, including General Antonio I. Villareal, a signatory of the 1906 Liberal Party program, finally brought about an agreement for discussions in Torreón with Northern Division delegates to resolve the differences between Villa and Carranza. This series of meetings concluded in the signing of the Torreón Pact on July 8, 1914, shortly before the fall of Huerta. The mere fact that both sides signed a pact, when Villa's division was supposed to be under Carranza's high command, shows both that the split had reached major proportions and that Carranza still needed some kind of reconciliation in order to avoid an open clash. He was thus acting upon a relationship of forces which found expression in the clauses of the pact itself.

In essence, the Torreón Pact affirmed (1) that the Northern Division would recognize Carranza as commander-in-chief and end the insubordination it had shown prior to Zacatecas; (2) that the Constitutionalist commander-in-chief recognized Francisco Villa as the sole commander of the Northern Division; (3) that, according to availability, the Northern Division would be supplied with all the necessary material for combat; (4) that both sides would communicate with Maytorena, Sonora State governor, who for some time had been in conflict with Obregón and Carranza, and try to persuade him to resign in favor of a third person impartial to himself and his opponents; (5) that once the commander-in-chief had assumed the executive power following Huerta's defeat, he would call a convention of Constitutionalist leaders from the different armies on the basis of one elected delegate per thousand soldiers; and (6) that the purpose of the convention would be to set a date for presidential and parliamentary elections, and to discuss and approve the governmental program which the newly elected president and representatives should follow.

The eighth and politically most important point is the so-called golden clause that Villa and his staff, among them the former Magonist Antonio Villareal, forced into the Torreón Pact. Here, for the first time, Villism found its way to the general formulation of a political program. Clause eight reads as follows:

> Since the present conflict is a struggle of the disinherited against the abuses of the powerful, and considering that the misfortunes afflicting the country stem from praetorianism, plutocracy and the clergy, the Northern and North-East Divisions solemnly undertake to fight until the ex-Federal Army disappears and is replaced by the Constitutionalist Army; to implant the democratic system in our country; to secure the well-being of workers; to bring about the economic emancipation of the peasants through just distribution of the land or other means that help to resolve the agrarian problem; and to correct, punish and make duly accountable those members of the Roman Catholic clergy who have given material or intellectual assistance to Huerta the usurper.

The Torreón Pact, and this clause in particular, fairly accurately reflects the military, social, and political relationship of forces between the different Constitutionalist sectors in the period following the battle of Zacatecas and just preceding the overthrow of Huerta. The superior military and social strength of Villism was fettered by the weakness of its politics vis-à-vis the Carranza leadership. In its turn, however, this leadership had to make concessions to general social demands, avoiding a break with Villism and the peasant base on which, through Villism, it rested as a nationalist leadership.

Yet again, Villa's experience in battle led him to use his strong side (the military relationship of forces imposed through swift and dramatic victories) in order to discuss and secure political concessions.

Some of Carranza's officers, particularly the revolutionary nationalist wing, also fought for these concessions as part of their own program. Thus, in clause eight of the Torreón Pact, we can clearly see the indirect presence of the earlier discussions around the Guadalupe Plan, in which Carranza had faced a group of young officers led by Múgica; the initiative taken a year later by Lucio Blanco and Múgica to redistribute land in Matamoros; and more remotely, through General Antonio I. Villareal, the general social aspirations of the 1906 Magonist program. It was this conjunction of forces that made possible not only clause eight but the pact as a whole, including the compromise agreement on a conference of military leaders to establish the program of the future government.

Through this signed compromise, the whole Constitutionalist Army openly expressed its role as a political "party" and a constitution-making formation; it was no longer just Carranza's high command, but all the officers in the northern armies who now assumed the representation of the revolutionary movement. Although the form was still a substitution, it did impose a petty-bourgeois army democracy upon the personal, centralized command of the Carranza leadership. It was the distant expression, within the army itself, of the mighty revolution then shaking the country.

As far as Villism is concerned, the pact involved a certain rapprochement with the movement in the South. For the influence of

Zapatism inevitably grew among the Villist soldiers, especially as the peasant armies scored major victories and the revolution neared its climax. Carranza had to balance upon this combination of forces.

In this balancing act, Carranza's aim was to win time by putting off a split, so as to win space by occupying more territory and consolidating state power in Mexico City. Thus he let the Northeast Army delegates conduct the negotiations in Torreón, keeping himself on the sidelines, while the Northwest Army marched at full speed on the capital, and the Northeast Army held its positions in order to control the movements of the Northern Division and, if necessary, to meet them with force. Making certain concessions, he also had to check the influence that Villism, the peasant masses, and, indirectly, Zapatism exerted upon a radical section of its own officers. But insofar as some of these factors seemed to come under his control, and insofar as any further general concessions might take concrete shape (like Lucio Blanco's land redistribution in an earlier period), Carranza hastened to disown the Torreón Accords on the grounds that he had never put his own name to them. He would only accept that part which referred to the end of the insubordination of the Northern Division, but not the programmatic points or the compromise call for a convention. By the time he made his position clear, Obregón was at the gates of Mexico City and the fate of the capital was sealed.

Obregón's army was already crystallizing as the military embryo of the future Mexican state apparatus. For although Pablo González was politically much closer to Carranza, a number of features made this force the principal military lever for the commander-in-chief: its superior organization and command; its base in economically and politically important regions, beginning with Sonora; the continuity of the Sonora State administration and its budget since the beginning of the revolution; and its line of advance to the capital along the Pacific railway. Above all, however, the tendency represented by Obregón offered Carranza some opening to the people. Thus, not only was Obregón the ablest general in Carranza's team, but he was also a possible intermediary between Carranza and Villa—although at a certain point his own political ambition and the objective conditions of equilibrium between the two leaders prompted Obregón to bid for the role of arbiter.

Among Obregón's officers was a section of the nationalist military tendency which, as in the cases of Lucio Blanco and Rafael Buelna, would later have a transitory and informal alliance with Villism. But the officer corps of both Obregón's and González's army developed as a military stratum that would be one of the foundation-stones of the new Mexican ruling elite. Obregón's own family became new landowners enriched by the revolution; Abelardo Rodríguez, a president for two years, became a multimillionaire; and Aarón Sáenz rose from a modest captain in Obregón's army to the richest sugar tycoon in Mexico. Many other names could be added to the list.

The officers began to adopt corresponding tastes and customs in the very course of the campaign, billeting themselves in the luxurious houses and mansions abandoned by rich landowners. They used their silverware, drank their wine, and were attended by their servants. They organized fiestas and receptions for society families, making connections here and there; and those families with the most initiative tried to arrange marriages for their daughters. As in the French Revolution, the old property-owning classes grew ever bolder in seeking family ties with these parvenus. From a social point of view, of course, the function was also to contain those petty bourgeois raised by the revolutionary wave, and to absorb their initial impetus into the old class wisdom of the exploiters. Although Obregón's officers retained much closer links with their rank and file than those of any bourgeois army, not to mention Huerta's corrupt federal army, they still developed as a separate layer enjoying multifarious relations with the less compromised class sections which had supported the enemy. This did not happen in Villa's army, divided as it was from the enemy by an unbridgeable class abyss. Conversely, although Obregón's army everywhere received local support as the armed, marching representative of the revolution, it did not arouse that wave of enthusiasm which accompanied the Northern Division on its way through the country.

Nevertheless, the underlying base of peasant hopes and mobilization was the same. It was an army of the revolution, and wherever it went the revolution was vanquishing the old regime. Even the differentiation of the officer corps, by no means a clear-cut process, was held in check while the revolution stayed at the full and the masses continued to dominate the arena. What later hardened into a distinct layer, and then into a social class, initially existed at the level of mere tendencies and inclinations. For the time being, these same officers were the bearers of a revolutionary force which, coming from their own peasant base, lifted them to the crest of the wave.

Obregón and his colleagues were therefore able to build from scratch an army which, though never matching Villa in spectacular military activity, did win a series of battles and show considerable boldness of movement. Such audacity was indeed crucial to its survival; for as the Northwest Army moved southward, it lost its initial operational base in Sonora, where Governor Maytorena withdrew support as part of his conflict with Carranza. Thus in mid-May, when Obregón received the order to advance rapidly on Mexico City and so gain the upper hand over the Northern Division, he really had no option but to push ahead. If he tried to withdraw through the difficult mountainous terrain, he ran the risk that his bases would be cut off. If he did not advance with sufficient speed, the federal forces might mass in his path and block the way. For he knew that after June 25, Villa would be forced by lack of supplies to halt his advance on Mexico City, thereby relieving the pressure on Huerta's troops.

Obregón decided to use his rapidity of movement to the full. Without pausing to attack minor towns, he left them surrounded and swept down to the capital with his trains. His driving conviction was that politics, and therefore the Mexican capital, were now the decisive factors; that the enemy's will to fight had already been broken by Villa's victories up to Zacatecas; and that, as Engels once said, "in revolution, as in war, it is absolutely necessary to stake everything at the decisive moment, whatever the probable outcome may be."

So it was that Obregón came up against the enemy army at Orendain, in the vicinity of Guadalajara, Jalisco, the second largest town in Mexico. On June 6, 1914, he completely routed the *federales* and drove them into Guadalajara itself. Two days later, when the remaining three thousand troops abandoned the city, Lucio Blanco's cavalry annihilated them at the battle of El Castillo. (Among the participants was a nineteen-year-old officer called Lázaro Cárdenas.) The Northwest Army entered Guadalajara without a fight and resumed its unimpeded advance on the capital.

Defeated on all fronts, Huerta handed authority over to an interim president, Francisco Carbajal, on July 15. Ten days later, the new man offered to negotiate the surrender of Mexico City and the government to the Constitutionalist forces.

Throughout the advance, the Obregón command had displayed great rapidity of movement, audacity of attack (even temerity in the case of the twenty-four-year-old General Rafael Buelna, for example), capacity for maneuver and initiative, and military discipline. Above all, General Obregón had been extremely skillful in exploiting the mistakes committed by the enemy. These qualities were, in turn, based on the revolutionary impetus of the peasant soldiers, which made it possible to ensure a level of discipline in marked contrast to the lack of an army tradition and the improvised clothing that could hardly be called a uniform. But the sharpest contrast was with the discipline of fear which the federal officers imposed on a demoralized soldiery devoid of any fighting spirit. As soon as the battle turned against them, this collapsed into total disorder.

Only this impetus from below can explain such features as the celebrated train that ran without a railway. The incident occurred in early 1914 in Sonora State. An army train had to run between two points controlled by revolutionary forces, but the line passed through the federal-held town of Empalme. The decision was then taken to pass on one side of the town, where there was no railway track at all for fourteen kilometers. The soldiers prepared five hundred meters at a time, the length of the rails available to them, and set in place the engine, rolling stock, and water tanks. As the train advanced, they picked up the rails and put them down again in front, special teams having been sent ahead to level the ground. The whole operation lasted fifteen days, during which time a number of enemy attacks had to be beaten off. But eventually the train returned to the normal line, having established a Mexican variant of Marx's idea that revolutions are the locomotives of history.

Actions of this kind were quite beyond the imagination of the passive and cautious federal command. Their movements were sluggish and conservative, when they did not take up purely defensive positions in the towns. The rank and file, essentially conscripted peasants subject to the brutal discipline of the old Porfirian army, lacked a fighting will and purpose. Besides, it was a corrupt and disintegrating army, whose commanders traded on the side with ammunition, supplies, and tents, as well as their soldiers' pay. Thus, although their formal military training was greatly superior to that of most Constitutionalist officers, they suffered defeat after defeat at their hands. And since defeats, like victories, have a cumulative effect, the federal army force in Mexico City, though tens of thousands strong, was incapable of fighting another battle in the days before its final dissolution.[6]

Some writers consider that United States intervention tipped the scales of the Mexican Revolution. Certainly Washington never ceased to intervene during the Madero period, as it had done under the Porfirio Díaz regime; and it certainly took a direct interest in the whole course of the revolution across its southern border. But such intervention was far from crucial in determining the evolution and outcome of the struggle.[7]

For many years, Mexico was one of the fields in the struggle between rising American imperialism and British imperialism. Washington had sided with Madero against Díaz, but then, acting through its ambassador, it backed Huerta against Madero; and later, President Wilson was hostile to Huerta and favored Carranza.

As the revolution gathered pace, the U.S. government sent permanent or semipermanent representatives not only to Carranza but also to the Villist and Obregónist commands. These sent back detailed reports on the course of the struggle, as well as on their discussions with senior officers. Emissaries even managed to hold talks with the Zapatist high command. On the other side, Carranza was especially active and had a permanent mission in the United States.

U.S. border towns provided a meeting-place for revolutionaries. Whereas Huerta's war materiel mainly arrived through the port of Veracruz, the early supplies of arms and ammunition to the Constitutionalists came across the United States frontier. In the other direction, Mexican cattle that used to belong to pro-Díaz ranch owners were sent north in payment for the weapons.

On August 27, 1913, however, President Wilson intervened more directly by ordering an embargo on arms sales to Mexico. This mainly affected the Constitutionalist Army, since most of Huerta's military supplies came by sea from Europe. But the required materiel was still smuggled across the long border, obviously at a higher price.

When the impotence of the regime began to make itself felt, and when Huerta decisively turned to Britain in exchange for certain concessions, the United States took a number of direct steps against him. In doing this, however, Washington effectively declared its readiness for military intervention against either side if any attempt was made to attack or expropriate the oil, mineral, or other holdings of U.S. capitalists. On April 21, 1914, using the pretext of a minor incident with some U.S. soldiers in Tampico, a marine force under Admiral Fletcher occupied the port of Veracruz after a brief tussle with the garrison. As a result of this U.S. invasion—the second in history, if we leave out minor cross-border incursions—Huerta's supply-port was in effect closed.

Meanwhile, on February 3, 1914, a month before the great

Villist offensive, Washington had lifted its arms embargo in the North. Huerta, acting in the name of the federal government, appealed for resistance to the invasion and called on the Constitutionalists to join in a national front against the invader. But the revolutionary forces, aware that the marines were not about to push deeper into the country, could already see victory on the horizon and naturally declined the offer. Besides, Huerta suffered most from the occupation of Veracruz.

In the camp of the anti-Huerta revolution, the leader who most clearly assumed the representation of the nation was Venustiano Carranza. Addressing himself to the U.S. government, he demanded the withdrawal of the marines from Veracruz and stated that the defense of Mexican territory was above internal conflicts. The peasant leaders Villa and Zapata, who were naturally also opposed to the invasion, functioned only as a local or regional, rather than national, force vis-à-vis the Americans. Here, too, appeared one of the elements that influenced the final outcome of the struggle in Carranza's favor: his leadership took up the representation of the nation, whereas such a task was beyond the capacity of the peasant leadership.

Washington saw that any further action would arouse the whole nation against the invaders, and so it evacuated Veracruz in November 1914, three months after the fall of Huerta.

At the time of Huerta's fall, the four revolutionary armies embodied, from left to right, the factions that would enter into political and then military conflict with one another. On the left, controlling the southern part of the country, Zapatism and the Southern Liberation Army called for a deepening of the social content of the revolution and the implementation of the Ayala Plan.

Villism, with its Northern Division, was then breaking with Carranza and moving into an ever closer alliance with Zapatism. It was firmly entrenched in the North, above all in its operational base in Chihuahua and Durango.

On the right was Carranza, with Pablo González and his Northeast

Army. Although the army had little military prestige or authority, it provided a direct lever and form of military representation for the Carranzist tendency, also securing the port and oil region of Tampico.

In the center, actually occupying Mexico City, was Alvaro Obregón with his Northwest Army. This tendency represented the two wings of the nationalist petty bourgeoisie: both those, including Obregón himself, who were favorably disposed to capitalist development and those who, feeling attracted to the peasants' and workers' demands, constituted a bridge toward the Villist movement and, in the case of Lucio Blanco, for example, would later form a temporary alliance with it. For its part, the Northern Division had officers like José Isabel Robles and Eugenio Aguirre Benavides who felt the attraction of Obregonism. When the decisive military clash erupted between Villa and Obregón, these last two currents eventually found themselves on shaky middle ground.

At the moment of Huerta's overthrow, Carranza was counting on Obregón and González as a force against Villa and Zapata. But although Obregón supported Carranza, he was trying to forge an independent policy of negotiation with the Northern Villista leaders, as opposed to Carranza's policy of bloody repression. Until the military clash broke out, he therefore sought to attract Villa and some of his officers in an effort to isolate hard-core Zapatism. This involved concessions, however, that Carranza was not prepared to make.

In August 1914, this contradiction was still obscured and overshadowed by the fundamental class division setting both them and González against Zapata and Villa. It was the Obregón and Carranza–González tendencies which occupied the capital, established a provisional government of Mexico, and drove a military-cum-geographical wedge between the Villist North and the Zapatist South.

However, the problem was not just military or even political, but above all social in character. The fall of Huerta was a major turn that echoed with tremendous force throughout the country. The

peasants felt triumphant. Armed peons and peasants were en-
trenching themselves on the lands they had just won, redivided, and
sown, or were completing the redistribution of those they had not
yet taken by assault. The peasant high tide was rising in the whole
of Mexico, pounding any political or military obstacle in its path,
imposing its colossal weight to alter the relationship of forces established in the hour of victory through political maneuver and
military action. But at the same time, its own leaders had not anticipated this and were not clearly aware of its implications. Only
when the social upsurge imperiously required a political, class expression, without actually finding one, would the policy of the faction opposing this upsurge come to the forefront. Only at this
point would the situation be ripe for a military solution.

It was not the occupation of Mexico City but this huge social
rising that dominated the next few months, prompting a leftward
shift in the whole political and military relationship of forces.

5

THE CONVENTION

Obregón's entry into Mexico City on August 15, 1914, followed a few days later by the installation of the Carranza government in the capital, opened an interval of political struggle between the opposing factions. The Constitutionalist leadership, conducting a national-scale politics, took the initiative by trying to neutralize and politically subdue the peasant leaderships. Carranza's aim was to stabilize the political situation, to control the military situation, and to gain time in relation to the peasant armies, one back in its northern Chihuahua base, the other held in check in the South.

As it took up positions in Mexico City, Obregón's army replaced the federal army marked down for dissolution under the terms of the surrender. It also took over the federal outposts against Zapata's forces in such a way as to curb any intended advance. From this position of military strength, Carranza prepared for talks with the Zapatists to demand that they submit to the new government. For their part, the Zapatists had occupied Cuernavaca, the last Morelos town in federal hands, and now faced the Constitutionalist advance posts on the border of the Federal District.

In the states where they established their own administration, the Constitutionalists passed a series of decrees to satisfy the most immediate demands of the people: abolition of employers' shops and cancellation of all debts owed by the peasants and peons; a minimum wage; an eight-hour day; and a compulsory day of rest. However, no legal measures were taken to solve the land problem or to sanction the vast land distributions already undertaken by the peasantry on their own account.

In Mexico City, the trade-union movement resumed public activity; and on September 26, 1914, the new authorities allocated the St. Brigitte and Josephine Convents to the Casa del Obrero Mundial, in place of its old headquarters, which had been closed by the Huerta regime in May and reopened on August 21. There the unions held their various meetings of organization and reorganization.

Like Villa in Chihuahua State, Zapata and his general staff formed the only government in the South, particularly in Morelos, Guerrero, and part of Puebla. The de facto land redistribution was virtually complete, or else was nearing completion in those localities which had remained till the last under federal control. In Cuautla, for instance, Eufemio Zapata sent the following message to Emiliano Zapata's headquarters:

> Mexican Republic, Liberation Army.
> I report that the irrigated land is already being suitably redistributed in the area surrounding this and other towns which have requested it. The people appointed to this task have an expert knowledge of the reference-system for redivision. I report this for your information and other purposes. Reform, Liberty, Justice and Law. Cuautla (Morelos) Headquarters, 19 September 1914. General Eufemio Zapata.

Once Carranza was installed in Mexico City, he had a number of discussions with Zapatist representatives, while delegates like General Villarreal and the lawyer Luis Cabrera held other talks with Emiliano Zapata and his general staff. In every case, however, the negotiations ended in deadlock. Zapata insisted that, as the basis for any agreement, the Constitutionalists should endorse the principles of the Ayala Plan, above all those concerning land redistribution. Carranza would only accept the submission of the Southern Liberation Army to his own forces, refusing any discussion of land distribution. "The *hacendados*," he argued, "have legally sanctioned rights; it is not possible to take away their property and give it to those who do not have the right." A Zapatist delegation sent by General Genovevo de la O received the following reply: "This land-redistribution business is absurd. Tell me which haciendas you own and are able to redistribute, so that each of you can redistribute what belongs to you and not to someone else." Here the discussion came to an end. In December 1910, more than two years before Carranza, General Genovevo de la O had risen in armed revolt with twenty-five men and a single rifle: he was a peasant then, and would still be a peasant when he died in the 1950s. But the man who had the perfidy and insolence to ask which haciendas he had to redistribute was himself a big Coahuila landowner.

Such, then, were the last discussions between the bourgeois and Zapatist leaderships. Each now dug into their positions and waited for the time to resume the struggle.

While they were completing the land redistribution in their own region, the Zapatists adopted a number of political positions, also related to the agrarian problem, which were part of their own preparation for the country's reorganization and made them the functioning government in the South.

In August 1914, the Zapatist command again set forth its political positions in a call "To the Mexican people." The peasantry, so the document states, "took to revolt not in order to conquer illusory political rights that give it nothing to eat, but for the patch of land that should provide food and freedom." Rejecting any form of military government, or any merely electoral solution not involving social reforms, it reaffirmed the arguments and demands of the Ayala Plan. It proposed that all "the leaders of combat groups, the representatives of the insurgent people in arms," should assemble to appoint an interim president, who should "sincerely and unreservedly" accept "the three great principles of the Ayala Plan: expropriation of land by reason of public utility, confiscation of property belonging to enemies of the people, and restitution of land to dispossessed individuals and communities." Otherwise, the manifesto warned, the armed struggle would continue until these goals were accepted.

General Manuel Palafox was at this time in correspondence with Atenor Sala, a wealthy Mexico City gentleman who argued that Zapata should adopt his utopian "Sala System" for legal land redistribution and countrywide settlements of small farmers. Palafox, then a growing influence in Zapata's high command, closed the exchange of letters in September with a lengthy programmatic statement. It is worth reproducing this in full, since it reveals the scope of Zapata's policy in 1914 and the way in which his leaders envisaged the practical application of the Ayala Plan.

Mexican Republic, Liberation Army.
Cuernavaca, Morelos Headquarters, 3 September 1914.
Señor don Atenor Sala, Mexico City, Federal District.
Most worthy sir,

I have received your much-awaited letter of 28 August and read it with attention and careful consideration. I would now like to make the following points. Having read quite closely the pamphlets and other documents, based on your study of the agrarian problem, which you kindly sent to Revolutionary Headquarters, I realize that they pose agrarian principles very different from those outlined in the Ayala Plan.

Many million pesos would be required to implement your system—more than our unhappy country has at its disposal. For according to your plans, the government would have to lay out large sums of money on the essential land-redistribution measures, especially those relating to new farming settlements. But the country is in no position to make such payments, *and it would be unjust to purchase the landholdings which enemies of the Revolution have illegally possessed for many years.* The Agrarian Revolution is working with complete justice to inscribe on its banner the three great principles of the agrarian problem: namely, *redistribution of the land to the villages or individuals dispossessed in the dark days of bad government; confiscation of property belonging to the enemies of the Ayala Plan; and expropriation by reasons of public utility.*

The Revolution advocated by the Ayala Plan simplifies *the*

agrarian problem into the three preceding principles *without wasting one centavo.* Its aim is that tomorrow, when the Revolution forms a government, *it will not be necessary for anyone, including the proletariat, to pay a single centavo.* Money is not needed to return the land which someone took from another with the support of a bad government; MONEY IS NOT NEEDED *to confiscate property from those who, for so many years, have directly or indirectly supported the government in the struggle against advocates of the Ayala Plan.* It will only be necessary to pay small sums *to compensate foreigners* whose rural holdings have to be expropriated by reason of public utility; and this will apply solely to *foreigners who have not meddled in political affairs.* On closer analysis, however, such expropriations will not cost the nation a single centavo, if we take into account that *payment will be made* with THE VALUE OF URBAN PROPERTY CONFISCATED *from enemies of the Revolution.*

You will not deny that most *hacendados* in the Republic have committed hostile acts against the Revolution, even giving financial assistance to previous governments. It is therefore just that article eight of the Ayala Plan should be applied to them: even though you say that this system is not noble, it is necessary if the millions of disinherited Mexicans are to be given something to eat. It is better for humanity that thousands of bourgeois, rather than millions of proletarians, should die of hunger—this is what a right moral sense tells us.

The distribution of the land will not take place exactly as you indicate, through parcellization. *Instead, such redistribution will be effected in the most just way, in accordance with the customs of each village.* Thus IF A PARTICULAR VILLAGE WISHES THE COMMUNAL SYSTEM, *this is how it will be done; and if another village wishes parcellization of the land to establish* ITS SMALLHOLDINGS, *this will be done.* Supported by the Revolution, they will then till the land with zeal. And after some years have passed, *any bourgeois who seek to acquire their confiscated property with the help of some government* will not succeed, because the villages with arms in hand (arms they will always retain) will be able energetically to impose their will on the government and to protect their rights. Time itself will prove that this is so. But if something goes wrong and the villages let themselves be despoiled of their land, that will not be our fault. *We are now handing them back their land; we are teaching them how to keep it and to ensure that their rights are respected.*

The southern revolutionaries are filled with a sense of the evil and corruption of governments. The long four-year struggle has taught us the hard way that we have the just right to ensure that village interests are not tomorrow spurned by some nefarious government. If we are to avoid this, we must pass on these agrarian principles, firmly guaranteed, to the next and future generations. THE GUARANTEE IS TO DEMAND AT ANY PRICE THAT THE COMING REVOLUTIONARY GOVERNMENT RAISE TO THE LEVEL OF CONSTITUTIONAL PRE-CEPTS *the three agrarian principles mentioned above*, so that the agrarian question remains both *de facto* and *de jure* implanted in the country. *We shall not entrust these agrarian principles*, for which so much fighting has been done, *to any government not identified with the Revolution.* We therefore demand of Mr Carranza that the interim government of the Republic should have a clearly revolutionary character, in keeping with article twelve of the Ayala Plan and other well-defined points; *that the program of the interim government should be discussed* AT THE CONVENTION FORMED BY REVOLU-TIONARIES OF THE REPUBLIC; *and that this program should naturally* EMBRACE QUESTIONS NOT INCLUDED IN THE AYALA PLAN, such as the creation of AGRICULTURAL BANKS, *the large-scale* IRRIGATION *works needed in some states of the Republic, the improvement of* PUBLIC EDUCATION, *improvements for* THE WORKER, *improvements for the small trader, and lastly,* A CAMPAIGN AGAINST CLERICALISM.

As you see, these aspirations go beyond what Mr Carranza has in mind. If there is not a satisfactory solution, the sixty-five thousand southerners will shoulder their Mausers and march off against the new enemies of the Ayala Plan, against those Carranzists who think they can treat with contempt the trust and hopes of the

Mexican people. And if, as may happen, I have to take responsibility for such a course, then History may judge me and I will respect its verdict.

I hope that this hastily written account will give you some idea of the real tendencies of the southern-led Revolution.[1]

This letter written by Manuel Palafox is one of the most advanced texts of the Zapatist movement, anticipating everything essential in the agrarian law that would be decreed in Cuernavaca a year later, in October 1915. Nevertheless, it is locked in the same internal contradiction that characterized the Ayala Plan. Zapatism directed the slogan of expropriation without compensation against all the property of the bourgeois landowners, beginning with the latifundia. But although the Mexican economy of the time was still based on agricultural production, its command-levers were to be found in the towns and industry. At this point, the present program becomes imprecise and confused.

Notwithstanding the permanent duality at the heart of Zapatism, however, this letter clearly expresses its will to go beyond the confines of bourgeois law, its egalitarian moral norms irreconcilable with Maderism and Carranzism: "It is better for humanity that thousands of bourgeois, rather than millions of proletarians, should die of hunger—that is what moral sense tells us."

These principles did not wait for "the hour of victory": the Southern Liberation Army put them into practice wherever it held sway. Thus on September 8, 1914, at the height of the political confrontation with Carranza, the Zapatist government in Cuernavaca issued the following decree:

> Art. 1. Property belonging to enemies of the Ayala Plan Revolution who directly or indirectly oppose, or have so opposed, the application of its principles, is hereby nationalized in accordance with art. 8 of the Plan and art. 6 of the decree dated 5 April 1914.
>
> Art. 2. Liberation Army generals and colonels, in liaison with

Revolutionary Headquarters, shall issue nationalization orders for both rural and urban property.

Art. 3. The municipal authorities shall keep a record of nationalized property and, having publicly announced the nationalization order, shall report in detail to Revolutionary Headquarters about the category and state of such property, as well as the number of former owners.

Art. 4. Nationalized rural property shall pass into the possession of villages with no land or other elements of labor, or shall be entrusted to orphans and widows of those who have fallen in the struggle for the victory of the ideals of the Ayala Plan.

Art. 5. Nationalized urban property and other such holdings of enemies of the agrarian revolution *shall be used for the establishment of agricultural promotion banks, whose task will be to ensure that small farmers are not at the mercy of usurers* and are at all costs able to prosper, as well as to provide pensions for the widows and orphans of those who have died in the present struggle.

Art. 6. Nationalized lands, woodland and waters taken from enemies of the cause *shall be distributed to villages either in common or in parcellized plots, according to the preference expressed.*

Art. 7. The redistribution lands, woodland and waters *may not be sold or alienated in any form; any contract or transaction tending to alienate such property is null-and-void.*

Art. 8. Rural property redistributed in parcellized plots *may only change owners by legitimate succession from father to son*, every other circumstance being subject to the preceding article.

Art. 9. This decree shall take effect immediately. Communicated to you for publication, circulation and due observance.

Reform, Liberty, Justice and Law. Issued at the Cuernavaca Headquarters, on the eighth day of September 1914. Commander-in-Chief of the Liberation Army, Emiliano Zapata.[2]

The dispatch from Enfemio Zapata quoted earlier was one of the first applications of this decree. It should be remembered that although the northern peasantry was then seizing land on its own initiative and cultivating it under the protection of its own rifles, no similar decree had yet been issued by the Villist command. The conflict between Zapata and the bourgeois leadership did not just refer to intentions and programs, but directly focused on the actual situation and regime in the zones of the respective armies.

The conflict with Villa followed a more sinuous but equally irreversible course. As always, the unstable alliance between bourgeois and peasant leaderships broke down in the hour of victory. In this case, however, when the Carranza leadership tried to turn round and butcher those who had carried it to victory, it found them in Villa's powerful and militarily independent army. This, together with the political support of Zapata's intransigence, was able to find the form and resolution to stand up to their recent ally and leader.

General Obregón played a singular role in the breakup, his first impulse being to avert it through mediation. He went off to Chihuahua on the authority of Carranza, as well as his own as a revolutionary army commander, and tried to persuade Villa to submit in return for certain promises that essentially reiterated those of the Torreón Pact.

Secondly, however, Obregón was playing another game, which diverged from the aims of the bourgeois leadership and foreshadowed his later Bonapartist policy. Thus, he sought to lean upon Villa in order to force Carranza into a policy of social concessions, through which he might broaden his social base and channel the revolutionary upsurge then breaking through on all sides.

Thirdly, Obregón went in person to the heart of the Villist bastion in Chihuahua, testing the strength of Villa's authority over his officers, trying to gain influence among some of them, and directly assessing the military strength and state of mind of the Northern Division. In other words, Obregón engaged in a kind of factional activity in which nothing less than his own skin was at stake. Having greeted him with a military parade, Villa saw the double game and was on the point of having him shot. But after he had already summoned the firing squad, he hesitated to take on the responsibility and eventually invited Obregón to supper instead. Nearly up against a wall, Obregón moved straight on to a reception at which he was the guest of honor, and from there to a political agreement with Villa set forth in a letter to Carranza dated September 21, 1914. Then, as he was on his way back south, Carranza rejected the agreement in a telegraph message to Villa. Interpreting all this as a murky maneuver, Villa gave orders for Obregón to be brought back and shot without more ado. But some sympathetic Villist leaders allowed him to continue on his way, and Obregón escaped the death penalty demanded by the peasant wing of Villa's general staff as the price for his intrigue and espionage. (Besides, Obregón was Villa's guest, and in peasant countries guests are sacred; it is not polite to shoot them.) The whole of this famous episode sums up well the political instability of Pancho Villa.

It is not simply Obregón's personal audacity which explains why the chief military commander and second political leader of the victorious forces in Mexico City should have embarked on such a hazardous venture. Not having the forces to oppose the Northern Division, he needed to gain time and avert a head-on confrontation. At the same time, he felt that he had to impress his own policy on Carranza if he was to have the minimum social base with which to take on Villa. All Obregón's initiatives, together with his hardiness, or foolhardiness, dictated by his unstable situation between two antagonistic forces, reveal the great apprehension which his own people, Carranza's team, and the whole Constitutionalist high command felt with regard to Villa's forces and movements.

All these maneuvers were doomed to failure. For the crucial element here was not political skill in beguiling the peasant leaders—the old tradition of bourgeois and petty-bourgeois lawyers and politicians—but the real-world relationship of forces. Although direct struggle would eventually decide the issue between the opposing forces, the hour of Obregonist Bonapartism was still several years in the future. The strength of the mass movement had not yet been consumed: its energies were burning throughout the country, and the real class relationship of forces still had to be tested through the clash of arms. Still without a base to act as arbiter, Obregon continued to give political and military support to the Carranza government as its principal army leader. In this capacity, he was able to wrench concessions but not the command-post itself.

Since the Torreón Pact, and even before, the need for a congress or convention to draw up a postvictory program began to make itself felt among the Constitutionalists and in the Zapatist documents and publications. Such an assembly appeared as the ground on which factional differences, held back in the struggle against the common enemy, could be peacefully resolved.

In a letter written in mid-September 1914, Carranza informed Obregón and Villa that he had decided to call such a meeting of all military leaders in Mexico City on October 1. This was a concession to the combined pressure of the senior Northwest Army and Northern Division officers, this time headed by Obregón. It was this letter which Obregón carried to Chihuahua on the occasion when he narrowly escaped the firing squad. The letter from Obregón and Villa to Carranza was dated September 21, just a few days before the final break between the Northern Division and the new government.

The joint reply rejected the idea of a meeting on October 1 on the grounds that the officers present would be appointed from the center instead of representing their troops; that since the questions for discussion had not been specified, "the agrarian problem, which may be said to have been the soul of the revolution, risked being downgraded or even excluded in favor of less important matters"; and that "the immediate calling of federal and state elections and the implementation of the agrarian reform" had to be declared as the "primary objectives" of such an assembly. It further stressed that the Northern Division could not attend the meeting until it was assured that "redistribution of the land" would be discussed. The letter was never answered, for the break came the next day, and Pancho Villa sent a telegram to Carranza stating that he no longer recognized his leadership. In a public declaration, he specifically charged that the commander-in-chief "refused to accept a Convention on the bases proposed in the Torreón Pact" and was no longer abiding by the program outlined in his letter to Obregón and Villa.

A meeting of Constitutionalist officers headed by Lucio Blanco proposed that a convention be held in Aguascalientes or "other neutral ground" as a way of avoiding an armed confrontation. This town, straddling the way between Mexico City and the advance post of the Northern Division in Zacatecas, therefore became a symbol for the negotiations with Villism favored by part of the radical wing of Carranzist senior officers. Carranza himself flatly rejected the idea, arguing that "the principle of authority must be upheld at the cost of any sacrifice." On September 26, already back in the capital, Obregón joined those who had set up a "peace making commission" between Carranza and the Northern Division; so that now the most important Carranzist military leaders were also pressing for an agreement. Lucio Blanco even took care to inform Zapata of the conflict under way, suggesting that he, too, should send delegates to a convention on neutral ground. Finally, at a meeting in Zacatecas between delegates from the peacemaking commission and the Northern Division, including Villa himself, it was agreed to open a convention of military leaders in Aguascalientes on October 10, 1914. By this very token, the two sides accepted an armistice suspending all hostilities and troop movements.

The position of certain officers who joined the peacemaking commission was rather more than a maneuver. They were afraid of a clash with Villa, but they also felt influenced by the peasant revolution and repelled by Carranza's narrow-mindedness and inflexibility. They realized, or suspected, that his policy not only ran counter to the revolutionary impulses that had carried them into the armed struggle, but would require the massacre, in tens and hundreds of thousands, of the very peasants who had made the revolution.

But they also shrank from the rough, "uncultured," radical features of Villism and Zapatism—from that thoroughgoing revolutionary prospect of mass power which, though imprecise for want of a clear program, had been brought closer by the nationwide peasant uprising. They could see the levelling thrust of the revolution, but not its future. The peasantry could not show it to them, nor could they go beyond the ideological horizon of the bourgeoisie, however much they tinged it with Jacobin hues.

This whole tendency sought a rapprochement with Villa that would not entail a break with Carranza. It was the strongest force among the Constitutionalist officers, owing not only to its own weight, but also to the borrowed weight of the upsurge, and of the Villist and Zapatist movements. In the end, then, they were able to force Carranza to accept the Aguascalientes Convention.

Officers like Lucio Blanco saw the projected gathering as a kind of Mexican counterpart to the Convention of the Great French Revolution, which would issue forth a series of revolutionary programs and laws. When the delegates finally assembled, however, none would have a concrete idea of the programs and laws to be adopted. Obregón, his feet more firmly on the ground, saw the Convention as a way forward which, with the support of the petty-bourgeois wing of Villist officers and the radical wing of Constitutionalists, would discard the peasant Villa at one extreme and the bourgeois Carranza at the other. It would then call upon the arbiter, General Obregón, to resolve the conflict. In pursuit of this aim, he threw all his weight behind the idea of the Convention, which allowed him to continue the political "grand maneuvers" interrupted by his near-execution in Chihuahua. Luis Cabrera believes that "most probably, the only way out for the Convention will be a new war, and demand from the conventionists the sanction of radical reforms."

All these factors eventually combined to force Carranza to yield. However, the Convention actually opened in Mexico City on October 1, 1914, with Carranza's own civilian and military delegates, and with an agenda not at all like the one agreed on with Villa at the recent armistice. The delegates quickly ratified the commander-in-chief as head of the Executive Power. But when the Northern Division threatened to march on the capital from Zacatecas, Carranza gave in to Obregón and on October 5 accepted that the Convention should move to Aguascalientes, a "neutral" town but with the Northern Division stationed outside its gates.

The Military Convention of Aguascalientes began its work on October 10, 1914. Now that the civilians had been excluded, all the delegates were military men: Carranzists and Villists, under the leadership of Obregón and Villa, respectively.

A few days later, the Convention declared itself a sovereign and supreme body, and sent a commission to invite a delegation from Zapata. Lengthy sessions were meanwhile devoted to secondary and procedural matters, from which the conflict between Carranza and Villa already began to emerge as the central focus. These sessions reflected the delegates' lack of parliamentary experience. But they also indicated something much deeper: namely, the lack of a clear program and perspective among the tendencies participating in the assembly. These military men were there because the peasants had borne them to victory over Huerta. And yet the peasants, the true protagonists of the revolution, were not present: no one directly represented their concerns and their demands, even though these shone through all the surface debating. Obregón's aim was not to solve this contradiction, but to gain time by exploiting it and eventually to break Villism apart by playing on its political weakness. The delegates swelled up in speeches full of big words and devoid of ideas. While the Convention became bogged down, the prevailing expectation and indecision undermined the confidence and the expectations, and inactivity began to weigh heavily on the Northern Division itself.

On October 27, after a delegation headed by two Villista generals, Felipe Angeles and Calixto Contreras, went to Morelos to invite and convince them, a Zapatist delegation took its place in the Convention. Although it did not take part in the voting, since Zapata had insisted as a precondition that the Convention support the Ayala principles, its presence nevertheless transfigured the assembly. It was the only tendency to come forward with a program that bore some relation to the real demands of the peasantry.

The arrival of the Zapatists produced at a political level what

Carranza, and above all Obregón, had been concerned to avert only at a military level: namely, the junction of Zapatism and Villism. So decisive was this development that it immediately dragged along the whole Convention, including the Carranzist delegates left with neither a program nor coherent arguments with which to oppose it. On October 28, the Carranzists, whose radical wing had suddenly found a lever of support, were forced to join the Villists in a unanimous acclamation of articles 4, 5, 6, 7, 8, and 9 of the Ayala Plan—all those containing political and social demands—and soon after, articles 12 and 13 as well. (While his senior officers were voting in this way, Carranza's own letters and documents continued to refer to Zapata as "the enemy.") The session ended with cries of "Long live the Revolution! Long live the Ayala Plan!"

The Convention had reached its climax, although the ensuing crisis would take a couple of days fully to mature. The question of Carranza's withdrawal from the Executive Power provoked an ever sharper conflict. Carranza maneuvered with letters, telegrams, and legal arguments, asserting that until Villa and Zapata resigned their command, the Convention could not decide on his fate. It was an impossible discussion, for it was quite obvious that, so long as the clash of arms had not demonstrated the true relationship of forces, no one would dream of relinquishing his command and destroying his own tendency.

On October 30, the Convention approved a motion, drawn up by a commission including Alvaro Obregón, Felipe Angeles, Eugenio Aguirre Benavides, and Eulalio Gutiérrez, to the effect that Carranza should cease to be in charge of the Executive and that Villa should give up his command of the Northern Division. At the same time, the Convention was to name an interim president who would call elections within a fixed space of time. Concerning Zapata the assembly declared itself without jurisdiction, since his forces had not sent an official voting delegation. Carranza continued to maneuver over his resignation, posing a number of conditions which indicated that he had absolutely no intention of accepting the decision. On November 1, the Convention elected

General Eulalio Gutiérrez president of the Republic—a man who could count on the support of the Villists and the unofficial good will of the Zapatists.

On November 3, Villa proposed a characteristic solution to the conflict between himself and Carranza: not a few days' exile in Havana, as Carranza suggested, nor straightforward dismissal of them both, but a decision by the Convention to shoot the two simultaneously. The gesture met with applause and hurrahs, in the best style of the Sovereign Military Convention of Aguascalientes. But, of course, nothing was resolved.

On November 10, finding no agreement possible, President Gutiérrez declared Venustiano Carranza a rebel and appointed Francisco Villa operational commander of the two Convention armies, essentially the Northern Division. Obregón, whose role as arbiter was now aborted, joined up with Carranza and gave him his support. Carranza, in fact, had already left Mexico City. On November 12, from Córdoba, Veracruz, he branded Villa and Gutiérrez representatives of "reaction" in rebellion against his government—a characterization Obregón would use throughout the coming campaign.

For his part, Villa informed Zapata that he was going to advance on Mexico City, and requested that he mobilize his own forces in order to prevent the Carranzists from reinforcing the garrison in the capital with troops from Veracruz and Puebla. Meanwhile, all the Carranzists had abandoned the Convention, and by about November 20 any possibility of a political solution had disappeared. The crisis now took the form of an openly military conflict between the Conventionist government headed by Eulalio Gutiérrez and the Constitutionalist government headed by Venustiano Carranza, and between their respective army commanders, Francisco Villa and Alvaro Obregón.

When the break with Carranza was consummated in mid-November, the Convention issued a manifesto reaffirming that the people had embarked on the revolution in pursuit of "deep social needs" rather than a merely political formula; and that in epochs "of profound social and political turmoil, when institutions totter and come crashing down, sovereignty . . . resides in the armed people." The manifesto enunciated a "minimum program" that included the following: withdrawal of United States forces from Mexican territory; restitution of communal lands to the villages; "the destruction of latifundism, so that large landed property is disentailed and redistributed among the people, who bring forth the produce of the soil through their own exertion"; nationalization of property belonging to enemies of the revolution; and freedom of association and the right of workers to go on strike.

The military crisis was the natural continuation of a political crisis that proved insoluble as soon as the Convention, instead of serving as an instrument for Obregón's maneuvers against the peasant leaderships, became the meeting ground between the two and moved to the left through its adoption of the Ayala Plan. The Convention, which never was nor could have been a body representing the aspirations of the peasant base of the revolution, was nevertheless in no position to set itself up as a juridical structure for containing that base. The revolutionary upsurge and the military strength of the peasant armies were much too strong, while the bourgeois leadership had too weak a social base, and the petty-bourgeois tendencies, like the petty bourgeoisie in general, were too politically unstable and too much under the social influence of the revolution. Its incapacity to carry out either of the two opposite functions is the essential reason for the characteristic innocuousness of the Aguascalientes Convention.

Obregón, who fought for the Convention within the Constitutionalist forces, had mainly, if not entirely, used a military-bureaucratic apparatus yardstick to assess the probable strength of Zapatism within the assembly. His assessment was therefore wrong. Like everyone else, he was aware that Zapatism enjoyed the support of the peasant masses. But in his militarist view of things, this support had to find a mediation if it was to carry weight in the sphere of "high politics." In other words, it had to express itself through a bureaucratic, intellectual, and military apparatus, a body of lawyers and officers such as the Constitutionalists were then developing.

An apparatus—that is what Zapatism lacked. Its few well-dressed intellectuals were subject to the firm, unyielding will of Zapata, the armed representative of the peasant base. Its officers and generals were peasants, with the clothing and habits of peasants, and only the word "general" before their name distinguished them from the ranks. The Zapatist delegation arrived almost penniless in Aguascalientes, since the Liberation Army did not have the money to pay the costs of the trip. Zapata wrote to Atenor Sala, asking him to lend the delegation a few thousand pesos as it passed through Mexico City. But that rich "friend of the peasants" invoked the flimsy financial excuses such people usually offer. "He's bourgeois to the bone: he didn't give us one centavo," one delegate wrote to Zapata, adding that their first funds came through Angeles from Villa in Zacatecas. The clothing and habits of the Zapatists, just arrived from the impoverished South, sharply contrasted with the cars, uniforms, and lavish spending of the nascent military bureaucracy that formed the Carranzist delegation in Aguascalientes.

It is not strange that Obregón thought he could continue his own game and keep control of the Convention after the arrival of the Zapatistas, and perhaps even run rings round them politically. For he was unable to grasp the historical essence of Zapatism. What Obregón did not see was that the Zapatists were bringing the elemental program of agrarian revolution with them onto the Convention floor.

Zapatism proved to have a social power of attraction beyond the ken of its opponents. Not only did it win over and politically focus the powerful Villist forces, but the junction of the two movements in turn created a transitory pole of attraction for part of the radical wing of Constitutionalist officers. Carranza had been able to control them so long as Constitutionalism, through Villa's military and political subordination, could keep the Villist peasant base under control. But once Villism met up with Zapatism, it shattered that control forever.

This whole regrouping of forces took shape not through hollow, interminable debates in the Convention, but in the relationship of real-world forces politically expressed in the unity of Villists and Zapatists under the banner of the Ayala Plan. Political program weighed more than the army mergers in the process of unification, at a time when the two forces were still militarily separated from each other by the armies of Obregón and Pablo González occupying Mexico City, Querétaro, and the whole central region between Zacatecas in the North and Morelos in the South.

Once the Villists and Zapatists had united at a political level, the Constitutionalists could try to maintain their *military wedge* between the Northern Division and the Southern Liberation Army, but they could find no *social wedge* to drive between the two. The *political wedge* of Carranzism, notwithstanding its left wing, appeared too weak and lacked both a program and a base; some of its own army officers were even feeling the attraction of the united Villist and Zapatist movements. Since the social power of the revolution now operated through a military and political center that, for all its limitations, was an effective material force, the Constitutionalist military wedge was now itself in danger of falling apart.

Obregón had sought to use the Convention as a political wedge, but did not have an adequate program to equip it with a social base. Nor could he conjure one up by relying on the military-bureaucratic apparatus or on short-winded maneuvers among the peasant delegates. He therefore had to fall back upon Carranzism, the bourgeois side of the class line.

This was the time for weapons, not for compromise. And so, the Constitutionalists, particularly those who followed Obregón, withdrew from the assembly a few days after they had voted by acclamation to back the Ayala Plan. The Convention was a political disaster for the bourgeois leadership—above all for Obregón, who had embraced the whole project only to see it slip completely out of his hands.

Apart from keeping the Zapatists at bay on the outskirts of Mexico City, the Constitutionalists had done very little since they arrived in the capital. The months since August 1914 had been a time of political and military paralysis, unshaken by the war of verbal maneuver around the Convention and all the parallel negotiations. Instead of working in their favor, as they had hoped, time had turned against them, since the unification of the Villists and Zapatists opened an apparent way forward for the masses. The Constitutionalist government had taken no effective measures to win the population of Mexico City to its side. Thus, when Carranza broke with the Convention, he set off for Veracruz State and conducted his last delaying tactics by telegram while negotiating the U.S. withdrawal scheduled for September.

The Constitutionalists were in no position to defend the capital: Lucio Blanco, the military commander of Mexico City and head of the Northwest Army cavalry, had leanings toward the Conventionist side; and Obregón was himself preparing for his troops to abandon the town. Meanwhile, Pablo González, whose Northeast Army faced the advancing Villists, had already withdrawn southward from Querétaro without offering a fight.

On November 23, the U.S. Marines fulfilled their agreement with Carranza and evacuated Veracruz. The next day, Obregón's army trains evacuated Mexico City for Veracruz, and Lucio Blanco assumed command of the city in the name of the Convention. A number of like-minded officers also broke with Carranza and took their troops over to the Conventionist side, thereby weakening still further Carranza's much-reduced army. That same night, November 24, 1914, Zapatist forces entered the capital and gave assurances to the whole population.

On December 3, the Northern Division, together with the Convention and its government, moved into the city through Tacuba and Atzcapozalco. The next day witnessed the meeting between Villa and Zapata at Xochimilco.

The peasant armies now occupied the capital and the whole of the North and Center, while Carranza's forces were a mere segment of an army, routed and driven into a coastal strip to seek refuge in the port of Veracruz. The entire country shifted to the left under the violent impact of a revolutionary upsurge that seemed to know no obstacle. In December 1914, the armed peasants were the masters of Mexico and of its seat of power, the National Palace in the capital of the Republic.

6

Mexico City, December 1914

The occupation of the capital by the peasant armies synthesized what was going on in the country. The peasant war had now reached its highest point. The old oligarchy had lost its power forever, together with much of its property—nothing like this had happened before anywhere in Latin America, nor would it again for many decades. The representatives of the new bourgeoisie had not yet managed to consolidate this power in their own hands. Indeed, faced with the mighty onrush of armed peasants, they had been forced to abandon the political center of the country, Mexico City, and the material symbol of power, the National Palace.

In reality, there was a vacuum of power. For it was not enough that the oligarchy should lose power and that the bourgeoisie should be incapable of holding it: someone still had to take it. The peasant leadership did not take power: it merely kept it "in custody," as at the National Palace, in order to hand it over to the petty-bourgeois leaders of the Aguascaliente Convention. The exercise of power demands a program. The application of a program requires a policy. A policy means a party. The peasants did not have, could not have had, any of these things.

The urban working class, as an independent political force, was absent from the arena. There were workers in Villa's army, particularly miners and railway workers; but they were there as individuals, not as an organized force. Anarchists and Magonists existed as a diffuse current within the leadership of the incipient unions. And the inclination of the anarcho-syndicalist leaders was to entangle themselves with the state rather than to risk uniting their fate to the uncertain destiny of the armed peasants. In fact, they did not even have a program to offer the peasantry, since the revolutionary Magonist appeals, filtered through the prism of the union leaders, were not anchored in the class struggle as it existed in the real world, as opposed to the world of ideological speculation.

The workers and artisans of Mexico City looked with sympathy on the peasant armies, greeting their arrival with countless spontaneous expressions of friendship and solidarity. Yet feelings were not enough to establish a worker-peasant alliance. The new unions did not have the necessary program and political organizational expression, while the peasant leadership, torn between the revolutionary impetus of its armed base and its own illusions about "good laws" and "good, illustrious men," did not grasp the necessity of such an alliance. This was also true of the peasant masses themselves, despite their natural suspicion of the new *catrines*.

In that year, 1914, the world socialist movement was at its lowest point in many years: the first great imperialist war had just broken out, and the peoples of Europe were paralyzed and caught up in the slaughter of World War I.

Not only did this determine the isolation of the Mexican Revolution at the critical moment; it also served as a measure of the historical achievement of the Mexican peasantry. For without realizing it, they were the high point of the revolution around the world when they took control of the capital in December 1914. With ingenuousness, but also with determination, they then tried to carry further the task that history and their own courage had placed on their shoulders.

The occupation of Mexico City by the peasant armies is one of the finest episodes of the entire revolution—an early, impetuous yet orderly expression of strength that has left its mark on the country; one of the foundations that, unshaken by setbacks, treachery, and conflict, uphold the pride and self-respect of the Mexican peasantry.

Martín Luis Guzmán, a fine writer who, having joined Villa in the hour of victory, deserted at the approach of defeat, left an outstanding literary chronicle of the revolution, *The Eagle and the Serpent*. In a vivid description of the period, "The Zapatists at the Palace," he displays all the feelings of fear, hatred, doubt, incomprehension, and ambivalence characteristic of the petty bourgeois who formed the Conventionist government. It is worth quoting at length from his account, which also highlights the internal contradiction that would soon bring the unstable government to the point of collapse. Guzmán was undersecretary of war in this government, the secretary being General José Isabel Robles.

> Eulalio Gutiérrez wanted us to visit the National Palace before his government was installed. So José Isabel Robles and I presented ourselves that very evening. Eufemio Zapata, who kept guard of the building, came down to welcome us at the main gate and started to do us the honours of the house.
>
> Judging by his behavior, Eufemio seemed very full of his temporary role, which was to settle the new president into his own government house and to initiate him into the splendors of his future rooms and offices. As we are stepping out of the car, he shook our hands and said a few words of rough yet friendly welcome.
>
> I looked around me. Moving off slowly, the car was scarcely through the gates which lay under one of the courtyard arcades. Further back, the spandrels formed by the compact white of the arches and the penumbra of the wall-opening met each other at an angle. A group of Zapatists were watching us from the guardroom, while others looked at us through the pillars. Were these groups humble or suspicious? What they aroused in me was rather a strange sense of curiosity, due in large measure to the setting of which they formed part. For that huge palace, which had always struck me as so unchangeable, now seemed almost empty, delivered for some incomprehensible reason to a band of half-dressed rebels.
>
> We went up the staircase of honor rather than the old one. Eufemio walked ahead, like a caretaker showing a house to prospective tenants. As he claimed each step, with his tight wide-seamed trousers, his drill-shirt open below the waist, and his excessively

broad *sombrero,* he seemed to symbolize the historic days through which we were living. For his boorish, not humble, figure contrasted with the refinement and culture heralded by the staircase. A palace footman, a coachman, an office-holder, an ambassador would have moved respectfully up these stairs, with the greater or lesser dignity inherent in his position and congruous with the hierarchy of more exalted ranks. Eufemio moved like a young stableman who thinks he will suddenly become president. There was a discord between shoe and carpet in the way his shoe trampled the carpet; a discord between hand and stair-rail in the way his hand rested on the stair-rail. Every time he moved his foot, it seemed surprised not to stumble on broken ground; every time he stretched his hand, it groped in vain for a tree-trunk or a rough edge of stone. One had only to look at him to realize that all his rightful surroundings were missing, and that what now encircled him was too much for him.

But then a tremendous doubt came over me. What about us? What impression would our small group, Eulalio, Robles and I, have made upon an observer as we followed behind Eufemio—Eulalio and Robles with their Texan hats, their ungroomed appearance, and their unmistakable lack of refinement; I with the timeless air of civilians who plunge into Mexico City politics at a time of violence, to become presumptuous intellectual advisers appointed, at best, to successful *caudillos,* or at worst, to criminals who pose as rulers?

When we reached the top, Eufemio took tireless pleasure in showing us each one of the presidential rooms and apartments. Our footsteps echoed by turns on the shining wax-floor, which reflected the shape of our bodies broken by the multi-hued rugs. Behind us, the click-clack of two Zapatists following at a distance rose and fell in the silence of the empty halls. It was a soft, low sound. Occasionally, the click-clack stopped for several moments, as the Zapatists paused to look at some painting or piece of furniture. I then turned round to observe them: from that distance, they seemed encrusted in the broad reach of the hall, forming a curiously still and remote double shape. They stood very close to everything, silent, bareheaded, with long, shiny, compressed hair, modestly holding their broad hats in both hands. Their mild, uneasy, almost religious concentration certainly rang true. But what did *we* represent, Eufemio, Eulalio, Robles and I? Did we represent something fundamental, sincere and profound? We commented on everything with smiling lips and firmly placed hats.

Whenever he came to something, Eufemio did not hesitate to give his often primitive opinion. His remarks displayed an optimistic and ingenuous view of high office. "Here," he said, "is where the government people meet to chat." "Here is where they dance." "Here is where they eat supper." It gradually became clear that, in Eufemio's mind, we had never known the feel of a carpet, never had the slightest idea of the function of a sofa, a console-table or drawing-room furniture. And so, he explained it all to us, in a tone of such simplicity that I felt a real tenderness towards him. In front of the presidential chair, his voice reached a pitch of triumph bordering on ecstasy: "That's the chair!" And he added, with an enviable rush of candor: "Since I've been here, I come to see this chair every day, so that I can get used to it. Just think: I always used to imagine that the presidential chair was for riding on!"[1] Eufemio burst out laughing at his own simplicity, and we joined in the laughter. But Eulalio, who had been itching to make a joke at the Zapatist general's expense, now gently put his arm round his shoulder and made [a] barbed remark in his caressing honey-toned voice:

"It's not useless, comrade, for you to be a good rider. You, and others like you, can be sure of becoming president on the day when horses are fitted with this kind of seat."

As if by magic, Eufemio stopped laughing and grew sullen and taciturn. For Gutiérrez's repartee, extremely cruel and perhaps extremely apt, had touched him to the quick.

"O.K.," he said moments later, as if there were no longer anything worth seeing, "let's go down to the coach-houses and stables. We'll have a quick look round, and then I'll take you to the rooms where I and other comrades live."

We spent some time looking at the coach-houses and stables,

more to please Eufemio than for our own pleasure. Once among the horse-collars, reins, bits and bridles—and the smells of creaking and greased hide—he displayed an incredible amount of precise knowledge. He seemed to know no less about the breeding, training and grooming of horses. Above all, he spoke to us with an enthusiasm that made him forget the incident of the chair, and he then took us to the part of the palace occupied by himself and his colleagues.

It was a fair indication of his sincerity that Eufemio had found rooms to his taste in the poorest and most remote of the inner patios. No doubt he was well aware of the excessive modestness of his shelter, for he tried to pre-empt criticism by giving us an advance description.

"That's where I am," he said. "Since I've always been poor, I wouldn't be able to live in bigger rooms."

This is the account of an enemy within, who could not in spite of himself help feeling a certain respect. These people were, and felt themselves to be, intruders, and Guzmán says as much. Yet they could not resist expressing their bitter sense of irony at the peasants who trample on "culture." In their view, "a footman, coachman, office-holder or ambassador" was able to represent "culture" in the inner sanctum of the state—in other words, any servant of the bourgeoisie subject to its class values. But they felt insulted by the presence of a peasant leader who, in his very manner of climbing the stairs, cancelled the whole bourgeois "hierarchy of ranks."

The most important factor in this account is one that does not register in the author's consciousness: the palace is empty; the new president and his secretaries represent no one and have no force of their own; and yet, Eufemio and the Zapatists, who do have this force, speak of the government as an alien body—"the government people"—and have not fully cast off their respect for the symbols of bourgeois domination enshrined in the palace. They have not made this their own: they have just occupied it. (In the incident of the chair, Eufemio indirectly reflects the peasant will to exercise power, eliciting from the others an instinctive and aggressive reaction in the form of contemptuous irony.) Their meetings do not take place here, nor any other events in their political and social life. Although the old command center of the ruling classes stands silent and empty, and although the petty-bourgeois Conventionists seek refuge in jokes in the face of the enormous tasks ahead, the victorious peasant armies do not have a seat for their government in the palace or any other building in Mexico City.

In short, there is a vacuum of power.

On December 6, from the National Palace balconies, Villa and Zapata reviewed a march-past by troops of the Northern Division and the Southern Liberation Army. Later, having posed together for a photograph, they took turns sitting in the presidential chair. "We'll see how it feels," they said.

Two elements now dominated the political situation in the capital: the alliance of the peasant leaderships, and the government they had set in place. Then there was the state apparatus, without an apparent head but with all its ministries, functionaries, and bureaucrats. Not knowing what to do with it, the peasant leaders entrusted the Convention government to administer it "to the people's benefit." The members of the government said yes; but apart from a few nebulous and vaguely democratic notions, they too did not have an idea of what to do. Indeed, they felt that the peasant leaders were treating them not as dignitaries but as mere administrative employees, and to an increasing extent as prisoners of the very people who had to be prevented from going beyond the law. The property of the old oligarchy was placed under control and occupied. The president, as well as the generals, ministers, and top civil servants, had moved their homes and offices into the old mansions abandoned by their bourgeois owners: they slept in their beds, ate at their tables, and drank their wine. But the structure of private property was intact—or at best, in controlled suspension until the skies cleared—and the continuity of the state apparatus ensured that it would remain so. Although the peasants had redistributed the country haciendas, the turmoil in Mexico City unfolded in the lofty realm of politics, barely touching the property bedrock of the social class structure.

Zapata and Villa first met in Xochimilco, on the southern outskirts of Mexico City, on December 4, 1914. Their meeting resulted in the so-called Xochimilco Pact, really more of a verbal agreement on the general course of the struggle.

There is a stenographic record of the first part of this meeting, in which the main conversation involved various stories from the war. The only political perspective was that the government should be entrusted to "educated people," while they themselves continued military operations, each in his respective zone. Of course, they agreed that "the lands of the rich should be redistributed" and "given to the people." As Villa put it in the discussion: "Our people have never had justice, nor even freedom. The rich have got all the major landholdings, while the poor wear rags and work from dawn till dusk. I believe that life must be different in the future—otherwise, we're not worth the Mausers we carry."

However, political power was to be given to the petty-bourgeois Conventionists, who were in turn preparing to hand it back to Carranza. The peasant leaders would try in vain to keep them under control: the petty bourgeois went on maneuvering; and when the peasant machete threatened to put a stop to their maneuvers, they simply decamped and left behind as much damage as possible. The dialogue between Villa and Zapata is enough to show that their own political limits left them with no alternative but to trust in those *catrines* of whose future betrayal they already had some foreboding. The stenographic record contains this exchange:

VILLA: I don't want public positions, because I don't know how to deal with them. We'll see what these people are up to doing. We'll just appoint the ones who aren't going to make trouble.

ZAPATA: I'll advise all our friends to be very careful—otherwise, they'll get the chop . . . (*laughter*)

SERRATOS (a Zapatist general): Of course . . .

ZAPATA: Because I don't think we'll be fooled. It's been enough for us to rein them in, keeping a very close watch on them, and to keep feeding them under our control.

VILLA: It's very clear to me that we ignorant men make the war, and the cultured people have to make use of it. But they should not give us any trouble.

ZAPATA: The men who've worked the most have the least chance to enjoy those city sidewalks. Nothing but sidewalks. As for me, each time that I walk over these sidewalks, I feel like I am tumbling down.

VILLA: This ranch is too big for us; it's better out there. As soon as this business is sorted out, I'll be off north to the country. I've got a lot to do up there. And the people there will fight hard.

This dialogue contains the seeds of both political and military defeat. Unable to keep power in their hands, the two leaders are prepared to hand it over. They therefore give up the idea of a centralized army, which would require a centralized state power, and decide to forsake the center that is already in their hands: each will return to fight in his own region, whose horizon they have not been able to transcend in a vision of the nation. As Villa puts it, "This ranch is too big for us; it's better out there."

For their part, the members of the Convention government were as if suspended in midair. The peasants could hoist them into government, but real power required a national program which, apart from restitution of the land, was beyond their capacity to provide. For however radical its methods may be, Jacobinism still needs a bourgeois class mold. In the same way, although a river may temporarily flow out of its bed, it is still that bed which determines its basic course. If Jacobinism were to destroy the bourgeois class mold, instead of merely racing ahead, then it would cease to be Jacobinism: it would change its base and be changed into socialism. At one point, the revolutionary strength of the armed peasantry was able to create a government of its own, separate from the Carranza government. This demonstrates, above all else, that although the prospect of revolutionary seizure of the land formally corresponds to a democratic demand, it already transcends the limits of the bourgeoisie and necessitates a confrontation with the ruling class. Yet the peasantry could establish a government, but it could not establish a stable national power of its own.

The Carranzist government, driven to the sea, weakened militarily by defections and socially by its open clash with the peasant armies, was nevertheless the only one with a national perspective. Here lay the essence of its superiority. For just as the unstable, vacillating elements in the Convention heights had been attracted by the social dynamism of the revolutionary upsurge embodied in the peasant military thrust, so now the uncertainty and inner paralysis of the Convention government, unable to translate this dynamism into a revolutionary policy, would soon fragment and soften them for the attraction of the Constitutionalist movement.

This attraction was all the more powerful in that Obregón's line was becoming dominant among the Constitutionalists. Indeed, it was only his radical-tinged policy which, in the absence of an independent course on the part of the peasant leaderships, could actually exercise this attractive power and politically weaken the enemy forces.

The powerful thrust of the revolution is shown by the fact that the peasantry tried to become politically independent of the government of the bourgeoisie, installing a new government in the occupied capital rather than simply keeping up the war in the countryside. It stood in contradiction to Carranza's genuinely bourgeois government, but the contradiction was even more profound with the insurgent peasant base that supported it against Carranza. In the end, therefore, the Conventionist government came to act as an agency of Carranza against the peasant leaderships.

Years later, the chronicler of Conventionist indecision, Martín Luis Guzmán, gave a lucid and cynical account of this process.

Eulalio, who was far from being a fool, took in our situation perfectly; three or four weeks in power (or whatever it might be) were enough to confirm him in his original idea: all that could be done for the moment was to play for time and to seek a way of escaping from Villa without falling into Carranza. But to wait meant to defend ourselves—and to defend ourselves against the most immediate threat, who was Villa and Zapata. We therefore had to work out one of the most incongruous policies imaginable: to help our declared enemies, the Carranzists, to subdue our official supporters, the Villists and Zapatists, so that we might relieve ourselves a little from the tremendous pressure with which the more immediate power was weighing us down.

The Conventionist government in the capital was thus not an institution of power—Guzmán recognizes this when he talks of "three of four weeks in power (or whatever it might be)"—but an unstable, conflictual alliance with a section of the radicalized petty bourgeoisie. It was a kind of pre–Constituent Assembly, and like all such bodies, it posed two problems without being able to resolve them: where is the country going, and who is to steer it on course? It could not answer the first question, and still less the second (which ultimately settles the first). This situation could not last long, nor did it.

The government itself fully reflected this contradiction. The perspective of its more conscious elements was to use the peasants' strength as a bargaining point with Obregón, and hence with Carranza. Merely in order to be accepted as parties to negotiation, they had to show that they controlled this strength. But since, in reality, they did not control anything, all they could demonstrate was that they were engaged in underhand sabotage. Other members of the government had a completely volatile and nebulous perspective. In general, however, it was a gathering of careerists, illusionists, adventurers, waverers, and spongers; or, in the best of cases, disoriented and "presumptuous intellectual advisers appointed to successful *caudillos*," as one of them, Martín Luis Guzmán, would write years later. It differed from the summit of other "peasant parties" in history only insofar as the armed peasant base was not just an electoral mass, but a force actually dominating the country. Through its own leaderships, of which Zapatism was the politically decisive one, it kept a deeply suspicious watch over these heights, placing rifles in the way of their maneuvers. Inevitably the contradiction would soon reach bursting-point.

These politicians, too impotent even to issue an agrarian reform law, were an impediment by their very presence. They looked on Villa and Zapata with a mixture of fear and hate. Through their actions, methods, and inaction, they placed a barrier between the urban workers and the Villist or Zapatist peasantry, joined in this endeavor by the union leaders who could see some career prospectus with Obregón. They paralyzed and betrayed everything. The most corrupt lived in the abandoned luxury of the bourgeoisie, while the more gullible lived in the clouds. None of them represented anything, save the lack of a politically independent national perspective.

Nevertheless, the formation of the Conventionist government expressed something deeper and longer-lasting than the men who joined it, something unique in the history of peasant wars. For through Villa's military organization and centralization, and through Zapata's political intransigence, the insurgent peasants were capable of a supreme effort to step forward as an independent national force; to draw along a section of the petty bourgeoisie, if only on a conditional and temporary basis; and to exert such a powerful influence on the Jacobin current within Constitutionalism that the peasants' weight in the revolution would eventually find a more permanent political expression.

This supreme effort, though inevitably disappointed, heralded the coming era of revolutions that would formally begin three years later in Russia.

The military situation appeared altogether favorable to the armies of the Convention: they dominated the capital and the entire center of Mexico, virtually all the northern regions, nearly all the richer and more important states (with the notable exception of Veracruz), and the great bulk of the railway network. For their part, the Constitutionalists retained their last bastion in Veracruz and nearby areas, as well as a few northern ports and frontier towns and some southern regions that played no significant role in the revolution. During the weeks after the capture of Mexico City, Villa took Guadalajara and the state of Jalisco from General Diéguez, while Zapata drove General Salvador Alvarado back from Puebla to Veracruz. At the same time, Felipe Angeles fought another successful campaign, capturing Saltillo and Monterrey, among other towns, defeating the Constitutionalists at the battles of General Cepeda and Ramos Arizpe, and bringing virtually all the northwest territories under his control.

In late December and early January 1915, the country was one huge battlefield on which units of the Northern Division and the Southern Liberation Army were simultaneously fighting the Constitutionalists in the North and Northwest, along the Pacific coast, in the Gulf region, on the borders of Puebla, and in the center of the country.

In doing this, however, the Conventionist armies converted all the advantages of their central position into disadvantages, completely dispersing their forces on several fronts against secondary enemies. Nothing could have been of greater benefit to the weakened Constitutionalist center in Veracruz, which needed time for both military and political reorganization.

A Constitutionalist general, Juan Barragán, described the military situation in these crucial days as follows:

> A brief analysis of the topography in which the belligerent armies were operating is enough to show that the Constitutionalist forces were in the worse military position. Let us begin with the *northern states*: in Sonora, Agua Prieta was the only town in the hands of Constitutionalist troops; Chihuahua, Coahuila and Nuevo León were entirely controlled by the Northern Division; in Tamaulipas, the Constitutionalists still held Nuevo Laredo, Matamoros and Tampico, while the capital and the rest of the state were in Conventionist hands. *The Gulf states*: Veracruz, Tabasco, Campeche and

Yucatán, dominated by the Constitutionalists; Yucatán subsequently lost. *The Pacific states*: Chiapas, controlled by the Constitutionalist government; Oaxaca, partially dominated by the enemy, but the Isthmus and the rest by the Constitutionalist army; Guerrero, in enemy hands, except for the port of Acapulco; Colima, controlled by troops loyal to the High Command; Sinaloa, dominated by the enemy, apart from the port of Mazatián. *The states of the Mexican interior,* all in enemy hands, including the capital of the Republic.

It will be clear from this description that Constitutionalist forces occupied what we might call the periphery of the Republic, while the Villists and Zapatists had installed themselves in the center. Strategically speaking, this placed the former in an inferior position. It is certainly true that the Constitutionalists, controlling ports on both coasts and a number of frontier towns, could obtain adequate supplies of war materiel from abroad and distribute it, mostly through Veracruz, to the various military columns. But it is also undeniable that they had to overcome numerous time-consuming problems in transporting men and materiel to reinforce their weak points. The Villists and Zapatists in the center of the country dominated the railway network, as well as holding various towns on the northern frontier. They could therefore rapidly shift their troops to any point they needed to attack or defend, and were also in a position to receive regular supplies of war materiel produced in the United States.[2]

General Francisco Grajales, who considered Obregón a "military genius of the revolution," has left this account of the same period:

It is a hard task to outline the general picture offered by the country in those days. The belligerent armies scattered over the whole territory of the fatherland, deprived of organic stability as a result of constant defections, and equipped with a troop-force of uncommon mobility, appear to the observer in an inextricable confusion. But, from a geographical point of view, it is possible to note a number of theatres of operation. The principal one was in the Center, with Puebla as the battle-front; secondary theatres took shape in Jalisco, Tepic, Sinaloa, Sonora and Baja California; and still others very soon appeared in the North East (Coahuila, Nuevo León, Tamaulipas and San Luis Potosí), Yucatán and the Tehuante-pec Isthmus.

In the Center, the Constitutionalists could only count on the remnants of the North-West Army Corps located at various key-points along the railway between Veracruz and Puebla. The North-East Army Corps (General Pablo Gonzaléz) had virtually disintegrated in its retreat from Querétaro to Pachuca following clashes with the Northern Division. Some fragments set off in the direction of Tuxpan and Tampico, while others passed over to the enemy.

The Convention government resolved that the Southern Liber-ation Army should take charge of the campaign against Constitu-tionalist forces operating in the states of Puebla, Veracruz and Oaxaca, the operational theatre in the Center; and instructed Gen-eral Villa to conduct the campaign in the West, North-West and North East.

This absurd dispersal of forces, stemming from Zapata's obtuse criteria of localist jurisdiction, brought a miraculous salvation for the Constitutionalist side. The dispersal of forces combined with the greatly inferior quality of the Zapatist officers and soldiers, who had to face none other than the war-hardened legions under the personal command of General Obregón.[3]

Who and what was responsible for this "absurd dispersal of forces"? We have already seen that on December 4, at their very first meeting, Zapata and Villa agreed to fight in their respective zones. General Angeles, who had long discussions with Villa on the further course of the campaign, was in disagreement with this de-cision. As soon as the Villist forces entered Mexico City, he pro-posed that, instead of pausing, they should pursue Obregón's battered army and focus the entire thrust of the Northern Division on its annihilation. But Villa opposed this plan: since his base was in Chihuahua, he argued, and since his supply lines stretched from Ciudad Juárez to Mexico City, the first task should be to protect these lines against enemy attack, while Zapata took charge of attacking, or at least bottling up, Obregón's forces. Angeles insisted that this absurd and dangerous division of forces would dissipate the sustained momentum of advance; that the national capital had now replaced Chihuahua as the principal base; and that it was necessary to reach the sea and shatter the enemy center in Veracruz, since Obregón would again use any short respite in order to regroup his forces. The other Constitutionalist forces scattered about the country were an element of secondary importance, whose surrender would follow the annihilation of the Veracruz center. "They are like hats hanging on a rack," he said by way of analogy. "There's no point in pulling them off one by one, when a single blow at the rack, I mean Carranza, will bring them all down by themselves."

Although the rack was a very graphic image, the task of convincing Villa involved not images but class questions. However we look at it, Felipe Angeles was clearly right. Being a professional solider who saw the war and the country in national terms, he inevitably had a broader political horizon. Villa, like Zapata, was dominated by regional peasant criteria. He was extremely uneasy at the thought of being cut from his regional base in the North, not only for logistical reasons, but also because his prestige and authority were those of a peasant leader. In his view, seizure of the capital ("too big for us") could not possibly compensate for the distance from his base. The roots of his assurance were in "the land"—that is, in his native region.

For his part, Zapata not only shared these feelings but regarded the South as his own military jurisdiction. Villa was prepared to accept this division, sharing as he did the regionalist peasant logic in which it originated. But he did not have the same confidence in the military aspirations of the Zapatist army, which he knew to be inferior to both the Northern Division and Obregón's forces.

Thus, at a time when the peasant armies could and should have concentrated all their strength on the annihilation of the enemy center in Veracruz, their alloted task of protecting long supply lines and fighting in their respective zones inevitably led to dispersion.

On the opposite side, Obregón viewed things according to the same criteria used by Angeles. Fearing, as the most logical course, a concentrated assault by all the Villist and Zapatist forces, he prepared for resistance with grave doubts about the possibility of success. When the assault did not take place, he understood that the Conventionists were losing momentum and giving him the respite vital to survival. Throughout the first half of December, he feverishly reorganized his troops for the counteroffensive. On December 13, Carranza appointed him commander of the operations against Villa, setting the recapture of Mexico City as the first objective.

Meanwhile, the delay and dispersion of the offensive lost Villa some of his authority over such wavering Conventionist offices as Lucio Blanco, and helped to speed up their defection. Previously, they had been swept along by the strength of the peasant upsurge and the irresistible advance of the Northern Division, although they had still harbored many reservations about Villa and Zapata. Now that the offensive had slowed down, and the Convention government was politically paralyzed, these doubts rapidly gained the upper hand.

This difference in strategic vision between Villa and Zapata on the one hand, and Angeles and Obregón on the other, essentially came down to an irreducible divergence of aims. Villa and Zapata were fighting for land, Obregón for power. Villa and Zapata did not know what to do with Mexico City, while Obregón needed the capital as a national political center and a social base. Obregón was still in a position of military inferiority. But since it is political power that ultimately settles the question of land ownership, the advantage was already completely on his side—although there would have to be great battles before he asserted it in reality.

Angeles's military arguments, expressing a national political perspective, would never convince a man who, like Villa, did not share this perspective and was unable to rise above his regionalist vision. Angeles bowed to his leader's decision, engaged and won some magnificent battles, and eventually lost the war alongside Villism and the Northern Division.

In considering the peasant occupation of Mexico City, one is immediately struck by the fact that they had no organic expression of power at a time when they mastered the greater part of the country. Everyday life continued in the capital, as it always does after, and indeed during, a revolution. Two powers, the Conventionist and the Constitutionalist governments, nominally controlled distinct parts of the country, while in the capital itself another duality of power had arisen between the Conventionist government and the peasant leaderships. These leaderships could not impose a policy on the government, because they did not have one; and Eulalio Gutiérrez and his ministers were not in a position to control the activity of the peasant leaders.

The Villist-Zapatist occupation of Mexico City was distinguished by its orderly character. There was no looting, and the troops neither committed excesses nor provoked disorders. Their discipline owed more to a basic feeling of solidarity with the workers and the "poor" of Mexico City than to the existing army regulations. Disorder and even crimes, when they happened, came mostly from the officers enjoying their new "power" in bars, restaurants, and similar places.

Whereas this relative order prevailed in social life, the opposite was true of political and economic life: no one assumed command or took initiatives; and the two powers wasted much of their time in conflicts that paralyzed them both. Gutiérrez and his ministers wanted to impose forms of bourgeois legality, but the peasant leaders essentially retained the laws of war, including the elementary laws of revolutionary terror through which they ensured their rule. Unlike the terror used against the masses by Díaz and Huerta, and by Juvencio Robles in Morelos, this was directed against the political enemies of Villism and Zapatism and the tiny, clearly identifiable minority of rich people. The workers, poor petty bourgeois, semi-peasants, and artisans felt safe under the occupation of the peasant armies.

Every day, however, these same people experienced the government paralysis, the ineffectiveness of president and ministers, the lack of initiatives, and the incapacity for political action displayed by Villism and Zapatism. They saw, felt, and endured the progressive worsening of the political situation, the administrative chaos, and the growing shortage of supplies.

The dual power expressed itself in some striking ways. The peasant leaders were nominally in the service of the government, which had to approve the economic measures necessary for them to continue the war. In practice the reverse was true, at least as far as Villism was concerned. For Villa continued to draw his resources from the northern territories, especially through the sale of expropriated livestock in the United States and through a special tax on rich traders living in towns under Northern Division control. In Mexico City, senior officers such as Villa's old friend, General Urbina, would finance their units, and occasionally themselves, by kidnapping rich people and demanding a ransom. It was curiously symptomatic that the supposed rulers of the capital, who could have raised the necessary funds simply by confiscating them from the same people of wealth, nonetheless resorted to the clandestine kidnapping tactic used by hunted peasant bands.

The settling of accounts with political enemies proceeded in the same way. For Villa and Zapata, as their Xochimilco conversation already showed, the main function of the Convention government was to give "legality" to the power of the peasant armies. Thus, given that Gutiérrez and his cabinet opposed radical measures in this or any other field, the revolutionary terror and reprisals had to be conducted behind their back. This empirical, unstructured form of "dictatorship of the peasantry" had to operate in a clandestine manner, because it did not have the sanction of its own government.

The enemies of Villism and Zapatism raised a hue and cry over the "anarchy" reigning in the capital at that time. There was no such "anarchy," and most of the city's population did not live in a climate of fear or uncertainty. Indeed, having experienced all the former governments, from Díaz to Huerta, they at last felt that people like themselves, the armed peasants, had the material force on which political power depends. Although the peasant leaderships did not exercise power and handed it over to Gutiérrez and his ministers, their troops provided a degree of protection from state abuses that the poor people had never previously enjoyed.

"Anarchy" and the settling of accounts essentially represented a disorderly attempt by the peasant leaders to counter the growing weight of bourgeois tendencies within the Convention government. They were part of what Guzmán called "the tremendous pressure with which the more immediate power is weighing us down." "Very careful, otherwise they'll get the chop," Zapata had said in Xochimilco, but the peasant machete fell without a clear plan to direct its blows and make them politically effective. Although distrust and lack of structure gave rise to mistakes, a class intuition generally guided the settling of accounts. This is clear in the case of the Conventionist David Berlanga. When Villa ordered him to be shot, it was because he had continually criticized Villa's "abuses" and argued that Gutiérrez and his ministers should break with the "bandits," Villa and Zapata.

Much clearer, however, is the case in which Juan Banderas—a general from Sinaloa nicknamed El Agachado (Stoopy) for his bent back—waged a campaign of persecution against Gutiérrez's appointee as secretary of education, the lawyer José Vasconcelos. One day, it was reported to Villa that General Banderas was looking for the secretary of education "in order to shoot him." When Gutiérrez protested that such a situation was inadmissible, Villa called in El Agachado, a former peasant like all the officers in the town, and asked him if the reports were true. He further demanded to know what Banderas had against Vasconcelos, who a few months earlier had been full of praise for Villa. Banderas replied that before the

revolution, he had been arrested in Mexico City in connection
with a land dispute. Vasconcelos had then visited him in his cell,
offering to defend him and secure his release in return for a large
sum of money. Banderas raised the money at great cost to his family. But once he had handed it over, Vasconcelos never reappeared
in the prison and left him to rot.

Villa suggested that Banderas leave the minister alone, so as not
to provoke a government crisis, offering to reimburse the sum out
of Northern Division funds. Banderas refused. The money did
not concern him in the least—it was just that such an immoral
man should not be secretary of education and responsible for the
upbringing of children and young people. If he was going to
"break" this "little lawyer," it was to do some good for the youth
of Mexico.

Villa must have found the argument irrefutable, because he did
not insist any more. Instead, he summoned Vasconcelos and, offering to find him a temporary job in Northern Division territory,
told him that he should give up his post and leave the capital. For
El Agachado was "very much a man of principle," not to be trifled
with, who would kill him if he remained. "Now," Villa added,
"you are reaping what you once sowed." Vasconcelos did leave the
capital, but as an open enemy intent on making propaganda against
Villism and Zapatism.

This incident played a part in triggering the crisis of the Conventionist regime. Eulalio Gutiérrez complained that Villa had allowed a peasant general to drive out "at pistol-point" none other
than the minister of education in his government. Villa pointed
out that he had offered Vasconcelos a bodyguard, only to be turned
down. But Gutiérrez kept up the pressure. What kind of government was this, he asked, which had to use a bodyguard to defend its
officials against pro-government troops? (Indeed, what kind of
government was it?)

After a number of similar incidents, Villa finally placed his most
select troops, *los dorados,* on guard over the presidential residence. At
the same time, he informed Gutiérrez that he was now a prisoner,

and that if he attempted to escape "in order to steal back legality," he would find Villa's troops in control of the house, the city, the streets, and the trains. Gutiérrez, it is said, replied that he would leave by donkey if necessary, thereby consummating the break with Villa. The dual power inherent in the Convention regime thus entered into the most dramatic form of crisis. Since Gutiérrez was "the president" and "the law," Villa did not want to apply his normally radical method and have him shot. It was therefore just a question of days before Gutiérrez found a way of escaping, even on the back of a donkey; and with his departure, the untenable phantom government finally broke apart.

Yet this phantom government, useless for any positive initiative, was a very real force in all its negative aspects. It was a center of organized sabotage against the peasant armies—particularly the Southern Liberation Army, whose lack of independent funds made it dependent on the Convention government for the new, more formalized warfare against an enemy greatly superior to Huerta's corrupt armies. This sabotage, combined with the military weakness of the Zapatist guerrillas and the geographical dispersion of the peasant armies, left the road almost open for Obregón to march on the capital from Veracruz.

Again, Martín Luis Guzmán has left a frank report of this treachery. He presents himself as one of the main operators of a policy through which "we functioned more as allies of Obregón" than of Zapatism and Villism. He writes:

Robles, Aguirre Benavides and I conducted operations from the ministry of war, with a cool precision whose good results compared with the vexations and dangers of our endeavor. These particularly affected myself; for although I was not an army man, had no guard, and was not surrounded by watchful officials, I had to contend with the ill-will of innumerable Zapatist senior and junior officers who saw me as the infamous author of their defeats. This was at a time of utter personal insecurity, when Mexico City—as so often before in our long history of political crime—woke up each morning to ask who had been murdered during the night, and when every night it considered the most cruel and treacherous murders to be feasible.

Robles had said to me: "As you are aware, we won't achieve anything against Villa for the time being. What does he need us for, except for a banner? But things are different with the Zapatists. If they ask for money, hand it over and just make sure they don't get their hands on the account. But if they ask for guns, or ammunition, or trains, don't even give them water."

It had to be seen how some of Zapata's subordinates (usually generals in blouses and cotton trousers, with a rifle on their shoulder and a cartridge-belt across their breast) would grow increasingly agitated at me; and how others (this time, generals with tight-fitting trousers, a drill-jacket and a pistol in a silver-embroidered holster) would try to make financial gain out of the situation.

During the days when the Zapatists were fighting to wrest Puebla from Alvarado's forces, I used all imaginable resources to avoid supplying them with guns, bullets and locomotives. Since neither Robles nor Aguirre Benavides appeared much in their offices, I was the one besieged by the commanders of the Southern Liberation Army. They would come to see me with their numerous general staff: the semi-darkness of my office was broken by the large, conspicuous patches of their beltless cotton pants; their steps made a soft, mellow sound; and they filed past like a huge crowd on an invisible road, their enormous, wide-brimmed hats producing a breeze in the stale, confined air. I made them sit down without distinction of rank, and became entangled in highly intricate disquisitions on the modern art of fighting with and without bullets, with and without rifles, with and without trains. Everything went very well as I convinced them that the arms, explosives and ammunition factories did not provide a hundredth of what we needed, or as I made them understand why, within our alliance, only General Villa was equipped to produce enough. But if they thought, or even suspected, that I wanted to refuse help, they would put me in great danger and mount a huge scandal. One disappointed group took its revenge by doing a kind of "rifle-and-pistol dance" in the waiting room, sowing fear among the fifty or so people present. And these were the mildest cases. One general, for example, without beating about the bush, simply threatened to kill me if I did not provide trains for the relief of Amozoc, then under attack by the Carranzists. When I assured him that I had no locomotives, he replied that he had seen some in such and such a station. And when I tried to compromise by offering him an antiquated and almost unusable engine, so old that it still needed firewood, he calmly replied with great exasperation:

"O.K., boss, I'll take it. But if they beat me, you'd better watch out, you son of a bitch! Because then I'll come and deal with you."

Hearing the insult, I gripped a crystal paper-weight on my table and prepared to hurl it at the Zapatist general's head. "Son of a what?" I said angrily.

"Nothing, boss, nothing; don't get upset. It was just a manner of speaking. But I'm not joking. If they defeat me, I'll be back to rub you out."

It is true that Guzmán may have later exaggerated his own treachery in order to boost his reputation among the victors and, more curiously, in the eyes of history. It is also true that this and the numerous other acts of betrayal did not play a decisive role. But they were still rather important. A genuine dual power, falling on either side of the class lines, then opposed the peasant leaderships to both the Constitutionalists and the Convention government, although these two formally appeared as mutual enemies. Once again, the apparent battle line did not coincide with the deeper class line of division; and once again it was the latter that eventually shaped the former, when the Conventionist politicians either abandoned all struggle or went over to Obregón. On January 7, 1945 Eulalio Gutiérrez, acting on behalf of ministers Robles, Lucio Blanco, and Aguirre Benavides, wrote a letter to Obregón in which he offered to join his ranks and relieve Villa of his command. On January 15, all four fled from Mexico City after formally decreeing the "dismissal" of Villa and Zapata.

The essential reason for the coming defeats lay in much deeper aspects of the situation: above all, the sense of disillusion the masses felt in their hearts at the political impotence of their leaders. The revolutionary tide had reached its peak with the occupation of Mexico City, the Xochimilco discussions between Villa and Zapata, and the march past the National Palace. From that time, the subaltern classes instinctively or half-consciously looked forward to a political transformation in their favor. Their enemies were routed. And now that their leaders had seized the formal attributes and national seat of power, they expected them to exercise it in their interests. At the very least, a law should be passed to give them ownership of the land they had occupied and were already tilling—a law similar to Lenin's first decree on the land. They did not, of course, formulate things in this way, but in practice they expected it to happen. (Obregón and Carranza understood this, and turned it to account with their agrarian law of January 1915.) The peasant leaders should also have taken measures to win the support of the urban population, first of all limiting the length of the working day and fixing a minimum wage (as Obregón would do a few months later in Celaya). They should have fulfilled the hopes which, having drawn huge masses for four years on to the path of revolution, now seemed as close at hand as the presidential chair visited by Eufemio every day and tried by Villa and Zapata in turn. Yet nothing of the kind happened.

Although the process was not directly apparent, disillusion began to sink into the deepest layers of consciousness. The nationwide upsurge continued; more land was still being occupied—the revolution seemed to be pursuing its course. But no, it had run up against an obstacle. The lack of a national political program (apart from land ownership) was now weighing with all its force upon the people. They felt that they had already done the maximum, taking by assault the distant, glittering capital of their oppressors; and that here, an invisible stumbling-block had nevertheless arisen in their path. "We ignorant men make the war," Villa had said at Xochimilco. "The cultured people have to make use of it."

The disillusionment was political in character, since the revolutionists could not see a political way forward once the gigantic social upsurge had reached its peak. This in turn reacted upon the upsurge itself, starting to break up the perspective which had momentarily seemed to offer itself through the alliance with the petty-bourgeois sector of the Convention. Thus, the immediate dispersion of military forces had deep social roots: it expressed the historical impossibility of a national peasant government and foreshadowed the slide into a form of large-scale guerrilla warfare conducted by retreating peasant guerrillas. In other words, it announced that the revolution had reached the highest point attainable under the existing leadership and would now start to decline, however great the heroic, yet defensive, mass struggles still ahead. All this was written in the events of December 1914, although naturally no one was able to read the writing.

When Obregón broke with Villa and abandoned the Aguascalientes Convention, it seemed that the failure of his balancing-game between Villa and Carranza had left him a prisoner of Carranza within the Constitutionalist camp. Villa had changed from an opponent within the Constitutionalist ranks to an enemy outside. This shift not only strengthened Obregón's unity with the commander-in-chief, but also forced Carranza to lean upon the policy of Obregón and the radical wing in order to meet the threat of Villism and Zapatism.

Thus, instead of accentuating the hold of Carranza's right-wing tendency, the break with Villism actually produced a radicalization of Constitutionalism, the function of which was to provide a social counterweight to the peasant armies during the culminating phase of the revolution. There were a number of further reasons for this radicalization. First, since it no longer had the cover of Villism and its alliance with the Northern Division, the Constitutionalist movement had to come forward with concrete promises: a program of social reforms addressing the interests and concerns of the peasantry. Secondly, the fiasco of Obregón's "grand maneuvers" at the Aguascalientes Convention, directed against the Zapatist program, undoubtedly convinced him that certain concessions had to be made to the peasantry. Thirdly, the retreat from Mexico City, in the midst of partial military disintegration and the indifference of the population, indicated a return to Obregón's initial line of assisting trade-union activity in the capital. The aim, then, was to use various social measures to build support among the workers, artisans, and urban poor, not only in Mexico City, but also in Veracruz and at a national level. Fourthly, as the revolutionary upsurge reached its height, the weakening of the Constitutionalist apparatus and military positions had augmented the influence of the radical wing which sought to link the movement to the masses. As Lucio Blanco had seen, it also forced a number of concessions from Carranza, designed to counteract the attractive power of Villism upon the radicals, or at least to soften their dissatisfaction that the break with Villa had not been averted.

All these factors were operating as the battered Constitutionalist army regrouped its forces in Veracruz, and in the region controlled by the Eastern Army under General Cándido Aguilar, who many years later would be the undisputed political leader of Veracruz State. From Veracruz, Obregón applied all his energy in reorganizing the Constitutionalist forces for a counterattack on Mexico City. The first stage was to be the recovery of Puebla, which the Zapatists had captured in mid-December from General Salvador Alvarado.

In Veracruz, the capital of the Constitutionalist government, Obregón could count on two advantages: his control of the port and its entrances, through which arms and ammunition could be freely imported; and, for the purchase of these supplies, tax revenue from the wealthy Minatitlán oil region and from Yucatán henequen exports. These provided a much more secure source of funds than the already dwindling livestock reserves that were Villa's financial mainstay. The port also assured an escape route by sea if, as was then expected, the Northern Division and the Zapatist army managed to encircle the town. Lastly, whereas the Northern Division supply lines were remarkably extended and imposed a major burden for their defense, the extreme compression of the Obregonist lines partly offset the advantages of the central position, in any case neglected by the Villist and Zapatist forces.

The crucial element in the preparations, however, was not military but political in character.

First, the Carranzist Luis Cabrera wrote up a series of programmatic goals for the revolution, amplifying the Guadalupe Plan in a way that revealed the political infuence of the Obregón tendency. This new formulation, promising land redistribution as its main point, signified that the main struggle against Villa and Zapata required the adoption of some of their objectives, albeit in a circumscribed manner. At the same time, the objectives were more precisely defined and placed within a national perspective and juridical frame.

A series of further demands, absent from the Ayala Plan and the Zapatist decrees, were introduced to attract the support of the workers and urban masses. Thus the radical wing of the Constitutionalist movement, whose influence could not have failed to be dominant in this period, sought to shape from below a *sui generis* workers' and peasants' alliance around the leadership of Constitutionalism—an alliance remaining under its control and serving its partisan interests.

All this would have been pure illusion without the second aspect of the preparations. If the attempt to win a sector of the revolutionary masses through concessions had sufficient resonance to lift Constitutionalism from the mire, this was above all because the lack of a national program deprived the other camp of a real and much-needed urban workers' and peasants' alliance. Moreover, the impact of the new Constitutionalist program, issued so late in the day, was reinforced by an objective experience of decisive weight in the consciousness of the people: namely, the paralysis affecting the Conventionist government established with Villa's and Zapata's support.

On December 12, 1914, just before the Zapatists captured Puebla, Carranza formally approved the additions to the Guadalupe

Plan in his capacity as commander-in-chief of the Constitutionalist Army and head of the Executive Power of the Mexican Republic. In its preamble, the decree ran through the Carranzist version of the conflict with Villa and the Northern Division, typically not even mentioning Zapata as part of the revolution. "Once the victorious revolution reached the capital of the Republic," so this version goes, "it tried to organize the provisional government in a proper manner, resolving to heed the demands of public opinion and to satisfy the people's urgent need for social reforms. But then it ran up against the difficulties which reaction had been preparing within the Northern Division, with the aim of frustrating the victories won by Constitutionalist Army forces." The term "reaction" was especially directed against General Felipe Angeles, whom Obregón singled out as the *éminence grise* of Villism. The accusation recurs throughout the text: "General Villa bases himself on the very elements who prevented President Madero from orienting his policy in a radical direction, and thereby bear the responsibility for his fall." Or again: "Since General Villa's reactionary troops mainly seek to obstruct the revolutionary reforms needed by the Mexican people," and so on.

The document also presents an account of the evolution and results of the Aguascalientes Convention. Its conclusion is as follows: "While the essence of the Guadalupe Plan must be upheld, the Mexican people and the Constitutionalist Army must very clearly define their present military goals. These are to annihilate the resurgent reaction headed by General Villa; and to implement the political and social principles inspiring this High Command—the ideals for which the Mexican people have fought during four years and more."

In the words of the preamble, the commander-in-chief also "has an obligation to ensure that, as before, effect is given to all the laws crystallizing the political and economic reforms which the country requires, and that such laws are issued during the fresh struggle about to develop."

This sudden urge for reforms changed the basic orientation of

the Guadalupe Plan: whereas it had previously talked of considering these problems at the end of the revolution, it now stressed that
the reforms measures should be taken "during the struggle about
to develop." Today, not tomorrow—that is that basic promise appearing in all key articles of the decree. Of the two conceptions
which confronted each other before the signing of the original
Guadalupe Plan, the one represented by Múgica's young officers
now had its revenge over Carranza's. The articles of the decree set
out a kind of "revolutionary dictatorship":

> Art. 2. The Commander-in-Chief of the Revolution and head
> of the Executive Power shall issue and enforce, during the
> course of the struggle, all the laws, regulations and measures
> designed to satisfy the economic, social and political de-
> mands of the nation, carrying out the reforms which public
> opinion considers necessary to guarantee the equality of
> Mexicans: agrarian laws assisting the formation of small-
> holdings, dissolving the latifundia, and restoring to villages
> the land of which they have been unjustly despoiled; fiscal
> legislation designed to establish a fair system of taxing
> landed property; legislation to improve the condition of the
> rural peon, the worker, the miner and the proletarian classes
> in general; the assurance of local government as a constitu-
> tional institution; the groundwork for a new system of or-
> ganizing the independent Judicial Power, both at federal and
> regional state level; revision of the law relating to matrimony
> and civil status; regulations ensuring strict compliance with
> the Reform Laws; revision of the civil, penal and commer-
> cial codes; reforms in judicial procedure, with the aim of
> guaranteeing the swift and effective administration of jus-
> tice; revision of the law on the exploitation of the country's
> mines, oil reserves, waters, forests and other natural resources,
> so as to dissolve the monopolies existing under the former
> regime and to avoid the formation of new interests in the
> future; political reforms to guarantee real enforcement of the

Constitution of the Republic, and, more generally, of all the other laws deemed necessary to ensure that all inhabitants of the country may fully and effectively exercise their rights, with equality before the law.

Art. 3. In order that he may continue the struggle and accomplish the work of reform to which the preceding article refers, the commander of the Revolution is expressly authorized to assemble and organize the Constitutionalist Army and to direct its operations in the campaign; to appoint the governors and military commanders of each state and to remove them at will; to carry out expropriations in the public interest, wherever they are necessary for land distribution, village building and other public services; to contract loans and issue National Treasury bonds, with an indication of the underlying securities; to appoint and remove at will the federal staff of the regional state administrations and to prescribe their individual assignments; to carry out, directly or through senior officers so empowered, the requisitioning of land, buildings, weapons, horses, vehicles, provisions and other war supplies; and to introduce decorations and award remuneration for services to the Revolution.

All these goals, important as they may seem, trailed behind the mass strength of the revolution at that time. Still, they were a far cry from Carranza's statement four months earlier to General Genovevo de la O: "Tell me which haciendas you own and are able to redistribute, so that each of you can redistribute what belongs to you and not to someone else"; or from his previous order that Villa should return the land redistributed in Chihuahua ("That won't be possible," Villa had replied, "because the soldiers of the revolution have it!"); or from his action in transferring Lucio Blanco after he had carried out land redistribution in Matamoros.

However limited these objectives, then, it was a program which one sector of the revolution addressed to the Mexican people. In the months to come, it would find its target. Moreover, it identified the struggle to conquer and exercise national policy power as the pivot of any reform program, effectively contrasting this with the contradictions and paralysis of Eulalio Gutiérrez's phantom government.

Carranza's new program, whose full application he would always resist, went beyond the Torreón Accords that had been roundly condemned for their radicalism just six months earlier. This fact is the best illustration of the power of the social upsurge, and of the generally radical situation that had developed in the country. In the open struggle between the two tendencies of the revolution, the moderates had to adopt crucial demands of the Villist wing which the peasant leadership had not managed to express in programmatic form, while at the same time branding Villism as a "reactionary" force responsible for Carranza's resistance to social reforms after the fall of Huerta. Through this cynical explanation, the Constitutionalists reversed the true roles played by Villism and Carranzism in the Torreón discussions and subsequent events. Nothing stood in the way of this unscrupulous falsification, since the other side was in a state of political paralysis, issuing neither proclamations nor manifestos and offering no political line or program.

Frank Tannenbaum argues that the new declaration of objectives, issued four years after the beginning of the revolution, "was the voice of a defeated military group that assumed to speak for the country." "It was a cry of despair," he continues.

> The Carranza group had been driven from the City of Mexico, and clung to a very narrow strip of coast, with the intention of escaping to sea if Pancho Villa or Zapata came nearer. It was not a proclamation by a victorious revolutionary army ready to establish a government for the purpose of bringing these reforms to pass. It was a bait for attracting adherents to the cause, a means of justifying the independent existence of an army. Had it not been for the loyalty of Alvarado in Yucatán, who supplied Carranza with large sums of money derived from the high price of henequen (which was at that

time in great demand because of the European war), even this policy might not have saved him. But the program did bring to Carranza elements that hitherto had remained outside of his camp. It attracted the workers in Mexico City and Orizaba. It gave him the support of the *agraristas* who believed in Zapata's cause, but who, for one reason or another, did not follow Zapata in his ruthless and violent struggle against great odds.[4]

A turning-point appears in the course of every popular revolution: if the radical wing does not then grasp political power, the movement inevitably begins to fall back, though never to square one. When this point is reached, it is the task of a conscious leadership to become aware of it and to raise adequate slogans and concentrate all its forces on the key objectives attainable at the time. Over a few days, over even a few hours, the slogans of the leadership then play a decisive role in either the triumph of the movement or the beginning of its dispersal. The disintegration is not at once apparent, because furious battles continue to dominate the arena. But even if the leadership does not perceive that the critical point had passed, its insecure allies—the ranks and leadership of intermediate classes attracted in the period of rising movement—never fail to register the ebb and are always the first to desert.

This truth may be seen in the flight of Eulalio Gutiérrez and his ministers. Although the decisive military blows were still a few months away at the beginning of 1915, the revolutionary forces were already entering a period of broad if uneven downturn, in which they would wage a bitter struggle and safeguard some of the basic gains of the revolution—above all, the experience of their own strength. For, as we have seen, the Constitutionalist leadership could not check the advance of the revolution by military force alone: it was compelled to carry through basic tasks entailing the destruction of the old regime against which the nationwide uprising had taken place. Before they entered fresh battles, all the opposing factions of the revolution had to recognize principles which, though not sanctioning the definitive victory of the revolution, essentially proclaimed the irreversible triumph of its initial objectives.

All this should be added to the historical balance sheet of the Northern Division, the Southern Liberation Army, and that high point of Mexican history: the occupation of the capital by the peasant armies.

The peasantry took four years to acquire sufficient strength for the capture of Mexico City. This was the necessary time span in which their experience reached maturity and the whole revolution climbed to its peak of radicalization. The seizure of the capital therefore came as a necessary conclusion to all the prior battles in the North and South.

It was a broad upsurge that shattered the very foundations of the old regime, sweeping the whole country and pulling all into the struggle. This process condensed in the destruction of the repressive core of the old regime, the federal army and its auxiliary forces: it was a blow from which the old oligarchy did not recover, since it thereby lost the continuity of a caste army.

The peasant occupation of Mexico City also broke the institutional continuity which Díaz and Madero had sought to preserve with the Ciudad Juárez Accords, and completely thwarted Carranza's original aim of restoring it, as he intended to do through the Guadalupe Plan and his own entry into the capital in August 1914. This development marked off the peasant revolution in Mexico from all previous peasant wars.

Instead of dispersing in a huge, frantic, centerless *jacquerie*, the peasant war concentrated on the capture of Mexico City its own national role and the entire transformation which had stamped the country during four years of revolution. This historical action could not have been accomplished by the peasantry alone. It was therefore not a wild product of "ignorance"—something Villa and Zapata recognized in their way when they referred to "cultured people" as necessary for the tasks ahead, thus voicing the historical experience that the city is the place where the final decisions belong. The only urban class then in a position to carry this out was the revolutionary petty bourgeoisie, even though it mainly supported Constitutionalism and nothing more than its shadow was in a doubtful alliance with the peasants. The watchful peasantry tried to control this layer, continuing to operate as a separate power. But then, in order to escape "the tremendous pressure weighing us down," the Conventionist politicians rapidly abandoned the cause. The peasantry had, it is true, been using them, as it used the radical Constitutionalist petty bourgeoisie, in order to give its insurrection a national character and raise it to a higher political level.

Still, this happened three years before the Russian Revolution; not at the dawn of the bourgeois revolutions, but at the dawn of the age of the national, agrarian, and socialist revolutions of the twentieth century.

The taking of the National Palace by the armed peasants was a hammer blow, a historical divide more important than all the laws, votes, and debates of all the conventions and congresses of those times. After four years of countrywide battles, it consolidated the new self-confidence of the peasants, urban workers, and Mexican poor, and gave them a degree of national consciousness that no other single action was able to impart.

Just these two gains, impossible to measure in economic terms, were worth ten years of armed struggle.

7

From Celaya to Querétaro

Obregón's army, now called the Operational Army, won its first victory in the new offensive by recovering Puebla on January 5, 1915. As he could see that the resistance would be weak and poorly organized, Obregón permitted himself quite a risky military maneuver. He divided his army into two big columns and sent them forward separately through the all but impassable Malinche Mountains, in such a way that they were unable to assist each other in case of danger. Then he attacked Puebla on both sides.

Zapata had already withdrawn to Morelos with his best troops; and through one of those absurd agreements reached during the Convention period, the Puebla garrison had been left under the command of the ex-Orozquists Juan Andrew Almazán and Benjamin Argumedo, old enemies of Villa and last-minute recruits to the Southern Liberation Army. During their time in charge of Puebla, they came to a deal with local supporters of Félix Díaz—the counterrevolutionary general operating in Oaxaca—and set free some hated Huertist officials who had been arrested when Puebla was in the hands of Constitutionalist forces under Salvador Alvarado. The disastrous policy of the local leadership not only provoked furious protests from the Villists in Mexico City, but debilitated the whole social base for the defense of Puebla. Combined with the treacherous activity within the Conventionist government, Obregón could capture the city after just one day of resistance which, though quite strong, was far inferior to what might have been expected of the Zapatists.

Puebla was a strategically important town, and the road to Mexico City now lay open. Its capture also affected the morale of the two sides, since Obregón's reorganized army had not yet scored a direct victory over the peasant forces. Stauncher resistance at Puebla would have greatly weakened the Constitutionalist Army and impeded its rapid surge of confidence. Yet the peasant armies had been unable to achieve that unified, centralized command essential to any warfare: each one operated according to its own criteria, its own limitations and immediate interests. Moreover, Zapata had never put up a last-ditch fight for a city, and he did not now attach sufficient importance to Puebla's defense. Perhaps he was also influenced by the crisis in his alliance with Villa, expressed in the ambivalent or treacherous policy of the Conventionist leaders, and by the flood of accusations and intrigue that normally accompanies such an unclarified situation. It is enought to recall the instructions War Minister Robles, a general in the Northern Division, gave to his undersecretary, Martín Luis Guzmán: if the Zapatists "ask for guns, or ammunition, or trains," he had said, "don't even give them water." The "military" operation of calumny and intrigue clearly had a prodigious effect in this short and concentrated period, easily confounding Villa and Zapata as well as their subordinate officers.

For the first time, a peasant army had to do formal battle not with the passive, corrupt forces of the old regime, but with an army representing one wing of the revolution that promised a glittering program of reforms to the workers and peasants. On this occasion, moreover, the peasant army was the weaker and less prepared.

With Puebla under his belt, Obregón did not wander into further clashes with the Zapatists. For it was quite clear to the Constitutionalist Army leader that control of the country would require an attack on the military center of gravity of the peasant forces: the Northern Division. This is why his various declarations ignored Zapata and concentrated their fire on the "reactionary traitors," Villa and Angeles. Moreover, he realized that operations against Zapata would enmesh him in a struggle with the Morelos peasantry, whose ubiquitous and tenacious guerrilla warfare, though incapable of stemming Obregón's advance at Puebla, had broken down all previous armies sent into its home territory.

Thus, Obregón merely left a small force in Puebla to maintain the vital rail link with Veracruz, and immediately advanced on Mexico City. The Zapatists were in no position to mount a defense and swiftly abandoned the capital, while for his part Villa was away fighting in the center of the country. The Conventionist government had deserted a few days earlier, on January 15; and its remaining members, including the Zapatist minister of agriculture, Manuel Palafox, and a new Villist president elected by the Aguascalientes Convention, Roque González Garza, moved the seat of government to the Zapatist-held town of Cuernavaca.

Obregón occupied the capital at the end of the month. This sealed the military-geographical separation between Villism and Zapatism, as well as their failure to keep political power in the Mexican capital. Still, this failure did not involve the arrival of a counterrevolutionary army, like those that put down the Paris Commune, the Hungarian Commune of 1919, or the Berlin uprising of January 1919. Obregón's army was not to butcher the masses but to grant them concessions, for its military victory depended on the partial incorporation of its enemy's program.

The most immediate sign of this was the Carranzist agrarian reform law of January 6, 1915. This law, written by Luis Cabrera, sanctioned the return of all the village land seized "in contravention of the law of 25 June 1856" (passed under Benito Juárez), requiring only that the village should present its original deeds to the appropriate authorities. In the case of villages that "have no communal land, or are unable to recover it because they lack the deeds or cannot identify it, or because it has been legally alienated," the reform law recognized their right to acquire sufficient resources through government appropriation of nearby land.

The law expressly decreed that village land should be divided among private owners. Clearly the intention was to foster smallholdings, and to develop a layer of well-off peasants as a social prop for the urban bourgeoisie. In this sense, its goals were historically

continuous with the Juarist laws that provided the basis for the liquidation of peasant communities and the development of latifundia. "The aim is not to revive the old communities," Carranza's
law spelled out, "or to create others of a similar nature, but only to
give land to the rural poor who presently have none. . . . Such
land shall not belong to the village commons: it shall be divided in
fee simple, although necessary safeguards shall ensure that avaricious speculators, particularly foreigners, are not easily able to lay
hold of such property, as happened almost invariably with the legal redistribution of communal land and village property under
the Ayutla Revolution."

These restrictions did not, of course, apply in practice, and the
Carranzist agrarian reform soon led to a huge-scale transfer of
agrarian property from the old Díaz oligarchy to the new bourgeoisie of Constitutionalist generals. Yet, at the time it was passed,
the law was a straightforward promise of land redistribution but-
tressed by the guns of the Constitutionalist Army. In its wording,
and above all in the prospects of nationwide implementation, it appeared much more concrete than the Zapatist decrees in Morelos
(where, it is true, no one was dazzled by the new law) and much
more real than the hazy Villist policy, which did not even have any
agrarian legislation. The Carranzist law, bourgeois through and
through, was nevertheless an effective political banner with which
to attract one section of the peasantry and neutralize the other. It
therefore hastened the weakening of Villa's peasant social base; and
as to the Zapatists, whose agrarian legislation was much more profound yet based on localist armed struggle, it succeeded in confin-
ing their influence to Morelos State and small neighboring regions.

The law had other features crucial to its eventual impact. Referring to the period of the Porfirio Díaz regime, it declared null and
void all the disentailments carried out by "companies, judges and
other bodies" which illegally invaded and occupied lands, waters,
and woodland with an existing owner. Thus it effectively called
into question the whole process of latifundia-building begun in
1876. At the same time, it resolved that all land restitution claims

should be addressed, not to elected village officials as in Morelos, but to the remote central governors of the relevant state. Given "the lack of communications" and "the state of war," however, claimants were also entitled to address themselves "to senior officers specially authorized by the Executive Power." This was the foothold for a huge land-seizure operation conducted by Constitutionalist generals, senior officers, functionaries, and politicians. The most direct beneficiaries of the "agrarian reform," they would enrich themselves with a voracity comparable to that of the bourgeoisie in the Great French Revolution, constituting a layer of new latifundists and "revolutionary" nouveaux riches later represented by the governments of the Mexican bourgeoisie, and fusing with the remnants of the Porfirian oligarchy through a variety of deals, marriages, and other such business contracts.

Despite everything, this operation had to cloak itself in an agrarian reform that did represent the very concession to the peasant masses so stoutly resisted by Carranza in the period between the Guadalupe Plan and the Torreón Pact.

The Zapatists and Villists did not fail to realize this. On the one hand, the agrarian reform program in Morelos received an indirect stimulus to its further radicalization. On the other, Guzmán plausibly described Villa's reaction on hearing of Carranza's divorce and agrarian legislation: "Right, sir. The people will benefit from these laws, whoever has passed them."

Mexico City had proved a dead weight for the peasant leadership—a center of weakness, indecision, and endless intrigue. The most radical minister in the Conventionist government, the Zapatist Manuel Palafox, had focused nearly all his attention and activity on matters relating to his ministry of agriculture, and he seemed far from understanding the importance of an alliance with the workers, artisans, and urban poor or the need to satisfy their immediate demands. If he did not see this—a man whom North American secret agents described as full of "rabid socialist ideas"—then how much less was it felt and grasped by the indecisive, intriguing bulk of Conventionist ministers? After Gutiérrez and his ministers defected, the peasant leadership made no effort to retain the capital, not knowing what to do with the city or how to tackle its basic problems.

Obregón did know. Right from the start, he understood that the role of Mexico City for the Constitutionalist cause was not as a center of political authority (since this had to be asserted in the coming battles), but as a popular social base for his faction and hence a recruiting ground for his Operational Army.

From his headquarters, Obregón took various measures to alleviate the material plight of the poorer sections of the population. Their situation was then very serious indeed: textile factories were often shut for lack of raw materials, others because there were no markets for their goods; the military absorbed the entire railway capacity, so that commodities could be moved neither into nor out of the city; absolute essentials were in short supply or simply unobtainable. The Constitutionalist Army immediately set up "relief stations" at various points in the capital, whose function was to distribute provisions, clothing, and money benefits. For this task, Obregón used the framework of the unions, acting as social mediators for his army. The first of these were located at the entrance to St. Brigitte's Convent, the headquarters of the Casa del Obrero Mundial. By February 8, 1915, the relief operation was already under way.

At the same time, Obregón issued regulations that placed the burden of costs on the capitalists, merchants, and clergy. And when they resisted the exactions, he began to apply drastic measures by imprisoning them until payment was made. He jailed and even shot a few marketeers who were doing big business out of the shortage of subsistence goods. Finally, he ordered that any merchant or priest who refused to pay his taxes should be conscripted into the army for the coming campaign against the Northern Division. The merchants paid up and were released. The priests operated as a political unit, pleading that ill-health made it physically impossible for them to fight. Obregón then ordered a medical examination, which showed that only a few of the 180 detained priests had some major complaint, and that the 60 or so with vene-real disease were fit enough to join the ranks. This ironical doctors' report was subsequently published.

Foreign businessmen also protested at the tax impositions, and Carranza went over Obregón's head and exempted them from payment. But this did not prevent the U.S. State Department from sending a vehement protest letter, which accused Obregón of "inciting the populace to commit outrages in which innocent foreigners may become involved," and of being responsible for "instigations to anarchy" just before the capital was abandoned. It further stated that "Constitutionalist officers have deliberately cre-ated this deplorable situation, in order to obtain the submission of the populace to their incredible demands, and to punish the city for its refusal to comply." After declaring that the United States could no longer "patiently sit and watch" this "intolerable" situation, the note concludes by saying that the U.S. government will hold "Generals Obregón and Carranza personally responsible" for any harm that comes to its citizens in Mexico, and that it will therefore "take suitable steps to demand an account from those personally responsible for what may happen." Since Washington did not have official relations with Mexico, although informal U.S. agents were in every army, the note was actually delivered by a Brazilian diplo-mat. In reply, Obregón merely told him that it would be forwarded to Carranza as the person in charge of foreign affairs, and he then turned back to his last-minute preparations for the campaign.

The Constitutionalists also took more direct measures to win the support of the workers' movement. The Mexican Electricians Union, affiliated with the Casa del Obrero Mundial, had declared a strike against the Mexican Telephone and Telegraph Company over its refusal to recognize the union as a legal entity and to hold talks on the workers' list of demands. On February 6, 1915, a meet-ing took place between representatives of the government, the workers, and the company, at which the latter refused to accept any of the demands. As a result, the official representative declared there and then, "In view of the company's intransigence, I hereby inform you that the Government of the Revolution is attaching forthwith the company interests and property and placing their management in the hands of the workers." Leaders of the Mexican Electricians Union immediately entered the company offices, assumed possession of its property, and took charge of its affairs. That evening, a strikers' general meeting at St. Brigitte's Convent acclaimed the government declaration and brought the victorious strike to an end. The electricians' leader, Luis N. Morones, was appointed general manager of the Mexican Telephone and Telegraph Company.

Obregón's policy in the capital culminated in an action that decisively shifted the balance of forces in his favor. This was the signing of the agreement whereby the Casa del Obrero Mundial (COM) unions gave their support to the Constitutionalists in the fight against Villism. The pact was signed in Veracruz on February 17, 1915, by a personal representative of Carranza and various COM leaders. The Constitutionalist government here reiterated its promise to improve workers' conditions contained in the Decree of December 12, 1914; and undertook "to pay careful attention . . . to the workers' just demands in conflicts which may arise between themselves and the employers." In return, the COM-affiliated unions resolved to form "Red Battalions" out of trade-based workers' contingents, integrating these into the Constitutionalist Army and politically supporting the fight against "reaction" through their own organizations. The agreement was published in Mexico City, in a manifesto that tried to use traditional anarchist-style phraseology to cover up the allegiance of the workers' leadership to the emergent leadership of a new national bourgeoisie.

The labor unions thereby submitted to the policy of the Constitutionalist Army, receiving in exchange organizational concessions and various immediate demands, as well as official recognition of the union leaders as political props, and therefore beneficiaries of the regime. Nor was this all. In the situation of the time, the pact concretely committed the unions to march into battle against Pancho Villa's peasant armies.

Nevertheless, the pact also expressed the social weakness of Constitutionalism and its Obregonist wing, which had to depend on workers' support, an alliance with the unions, and the incorporation of "Red Battalions" in order to make its will prevail.

The decision to go for the pact was not taken without an internal struggle. Indeed, since a large section refused to side with Carranzism, it actually provoked a split within the Casa del Obrero Mundial.[1] The crucial debate took place at St. Brigitte's Convent on February 8, 1915, two days after the unwise attitude of the telephone company had given the pro-Constitutionalists a golden opportunity to win support for their position. But at the meeting, which was attended by more than a thousand workers, a sizeable section opposed the idea of joining up with either Constitutionalism or any of the other forces in combat. Attacking those who made patriotic incantations, this faction declared that the COM knew no national flags or boundaries, that its cause was international like the class struggle and the proletariat itself, and that the alliance with Carranzism was a craven act in relation to a new faction of the bourgeoisie. Dr. Atl, a Carranzist agent who did not belong to the organization, then intervened to condemn the "extremist" opponents of the pact. His speech caused such an uproar that the meeting concluded without voting on a resolution. Thus the COM leaders did not succeed in winning the approval of the workers' general meeting for their proposed alliance with the Carranzists.

The leadership next called a secret meeting for February 10, to which only sixty-seven people were invited. But even at this select gathering, the two currents reemerged in violent confrontation with each other. The opponents of the pact put forward the anarchist idea of a social revolution against private property, the state, capitalism, and the Church, counterposing this to a Constitutionalist political revolution that "will merely serve to increase the domination and wealth of the new rich." They again insisted that to take up arms in this political revolution would be "to act as a tool of this new caste and to carry it to victory"; it would, in short, be an act of class capitulation. The pro-alliance tendency, which this time had a majority, argued that the workers' movement had to give armed support if it was to claim its rights after the victory of the Constitutionalist revolution. In the early hours of the next morning, the meeting finally voted not only to propose the pact to Carranza, but also to close down COM headquarters and suspend its organizing work until "the triumph of the revolutionary cause we are now reinforcing."

Once again, the underlying determinant was not Obregón's "skill" or even the willingness of the union leaders to yoke the unions to the city government. The final decision was essentially due to deeper class factors: the peasant leadership had no national program that represented or reflected working-class interests; the radical, anarcho-syndicalist leaders who expressed the workers' view of the pact as a submission to the bourgeoisie did not put forward an alternative policy or a concrete revolutionary-organizational method; and they did not grasp the need to oppose the pact by means of an alliance with the peasantry, limiting themselves instead to abstract statements about the future "social revolution." In these conditions, the wing of Constitutionalism was able to offer a concrete, reformist Jacobin perspective of organization, influence, and future gains. It therefore had some impact on the workers, and Obregón's description of Villism as "reactionary" did not strike them as mere invective.

So it was that four "Red Battalions" fought on the winning side in the decisive battles against the Villist army. They were composed of textile workers, cabinetmakers, stonecutters, tailors, masons, printers, mechanics, and steelworkers, while two more battalions, comprising armory workers, tram drivers, and other trades, were assigned to various other missions. A group of COM women workers formed a nursing corps and joined the Operational Army under the title Acrata Health Group. According to Obregón's memoirs, the Mexico City workers altogether supplied nine thousand men for his army, most of them belonging to organizations affiliated with the Casa del Obrero Mundial.

St. Brigitte's Convent changed from a union headquarters into a union-run army recruitment center. Every day, COM-affiliated unions met to approve the decision to join forces with the Constitutionalists. However, there was an important exception: a general meeting of the Mexican Electricians Union—the very union that, a few days earlier, had obtained the biggest government concessions in its strike against the telephone company—now voted against a proposal to support the Carranzist army and join the war. These workers felt that their strike victory was not a gift but the fruit of hard struggle, and that the Constitutionalist authorities were now trying to make political capital out of it. Their position transcended the horizon of their own union and, in effect, represented the same opposition current that had already appeared in the tumultuous meeting of February 8.

On March 10, 1915, the Operational Army again evacuated the capital, this time to march into battle with the Northern Division in central Mexico. Ever since they arrived in the city in late January, they had been harassed by Zapatist forces operating, as in 1912, at the very gates. During these two months, the Villists had scored a number of victories against various Constitutionalist units, particularly in the northeast, where the troops of General Pablo González were completely routed and demoralized. González had lost the whole of Nueva León and Tamaulipas before taking refuge in the port of Tampico and requesting sea transport to evacuate his remaining troops and artillery to Veracruz.

Obregón's advance on central Mexico was designed to provoke a decisive confrontation between his organized and strengthened army and the main Villist forces, so as to stem the defeats being suffered in the North. The main danger, in Obregón's view, was that the Villist forces would move fresh from their victories in Nuevo León and Tamaulipas to capture the port of Tampico from the shattered remnants of González's army. They would then be able to count on a major commercial and industrial center and one of the largest ports in the country, commanding the whole of a rich oil-producing region,

complete with refineries, that could supply them with not only locomotive fuel but a wide variety of other resources. At one stroke
they would then acquire most of the benefits Veracruz afforded Carranza, while still retaining control over the North and Center-North
and the advantage of free movement along internal lines of communication.

In order to draw out these Villist forces, Obregón completely
evacuated Mexico City and handed it back to the Zapatists on the
following day. His military calculation was clear: the relative weakness of his forces obliged him to concentrate them in one campaign; he could not both defend the capital against persistent
Zapatist attack and march out to engage Villa in battle. In any case,
he had no choice but to accept the Southern Liberation Army at
his back, although he did successfully defend his railway supply-
link with Veracruz against repeated Zapatist incursions.

This also involved a political calculation that Zapata would gain
nothing by occupying Mexico City, and that the character of his army
essentially tied it to its roots in the peasant warfare in Morelos State.

Finally, while Obregón could clearly see the crisis of the peasant
political leadership, his Bonapartist instinct also told him that the
state of mind of the masses had changed, that an ebb was beginning after the revolutionary high tide of December 1914.

Since Obregón's army was already as prepared for combat as it
could reasonably hope to be, any further period of military inactivity threatened to become a disadvantage instead of an advantage.
Thus, at the point when all these factors impelled him to seek a resolution on the battlefield, Obregón applied the elementary principle of concentrating his forces for the encounter.

Meanwhile, just as Obregón feared, Angeles suggested to Villa
that they complete the northeastern campaign by seizing Tampico
and the entire oil region, and that they seek the decisive battles
in their northern stronghold. In his view, they would be playing
Obregón's game and courting disaster if they were to accept battle
in central Mexico. In military terms, his was indeed the better plan,
involving as it did the concentration of forces, the shortening of

supply lines, the control of much of the oil revenue, and the occupation of the whole northern frontier and a major seaport. In a strong defensive position with untouched, battle-seasoned troops, they could then wait for the enemy to commit himself, to extend and weaken his supply lines, and to grow ever more uneasy at the size of a rear subject to attack by Zapatist guerrillas.

This plan also corresponded to a national view of the military and political situation. Seeing the nation as a whole, Angeles wished to accumulate the decisive elements for victory on a national scale: he therefore sought first to establish himself in a territorial zone, complete with its own resources, a port, international relations, and the basis of a state structure. In embryonic form, his plan contained the elements of a twin-based territorial conflict that would have modified the essentially kaleidoscopic character of the Mexican civil war. It was a plan for power, not for land: indeed, the general, as a true follower of Madero's politics, had always been opposed to redistribution of the land.

Once again, Felipe Angeles's political conception, and hence his military projects, were at odds with those of Francisco Villa. Seeing only Obregón's advance through land his army had controlled and his fellow peasants had redistributed, Villa thought that any further loss of ground would quickly swell the troops and resources available to the Constitutionalist Army commander. Since he lacked the national perspective of Obregón and Angeles, he could not understand the political weight attached by the latter to the port and region of Tampico. After all, a similar attempt had ended in fiasco with the occupation of Mexico City in December 1914. Villa could see no sense in repeating the experience.

Now, however, he was inclined to try what Angeles had proposed in December: an advance to meet and destroy Obregón's army. Of course, the circumstances had changed. But for this very reason, the apparent reversal of Villa's and Angeles's positions reflected their basic self-consistency. The national military viewpoint, which had previously suggested an offensive drive on Veracruz, now pointed to the capture of Tampico and the creation of a strong defensive position against the reorganized enemy forces. The peasant military outlook saw no reason to pursue Obregón to the coast instead of maintaining central control with widely dispersed forces, now logically minimized the political importance of Tampico and prepared to meet the enemy's advance in the central zone supposedly crucial to security, so that the enemy might be militarily defeated before he sank deeper roots in the land. Angeles and Obregón tended to see the country as a whole; Villa, as well as Zapata, saw it in regions.

Obregón's advance was a trap laid for Villa's peasant imagination, not for Angeles's military vision. It was successful. Discounting Angeles's arguments, Villa rushed to accept battle where Obregón was offering it. In a sense his peasant politics left no choice but to seek a military victory before the enemy could increase the size of his forces. For Villa evidently *perceived* the defection of the officer backbone of the Convention; the intrigues designed to separate him from Zapata; the conflicts between Zapatist and Villist political representatives; the Constitutionalist military barrier between the northern and southern peasant armies; the gradual change in mood among his troops and the local population he encountered; and many other symptoms of the same kind. In his own way, then, Villa also sensed that the ebb of the peasant masses had begun, and his natural inclination was to stem it through military methods and military successes. It was as if a decisive blow could check the weariness of the masses rooted in social and political conditions. He felt no other hope since his material resources, particularly the livestock traded for arms across the northern border, were sinking to a dangerously low level.

And yet, even if Villa had defeated Obregón, this would still not have opened a path independent of the bourgeoisie; and Angeles or others would in some shape or form have repeated the history of the Convention. But Villa did not and could not know this, although he may have had a foreboding about this possibility.

On April 6, 1915, the first Celaya encounters initiated the phase of the four great battles of Bajío. Obregón had entrenched himself in the town of Celaya, waiting to meet the assault of the Villist cavalry. The plan was for a defensive battle that would exhaust the enemy and subsequently allow the Operational Army to pass on to the counterattack. On April 6 and 7, the Villist infantry and cavalry, supported by intensive artillery fire, made repeated charges on the defensive positions of Obregón's army. The defenders had to face critical moments when some of their lines were on the point of collapse, but the waterlogged terrain helped them to hold the Villist troops over many hours of fruitless assaults. When the smoke cleared, they had managed to whittle down Villa's forces and consume most of his ammunition. Obregón now seized the opportunity to counterattack with the cavalry brigades he had kept in reserve. These fresh forces mounted a twin-pronged offensive maneuver against the tired, battered Northern Division, compelling it to flee in disorderly retreat.

This was not, to be sure, a decisive defeat. Villa quickly regrouped his forces and prepared for a second attack. On the other side, Obregón abandoned the idea of pursuit, since the Northern Division not only retained the bulk of its forces but had urgently called up reinforcements and a fresh supply of ammunition. (According to Villist sources, much of this new ammunition supply from the United States proved to be defective and unusable, thereby contributing to the eventual defeat.) Obregón refortified his positions in Celaya in such a way that his troops formed a 360-degree wall around the town.

The second battle of Celaya began on April 13, and rapidly assumed the characteristics of the first: Obregón's defensive stance; violent charges by the Northern Division, this time on a full defensive square; slackening of the offensive after thirty-six hours without success; a dawn counterattack on April 15, involving a twin-pronged cavalry maneuver, supported by three infantry brigades at the center of the battle area. The key to this counterattack, which Obregón had planned when he again decided to adopt a defensive strategy, was the fresh cavalry kept hidden in a wood several kilometers away. At the signal to attack, these forces arrived on the battlefield as one of the pincers that surprised and crushed the battle-weary Villist troops.

On this occasion, the Villist defeat was much more serious. Although sources quote different figures, it may be calculated that Obregón had as many as twenty thousand men, slightly more than Villa; that he deployed eighteen artillery pieces (half Villa's total); but that he had a great superiority in machine guns (sixty-four plus reserves, according to Obregón), crucial to the strengthening of his defensive positions. In its retreat, the Northern Division left in enemy hands virtually all its artillery, thousands of prisoners and light weapons, and several thousand dead and wounded. Here again, the exact figures vary considerably from one source to the next. Obregón's memoirs talk of four thousand Villist dead and as many wounded, while Villa's memoirs, compiled by Martin Luis Guzmán, set his total losses between three thousand and thirty-five hundred. What is certain is that the second battle of Celaya was the first complete disaster for the Northern Division. It already marked its definitive decline, forcing it, as nothing had previously done, to end its victory march and withdraw to its old Chihuahua bastion. Soon, fresh setbacks would turn this retreat into a rout.

Pancho Villa fell back on Aguascalientes, employing it as a base for the reorganization of his army. Meanwhile, Obregón's Operational Army resumed its northward advance from Celaya in pursuit of Villa's forces.

At this point, new differences arose between Villa and Angeles on the further course of the campaign. Now that the life-and-death battles had begun with Obregón, Angeles (who had not personally taken part in the Celaya battles) proposed that they should mass in Central Mexico all the Villist forces then fighting various Constitutionalist detachments in the Northeast, Jalisco, and El Ebano. Villa retorted that this would throw the way open for the enemy forces to move down to the Center. His overriding concern was not to leave the pro-Villist population in these areas without the protection of his forces, and to avoid any danger to his own lines of communication. If the enemy concentrated its troops for an attack on any of these areas, Villa argued, Obregón would be able to penetrate the North and cut off their operational base in Chihuahua. However risky it might be, the only solution was to confront Obregón with the forces already available in Chihuahua.

The second disagreement was of a more tactical nature. In Angeles's view, they should meet Obregón's advance by abandoning the town of León and securing defensive positions in Aguascalientes. They should then allow the enemy to wear itself down before passing on to the attack—in other words, reverse the roles played by the two armies at Celaya. Instead, Villa opted for battle in Trinidad, just above León. Once again, Villa demonstrated his concern with defending his social base above purely military considerations.

The battle of Trinidad formally opened on April 29, 1915. With various ups and downs, the fighting continued for more than a month until Villa's forces suffered a fresh defeat on June 5. In the course of the battle, General Obregón lost an arm and was on the point of losing his life. General Francisco I. Grajales, in his comments on Obregón's campaigns, wrote about this battle:

We have seen General Obregón conduct two defensive battles in Celaya. Both of these clearly display the two classical stages: resistance through the use of gunfire to wear down the attackers; and a counter-offensive designed to vanquish the enemy through gunfire and direct combat. When the leader from Sonora had to face the federal or Zapatist troops, the former slow and timorous, the latter disorganized and poorly officered, he always proved audacious and employed the offensive as his only form of combat. But now he had before him the brave, daring and excitable Pancho Villa, creator of a new army in which the dominant cavalry knew no tactic but the charge and hand-to-hand fighting, inspired by an offensive spirit of enormous savagery and ferocity. Obregón therefore exploited the advantages of defensive combat in order to crack the enemy before attacking him. Deliberately choosing the terrain of the next battle, he firmly applied his strategy and tactics of attrition.

But on this occasion General Villa, persuaded with difficulty by Felipe Angeles, decided to adopt the same battle procedure as the other side had been using.

This convergence of the rival commanders-in-chief lent the battle its slow character, spread it out in time and space, and gave an appearance of indecision to the two commands. Defensive battles save men, but they also swallow up ammunition. And in Trinidad the Constitutionalists had a very serious bullet-shortage, since the Zapatists had been conducting frequent attacks on their extended supply-line.

This is not the place to recount the twists and turns of the battle of Trinidad. In essence, Obregón again drew up a square around the town and beat off the Villist attacks; while at the same time, detachments from the two sides met in frequent encounters, during which the mobility, speed, and intensity of cavalry action played the dominant role. The climax came on June 1. Villa switched his main front from León to the southern side of the town and suddenly struck at the Operational Army's outer line of defense, occupying the station of Silao and cutting Obregón's rail link with the South. Simultaneously the fighting intensified on the rest of the battlefront.

Villa's large-scale maneuver compelled Obregón to postpone his counterattack and to reconcentrate his forces within the defensive square. Villa was unable to make any further progress, however, and although Obregón had been wounded and put out of action on June 3, the Constitutionalists launched a general counteroffensive two days later, striking north to León and south to Silao with their infantry and cavalry. The Villist troops had first to retreat and then to flee in disorder. That very evening the Constitutionalists marched into León, and on June 6 they reoccupied Silao. The Northern Division managed to salvage most of its equipment and withdrew to Aguascalientes with its trains.

In Aguascalientes, Villa dug into defensive positions and prepared to resist the hotly pursuing troops of the Operational Army.

This town, which less than a year before had been the seat of the Revolutionary Military Convention, now awaited the definitive battle between the Constitutionalists and the Conventionist Army (as the main Northern Division forces called themselves, after the Convention still sporadically functioning in Toluca).

Obregón's army reached Encarnación Station, south of Aguascalientes, on June 20, and came to a halt in expectation of a train that was bringing fresh supplies of fuel and ammunition from Veracruz. Meanwhile Villa concentrated his forces inside the town and greeted his generals as they brought reinforcements: José M. Rodríguez from the vicinity of Torreón; Rafael Buelna from Jalisco; José Prieto from Michoacán. Also there for their last great battle alongside Villa were Canuto Reyes, Rodolfo Fierro, Pánfilo Natera, Calixto Contreras, Manuel Banda, and General Felipe Angeles.

When Obregón heard of this concentration and the major defensive work in the town, he sent a force to protect and speed up the trainload of fuel and ammunition. Having repulsed a Villist attack on their rear, these troops finally escorted the train into Encarnación Station on the evening of June 30. Two days later, a lightning raid by General Reyes and Fierro cut Obregón's rail link with the South and left him trapped in Encarnación. On July 3, the Villist column captured León and, after pausing for a couple of hours, continued its southward advance, destroying railway and telegraph lines on the way. Reyes and Fierro progressed at dizzying speed through Irapuato, Querétaro, and San Juan del Río to Tula almost on the outskirts of Mexico City, all the time breaking Obregón's lines of communication. Along the way, they rallied a number of Villist and Zapatist units, and were soon at the gates of the capital.

On July 4, Obregón found himself cut off from his operational base, with supplies for only five days, an inadequate stock of ammunition, only four hours' fuel for his trains, and the principal enemy force just to his north. Nor was it possible to follow the Villist generals' lightning southward march of destruction. In these conditions, he decided to mass all his forces for an attack on the main enemy position in Aguascalientes. Since Villa's fortifications faced southward to Encarnación, Obregón tried a circling maneuver in order to attack from the rear and to drive the Villists out onto the open battlefield.

The operation began on July 6. But the next day, as the Constitutionalist column advanced through the flat, arid terrain, empty of water, trees, and vegetation, it came under constant fire from Villist units. By July 8, the main Villist forces were already launching an attack from their Aguascalientes base, boxing the Obregonists into an area six kilometers by four in which they had scarcely any water and only a day's supply of food.

Villa then decided to abandon his fortified positions, since they would be useless against an attack from the north, and threw all his forces into an assault on the Constitutionalist square-formation. Throughout July 9, his troops attacked on all sides—which at least eased the task of the defenders in blunting the thrust. Obregón's position was serious, as his supplies of both food and ammunition were nearly exhausted.

When he had no further way of maintaining the defensive, he resolved to advance on Aguascalientes itself. This is how he explained the decision in a dispatch dated July 9: "We have supplies only for tomorrow, and our limited ammunition is only enough to take a town by assault. Four leagues from Aguascalientes; impossible to retreat because there is not enough ammunition or provisions, and because it would be very irksome; perfectly aware of the risks I am taking, all our men will begin the advance on Aguascalientes at dawn tomorrow, with hopes but little assurance (given our ammunition shortage) of occupying the town tomorrow."

The almost pathetic tone of this communication, written a little with history in mind, should be contrasted with a letter of the same date originating from a member of the Villist general staff. After describing the critical situation of the Constitutionalists, beleaguered "in a very narrow area, where there is a lack of water and any kind of basics," the letter optimistically concludes: "I think that in a day or two, we'll have finished this immense battle with the complete extermination or dispersal of the main Carranzist column. At the moment, the enemy infantry is in very dire straits, short of water and other basics, as well as ammunition."

And yet, with the support of cavalry brigades, this very infantry successfully attacked and broke through the defense lines of Villist riflemen, possibly because the maneuver was not expected and because Obregón concentrated all his forces at the Villist weak points. At noon on July 10, Obregón entered Aguascalientes and captured an abundant haul left by the Northern Division in its disorderly retreat. Most precious, perhaps, were the four million rounds of ammunition, which solved the problem of the broken supply lines and allowed the Operational Army not only to hold the town but to push north to Zacatecas and east to San Luis Potosí.

So ended the series of four great battles in which the power of the Northern Division was broken forever. In all four, there had been moments when the scales seemed to be tipping in Pancho Villa's favor: in the two battles of Celaya, where the Villists gave as a crucial reason for defeat the defective ammunition supplied by U.S. arms dealers; in Trinidad, where Villa had seemed to launch a decisive attack on Obregón's rear just before his own rout; and in Aguascalientes, where, on the eve of his decisive breakthrough, Obregón's army had been encircled in a semi-desert, with virtually no provisions or ammunition. Each time, however, victory had been on his side.

Clausewitz said that "war is the province of chance; no sphere of human activity is so much in contact with it." And indeed, if we look just at immediate causes, the result of these four engagements does seem to have been due to chance. But the constant repetition of "chance" expressed a necessity, which stemmed from the fact that although Villa had the force of the peasant rebellion behind him, Obregón represented the possibility of organizing the country at the organic level attained by the revolution.

Thus, at the critical moments in Trinidad and Aguascalientes, General Obregón found what General Villa had displayed at the crest of the wave: the determination to face the most direct situation and to take the necessary measures for victory.

Clausewitz does more than merely identify the importance of chance and uncertainty in the field of war:

> From this uncertainty of all intelligence and suppositions, this continual interposition of chance, the actor in war constantly finds things different from his expectations. . . . Now, if it is to get safely through this perpetual conflict with the unexpected, two qualities are indispensable: in the first place an intellect which, even in the midst of this intense obscurity, is not without some inner traces of light, which lead to the truth, and then the courage to follow this faint light. The first is figuratively expressed by the French phrase *coup d'oeil*. The second is *resolve*.[2]

These qualities do belong to the individual, but only insofar as one finds them reflected in the guiding social goal that he more or less consciously represents. This social goal fuels "the traces of inner light," and when it vanishes the light goes out. Beyond any abstract comparison between the military capabilities of Obregón and Villa, this goal constituted the superiority through which the former was able to defeat the latter in four critical and successive battles.

Negative proof is provided by Angeles's attitude after the Celaya battles, which had been joined against his technical advice. According to his biographer and fellow member of the Villist general staff, Federico Cervantes, he sank into a state of deep pessimism, unrelieved even at those moments when the contest seemed to be going in Villa's favor. Although Cervantes, who also opposed Villa's tactics, may have tended to exempt Angeles from the military responsibility for defeat, his account does fit well with Angeles's general trajectory and military outlook.

Angeles was not present at Celaya and opposed the idea of a battle at Trinidad. Even toward the end of this long seesaw encounter, when Villa conceived the plan of an attack on the enemy rear, Angeles praised his audacity but objected that it would greatly weaken their battle line and expose them to a crushing enemy offensive. Later, when the Villists captured Silao and cut Obregón's link with the South, victory had seemed a close prospect. But even then, Angeles told his highly optimistic officers, "I believe the opposite—that we may be defeated within a week." Placing himself in the enemy's shoes, he could see where they might concentrate their offensive to take advantage of the dispersion of Villist forces to the north and south. Cervantes recalls that on the eve of the battle outside Aguascalientes, the likely outcome was discussed at a meeting of Convention representatives. Everyone expressed their confidence in Villa's victory except Angeles. "Obregón will win," he baldly stated.

This unbroken pessimism was based not only on his superior military-technical knowledge, but also on political factors. For although Angeles stayed alongside Villa, he could see no prospects for the struggle. His outlook brought him close to Obregón, and he knew what military steps he would have taken in his place. The split between Villa's peasant tendency and Angeles's political standpoint initially took the form of a military-technical disagreement. But although neither had consciously entertained the idea, it became an unstoppable process in the hour of defeat, reaching during the retreat to Chihuahua. Felipe Angeles then took his leave of the Northern Division and went to the United States as a Conventionist envoy. In reality the distance from Villa was even greater than this would suggest: Villa's uncertain plans for future struggle, involving a return to his Chihuahua roots in peasant guerrilla warfare, did not fit into Angeles's political-military conceptions.

Angeles's pessimism, the quenching of that "faint inner light," anticipated the evolution that began in Celaya and ended in Aguascalientes on July 10, 1915: namely, the breakup of the Northern Division as an organized army corps, and the termination of Felipe Angeles's role as its general with the greatest experience and professional military training.

From now on, only the class tenacity of General Francisco Villa was capable of maintaining, in the midst of utmost adversity, a years-long military struggle against Carranzism in the northern states of Mexico.

★   ★   ★

The Aguascalientes defeat initiated the final retreat and dissolution of the Northern Division. The bulk of Villa's army followed the railway line north—the only road still open to them. One of the army train-drivers on this route later recounted how the soldiers' cohesion and self-confidence gradually disappeared, and how the force disintegrating the Division on its retreat to Chihuahua was not so much the enemy's persistent harassment, as the certainty of defeat and the lack of a social perspective with which to face the already apparent ebb tide of the peasant masses.[3]

The driver further describes the tortured retreat from Aguascalientes to Zacatecas, when the eagerness to preserve as much material as possible produced such overloading that the trains nearly rested on the wheels. The coaches reserved for senior officers were empty, their windows shattered and their sides riddled by enemy bullets; while the officers themselves, beginning with Villa, preferred to avoid the enemy attacks on the railway by riding the 120 kilometers on horseback. This whole region, safe Villist territory a couple of months before, was now unable to offer them any security. And yet, someone standing on the Zacatecas station platform could have witnessed the arrival of the special wagon bearing the gilded inscription "General Villa" (just as Obregón's coach carried the name of his birthplace, Siquisiva), preceded by the famous Locomotive 135 that had once been assigned to Porfirio Díaz's presidential train. The train's engine and coach were riddled with bullets when it entered the town whose capture a year earlier— Villa's most famous exploit—had broken the back of the federal army. The stop did not last long. Obregón's advance cavalry entered Zacatecas on July 17, 1915.

The retreat now continued in the direction of Torreón, punctuated by incidents among the Villist troops themselves. Soldiers from Urbina's brigade had been involved in a shoot-out with some of Rodolfo Fierro's men over the possession of a flock of lambs intended as food. Equally circumstantial motives were behind a similar incident in Torreón, and there would be many a gunfight between officers or soldiers on even more trivial pretexts. These were all symptoms of the growing demoralization that affected a retreating army devoid of prospects. At the same time, the lack of fuel and repair materials made it ever more difficult for the trains to complete their journey.

The whole Villist zone of Central Mexico was being methodically occupied by Obregón's forces. On July 19 he established his headquarters in San Luis Potosí, using it as an operational base to clear the region of Villist units. By early August, when this task had been largely completed, the Constitutionalists controlled the whole of central and northeast Mexico; and by the end of the month, regular communications had been restored between the port of Tampico and San Luis Potosí. However, Villa still had all or part of the states of Coahuila, Durango, San Luis Potosí, Zacatecas, Chihuahua, and Sonora.

On July 11, the Zapatist forces who still occupied Mexico City abandoned it without a fight to Pablo González. A few days later, González withdrew and the Zapatists returned to the city. (The thrust by the Villists Reyes and Fierro had lost momentum just north of Tula, and they were already rejoining the main Northern Division force.) But it was clear that the Constitutionalists could recapture the city whenever they wished; and indeed, on August 2, 1915, Carranzist troops under González entered Mexico City, never to leave it again. While the Northern Division was retreating to Chihuahua, the Southern Liberation Army lost the capital forever, and the peasant war definitively recovered its regional forms in both North and South.

Defections continued to rise in the Villist ranks, and in mid-August Pánfilo Natera, one of their principal generals, took his troops over to Obregón. On August 12, some of these actually captured Durango City, forcing the men who remained loyal to Villa to retreat northward. But although the armed contest had been settled at the national level, fortunes still oscillated in the regions. Thus, Villist forces retook Durango ten days later, while in early September Obregón had to send urgent reinforcements to bolster González against the repeated Zapatist attacks around the capital.

The Constitutionalists entered Saltillo on September 4, and then moved on Paredón in an advance that retraced the steps taken by the Northern Division a year earlier. They captured Monclova on September 13 and Piedras Negras shortly after, ensuring control of the whole of Coahuila, and on September 27 took San Pedro de las Colonias without a fight. Over the next two days they marched into Torreón and Gómez Palacio, which the Villists had evacuated a few days earlier, and thereby brought the whole Laguna district under their sway. In every town it occupied, the advancing army found locomotives, goods and passenger wagons, other railway equipment, and a further supply of abandoned bullets. By October 10, Obregón could report that only Chihuahua and part of Durango remained in Villist hands. On the nineteenth of that month, Obregón's troops once again took the city of Durango.

In mid-October the remnants of the Northern Division gathered in Casas Grandes, Chihuahua, and decided to march west across the Chihuahua mountains into Sonora. Apart from the border town of Agua Prieta, where the Constitutionalist general Plutarco Elias Calles had repulsed all attempts to dislodge him, Sonora State was then controlled by Governor Maytorena, a passive ally of Villa. In the meantime, the ex-railwayman General Rodolfo Fierro had died in an accident while crossing a lagoon on his way to Casas Grandes.

There were more desertions before the column left for Sonora: senior officers defected to Carranza with all their troops, weapons, and equipment; and simple privates, who could see nothing but black in the future, merely vanished into the countryside. Still, it was a fairly sizeable column of some sixty-five hundred men that finally set off—this time without any women, ordered to stay behind on account of the extremely harsh journey ahead. Last to leave was a column of some two hundred men under General Manuel Banda, who had the task of recording the abandoned wagons and supplies and hunting for deserters. Whenever he caught one, he would personally shoot him on the spot with his revolver.

Villa attacked Agua Prieta in November. Obregón had guessed

Villa's plan to invade Sonora from the concentration of troops in Casas Grandes, and sent reinforcements to Calles by the North American Arizona railway, having just won U.S. recognition of the Carranza government on October 19, 1915. Villa encountered much stronger resistance in Agua Prieta than he had expected, and his forces were eventually repulsed with heavy losses.

On November 22 he marched on Hermosillo, the Sonora capital, but suffered a fresh defeat and had to withdraw to Chihuahua with the remnants of his column. The battle claimed the life of another career officer and disciple of Angeles—the young General José Herón González, who was shot just as he was ordering his men's retreat. In early December, General José Rodríguez's column of some four thousand men, the only sizeable force unable to join up with Villa, was beaten and dispersed by General Calles in the Sonora town of Fronteras. The various fragments then took another route into Chihuahua.

Just a year after its triumphal entry into Mexico City, the Northern Division was down to its last organized section. The retreat through wild, mountainous terrain, in the bitter cold of winter, finished many more of the Villist remnants along the way. By the time they reached Chihuahua, they had lost any collective will to fight. On December 20, the forces under Generals Banda, Limón, and others surrendered Ciudad Juárez, Guadalupe, San Ignacio, and Villa Ahumada, with four thousand men and their arms and ammunition. By December 31, 1915, the Constitutionalists controlled all the cities of Mexico, including Chihuahua. According to one of those who compiled Villa's memoirs, the Northern Division commander then left his generals and officers free to accept the government amnesty, himself deciding to continue the guerrilla struggle in the mountains.

The Soviet writers Alperovich and Rudenko give this account: "In December 1915, Carranza offered an agreement to Villa on the following terms: 1) a general amnesty for all his supporters; 2) surrender of all Villist-controlled territory to the Carranzist government; 3) integration of his troops into the Constitutionalist Army for the fight against Zapata; and 4) a guarantee that Villa could freely emigrate to the United States. Some commanders of Villist troops accepted these conditions. But Villa carried on with the struggle."

At the beginning of 1916, the Northern Division no longer existed. With a few hundred guerrillas, Villa returned to the mountains to continue the fight for another four years.

Not a few historians fail to mention U.S. intervention in the Mexican Civil War, merely referring to the role played by Ambassador Henry Lane Wilson in the Huerta coup. By contrast, Soviet historians like Alperovich and Rudenko imply that the fate of the revolution largely depended on U.S. interventionist measures taken at one time or another.[4]

In a broad historical sense, the presence of U.S. imperial power across the frontier did play a determining role throughout the revolution, as it has done in the whole of Mexico's history. But direct intervention was of secondary importance to the actual course of the revolution, while the clash between rival factions was essentially rooted in Mexican social forces and their respective leaderships. Furthermore, Washington's intervention was inconstant and partly contradictory in the various stages. To present it as if it were clear and rectilinear is to make an unwarranted transposition from a later period, when U.S. foreign policy assumed a more extensive world role, growing in self-confidence and understanding of how to confront revolution in agrarian countries.

The U.S. governments did not grasp the essence of the Mexican Revolution: they had never before seen such a phenomenon, apparently so confused and contradictory, in which the major decisions were not taken in cabinets and the realm of high politics, or through negotiations, pressure groups, diplomatic threats, and concessions. According to all their previous ways of thinking, battles were subordinate military continuations of top-level political decisions, settled by skill and chance and firmly placed in the service of clearly defined ruling-class interests. In Mexico, however, the masses were deciding the issue through methods of their own. Although they had no preconceived plan and no conscious direction, they imposed their will like a force of nature upon their leadership; their ebb and flow followed laws quite beyond the limited provincial comprehension of the newly emerging American empire, which lacked the experience and subtlety acquired by British ruling-class politicians over long years of colonial domination.

Washington gave no special support to Porfirio Díaz against the Maderist revolution, and even allowed its leader to organize the conspiracy on U.S. territory. Madero's rise to power was seen as a continuation of capitalist policy that might allow the revolutionary strength accumulated under the dictatorship to be channelled in a bourgeois direction. Only when Madero's government proved powerless to contain the revolution did Washington adopt a different line. Ambassador Wilson's letters, expressing ever greater alarm at the situation, then culminated in his government's decision to back the Huerta coup.

Since Washington did not understand the inner dynamic of the revolution, failing to realize that Madero's weakness mainly reflected the strength of the upheaval, it was surprised that his liquidation merely hastened the spread of the revolutionary struggle. The picture now became increasingly unclear, involving repeated oscillations in Washington's Mexico policy and government divisions on the way in which U.S. interests could best be defended.

Washington did, of course, have the clear objective of opposing the revolution and protecting its own interests and investments. The problem began when it had to define an appropriate policy. By late 1913 or early 1914, it was quite apparent that the most straightforward course—replacement of Madero by a strongman who would brutally curtail the revolution—had proved to be a disaster.

The outbreak of open conflict between the different anti-Huerta tendencies, all seemingly hostile to U.S. interests, more or less coincided with the onset of the 1914–18 war in Europe. The attention of European imperialist powers, especially Britain, France, and Germany, completely shifted away from Mexico, leaving the United States to defend not only its particular interests but also those of world imperialism (naturally rather secondary in Washington's eyes).

It was the first time Washington had had to face such a responsibility; and although it assumed it with gusto, the task exceeded its powers of political comprehension and maneuver and gave rise to an initially uncertain attitude toward the various revolutionary forces. On the one hand, the peasant leaders did not seem to have a national consciousness clearly opposed to any U.S. intervention, while their concrete actions struck at the pillars of capitalist order; and, on the other hand, Carranza and his officers had a nationalist policy opposed to any foreign intervention, but their national-scale policy would better guarantee order and property. So, in the end, it was inevitable that Washington should opt for Carranzism, albeit reluctantly and with the realization that the lesser evil was still an evil. What could not ultimately be changed was the basic reality, apparent since 1914, that the violent liquidation of the economic and political power of the landowning oligarchy removed the possibility of a government serving as the direct agency of foreign imperialism.

In the period between the marines' departure from Veracruz in November 1914 and the withdrawal of the punitive expedition in January 1917, Washington followed a policy that, however aggressive or insidious in method, had an essentially defensive character in the face of a hated revolution it could neither understand nor control. Apart, of course, from protecting direct U.S. interests, it set itself the limited yet quite precise objective of hindering the formation of a strong nationalist regime.

Even before Huerta's overthrow, the U.S. government sent envoys to all the revolutionary leaders: Carranza, Villa, and Zapata. But except in November and December 1914, when it withdrew from Veracruz and gave Carranza some relief in his confined coastal position against the thrust of the Northern Division, Washington did not show much concern at the prospect of victory by the two great peasant armies. After the first evacuation of Mexico City, in January 1915, it was clear anyway that such a victory could do no more than bring some kind of Conventionist government to power. Besides, nothing could be done to stem the peasant war: it had to run its own course.

At the political level, however, Washington very soon clashed with Carranza himself. While the struggle against Huerta was still in course, John Reed interviewed Carranza in Nogales, Sonora, and drew from him the following statement: "I tell you that if the United States intervenes in Mexico . . . intervention will not accomplish what it thinks, but will provoke a war which, besides its own consequences, will deepen a profound hatred between the United States and the whole of Latin America, a hatred which will endanger the entire political future of the United States."[5]

In late 1913, at the height of the struggle against Huerta, the Constitutionalist general in Tuxpan, Cándido Aguilar, was involved in an incident with the U.S. Navy. As his troops moved into the Tuxpan oil region in Veracruz State, U.S. Navy ships under the command of Admiral Fletcher were lying anchored off the island of Lobos. Fletcher sent the following message: "To General Candido Aguilar, commander of the rebel forces occupying the oil zone of Tuxpan region. I am instructed by my government to inform you that if you do not leave the oil zone within twenty-four hours, I shall land U.S. troops to safeguard the lives and interests of American citizens and other nationals."

The Mexican general replied: "To Admiral Fletcher. I refer to your insolent note of yesterday. The life and interests of North Americans and other nationals have been, are and will be fully safeguarded in the military zone under my command. Should the threat to land U.S. troops on Mexican soil be carried out, I shall be obliged to fight them, to burn the oil-wells in the region of which I have charge, and to shoot all North Americans in the region who, in the meantime, are to be considered hostages."

Simultaneously, Aguilar sent these instructions to his officers: "Urgently gather together all the families of North Americans living in the area. Put an officer and two soldiers on guard at each well, so that when the first cannon-shots are fired and you receive orders directly from me, you shall set fire to the wells and shoot all the temporary North American hostages." The landing did not, of course, take place. But this was one of a series of incidents that led to the occupation of Veracruz by U.S. Marines in April 1914.

The Constitutionalist government tripled the oil tax on July 20, 1914, and its decree of December 12, 1914, promised to revise legislation on the mines, oil reserves, forests, and other natural resources to the benefit of nationalist interests. Early in 1915, Carranza issued further decrees to control foreign investment in land, oil extraction, mining, and other such areas. This nationalist policy, which nevertheless stopped short of expropriation, became a permanent landmark of the Carranza government and a source of constant friction with Washington. At the same time, the Mexican bourgeoisie tried to profit from the 1914–18 war and the interruption of European exports in order to gain a firmer foothold in its own domestic market.

During the first half of 1915, when the war between Villism and Constitutionalism was at its fiercest, the U.S. government was shaken by an internal conflict over policy toward the different Mexican factions. One side, seeing the revolutionary implications of the peasant war, proposed that Washington should support Carranza. The other side, seeing Carranza as the most solid foundation for a strong nationalist government, denounced his oil policy and argued that some support should be given to Villa. For their part, the big oil corporations had already been conducting their own policy in Veracruz, giving financial support to General Manuel Peláez for his operations against Carranzist forces in 1914 and 1915. Later, between 1917 and 1919, these corporations would use the same general to direct a white terror against the oil-workers' unions.

Since early 1915, the idea had been maturing in President Wilson's mind that he should intervene as a "mediator" in the Mexican Civil War. On June 2, when the battle of Trinidad had still not been decided, Wilson announced to the American people that the United States would not tolerate continued civil war in Mexico, effectively threatening intervention if a stable government was not established. After Trinidad and Aguascalientes, however, every day that passed made it clearer that a Carranzist victory was the only possible outcome of the civil war. U.S. imperialists then tried to intervene in order to use Villa's retreating forces as a counterweight that might wrest concessions from Carranza's nationalist government. Alperovich and Rudenko give this account:

> [Robert] Lansing, who replaced [William Jennings] Bryan as secretary of state on 9 June 1915, wrote to Woodrow Wilson on 6 August that Villa should be encouraged to sell livestock in the United States on account of his rather difficult financial situation. On 9 August he sent another letter which explained his position in more detail. "We should help Villa for the following reasons," he said. "We don't want Carranza's coterie to be the only group in Mexico with which we have relations. Carranza has shown himself to be so intolerant that the mere appearance of opposition to his government would allow us to spread the idea that the various groupings are holding talks with one another. I therefore think that, until an understanding is reached, it would be useful to give Villa the opportunity to obtain the money for buying weapons." Approximately the same aim—to create a certain counterweight against Carranza—was discussed at a meeting between Villa and General Scott, chief-of-staff of the US Army.[6]

In the middle of August 1915, the U.S. government finally put forward concrete plans for mediation. On August 11, Secretary of State Lansing, together with the diplomatic representatives in Washington of Argentina, Brazil, Chile, Uruguay, Bolivia, and Guatemala, sent Carranza, Villa, Zapata, and other Mexican army leaders an official dispatch which has become known as the Pan-American Note. The proposal was that these countries should act as mediators in calling a conference of representatives of all the warring factions in Mexico, so as to "constitute a provisional government which may take the first steps to restore constitutional order in the country."

Villa accepted the idea on August 16, and put the name of General

Felipe Angeles on the list of prospective Villist delegates. (In fact Angeles, already distancing himself from Villa, had gone to the United States and would only return at the end of 1918.) Zapata also accepted on August 26, followed by various members of the Convention government, which was by now a mere shadow of itself. Among these was General Manuel Palafox.

Unlike the peasant leaders, however, Carranza saw himself as the representative of the nation and therefore rejected the note. Besides, since he was clearly winning the war, it made no sense for him to accept such a proposal of "mediation." On September 10, the Carranzist government replied to the signatories of the note: "[The government] cannot consent to discuss the internal affairs of the Republic with any mediator or on the initiative of any foreign government . . . given that acceptance of the proposals made by Your Excellencies would gravely damage the independence of the Republic, and set a precedent for foreign governments to interfere in the solution of our internal problems." At the same time, it called for itself to be recognized as the only legitimate government of Mexico.

The signatories of the Pan-American Note met in conference on October 9, at a time when Obregón's victorious campaign had placed the consolidation of the Carranza government beyond any doubt. The participants therefore decided to recommend that it be endorsed as the de facto government of Mexico.

On October 19, 1915, the United States officially recognized the Carranza government, banned further arms sales to its enemies, particularly Villa's forces, and allowed Obregón's troops to pass through North American territory for operations against Villa. As we have seen, this facility was of crucial importance in bolstering the Agua Prieta garrison to inflict a severe and decisive defeat on the Villist assault force.

The next year, the U.S. Army itself would launch a "punitive expedition"—a fruitless attempt to stamp out the tenacious remains of the Mexican peasant war represented by the Villist guerrillas.[7]

★   ★   ★

On July 31, 1916, the first general strike in Mexico's history broke out for a period of three days. But the workers went alone into struggle: the peasantry, which in its rise had stimulated the workers' movement, was now in retreat and in any case divided from it by the experience of the Red Battalions. For their part, the workers' leaders had used the first stage of the alliance with Carranzism—when it was a life-and-death question for the Constitutionalists to win the workers' support and prevent a linkup with the peasantry—in order to develop trade-union organization throughout the country.

Once the peasant armies had been defeated or thrown back, the bourgeois Carranzist faction quickly proceeded to confront the labor movement in a trial of strength that culminated in the 1916 general strike.

The Red Battalions agreement had involved certain concessions to the unions. Thus, on the eve of the battle of Celaya, Obregón decreed a minimum wage in the region and in all states under Constitutionalist Army control. The minimum was to be one peso a day—the very sum which, in early 1912, the Zapatist leaders had themselves forced the haciendas to pay their peons in areas controlled by the Southern Liberation Army. As Obregón's army was gaining ground in 1915, the Casa del Obrero Mundial (COM) sent out groups of organizers and agitators to unionize the workers. For although Carranza was an enemy of all forms of labor organization, he had to accept Obregón's political-military leadership of the campaign. And Obregón understood that the most important element in the pact with the unions was not the numerical addition to his army, but the secure social base that union activity provided at his rear. Moreover, it won him support in the towns that was crucial in offsetting the resistance of the pro-Villist peasantry.

In August 1915 the Casa del Obrero Mundial was reestablished in Mexico City, and Luis N. Morones became secretary-general of a reorganized Federal District Union Federation. The COM set up branches in San Luis Potosí, Yucatán, Veracruz, Tamaulipas, Coahuila, Puebla, Guanajuato, and Hidalgo. On December 5 it issued a manifesto that stated: "The armed struggle is coming to an end, and soon we shall begin to reap its fruits. We shall know how to use this freedom, won at the price of so many sacrifices, in order to form powerful unions sufficient in themselves to command the respect of our exploiters."

At the end of 1915, the Constitutionalist government awarded the Jockey Club building, once a redoubt of the Porfirian aristocracy, to the Casa del Obrero Mundial. It soon became the center for feverish union organizational activity, involving constant workers' assemblies and meetings. Here were founded or reorganized the unions of bakers, tailors, shoemakers, printers, tram workers, National Arsenal workers, and so on. Organizing groups continually set out for various parts of the country. At the same time, a flood of demands was presented by the bakers, printers, tailors (who opened a cooperative in the Jockey Club headquarters), carpenters, textile workers and others, usually together with a strike movement or the threat of a strike. Late in December, the Guadalajara tram workers and electricians struck in support of wage demands. In the El Oro mines in Mexico State, the strikers even replaced their superiors and took over the installations. Dockworkers walked out in the two chief ports of the country, Veracruz and Tampico.

Once the Northern Division collapsed in late December, the Carranza government no longer needed union support for the struggle with Villa. Paradoxically, the Red Battalions and the social cover of the Casa del Obrero Mundial had helped to destroy the military shield that indirectly prevented the Carranzists from concentrating their blows against the proletariat and the Zapatist bastion in Morelos. Now the Constitutionalist government was able to turn on its erstwhile allies.

On November 30, 1915, the railway workers were conscripted and brought under military discipline. At the beginning of the next year, the Constitutionalist high command dissolved the Red Battalions, disbanded most of their members, and incorporated the rest in the regular army.

On January 19, 1916, General Pablo González made a public

declaration against the widespread labor agitation. "If the revolution fought capitalist tyranny," he argued, "it cannot sanction proletarian tyranny." The declaration was accompanied by a series of measures against the organized labor movement. González's troops stormed the Jockey Club headquarters, violently evicted the workers' organizations, and closed down the magazine *Ariete*. In Monterrey, General Treviño shut the local COM offices; while in a number of other states, senior Constitutionalist officers followed orders from Carranza to arrest COM leaders, on the grounds that they were agitating for a general strike to receive wages in gold. Unionists arrested throughout the country were all brought to Querétaro prison.

By February the Red Battalions no longer existed, the workers had been driven from the Jockey Club, and many of their leaders were in prison or suffering persecution. The Veracruz alliance between Carranzism and the workers' movement had run its full cycle in the space of a year, proving that its opponents had been right to denounce it as an act of capitulation.

In these circumstances, the Federal District Union Federation decided to call a National Workers Congress in Veracruz. This congress, attended by delegates from all parts of the country, was the most representative gathering so far in the history of the Mexican workers' movement. It opened on March 5, 1916, and approved the founding of the Mexico Regional Federation of Labor. In its various resolutions, the anarcho-syndicalist current headed by the Veracruz leader Herón Proal prevailed over the reformist tendency led by Morones. Accordingly, Proal was elected secretary-general of the federation.

Article one of the statutes reads as follows: "The Mexico Regional Federation of Labor accepts the class struggle as the basic principle of workers' organization, and the socialization of the means of production as the supreme goal for the proletarian movement." Subsequent articles state that the organization will only employ "direct action," to the exclusion of "political action"; that its members are not entitled to occupy any public or administrative office; and that it will support the principles of the "rationalist school." The resolutions included one calling for the release of the union leaders jailed by the Carranza government. The Veracruz congress closed on March 17.

Mexico's economic crisis, stemming from the civil war, weighed ever more heavily upon wage-earning sections of the population. In war-affected regions, particularly in 1914–15, many factories shut their gates or reduced production for lack of markets or raw materials. The cost of food was continually rising, since there was not enough transport to carry even the reduced quantity of agricultural produce. The military commanders and state governors acted with discretionary powers, raising taxes, requisitioning goods, and issuing an uncontrolled supply of money. In the early part of 1916, more than twenty different currencies were circulating in the country, most of them accepted only in particular regions. The *veracruz*, one of the most widely used banknotes, was quoted in March 1916 as worth two gold centavos per peso. Demands for the payment of wages in gold therefore became the rule in every labor sector. On May 22 the Federal District Union Federation called a strike in support of this demand. But facing the threat of reprisals and the promise of concessions, the workers' leaders suspended the action on May 23.

As the promises did not materialize, the Federal District Union Federation renewed its preparations for a strike. Meeting in secret session in July, its federal council approved a strike call but did not set a precise date. Three strike committees were formed, so that they could succeed each other as repression struck their members.

The general strike began on July 31, 1916, spearheaded by the electricians' action in plunging Mexico City into darkness. Altogether, some ninety thousand workers in the federal district downed tools. Some made their way through the paralyzed city to attend a meeting at the headquarters of the electricians' union, where a presidential envoy invited them to send a delegation for talks with Carranza. When they arrived in the president's office, however, Carranza coarsely insulted them, described them as "traitors to the fatherland," and ordered their arrest and trial before a military tribunal. At the same time, the army broke up a meeting at the electricians' headquarters, and troops occupied the various trade-union offices. On August 1 the president decreed martial law and, invoking the Juarist law against "subverters of public order," instituted the death penalty for strikers. The vagueness of this law allowed any opponent of the government to be brought under its terms.

"The death penalty," states the decree,

> shall be applied not only to subverters of public order defined in the law of 25 January 1862, but also to the following categories: *firstly*—those who incite or spread a work-stoppage in factories or other enterprises designed to maintain the public services; who chair meetings in which such a stoppage is proposed, discussed or approved; who advocate and support such a stoppage; who attend a meeting of this kind and fail to withdraw as soon as they realize its purpose; or who try to make a stoppage effective once it has been declared; *secondly*—those who, seeking to suspend work in the aforementioned or any other factories or workplaces, and profiting from the subsequent disorders to worsen or impose such a suspension, destroy or damage property belonging to an enterprise whose workers are involved, or wish to be included, in such a suspension; or who, with the same intent, provoke disturbances against public servants or private individuals, or use force against the person or property of any citizen, or seize, destroy or damage public or private property; and *thirdly*—those who, by threats or force, prevent other persons from performing the duties normally discharged by workers in the enterprises against which a suspension of work has been declared.

The main strike leader, electrician Ernesto Velasco, was arrested on August 2. Bowing to the effects of repression and the death penalty decree, but also displaying the weakness of the strike leadership, Velasco ordered a return to work and the restarting of the

Necaxa power station that supplied the capital. The strike ended without any gains, and yet the repression did not abate.

The strike leaders were placed on trial. But since the court did not judge it expedient to pass the death penalty, Carranza ordered a retrial at which Ernesto Velasco was condemned to death. However, the sentence was first postponed and then commuted to a term of imprisonment. Eventually, after Velasco had sent various messages of recantation to Carranza, the government yielded to constant labor movement protests and allowed his release in February 1918.

While Carranza was conducting this repression, his war minister, Alvaro Obregón, was making various attempts at conciliation. As early as the evening of August 2, he secretly met with the second-line strike committee and presented himself as a "friend of the workers' movement" who had differences with Carranza. He argued that the situation was extremely difficult for an organized workers' movement, suggesting that union life should be temporarily discontinued "until things calm down." The workers' leaders accepted his advice, and the Casa del Obrero Mundial dissolved.

The collapse of the general strike brought to an end the history of an organization that, between 1912 and 1916, had been the center of organized working-class involvement in the Mexican Revolution.

In this whole episode, Obregón again played a dual role: on the one hand, there was a tacit division of labor in which Carranza repressed while Obregón contained and dissuaded; but on the other hand, Obregón did represent a current that sought support for its distinctive policy among the workers' leaders. The situation would repeat itself a few months later at the Querétaro Constituent Congress.

A new stage opened for the union movement in May 1918, when a national labor congress in Saltillo founded the Mexican Regional Workers Federation (CROM) under the leadership of Morones. This gave rise in December 1919 to the Mexican Labor Party, with roots in the ephemeral Federal District Union Federation of 1917. The CROM and its party immediately attached themselves to Obregón's policy and were one of the main props in his rise to power.

Early in 1916, the first incidents occurred between Villist guerrillas and the North Americans. Washington's recognition of the Carranza government, and the help it gave Obregón in the last battles against Villa, had definitively broken all relations between the peasant general and U.S. government representatives. Whereas a few months earlier the United States had sought to use Villa against the strengthening of Carranza's national government, direct experience now showed him much more clearly the goals and methods of U.S. policy in Mexico.

In January 1916, the Villist general Pablo López attacked a train at Santa Isabel, Chihuahua, and shot seventeen American passengers on board. This incident, which caused an outcry in the United States, was soon pushed into the background by a much more daring exploit. On March 9, 1916, troops under Pancho Villa himself crossed the frontier and raided Columbus, New Mexico. More than a hundred Mexicans and seventeen Americans lost their lives in the six hours of fighting.

In reply, Washington decided to send a "punitive expedition" into Northern Mexico, supposedly with the sole aim of locating and punishing Villa. But whereas Villa had raided Columbus with barely five hundred men, the force that entered Mexico on March 15, 1916, under the command of General John J. Pershing, numbered twelve thousand soldiers plus horses and artillery. Pershing was soon to lead the U.S. expeditionary force to the battlefields of Europe, and two of his sublieutenants, Dwight D. Eisenhower and George S. Patton, would become commanders of the U.S. Army in Europe during the Second World War. But all three registered their first setback in the fruitless search for Villa and his guerrillas.[8]

On March 29, in the first encounter between the U.S. military and a Villist unit, Villa himself was wounded in the leg and forced to spend many months recovering in a mountain hideout. But his men continued the guerrilla struggle against both U.S. and

Carranzist forces. It was during this period that General Pablo López was captured and shot by the Carranzists.

In its push into Mexico, the punitive expedition not only failed to track Villa down, but encountered growing resistance from the entire population. On April 12 the inhabitants of Parral, led by a woman, armed themselves with whatever they could find and confronted a U.S. column to cries of "Viva Villa!"

Although the Americans tried to obtain Carranza's consent, painting the invasion as an action directed purely against "the bandit Villa," the president expressed his opposition from the very beginning. On the day of the events in Parral, the minister for foreign affairs, General Cándido Aguilar, sent a strongly worded demand for the withdrawal of foreign troops. On April 29, talks began in El Paso between General Obregón, then minister of war in the Carranza government, and U.S. General Scott. But no agreement was reached, since the Americans demanded, as the precondition of any troop withdrawal, that the Mexican government should recognize their right to return in the case of further border incidents. On May 11, acting on Carranza's personal instructions, Obregón declared that the talks were suspended.

The Carranza government then began to face the invading column. Not only did this move accord with its own positions, but the rising tide of popular indignation and anti-imperialist sentiment had virtually forced the government's hand. The invasion had considerably boosted Villa's image in the North.

By June a force of ten thousand federal soldiers was already in Chihuahua, with orders to prevent any U.S. troop movements except in the direction of the border. On June 21, 1916, a Mexican Army detachment clashed with the punitive expedition at El Carrizal, forcing it to retreat and capturing a number of prisoners.

On July 4, the Carranza government again took the initiative of proposing negotiations, and these were opened on September 4. However, the Americans still insisted on various conditions for a troop withdrawal, while the Mexican representatives would only agree to negotiate on the basis of an unconditional withdrawal.

Other factors were now intervening to bring an agreement closer. Villa had been able to continue his guerrilla operations, and the mounting popular resistance to U.S. troops was harmful to both the Americans and the Carranzists. In the face of the invasion, the internal divisions Washington had hoped to exploit were giving way to a de facto alliance from below against the invaders and anyone who supported them. The Carranzist troops were themselves ever more reluctant to fight Villa and exerted considerable pressure for the expulsion of the invaders.

In mid-September, in an action that displayed his partial military recovery and the counterproductive effect of the U.S. operation, Villa entered the city of Chihuahua, released all the prisoners from jail, and seized arms, ammunition, and food supplies for his own troops and the local population. Martin López took special pleasure in riding his horse up the steps of the Chihuahua government house. Their objectives achieved, the Villist forces withdrew from the city.

In October 1916 Villa issued a manifesto to the nation that called for resistance to the invaders and expropriation of all foreign mining and railway companies, and stated that no foreigner with less than twenty-five years of residence should be allowed to own any property in the country. The manifesto ended with the slogan "Mexico for the Mexicans!" As always in Latin America, the anti-imperialist struggle radicalized the program of its protagonists—in this case the Villist faction.

At the same time, the course of the war in Europe was making U.S. intervention there an ever more imminent prospect. It was therefore necessary to end the invasion of Mexico, which had at least been a kind of trial run for European operations and served to increase the number of men under arms. In June 1916, for example, more than a hundred thousand soldiers were conscripted and deployed along the border with Mexico.

By the end of the year, it was already clear that the punitive expedition had failed in its objectives and become tied to its positions. It is estimated that Villa then had more than ten thousand

men in his guerrilla force. Carranza's government had not produced the expected concessions, and had continued its efforts to
structure the new regime. Since a decision had already been taken
to call the Constituent Congress for the end of the year, the further
presence of U.S. troops would merely help to push the Congress
delegates and resolutions to the left. On December 22, as if to
underline the complete failure of the expedition, Villa captured
the city of Torreón for the third time since the beginning of the
revolution, while the Constituent Congress was in session in
Querétaro.

On January 2, 1917, General Pershing finally received the order
to pull out; the withdrawal concluded on February 5 as the new
Constitution was being solemnly proclaimed in Querétaro. A well-
known ballad later recalled:

> Did the Americans think
> That war was a ballroom dance?
> Back to their land they went
> With shame writ all o'er their face.

Many explanations have been given for Villa's action. Some say
that Villa was enraged by the murder of a group of Mexican workers who had entered the United States. (They had been forced to
take a petrol bath for "sanitary reasons," and the tank had then
caught fire.) Others say it was a reprisal for the support given to
Carranza, when Constitutionalist troops had been allowed to cross
U.S. territory to defeat the Villist forces in Sonora. For their part, the
Soviet writers Alperovich and Rudenko argue that a section of the
U.S. bourgeoisie may have provoked Villa's "invasion" in order to
have a pretext for military intervention in Mexico.

The most convincing interpretation is provided by Friedrich
Katz, who cuts through emotional or conspiratorial factors to ana-
lyze Villa's military motivation. Katz argues that Villa took the decision to raid U.S. territory several months in advance. In return
for Washington's diplomatic recognition, Villa believed, Carranza

had been secretly negotiating a number of huge political, economic, and military concessions, including the opening of naval bases on the Pacific coast. Katz shows that although such talks really had taken place, they were conducted behind Carranza's back and directed against him. The parties involved were a group of Mexican conservatives linked to Porfirism and representatives of U.S. corporations, particularly oil companies with interests in Mexico, who had contact with the head of the Mexican Bureau of the U.S. State Department, Leon Canova.

The idea of a kind of U.S. protectorate in Mexico was not intrinsically unappealing to President Wilson: he several times considered plans to occupy all or part of Mexican territory, and ordered direct U.S. military intervention in April 1914 and March 1916. This time, however, he rejected Canova's plan on the grounds that it might prove inopportune. On November 5, 1915, Villa issued a statement that, basing itself upon various hints and conjectures, accused Carranza of selling the country to Wilson in return for his support.

A few weeks later, Villa wrote a letter to Zapata concerning the course of the northern war over the previous months. This letter, which contains many inaccuracies and an unwarranted triumphalism, expressed Villa's intention to attack the United States in response to its support for Carranza. Pancho Villa, again virtually an outlaw after his series of defeats, even suggested that Zapata should bring his troops north in order to prepare a joint attack! This naive and unrealistic proposal, addressed to the leader of an army that had never left Morelos at the time of its greatest triumph, does a great deal to explain the mentality and illusions of the peasant leaders of the Mexican Revolution.[9]

According to Katz, Villa hoped that U.S. reprisals would force Carranza either to reveal his alleged alliance with Wilson by permitting the entry of American troops, or to resist the Yankees and discontinue the alliance. In fact, although the attack on Columbus and the U.S. punitive expedition did not provoke a complete break between the two governments, the sharp conflict resulting from the

U.S. invasion and the Constitutionalist leaders' resistance did inflict lasting damage on the relationship that began with the recognition of the Carranza government in October 1915. Carranza did not receive the U.S. loans he so badly needed, and Washington reimposed a ban on arms sales to Mexico which, with a few short breaks, would persist until Carranza's fall in 1920. All Carranza's enemies drew some benefit from this situation—in some crucial respects, Katz concludes, Villa was thus successful in his plan.

The United States went to war with Germany on April 6, 1917. From then until the armistice in November 1918, the Carranza government resisted every pressure and maintained Mexican neutrality in the world conflict.[10]

The Constitutionalist campaign against Villa, so crucial to victory, had involved a number of major concessions apart from the decree of December 12, 1914, and its legislative follow-up. Not only was Zapata left free throughout 1915 to develop the Morelos Commune, not only was the organizational work of the unions greatly facilitated, but a number of leftist experiences developed in the outlying southeastern states of Yucatán and Tabasco.

In Yucatán, General Salvador Alvarado first defeated a local latifundist uprising in March 1915, and then, as governor of the state in December 1915, issued a series of laws and decrees that struck at the political and social power of the "divine caste" of local henequen oligarchs. Among these reforms were an order applying the January agrarian reform law to Yucatán; a local government law, and the introduction of a maximum workday and a minimum wage, retirement pensions and work-accident compensation, life and accident insurance, and improvements in hygiene and general working conditions.

Francisco J. Múgica, provisional governor of Tabasco between September 1915 and September 1916, also distributed the hacienda lands and decreed a number of progressive reforms. He would later use these experiences in Tabasco and Yucatán in leading the radical wing of the Querétaro Constituent Congress.

At the same time, remnants of the old regime still clung to life in remoter parts of the country untouched by the revolutionary wave. Thus on June 3, 1915, the governor of Oaxaca State, José Inés Dávila, issued a promulgation that "insofar as constitutional order is restored in the Republic, the Free and Sovereign State of Oaxaca reassumes its sovereignty." The state legislature adopted the 1857 Constitution and declared null and void all the reform measures approved by Carranza since December 1914. Naturally such counterrevolutionary foci had no chance of establishing themselves on secure popular foundations.

Carranza's main preoccupation, however, was to turn his fire against Zapatism and the workers' movement. In addition, he had to contend with the peasant detachments scattered almost throughout the country, whose peasant "generals" led a few dozen or a few hundred men in attacking trains, levying taxes, seizing towns, and harrying government troops. The peasant war was waning and fragmented, but it was not about to collapse.

Except in Morelos State, where, as we shall see, Zapatist peasants and agricultural laborers had created forms of popular power under centralized political leadership, the peasant war had no national objectives and no possibility of centralization and recovery. In this sense, its primitive, localist features could even appear reactionary in relation to the center of power, where a radical petty-bourgeois wing had been able to exploit the diffuse social strength of peasant resistance to demand and obtain a series of progressive reforms. The small groups of peasants who continued the struggle did not, of course, have reactionary aims or intentions: indeed, filled with rage that the petty-bourgeois and bourgeois Carranzists had usurped *their* revolution, they refused to lay down arms and be left without land or power. But since they were unable to express their aspirations in a national program and a centralized force, they fell into the hands of local peasant *caudillos* or officers who kept up a primitive, aimless, and often cruel pattern of struggle. This clearly and painfully expressed the nationwide downturn in the revolution and mass resistance.[11]

After 1916 the Zapatist leadership had to face the same problem, as is shown by the many statements against officer abuses. Zapata's own death finally unleashed this tendency in Morelos.

Where local or Indian traditions provided a lever for organization of the struggle, the armed peasantry was able to organize better resistance. This happened, for example, in the case of the Yaqui tribe. Initially, they provided a force of three hundred men, armed with bows and arrows and a few stray rifles, which became one of the pillars of Obregón's army. Particularly during the two very hard-fought battles of Celaya, their physical stamina, fighting capacity, and remarkable aim were all of inestimable importance. Like the workers of the Red Battalions, they thought that victory over Villist "reaction" was the occasion for them to claim the objectives of their struggle. Yet the Yaquis received the same answer as the urban workers. In October 1915, they asked for their lands in the Sonora Valley and the right to govern themselves in their own territory. Obregón answered with a military attack, but was unable to subjugate them. The Yaquis fought on throughout 1916, supported by remnants of the Northern Division. In the end, two federal columns crushed them through a frontal assault from both north and south.

In this patchwork quilt of struggles, the Constitutionalist Army was Carranza's only "party" or element of centralization, yet the army itself proved subject to internal tensions deriving from a clash between revolutionary factions that was much less clearly delineated than the bitter confrontation with Huerta. Carranza now decided to entrust a congress with the task of elaborating a constitution. In fact, this was an obligatory concession to the radical Constitutionalist tendencies, which demanded a legal expression of the revolutionary promises. It was also an attempt to unify the Constitutionalist movement by giving a juridical sanction to its military triumph.

The debates of the Aguascalientes Convention had had to make way for the clash of arms: the differences separating Carranzism from Villism and Zapatism could not have been resolved in the parliamentary arena. But once the true relationship of forces had been settled on the field of battle, the time came once again for words. What was out of the question in 1914 in Aguascalientes was now possible in Querétaro. Men who could not be forbidden to speak in 1914 had now been eliminated by force of arms; and only representatives of the victorious faction attended the new Congress with the right to speak and vote. The initial convocation had made this clear in September 1916, when it specified support for the Guadalupe Plan as a condition for election to the Constituent Congress.

Moreover, with the civil war embers still glowing throughout the country, the elections were not and could not have been very democratic or representative. In many states, a sham electoral process involved the straightforward appointment of local representatives. In others, a prior agreement between local Constitutionalist commanders and their secretaries and general staffs made it a pure formality. But even where the elections had greater content, the representatives were in effect representatives of the Constitutionalist Army and government, in its various tendencies. Only three of the two hundred deputies to the Constituent Congress came from the trade-union movement, and the few speaking for Morelos were sent straight from the capital. For in Zapata's southern stronghold, it had not been possible to organize even sham elections.

Still, the two years of civil war since Aguascalientes had not passed in vain. Enemies who fight each other for a certain length of time tend to influence and learn from each other. On the eve of the Querétaro Congress, the Constitutionalist faction was more than ever an amalgam of tendencies, fairly dissimilar and in some respects hostile to one another. The Zapatist and Villist peasant war, the Yaqui resistance, the workers' strikes and struggles, the social reforms in various states, the enrichment of a layer of Carranzist officers through plunder, land seizures, and corruption, the invasion by a U.S. punitive expedition—all these factors had prompted greater differentiation within the Constitutionalist movement. And in the absence of other forms of political manifestation, they found expression in the different tendencies and personalities of the victorious faction.

The Constituent Congress opened on November 21, 1916, in the city of Querétaro. Its declared purpose was to reform the 1857 Constitution, whose violation by Huerta's coup had provoked the emergence of the Constitutionalist movement. Yet this reform did not follow the procedure laid down in the 1857 Constitution, but involved the calling of a congress empowered, in effect, to issue a new constitution.

Soon after the Constituent Congress began, a split appeared between the progressive and conservative tendencies. Obregón proposed that the Congress should reject the credentials of the so-called renovation group, which included former members of the Maderist majority in the last parliament accused of collaboration with Huerta. Since this group embraced the drafters of the new Constitution (Luis M. Roja, Félix Palavicini, José N. Macías, and Alfonso Craviot) that Carranza intended to present to the Congress, the attack was directed against both them and the president. Carranza intervened in their defense, and their credentials were eventually accepted. But the dividing line had now been established.

After Carranza's project presentation, discussion began on the draft Constitution. In reality, it merely revised the 1857 Liberal Constitution on a number of political-organizational points, failing to mention any of the social gains and demands promised especially since December 1914. The conservative tendency naturally supported Carranza's draft, while the radical, "Jacobin" wing (a name given by their opponents and accepted by them) sought to integrate deep political and social reforms into the juridical structure of the country. One section even considered that these should fall into a socialist-type perspective.

The essential content of these reforms was to establish a very broad system of democratic safeguards and legal backup mechanisms; to create an exclusively state-run education system, with no private or clerical interference; to write into the Constitution the various measures on the liquidation of latifundia, the redistribution of land to the peasantry, the protection of smallholdings, the restitution of communal lands, and the encouragement of collective farming; to nationalize all the mineral and oil wealth of the Mexican subsoil, establishing the necessary legal principle for the eventual nationalization of all extractive industries; to limit the right to private property, subordinating it to the "social interest" (a vague formulation, which nevertheless gave a legal basis for the later push toward nationalization of basic industries and development of the economy through the state sector); and to express in the Constitution a system of workers' rights and safeguards (the eight-hour day, the right to strike, a minimum wage, etc.) which liberal constitutions never mention and, at best, leave for future legislation.

The main leader of the Jacobin tendency was Francisco José Múgica. He headed a group of Constitutionalist Army officers, and in his struggle for these reforms he drew support from deputies linked to the labor movement. With the backing of sympathetic centrist representatives, the tendency won a Congress majority that was reflected in the composition of various committees. Although the delegates generally accepted those clauses of Carranza's draft that involved a political reorganization beyond the framework of the 1857 Constitution, they effectively rejected his vision of a bourgeois-liberal constitution with no place for social questions. The Jacobin wing thus imposed its alternative position in a number of crucial articles: number 3, on education; number 27, on the land and public ownership of the subsoil; number 123, on workers' rights; and number 130, on the secularization of Church property.

These articles, particularly those referring to the agrarian question and workers' rights, cut across Carranza's intentions and converted his proposed modification of the 1857 text into a new constitution. Thus, when it was finally approved on January 31, 1917, the Mexican Constitution was undoubtedly the most advanced in the world. It was not socialist. Yet it virtually declared the big landowners and latifundia to be unconstitutional, thereby dismantling one of the former pillars of Mexican capitalism; it guaranteed the rights of workers and peasants, not just "the rights of man" in general; it was a nationalist document that favored nationalization reforms in the main branches of the economy.

The final text of article 27, for example, though embodying a compromise between conservatives and Jacobins, contains the following statement: "The lands and waters within Mexico's national territory originally belong to the nation, which has had and still has the right to pass them on to individuals in the form of private property. . . . The nation will always have the right to impose on private property those forms which are dictated by the public interest." It further declares that the nation has "inalienable and imprescriptible ownership" of the waters and subsoil minerals (oil, coal, metals, etc.) and that individuals may only be granted a concession to exploit such resources. After prescribing the norms of land redistribution, the article establishes the modern form of communal ownership, the *ejido,* as a constitutionally recognized addition to smallholdings (big landed property being excluded):

> The population centers which *de facto* or *de jure* retain the communal form, shall have the capacity to exploit in common the land, woodlands and waters which belong to them or have been, or shall be, restored to them." It then cancels all the seizures of communal land, waters, and woodland carried out under the Porfirio Díaz regime, and orders that these be returned to the villages in accordance with their previous title-deeds. "Population centers which have no communal land [*ejidos*]," it adds, "or which cannot have it restored because they lack the title-deeds or are unable to identify the land in question or have legally alienated it, shall be endowed with sufficient land and waters to constitute such communal property, in accordance with the requirements of the population. In no case shall the necessary extension be denied them, and to this end the federal government shall expropriate a suitable quantity of land situated near the village in question.

The most important provisions of article 123 are as follows: a maximum workday of eight hours, or seven at night; a ban on nighttime, dangerous, and insalubrious work for women and for minors below sixteen years of age; a ban on the employment of children below twelve years of age, and a maximum six-hour day for minors below sixteen; one compulsory day of rest per week; a month's rest after childbirth and special facilities during lactation; a minimum living wage ("the amount considered necessary, in the given conditions of the region, to satisfy the normal requirements of the workers' life, including his education, reasonable leisure activity, and his role as head of the family"); the sharing of profits "in every agricultural, commercial, manufacturing or mining enterprise"; equal pay for equal work, with no distinction of sex and nationality; compulsory payment of the full wage in legal tender; double payment of overtime (a maximum of three hours for no more than three consecutive days); an obligation for employers "to provide their workers with comfortable, hygienic accommodation at a monthly rent not exceeding half a percent of the property value, and to create schools, infirmaries and other necessary public services"; compensation for work accidents; hygiene and health measures in places of work; the right to associate freely, to form labor unions, and to hold strikes and stoppages (rights accorded to "both workers and employers"); the formation of workforce-management parity committees, to arbitrate in labor disputes together with a representative of the state; prohibition of unfair dismissal ("or dismissal for membership of an association or trade union, or for participation in a lawful strike"); nullification of any clause in a labor contract which contradicts these rights or restores employers' shops either directly and indirectly; a ban on the distrainment or alienation of a worker's family household (to be defined by specific legislation); and the ratification of social security laws.

Article 130 imposes severe restrictions on the churches, particularly the dominant Catholic Church. It stipulates that matrimony is a civil contract; that "religious groups calling themselves Churches" have no legal status; that "religious ministers will be considered as persons exercising a profession," their total number to be fixed by each state legislature; and that only Mexicans by birth are allowed to carry out this function. It forbids the clergy to take part in politics, to vote, or to associate for political purposes, and prohibits the publication of religious journals that involve themselves in political questions. "It is strictly forbidden for any kind of political grouping to bear a title or any token whatsoever which links it to any religious confession. Meetings of a political character are not allowed in churches."

The 1917 Constitution retained article 39 of the 1857 document, which stipulated that "the people shall always have the inalienable right to change or modify their form of government." It also reaffirmed the provision in article 10 to the effect that every citizen has the right "to possess arms of any kind for his safety and legitimate defense."

The Jacobin wing, which imposed these reforms on Carranza, looked to Minister of War Obregón for his indirect support. Possibly he had not intended to go so far, but in effect he did give them decisive backing in the conflict with Carranza. Of the members of the high command, it was Obregón who best understood that military victory had to be consolidated through major concessions to the crucial revolutionary forces; and that since the policy of the left had served to unite the social forces necessary for the defeat of Villism and the isolation of Zapatism, much of it had to be incorporated into the Constitution if the precarious unity of the Constitutionalist movement was to be maintained. Above all, after December 22, 1916, Obregón made a decisive intervention in the Congress to overcome resistance to article 27. For it was on that day that Villa's troops captured the city of Torreón, revealing the still-hot embers of peasant war and the mass discontent with the whole reactionary policy followed by Carranza in 1916. In the end, then, an alliance between the Obregonist center and the Jacobin left pushed through the final text of the Constitution.

Articles 27, 123, and 130 not only expressed the influence of local reforms applied by revolutionary Constitutionalist officers (Múgica, Salvador Alvarado, Heriber to Jara, and for a time Lucio Blanco), but went beyond the "golden" article 8 of the Torreón Pact by raising the most advanced Villist program to the level of a constitutional law backed by the full power of the central state apparatus.

Another factor in the adoption of article 27 was the need for a government program with which to confront the Zapatist law of October 1915 and its influence on the peasant masses. Most crucial of all, however, was the fact that the Jacobin tendency brought into the victorious faction the nationalist, popular, anti-imperialist features of the revolution, the diffuse power of the peasant war. Six years of national uprising, peasant war, mass irruption, armed land redistribution, liquidation of latifundia-based capitalist structures, elimination of their personnel at every level—all this had effected a deep and irreversible transformation in the structure of the country and the consciousness of its people. In the Mexican Revolution, like all revolutions, the youth burst onto the arena. Generals of twenty or twenty-five appeared at the head of the armies, and the vast majority of the men ruling Mexico were between twenty and thirty-five years of age. Frank Tannenbaum makes an acute observation on this characteristic:

The Constitution was written by the *soldiers* of the Revolution, not by the lawyers, who were there, but were generally in the opposition. On all the crucial issues the lawyers voted against the majority of the Convention. The majority was in the hands of the soldiers—generals, colonels, majors—men who had marched and counter-marched across the Republic and had fought its battles. The ideas of the Constitutional Convention, as they developed, came from scattered sources. The soldiers wanted, as General Múgica said to me, to socialize property. But they were frightened— afraid of their own courage, of their own ideas. They found all of the learned men in the Convention opposed to them. Article 27 was a compromise.[12]

It is not enough, then, to say that the 1917 Constitution was a bourgeois constitution. Undoubtedly it was, and under its protection the bourgeoisie and capitalism would undergo development in Mexico. But it is also an indirect, remote—in short, constitutional—testimony to the conquests of the mass struggle. The 1917 Constitution ratified the victory of the first nationalist revolution in Latin America.

After the constitution was adopted, successive U.S. administrations started a protracted struggle against this document that gave legal sanction to the triumph of the nationalist and agrarian revolution. Directing its fire particularly against articles 3, 27, 123, and 130, the U.S. government used all available means to force a change in the text or to prevent its application to American citizens and property. Carranza, acting on behalf of the national propertied classes rather than imperialism, also tried to restrict the range of these articles. On December 14, 1918, he presented two draft amendments to articles 27 and 123 with the aim of curbing the right to strike; and a week later, he sent the Congress a proposed revision of article 130 that would have deprived local legislative bodies of the right to limit the number of priests, removed the condition that they should be Mexicans by birth, and exempted their chattels from the requirements of article 27 of the Constitution. In support of the latter change, Carranza argued that article 130 was "a limitation of human conscience and a departure from national legal antecedents." The daily Excelsior commented that the presidential initiative was designed "to purge the Querétaro magna carta of its Jacobin exaggerations so inappropriate to our social-historical situation."

Although this "purification program" was not on the whole successful, the democratic clauses of the Constitution would largely remain a dead letter for subsequent governments, while its social clauses only received application insofar as popular organizations created a favorable relationship of forces.[13] Only during the second phase of the Mexican Revolution, in General Lázaro Cárdenas's presidential term (1934–40), with General Francisco J. Múzica as his closest friend and secretary in his cabinet, would the agrarian and social conquests gained through its own influence at Querétaro be actually translated into reality.[14]

8

THE MORELOS COMMUNE

During the high tide of the peasant revolution, expressed in the fragile unity of Xochimilco and the occupation of the capital, the northern and southern sectors were impelled toward the conquest of the centers of power and their own unification at a national level. After the withdrawal from Mexico City in January 1915, they definitively retreated into their separate regions of origin, with no other prospect than defensive battles and then guerrilla warfare.

As in every peasant war, however, which by definition lacks a single center, the rhythm and forms of the retreat were not identical. In 1915, as we have seen, the Carranzists concentrated their thrust against the Villist army—the decisive military force in the peasant revolution, which, through Felipe Angeles, potentially carried a bourgeois alternative based on the peasant masses rather than on the pro-Carranzist sections of the urban petty bourgeoisie, the working class, and even the peasantry. At this time, the military struggle against Zapatism was essentially a holding operation not yet designed to confront and smash it. Containment was a feasible objective because it corresponded to the nature of the Morelos movement, whose very forms of military organization reflected its attachment to the land and the local region.

It was not just by reason of military weakness that the Carranzist forces under General Obregón avoided a war on two fronts. Their social weakness was also a source of grave concern: the tumultuous peasant revolution had not abated; the tide was only just beginning to turn; and all the favorable signs did not add up to a guarantee, even for Obregón's Bonapartist political instinct. The Operational

Army was still a roving military fragment, no weaker but also no stronger than either of the two peasant armies. On the other hand, Obregón understood that the war against Villa had to be essentially a confrontation between two armies, whereas the plan against Zapata, entrenched in his own region, would have to be more than a social war with a military casing. Obregón would not be the man for that kind of war, his function being to reap its fruits through a later political deal.

For all these reasons, Obregón's campaign in central and northern Mexico gave the southern masses a certain respite to develop their peasant democracy in the Morelos region, of which they felt masters. This was to be one of the most important episodes of the Mexican Revolution.[1]

The Morelos peasants practiced in their home state the true essence of the Ayala Plan: revolutionary liquidation of the latifundia. Moreover, since the latifundia, with sugar mills as their economic heart, were the form in which capitalism existed in Morelos, they thereby liquidated the basic centers of capitalism in the region. Although they applied an old precapitalist view of the world, this took an anticapitalist form in the laws drafted by their leaders in the second decade of the twentieth century. The aim was to nationalize the sugar mills without compensation, placing them under peasant administration through the Zapatist army officers.

The armed struggle and land distribution since 1911 on, the victory over the federal army, the downfall of Díaz, Madero, and Huerta, the occupation of the national capital—all gave the Morelos peasants and their leaders enormous confidence in their capacity to take decisions, which they applied in their home territory. Although the national revolutionary tide halted and began to ebb after December 1914, the process combined with a continuing upsurge at the local level. This could not last for long. But the time limit was not, and could not have been, known to the peasants and agricultural workers who set about rebuilding Morelos society in accordance with their own conceptions.

The Morelos leaders, based on the strength and aspirations of the peasant army and villages, did what they had wanted to do at the national level through a government they were unable to sustain. In their own region, they knew the terrain and the people, and they felt secure from a social, organizational, political, and military point of view. The peasant revolution from which their strength came was much deeper than their own understanding, since its roots lay in old communal traditions and in traditional social Indian structures which had always been an instrument of struggle and resistance.

The leaders' actions again showed that the Mexican peasant war had developed not only as an individual struggle for land, but, much more profoundly, as a collective fight for land and power. The Southern Liberation Army, the Zapatist people in arms, was the essential instrument of this struggle at the level of politics, just as the Northern Division had been at a military level.

Officially Morelos came under the authority of the Convention government, which had still been functioning in the Federal District in early January 1915 and returned there after Obregón's army left for central Mexico in March. The Zapatist general Manuel Palafox had immediately joined the Convention government in December 1914 as minister of agriculture, and he remained in this post after Gutiérrez and his men defected in January and the Villist Roque González Garza assumed the presidency.

Palafox was on the left wing of Zapata's political general staff. His letter of September 1914 to Atenor Sala already showed that he had gone furthest in interpreting the ideas of the Ayala Plan and giving them a socialist content. In the days following the Xochimilco Pact, he had made a great effort to drive forward the agrarian revolution and the implementation of those ideas.

In the middle of December 1914, a U.S. agent in Mexico gave the following description of Palafox in a letter to the secretary of state: "He is intractable; and his rabid socialistic ideas would not help to solve problems in a manner beneficial to this country." When the agent had requested a safe-conduct to visit an

American-owned hacienda, Palafox refused him on the grounds
that "all these properties should be divided up to give land to the
poor." And when the agent protested that it was owned by an
American, Palafox said that "it was all the same whether it belonged to North Americans or to some other foreigner; that the
lands should be redistributed." The letter ends with some typical
threatening advice: "I can see he's the kind of man who will cause
the ministry of foreign affairs a great deal of work that could be
avoided."[2]

In January 1915, a month or so after he became minister of
agriculture, Palafox founded the National Rural Credit Bank and
ordered the creation of regional agricultural schools and a national
agriculture implements factory. In the middle of the month, he set
up a special land redistribution bureau and invited peasants from
states other than Morelos (Hidalgo and Guanajuato, for example)
to present their land claims.

Agrarian commissions, comprising young volunteeer agronomists from the National Agricultural School, took charge of de-
marcating the land to be redistributed, or already redistributed, in
the agrarian reform zones. Morelos was virtually the only state
where such commissions functioned on a regular basis. They sur-
veyed and delimited nearly every village in the state, allocating
agricultural land, woodland, and stretches of water. At the end of
January, some forty young agronomists arrived with all their equipment in Cuernavaca, now the seat of the Convention government.
Obregón's army had just occupied the capital, and some of them
had barely managed to escape the blockade between Mexico City
and Morelos State.

The commissions faced many other difficulties in completing
their task. In order to delineate the lands of each village, they had
to study age-old title deeds, many from the time of the Viceroyship, which were often very imprecise or mentioned land features
that were hard to identify. Much of this land had been seized by
the haciendas, and in some cases they had subsequently let it out to
peasants from another village. Whenever there was a dispute, the

commission would invite village delegates to a meeting and try to reach a satisfactory agreement. Some conflict was inevitable: but this collective method usually allowed it to be overcome in the end, thereby increasing the authority of the commissioners and the willingness of the peasantry to collaborate with them. Through this system of land distribution, the peasants themselves played an essential role in arguing their case and arriving at a solution that conformed to their traditions and requirements. This gave the whole process a strength that no state authority could have transmitted.

Marte R. Gómez, a member of one of these commissions, later recalled a typical story concerning the demarcation of land between the villages of Yautepec and Anenecuilco. General Zapata personally attended this discussion.

> "We reached the place where representatives of the two villages were assembled," Gómez writes. "He [Zapata] called over the old men who had been brought as experts. He listened with particular deference to Mr. Pedro Valero, showing respect for his age and his past struggle to defend the Yautepec lands against Atlihuayan hacienda. Then he turned to the engineer Rubio, and incidentally to myself: 'The villagers say that this stone-wall marks the boundary, so would you please draw its outline for me. You engineers can be very fond of your straight lines, but this wall will mark the boundary even if you have to work six months measuring all its twists and turns.' "

In March 1915 Zapata wrote to the Conventionist president, Roque González Garza: "The agrarian question has been solved once and for all. On the basis of their land deeds, the various villages in the state have taken possession of the land in question."

At the same time, Palafox kept control of land that was not distributed to the villages. His plan was to expropriate all this land without compensation, so as to meet the future needs of the peasantry or to satisfy collective requirements.

Marte R. Gómez explains that although the text of the Ayala Plan had not been changed since 1911, the underlying principles had grown considerably more radical. "In all justice," he writes, "it should also be recognized that General Zapata's promises in 1911, when he signed the Ayala Plan, were different from what he intended to practice in 1915 through his agrarian commissions. We were simply asked to draw the boundaries between different villages. It did not occur to anyone that we should pick up the hacienda plans and identify the two-thirds of their property that should be respected."

Palafox's measures went still further, involving nationalization without compensation of the Morelos sugar mills and distilleries. On the basis of decrees ratified in 1914, Zapata set these mills in operation as state enterprises. As soon as Palafox assumed office as minister of agriculture, he ordered that repair work should start on mills abandoned by their former owners and damaged by war, plunder, and neglect. By early March 1915, four of these were already functioning under the management of senior Zapatist officers: Temixco, under General Genovevo de la O; Hospital, under General Emigdio Marmolejo; Atlihuayan, under General Amador Salazar; and Zacatepec, under General Lorenzo Vázquez. Generals Modesto Rangel, Eufemio Zapata, and Maurilio Mejía later took charge of reopened mills at Puente, Cuatlixco, and Cuahuixtla, respectively. The profits that began to appear were handed over to Zapatist headquarters and used for military expenditures and assistance to war widows.

This kind of agrarian socialism, however, met an obstacle in the smallholder customs and inclinations of the peasant base. Having newly acquired their land, the peasants tended to revive the cultivation of subsistence crops (kidney beans, chickpeas, maize, vegetables) or the rearing of poultry—all of which could easily be sold in local markets. Zapata waged a campaign to convince at least some peasants that they should not merely grow vegetables but also plant cane for the sugar industry. In order to encourage this, he organized loans or grants of money and seed. "If you go on sowing chillies, onions and tomatoes," he told the peasants of Villa Ayala, "you will never escape the poverty in which you have always lived.

So you ought to plant cane, as I have advised you." Yet he seems to have had only limited success, and the further evolution of the war made it impossible to continue the experience.

All these measures and dispositions, involving state ownership of the centers of industrial production and individual or communal peasant ownership of the base, received codification in a law of October 1915 adopted by the Executive Council during a recess of the full Convention.[3] Inspired by Palafox and almost certainly drafted by him, this was the peak of Zapatism's socialist-style legislation. Emiliano Zapata's decree of September 8, 1914, had already formulated the essential principle that property belonging to enemies of the revolution should be used to buy out other landowners entitled to compensation.

Although these decrees therefore covered all capitalists and big landowners, they did not clarify whether industrial, as opposed to agrarian, property expropriated in this way should subsequently take the form of state enterprises, or whether it should revert to private ownership. Nevertheless, the case of the Morelos sugar complexes and distilleries, converted into de facto state enterprises or "national factories" (to use Zapata's expression), suggests that the agrarian expropriations would have followed a socialist dynamic if the Zapatist regime had had a pathway to the future. The history of other countries, especially Cuba, would confirm this many years later.

Palafox's agrarian law was the juridical expression of the land redistribution measures that the peasantry, in collaboration with the agrarian commissions, had already been taking in Morelos. Although the surviving fiction of a Conventionist government gave it a national form, its real field of application did not go beyond Zapatist territory. Still, it was more radical than any other agrarian reform law in Latin America, with the exception of the Cuban decrees of 1961 and later. Like all Zapatist legislation, it took care to leave ample room for the initiative of peasants and villages.

The preamble to the agrarian law begins by relating the law to the Ayala Plan. The initial Zapatist program, it declares, "concentrated the burning aspirations of the insurgent armed people, especially their agrarian demands which are the innermost source and supreme goal of the Revolution." Consequently, "it is urgently necessary to give these principles of the Plan a duly regulated form, so that they may pass straight into practice as general and immediately applicable laws." These references to the Ayala Plan underline the fact that the essential ideas of the agrarian law were already contained in Zapata's 1911 program. The revolution merely developed and enriched them, making them a reality through the distribution of the land.

The preamble concludes with this statement:

> The exercise of any public office in the present times imposes a sacred duty to perform revolutionary work, and yet not a few authorities are far from discharging this duty and thereby show that they are not identified with the revolution. They refuse to promote the measures taken for the economic and social emancipation of the people, making common cause with reactionaires, landowners and other exploiters of the working classes. In order to clarify where they stand, it is therefore necessary for the government to make a forthright statement that it will consider as hostile to the cause any authority which, forgetting its character as an organ of the Revolution, does not effectively assist in the triumph of the ideals of the cause.

Article 1 then declares: "Communities or individuals which have been despoiled of fields, woodland and waters shall have them restored if they possess legal deeds dated before the year 1856, so that they may immediately enter into possession of their property." Article 2 prescribes the form in which these rights should be claimed.

By virtue of article 3, "the Nation recognizes the traditional, historical right of villages, hamlets and communities of the Republic to possess and administer their communally owned lands [*sus terrenos de común repartimiento y sus ejidos*] in the form they consider most advantageous."

Article 4 defines the rights of smallholders: "The Nation recognizes the unquestionable right of every Mexican to own and cultivate an expanse of land whose produce shall allow him to cover the needs of himself and his family. For the purpose of creating small-scale property, all the land in the country shall be expropriated by reason of public utility and with appropriate compensation—the only exceptions being land owned by villages, hamlets and communities, and landed property which, not exceeding the legal maximum, is to remain in the possession of its current owners." Article 5 establishes the maximum that may be owned by "proprietors who are not enemies of the Revolution." There is a table of eighteen categories, ranging from "prime-quality irrigated land in a warm climate" (with a limit of 100 hectares), through "poor-quality seasonal land in a temperate climate" (200 hectares) and "poor pastureland" (1,000 hectares), to "uncultivated land in the North of the Republic" (with the absolute maximum of 1,500 hectares). Article 7 stipulates that land in excess of these limits "shall be expropriated by reason of public utility, with appropriate compensation based on the 1914 fiscal census, and at a time and in a form prescribed by regulation."

However, article 6 is the clearest and most decisive: "The rural holdings of enemies of the revolution are declared national property." In other words, they were nationalized without compensation.

The same article goes on to define "enemies of the Revolution for the purposes of this law." The list includes *científicos* or supporters of Porfirio Díaz; officials of Díaz or Huerta who "acquired property by fraudulent or immoral means"; "politicians, public servants and businessmen" who enriched themselves under the Díaz regime by carrying out "felonious operations or granting concessions especially harmful to the nation"; supporters of Huerta; and "high members of the clergy who helped to sustain the usurper Huerta." The final category is so broad that it covers virtually all the big agrarian and industrial property owners of the time: "g) Those who directly or indirectly assisted the dictatorial governments of Díaz and Huerta and other hostile governments in their struggle against the Revolution. Also included in this clause are all those who supplied funds or war-taxes to such governments, sustained or subsidized newspapers fighting the Revolution, attacked or denounced supporters of the Revolution, carried out divisive activity among the revolutionary forces, or in any other way entered into complicity with governments combating the revolutionary cause."

According to article 8, the Ministry of Agriculture and Land Colonization would appoint commissions to establish which persons in each state were enemies of the Revolution under the terms of article 6 and therefore "liable to the penalty of confiscation, to be applied forthwith." A single appeal could be made to the Special Land Tribunals, whose creation was signalled in article 9.

Article 10 stipulated that all land acquired under articles 5 and 6 should be "divided into lots and distributed among those Mexicans who request it, preference being given to peasants in all such cases." Each lot was to be sufficiently large to satisfy "the needs of one family." Articles 11 and 13 establish the methods of implementation, giving absolute priority in adjudication to "those who are presently sharecroppers or tenants of small farms."

Articles 14 and 15 state that land allocated to communities or individuals "is not alienable and cannot be mortgaged in any way," and that the rights over such property can only be transmitted "through legitimate inheritance."

Many of the remaining articles, numbers 16 to 35, defined the authority of the Ministry of Agriculture and Land Colonization, concentrating such great power in the hands of the minister for agriculture, then Manuel Palafox, that it effectively involved a revolutionary dictatorship along Jacobin lines.

Article 16 states: "In order that this law may be executed in the most rapid and adequate manner, the Ministry of Agriculture and Land Colonization shall have the exclusive power to implement the agrarian principles contained in the law, and to learn and direct all the affairs of the branch. This does not involve an attack on the sovereignty of the individual states, but is merely designed to ensure that the ideals of the Revolution are speedily applied to improve conditions for the disinherited farmers of the Republic."

Articles 17 and 18 resolve that the Ministry of Agriculture, and it alone, shall establish agricultural colonies and create a National Irrigation and Construction Service.

Article 19 decrees: "The woodlands are declared national property, and the Ministry of Agriculture shall ensure their inspection in a form regulated by it. They shall be exploited, according to the communal system, by the villages under whose jurisdiction they lie."

Articles 20 and 21 direct the Ministry of Agriculture to found an agricultural bank under its own exclusive management. To this financial end, stipulates article 22, "the Ministry of Agriculture and Land Colonization is authorized to confiscate or nationalize urban property, the equipment of nationalized or expropriated property, or manufactures of any kind, including the chattels, machinery and other objects therein, always provided that they belong to enemies of the Revolution." Article 27 adds that "20 per cent of the funds raised from the nationalized property specified in article 22 shall be used to pay compensation for expropriated property on the basis of the 1914 fiscal census." (The latter is the property belonging to nonenemies of the Revolution, as specified in article 5.) These financial measures have their origin in Palafox's letter to Atenor Sala of September 1914.

Article 23 cancels all existing agricultural concessions and authorizes the Ministry of Agriculture to sanction "those which it judges beneficial for the people and the government." Article 24 further authorizes it to establish "regional schools for agriculture and forestry, as well as experimental stations."

Articles 25 and 26 lay down an obligation to till the newly allocated lands, ordering that they be forfeited if, without justification, they are not cultivated for two years.

Articles 28 and 29 authorize smallholders to form production or marketing cooperatives, but it debars these from becoming share companies or involving anyone who is not a direct agricultural producer.

Articles 32, 33, and 34 declare all waters to be national property and prioritize their use for agricultural purposes. The thirty-fifth and final article renders null and void "all contracts involving the alienation of property owned by enemies of the revolution."

This is followed by a final stipulation designed to ensure that the villages themselves immediately apply the law. In effect, it gives legal sanction to land distribution from below, and even encourages the peasants to implement it without waiting for the central authorities to intervene. Here, as in the whole text, can be seen the profound difference from the Carranzist agrarian law of January 1915.

"All municipal authorities of the Republic," states this article, "are under an obligation to fulfill and make others fulfill the dispositions of this law, without losing time or invoking any excuse. They must immediately place villages and individuals in possession of land and other property belonging to them under the terms of this law, even though the Agrarian Commissions appointed by the Ministry of Agriculture and Land Colonization may later make appropriate rectifications. Let it be understood that municipal authorities which fail or are negligent in their duty will be considered enemies of the Revolution and severely punished."

The law is dated October 28, 1915, Cuernavaca, and signed by Manuel Palafox, minister of agriculture and land colonization; Otilio E. Montaño, minister of public education and the arts; Luis Zubiria y Campa, minister of finance and public credit; Jenaro Amezcua, representing the War Ministry; and Miguel Mendoza L. Schwerdfegert, minister of labor and justice.[4]

The importance of Palafox's agrarian law resides not in its effects— which did not have time to make themselves felt—but in its programmatic content. Although it merely condensed the peasants' actions into general legal articles, its various dispositions amounted to a clear-out government program. The Convention government, however, was not only a fiction as a national entity, but had already split into Villist and Zapatist wings; while the Northern Division, the only military force that could have guaranteed its existence and enforced the agrarian law, had already suffered its decisive series of defeats.

Nevertheless, this program set forth a full-scale transformation of the country, with a revolutionary dictatorship based upon liquidation of the latifundia and land redistribution under the control of the peasants' local organs of power. It was not a socialist but a radical-Jacobin program. Yet it established a dynamic that corresponded to the anticapitalist thrust of the Mexican peasant war—*a petty-bourgeois dictatorship* from above, wedded to *mass initiative* from below and an onslaught on the enemy involving *expropriation without compensation*. This combination had set up a socialist dynamic which, above all in 1915, magnified the original revolutionary import of the Ayala Plan. The new law would have undergone a similar revolutionary inflection as it was applied from below in accordance with its final section.

However, it was issued at a time when the main task facing the Zapatists was to defend the gains already achieved. By October 28 they had long since abandoned the capital, and the Convention had entered its phase of disintegration. In fact, it was the minority Zapatist wing that approved the law, profiting from the fact that the Convention was not then in session.

The national ebb of the revolution was already visible to all. On October 19, the United States had recognized the Carranza administration as the only legitimate government of Mexico. At the end of the month, Villa was leading the remnants of the Northern Division in their final retreat across the Chihuahua Mountains. The agrarian law therefore signalled that the most radical fraction was trying to accelerate on paper what it was losing in the real struggle. Hence the law's air of unreality, which, as we shall see, went together with Palafox's personal sense of exasperation.

It is possible that Palafox was seeking to leave behind some codification of his ideas on the country's government. But it is also likely that he believed in the law's magical capacity to stimulate the revolution, just as Villa hoped to revive it a few months before with a military victory over Obregón. The law should really have been issued in December 1914, at the height of the revolution, as a Conventionist government program underpinning a military offensive against Veracruz.

Unlike so many projects in the Mexican Revolution, however, the law was not merely a theoretical lucubration. It was actually applied to the lands and sugar mills of Morelos, being complemented by other measures that established forms of village self-government and decision making. Its importance lies in the fact that it expressed a revolutionary social reality and the urge to extend that reality to the whole country.[5]

In order to gauge its significance, we should remember that all this happened during World War I. There was nowhere in the world anything that could serve as a precedent. Although Palafox may or may not have been familiar with the theoretical texts, he could not build on any actual experience. The Paris Commune, which had taken nationalization measures, armed the people, and introduced citizens' government, was a remote and fleeting episode. Its world echo did, to be sure, reach Mexico. Yet there is no evidence that it had more than a faint impact on Zapata, not to mention the peasants of Morelos. Perhaps some history of the Commune had figured in the reading of Palafox or other Zapatist intellectuals. But their rhetoric, even the choice of the name "Convention," harked back more to the Great French Revolution.

Had it not been for the socialist-type positions of the radical wing, however, they could never have been generalized in the form of a juridical and programmatic text. Palafox and his fellow radicals proved capable of this task, even though Gutiérrez and the urban core of the Convention had deserted the cause, and even though they were themselves already divided from the Villists.

In this period, Zapatism entrenched itself in its peasant state, abandoned by unstable allies and dependent solely upon the armed villages of Morelos. It remained alone: this was at once its weakness and its strength. The Morelos peasants and agricultural workers created a commune of which the precedent was Paris 1871. They established it not on paper but in reality. If the Zapatist agrarian law was so important, this is because it revealed a radical wing that going beyond the local peasant horizon, had the will to remold the whole country.

In their home territory, the Zapatists created an egalitarian society with communal roots (very different from the individualist utopia of "rural democracy"), and they maintained it until they finally lost power. Whereas the radical Constitutionalists of the Querétaro Congress called themselves Jacobins, the radical Zapatists might with as much justice have called themselves "the Equals." For they were to the Querétaro Jacobins what Gracchus Babeuf's "Equals" had been to the Jacobins of the French Convention—except that the more rural Zapatists were not a conspiratorial group in the line of the French Revolution, but the leaders of a peasant revolution that had assumed local power and still aspired to national power.

The struggle of the Morelos Commune was the most far-reaching episode of the Mexican Revolution. In order to erase every trace of its existence, the Carranzist army therefore had to exterminate half the Morelos population, with the same wild fury that Thiers's troops displayed against the workers of Paris in 1871.

While the peasant revolution was following its course in Zapatist territory, the defection of Eulalio Gutiérrez led to a continual decline in the political power of the Convention and a corresponding rise in internal strife and intrigue. Early in April 1915, when the Convention returned to a Mexico City abandoned by Obregón's Operational Army for the central battlefields, a conflict erupted between Palafox and the new Conventionist president, Roque González Garza. At the beginning of May, Palafox had to step down. Zapata was so angry at the turn of events that, breaking with his usual custom, he made a special journey to the capital in an unsuccessful effort to have Palafox reinstalled. It was to be the last time he entered Mexico City. A month later, González Garza was defeated in the Convention and had to resign. Palafox retained his post at the Ministry of Agriculture, but within a government weaker than ever before.

In the North, Villa had already lost the two battles of Celaya. In the South, Zapata had his headquarters in the small town of Tlaltizapán—true capital of a state where the *catrines* dared not tread, or, if they did, were soon put out of circulation.[6] Womack condenses the graphic description of the town given by a North American agent who met Zapata in May 1915:

> Here, unlike in Mexico City, there was no busy display of confiscated luxury, no gleeful consumption of captured treasure, no swarm of bureaucrats leaping from telephone to limousine, only the regular measured round of native business. The days Zapata passed in his offices in an old rice mill at the northern edge of the town, hearing petitions, forwarding them to Palafox in Mexico City or ruling on them himself, deciding strategy and policy, dispatching orders. In the evenings he and his aides relaxed in the plaza, drinking, arguing about plucky cocks and fast and frisky horses, discussing the rains and prices with farmers who joined them for a beer, Zapata as always smoking slowly on a cigar.[7]

When in June 1915 Obregón routed the Northern Division in León, military activity in the South was at a purely local level, at the most involving attacks on the supply routes between Veracruz and the Operational Army forces. On July 11, Pablo González occupied Mexico City, and the Convention withdrew to maintain its ever more fictitious existence in Toluca. Some days later, the Carranzist troops again hastily abandoned the city to the Zapatists in order to stem Fierro's attack on Hidalgo. But they returned to take the capital on August 2, this time holding it for good. Villa had already suffered in Aguascalientes the last of his four successive defeats, and Obregón was in vigorous pursuit of his retreating army. Zapata then resumed his military harassment of the forces in the capital, and at the end of September he took the Necaxa electric power station on the very outskirts of the city. But he was very quickly forced to surrender it, while the Carranzists established firm control over the whole Mexico Valley.

The Convention finally split up on October 10 in Toluca, the Villists going to the North and the Zapatists taking refuge in Cuernavaca. Palafox there reorganized the Convention as if it were still the legitimate national government. But on October 19, Washington officially recognized the Carranza government and prohibited the sale of arms and ammunition to any other faction. Although this did, of course, correspond to the new relationship of forces, it above all involved a political decision to support Carranza's side. Whatever our past differences, Washington seemed to be saying, the U.S. government now recognizes the Carranzists as "the party of order" in the Mexican civil war.

This in turn accelerated the regrouping of all the property-owning classes behind Carranza's fight against the peasant "bandits" in the North and South. At this point, then, his government could count on support, varying in enthusiasm, sincerity, and durability, from quite a wide spectrum of forces. At one end of the spectrum were the workers of the Casa del Obrero Mundial; peasants attracted by the law of 1915; the radical petty bourgeois who later formed the Querétaro Jacobins; young officers who, like Lázaro Cárdenas, would be in the forefront of the new revolutionary rise in the 1930s; and young Constitutionalist Army men, such as Obregón, Calles, and Aarón Sáenz, who were eager for riches and would become the nucleus of the new bourgeoisie. At the other end were the Mexico City industrialists, big landowners who hoped to recover property in Morelos or at least to preserve their urban property, and the government of the United States.

Against this heterogeneous front, the Zapatist movement stood alone and encircled in its home territory, proving the depth and tenacity of its revolution. The Morelos peasantry, led by Zapata and other military leaders, had entrenched itself on the land, created its own village authorities, and entered a military organization that was half-army, half-militia. Apart from the peasants, only a tiny handful of urban intellectuals had rallied to the cause, becoming, in a sense, its loudspeakers within Zapata's political general staff.

The most intransigent, and hence at that moment the most important, of these intellectuals was Manuel Palafox. He was the dominant figure in the Zapatist Convention. Abandoned by, or isolated from, all its insecure allies, the Zapatist leadership again moved to the left. But whereas the revolution had been in full national flood in October 1914, it was in general decline by October 1915. In that crucial twelvemonth, Morelos had carried out the deepest revolution in Mexican history; and yet, all the efforts of the Zapatist leadership had been unable to discover a national way forward.

Thus, although the national ebb of the revolution had removed the blocking power of unstable allies, allowing Palafox to promulgate his agrarian law through the Cuernavaca Convention, it had also deprived him of the nationwide forces that could translate it into reality. This was the internal contradiction of the agrarian law and the Mexican peasant revolution as a whole.

In such a violent and confused civil war, however, there is never a watertight division between the camps. Zapatism materially rested upon the social, political, and military organization of the Morelos peasantry, but its social forces were actually rather broader. In Constitutionalist areas, the peasantry and some of the urban workers, as well as impoverished petty-bourgeois layers, still opposed the Carranzist government in a thousand different ways, denying it support and following with sympathy or hope the tenacious struggle in the South. Although Obregón's military campaign against Villa had been a thundering success—barely eight months between Celaya and Hermosillo and Fronteras—the campaign against Zapatism was to be long and costly for the Carranza government.

Furthermore, the broad Carranzist front included various forces in its ranks. One sector was under the influence of Zapatism and its agrarian principles; while another preferred to attract the Zapatist leaders through concessions, knowing that war in the South would not pit them against a conventional army like the Northern Division, but enmesh them in a struggle with a whole population strengthened by recent agrarian and social conquests. When the military decision was taken, then, the operational command was not given to Obregón, the most brilliant Constitutionalist military leader. The man who headed the war would be Pablo González, not the most competent but certainly the most reactionary and bloodthirsty of Carranza's generals.

In October 1915, the political confrontation between the two sides had not yet acquired a sharp cutting-edge. The Constitutionalist left, ideologically influenced by Zapatism, was a factor restraining military attack, but it also encouraged defection from a Zapatist periphery disoriented by the growing lack of prospects for the peasant revolution. Local leaders in Puebla and Mexico State began to accept the government amnesty. The most recent supporters, who had rallied to Zapata at the height of the revolution, were the first to abandon the southern ranks. Naturally it was a one-way flow.

The situation did, however, arouse hopes in the Zapatist general staff that they could make a political intervention in the conflict between Constitutionalist tendencies. For their part, the Zapatists then displayed three clear currents: Manuel Palafox represented the left, Antonio Díaz Soto y Gama the center, and Gildardo Magaña the conciliationist right. At the time, Palafox still held the leadership with the support of Díaz Soto y Gama. Zapata gave his backing to this leadership. But whereas Palafox tended to reject any negotiation, and Magaña waited for better times to exercise his conciliatory talents, Díaz Soto y Gama thought that political concessions could be used to influence the Carranzist internal struggle and to win fresh allies. It was an illusory hope, but no more so than the plan for nationwide application of Palafox's agrarian law.

A *Manifesto to the Nation*, probably drafted by Díaz Soto y Gama, appeared at almost the same time as the agrarian law. It exclusively attacked the big landowners, and gave a place to "industrialists, tradesmen, mine-owners, businessmen and all the active entrepreneurial elements who open new paths for industry and provide jobs for large groups of workers." This document was effectively counterposed to the agrarian law. It could not fail to weaken the propaganda impact of this law among the poor urban layers. Nor was there any chance that it would win support from the rich or middle sectors. For these could see that the "ample guarantees" were being offered by the Carranza government, not by the southern peasant revolution, which had expropriated the land and sugar mills and shot or hanged *catrines* without even asking to which of "all the other social layers" they belonged.

In late 1915, having shattered the Northern Division, the Carranza government forces turned their attention to Morelos. In November they announced a campaign to put an end to Zapatism "once and for all." Zapata made defensive preparations and transferred to his own headquarters the primitive munitions factory the Southern Liberation Army ran in Atlihuayan. Partly as a result of the U.S. embargo, the supply of war materiel was then so low that spent Mauser or 30–30 cartridges were being fitted with pieces of tram-wire instead of bullets.

The government announcement first produced a psychological effect, prompting more officers to desert in all the weaker zones of the Southern Liberation Army, and fueling mistrust, rivalry, and conflict among those who remained. Nearly all the members of agrarian commissions now crossed the lines and returned to the capital, while a very small number took up arms alongside the Zapatists. Redistribution work in Morelos was already complete, and the specialists had either to withdraw or to exchange their theodolite for a gun.

The Zapatist old guard, sustained by the peasant resolve to defend their territory, reacted energetically against the defection of eleventh-hour supporters. Just as the Carranzists were starting their offensive into Morelos from Acapulco and Guerrero State in the southwest, General Genovevo de la O launched a violent counterattack. His men recovered all the lost ground and forced the enemy to take up defensive positions in Acapulco at the end of 1915. But the pressure continued to mount on Morelos from forces based in the capital. The Carranza government adopted a broad political strategy, rather than a purely military tactic, when it dissolved the Red Battalions and opened its twin-pronged offensive against the workers' movement and the southern revolution.

Ever since the major defections began, Genovevo de la O had repeatedly accused the Conventionist minister of war, General Pacheco, of being involved in treacherous activity. At the end of February 1916, however, Zapata authorized Pacheco to hold secret talks with Pablo González, whose troops were stationed on the borders of Morelos. Suddenly, on March 13, Pacheco surrendered his positions and retreated with his troops, thereby allowing the Constitutionalists to advance until they were stopped by de la O some twelve kilometers from Cuernavaca. Still Zapata did not believe the charges of treachery. Pacheco then grew bolder and proposed an attack on Jojutla in order to capture the Convention members who had withdrawn from Cuernavaca at the time of danger. But Genovevo de la O caught him in the act and, without more ado, had him shot. The demise of the war minister was a symptom of the crisis within the Zapatist movement, boding ill for the battles just ahead.

In these days, the Convention gave a last sign of life. A Plan of Revolutionary Political and Social Reforms was launched in Jojutla on April 18, 1916, most probably inspired and drafted by Díaz Soto y Gama. A programmatic expression of the October *Manifesto to the Nation*, it was yet another grave token of the Zapatist political crisis. Unstable supporters were defecting, the agrarian commissions returning to Mexico City, the authors of documents retreating and vacillating. Only the villages and the movement's military leaders were preparing for resistance.

The Jojutla Plan was a program far behind the advanced Zapatist texts and even the Ayala Plan, which it nevertheless mentions in passing. Its clear aim was to give the southern revolution a "respectable" and "legal" character. The principal reforms were to be the development of smallholdings, compulsory purchase of landed property required by the government, labor legislation to protect the workers, a divorce law, reform of the education system, changes in limited company law "so as to prevent abuses by management boards and to protect the rights of minority shareholders" (a matter of great concern to the southern peasantry!), some timid fiscal measures in relation to foreign companies, and "adoption of the parliamentary system as the governmental form of the Republic." The plan did not bear the signatures of Zapata, Palafox, or Genovevo de la O. In fact, Díaz Soto y Gama, later to be a deputy in the Obregón regime, was the only significant political figure to sign the text. The Convention was nearing the end of its existence.

By contrast, all the combat forces were preparing for the defense of Morelos, encircled by thirty thousand men under Pablo González. By then he had won his first "battle" by occupying the Casa del Obrero Mundial headquarters at the Mexico City Jockey Club. Events in the North, where Villa's raid on Columbus had just given the United States a pretext for intervention, did not relieve the pressure on Morelos. The Zapatists evacuated the villages, preparing for a long struggle in the highlands. Cuernavaca itself was surrounded by Constitutionalist troops on April 29 and fell to a direct assault on May 2. All the main population centers were captured in the next four days, only Jojutla, Tlaltizapán, and a couple of other towns remaining in Zapatist hands.

The Carranzists entered Morelos as an occupation army. Like the federal troops of General Robles, they stole, burned, and pillaged wherever they passed. Hundreds upon hundreds of prisoners were shot—combatants and noncombatants, men and women, children and old people. Whole towns flooded the roads to the high mountain villages, where González's troops could not reach them.[8] Thousands of prisoners were sent to Mexico City, there to be deported as slave labor for the murderous henequen plantations of Yucatán.

In June 1916, Tlaltizapán fell with its munitions factory and greater booty into the hands of González. The Carranzists there killed 132 men, 112 women, and 42 children—a full-scale massacre. Emiliano Zapata and his remaining men left to organize resistance in the mountains. Morelos was occupied territory.

At the same time, the Carranza government was engaging in those open clashes with the workers' movement which led to the general strike of July 31, 1916. But the Mexico City workers and Morelos peasants were fighting on two totally isolated and distant fronts. Unable to help each other, they were separately defeated by the Constitutionalist central government.

With all the population centers occupied, Pablo González reported to the Ministry of War in Mexico City that the Morelos campaign was over. His officers now devoted themselves to systematic plunder, shipping everything movable to the capital and selling it on the black market for their own gain. Livestock, sugar, alcohol, sugar mill machinery, the contents of the munitions factory, furniture— all this could be, and was, carried off and sold. The inhabitants of Morelos were subjected to systematic persecution: murder, imprisonment, rape, exile, a whole wave of terror designed to subjugate them and to facilitate the plunder. In this way, the new bourgeois army that emerged from the revolution inaugurated one of its most constant practices.[9] The Mexican people erected its own indelible monument to Carranza and his officers by coining the term "to carrancize" (*carrancear*) as a synonym of "to plunder."

The González military administration further cancelled all the land redistribution work of the agrarian commissions and announced that new measures would be taken in accordance with Carranza's agrarian law of January 1915. Nothing would ever come of this promise.

The Carranzist terror did not subdue the whole state, however, but only the centers of population. For six years the Zapatists had redistributed the land to the villages, eradicated the latifundia, and turned the sugar mills into "national factories" under the management of their own representatives. Now they were preparing to defend these gains, rooted in their social relations, against the force of military occupation. The experience of revolution had imparted a sense of solidarity to the whole of social life. No purely military action could destroy this social fabric in a couple of months. The revolution was still bubbling throughout the country, and the capitalist norms imposed by the Carranzist army had to be reasserted not just through military domination but at the level of social relations.

It seemed to González that he had won, since the military strike was followed by a brief period in which his authority was unchallenged. The Zapatists, however, were busy reorganizing their army. They dispersed their twenty thousand men, who could no longer fight in the mode of a centralized army, and returned to small guerrilla detachments one or two hundred strong. These units spread over the whole region, restoring their base in the local population and establishing themselves in inaccessible mountain camps. The first attacks and ambushes had already begun by early July 1916. The people of Morelos fought with them, as lookouts, informers, or suppliers of food and shelter, while many would take up arms for a single action and then return to work in the fields. The guerrilla experience against the federal army of Díaz, Madero, and Huerta was now applied by the Zapatist army. The Carranzist troops soon felt that they were caught in a trap, and that the state was still in Zapata's hands outside the main centers and lines of communication.

At the same time, a new selection process was taking place within the Zapatist movement. Now that the plan was to no longer return to the capital, but only to defend the peasants' gains and their very villages and land, some of Zapata's officers felt reluctant to face the uncertainty that had seemed a thing of the past in 1914. Zapata, himself, had to send a number of letters and circulars condemning officers who wanted to continue living off the villages rather than fight the war. Such people, he said, are not worthy to lead "an armed movement which is fighting for the good of the people, not for the formation of a new class of useless idlers." He therefore decreed the expulsion from the Southern Liberation Army of "all senior and junior officers and soldiers who, instead of fighting the enemy, use their weapons to commit abuses against the village population and to carry off their scant means of subsistence," or who retreat without authorization in the face of the enemy. Lorenzo Vázquez, an officer in Zapata's army since 1911, was expelled in mid-August for his lack of fighting spirit. A short time before, Vázquez, Montaño, and Pacheco (the ex-minister of war shot by Genovevo de la O) had accused Palafox and Díaz Soto y Gama of preventing an agreement with the Constitutionalists and being responsible for the difficult position of the Zapatist movement. Thus, Vázquez's inactivity had a political rather than a personal cause and expressed the sharp struggle within the movement.

In September 1916, Zapata's reorganized guerrilla forces repeatedly struck at the Constitutionalists throughout Morelos. The resistance was gradually breaking up the occupation army. Now, however, unlike in the 1914–16 period, there was no clear prospect of a national revolutionary victory. The energy came solely from the peasants' stubborn will to defend existing conquests and to resist a better-armed enemy whose rule stretched over the key centers of the country and most of their own territory. It was an enemy which, for part of the population outside Morelos, nevertheless embodied certain gains of the revolution, and, for another part, represented the only serious hope of a nationwide restoration of order. The workers had been defeated in the strike of July–August 1916, and broad anti-Carranzist sections of the population, though sympathetic to Villa's and Zapata's fight, were reduced to forms of resistance they had earlier used against the *federales*.

The left-wing tendency in Zapatism, which had drawn up the great national plans in the period of ascent, could not be the political expression of the local resurgence in Morelos State. The tendency of Antonio Díaz Soto y Gama, this time represented by his brother Conrado, tried to reconcile the peasant goal of self-administration with the program endorsed by the Convention in Jojutla some months earlier. This attempt crystallized in a municipal government law designed to safeguard the existence and independence of village structures and communal administration, within a parliamentary-democratic perspective completely devoid of major "nationalizing reforms."

Still, when it came to local government, the sphere most directly related to village life, the law did propose a number of measures to ensure popular control through neighbors' assemblies. Other clauses stipulated that only local residents could be elected to the local council; that at the end of their one-year term, they could be re-elected only after an interval of two years; and that such important matters as "the alienation or acquisition of landed property, the approval of council salaries and expenditure, and contracts relating to street-lighting, paving, water supplies and other public services" should be submitted to the whole community for its approval. Furthermore, the law authorized the use of national tax revenue for local public works and self-government administration. By providing the financial means for villages to exercise the real power in their hands, it therefore effectively sanctioned a situation which, like the southern revolution as a whole, conflicted with the existence of a bourgeois central power.

At this time, about the middle of September 1916, General Pablo González issued a new order against the villages, directing that peasant families should gather in the main cities for deportation. In other words, he revived the "strategic hamlets" policy of Juvencio Robles, with the same illusion that this would destroy the roots of Zapatism.

The González terror did not indicate that he was on the point of overcoming resistance—quite the contrary. The Morelos peasantry sustained the new Zapatist counteroffensive, in a national situation which did not allow the Carranza government to assert its policy against the opposition echoed even in the Constitutionalist left wing. Carranza struck out at the July–August general strike, but in September he already had to make wage concessions to the workers. The U.S. punitive expedition brought more problems in the North, where resistance to the invasion grew among the people and a section of the Constitutionalist Army. The Constituent Congress, which met between December 1916 and January 1917, was an attempt to stabilize the Carranza government by reconciling the sharply divergent Constitutionalist tendencies in work on the Constitution itself. Finally, General Félix Díaz, Porfirio Díaz's nephew and one of the leaders of the 1913 military coup against Madero, had organized a rightist antigovernment rebellion in Oaxaca directed against the revolution *en bloc.* Díaz sought an alliance with Zapata; however, the peasant leader not only rejected the offer but ordered all Southern Liberation Army officers to refrain from establishing relations with Díaz or giving him any kind of recognition.

Thus, it was becoming ever more difficult to maintain the terror in Morelos. It was ever more apparent that the Zapatists controlled the countryside and were able to inflict frequent casualties on local garrisons. Yet the deportations and massacres continued. On September 30, Colonel Jesús Guajardo, the future murderer of Zapata, killed 180 men, women, and children in Tlaltizapán. They had allegedly refused to pay taxes, and they were supporters of Zapata.

By October, when Zapata stepped up his offensive, he is said to have had some five thousand men under arms, spread throughout the state and commanded by old-guard Zapatist officers. Instead of attacking local garrisons—which would have caused problems for the villagers—they conducted ever bolder raids on the railways, sugar mills, and factories, and on the areas surrounding the Federal District. On October 4, a Zapatist unit seized the Xochimilco pumping station, which supplied the capital with water. In November, they blew up a train within the Federal District. González's forces proved incapable of guaranteeing security even within the limits of the capital.

By December, the thirty thousand Constitutionalist troops who had occupied Morelos in May were demoralized and beginning to disintegrate. Believing that evacuation would soon be necessary, their officers worked round the clock to steal everything they could. The ranks had been whittled down by malaria, dysentery, and a typhoid epidemic, while the officers sold on the black market the meager supply of drugs that arrived from the capital. More than disease and officer corruption, however, it was the revolution itself that shook and dissipated González's army of occupation. Morelos's people laid political siege to the Constitutionalist troops stationed there, trying to win them over. Since the revolution was still alive, this stubborn force broke down the occupation army and caused its military withdrawal.

Zapata, who had already recovered Tlaltizapán, launched an offensive on December 1 against all the main centers in the state. Jojutla fell in the first attack, and at the end of the month González's troops began a formal retreat. At the same time, the Carranza tendency and the Jacobin wing of Constitutionalism were moving into their sharpest conflict at Querétaro over the key articles of the future Constitution. And, rather more important from a military point of view, a five thousand-strong Villist force captured Torreón City on December 22, 1916.

As González's ill-starred army retreated from Morelos, it came under constant attack from Zapata's forces. The guerrillas regained one main town after another: Cuautla on January 10, and the capital, Cuernavaca, a short time after. But although the Zapatist leadership was now full of illusions, the Constitutionalist withdrawal was only a respite, not the beginning of victory. It signalled that the military isolation of the southern revolution was not a social isolation from the climate in the rest of the country, and that the conditions were not ripe for the government to stamp out armed resistance. Weariness was growing in the ranks of the Morelos peasantry, yet the sorely tried population was still determined to fight after six years of war.

The Zapatists soon realized that their military and social forces did not permit them to go beyond the state borders. Having recovered Morelos, the southern revolution was still encircled. The U.S. punitive expedition had pulled out of northern Mexico. The social reforms written into the Querétaro Constitution had enlarged the government's base and temporarily resolved the factional struggle within the Carranzist movement. The central government had gained in stability. On a world scale, the war further accentuated the isolation of the Zapatist revolution.

During the late 1916 offensive against the Constitutionalists, Zapata saw that his forces required some form of political organization.

Experience showed that military organization was not enough to maintain popular cohesion, and that the traditional village structures had been completely overturned or eroded by deportations, massacres, and population transfers. Moreover, these forms of local power were quite inadequate for directly political tasks that went beyond village land problems.

Without using the name, Zapata was really thinking in terms of a political organization. But although everyone could agree on the Ayala Plan, it was not clear what else should serve as its programmatic basis. Hence the contradictory character of Zapata's proposal, as of other measures taken at this time. It sought to forge a closer link between the leadership around Zapata and a peasant base which, though supporting him, then had no organization other than traditional village structures or the guerrilla army.

A body along the lines suggested by Zapata was established in Tlaltizapán toward the end of November 1916: the Consultative Center for Revolutionary Propaganda and Unification. Its main leader was Antonio Díaz Soto y Gama; and among its fifteen founder-members were Palafox, Montaño, and Gildardo and Rodolfo Magaña. On the basis of contemporary documents, John Womack has given the most detailed account of its work. We can do no better than quote it at length:

> The consultants' duties were generally as Zapata had outlined them, to give the pueblos their bearings again. They were to deliver lectures in the villages on the mutual obligations of revolutionary troops and *pacíficos*; to give public readings and explanations of headquarters manifestos, decrees and circulars; and to mediate feuds between chiefs, between chiefs and pueblos, and between pueblos. And from this experience they were to advise headquarters in the framing of laws and reforms. Most important, they were to organize subsidiary juntas in all villages under revolutionary control, as Associations for the Defence of Revolutionary Principles.
>
> The first association Soto y Gama, Gildardo Magaña and

Enrique Bonilla set up on 12 December at Tochimilco. In the following weeks many others formed throughout southwestern Puebla and central and eastern Morelos. There they functioned as local branches of the Zapatista party, the first popular organizations both civilian and secular that had ever existed in many villages. Associates had no official authority, and they were under strict orders not to interfere with municipal government business; but in practice they dominated local society. On paper each association comprised four officers and six voting members, elected every four months by direct vote in the pueblo. Re-election for a year after leaving office was forbidden. Candidates had to be "revolutionary or at least to sympathize with the principles which the revolution defends." Other qualifications were local residence, majority of age, literacy, and no record of having exploited local people either from public office or through "influences . . . with past governments." But since only a few villages still contained ten such men not already in the Liberating Army, and even fewer had the forty whom a year's round of elections would require, the associations remained simple cadres. In almost all of them, the dominant figures were a few brothers or cousins who had retained local respect without having gone off to war. Together they filled maybe half the seats, which they traded around at each term.

The associates' responsibilities were various. Among them was that of taking part in "the elections of all classes of authorities, formulating candidacies which guarantee the interests of the pueblo, exhorting citizens to fulfill their electoral duties, and organizing them for the elections." The upshot was that associates controlled the irregular municipal elections in Morelos in 1917 and 1918 and probably exerted secret but nonetheless real influence in the regular elections in Puebla.

In routine matters the associates served as commissars. Their principal business was to make sure that the military respected the civil authorities. And they managed mediation in scores of disputes between municipal officials and chiefs of garrisons. The conflicts were usually over the control of local resources—crops, pasture,

draft animals, vacant plots. Because of all the migrations and reset-
tlements, it was harder now to say who had the best claim to use a
certain field or team of oxen. The soundest claim in a pueblo was a
reputation for having used the thing in question before. Yet the revolutionary troops, who had put no more than a rifle to use for the
past year, also deserved support or the means to support themselves,
and their *jefes* were quick to protect their interests. So rival authorities competed, each for its own constituency and each professedly
for the sake of the revolution. To specify the respective rights and
obligations of the villagers and the *guerrilleros*, the Tochimilco
associates sponsored negotiations between the town council and
Ayaquica's headquarters. Under a special charge to fulfill revolutionary promises on "the agrarian question," they obtained a treaty
on 21 December distinctly in the pueblo's interest. The agreement
became a model for other villages throughout the Zapatista zone.
And associates corresponded frequently to report on its working.
A warm camaraderie caught on among these commissars, who
began to fancy the notion that they were the true guardians of the
revolution.[10]

Womack then refers to the village education work of the Associations for the Defense of Revolutionary Principles, and calculates
that fifteen to twenty primary schools were created or re-created in
the first months of 1917. This was a feat no previous regime had
been able to achieve. The aims of the associations were, in their
own words, "to get propaganda into the bosom of the families and
to get the heads of these families to inculcate good principles
in their children and other relatives, to make them take an interest
in the Revolution and understand that on its triumph depends the
happiness of honest workingmen and the progress of Mexicans in
the material order as well as in the field of social and political liberties and rights and in the moral and intellectual order." In some
villages, night schools were also established for adults. Womack
concludes: "The academic lessons that students in the Zapatista
schools learned were rudimentary but still valuable. Besides, for

country folk the experience of hearing a teacher say that the resistance still going on was for the fatherland and for poor people, and that the Zapatistas were national heroes—this was unforgettable."[11]

As each village association gained experience, it assumed many of the tasks of the Consultative Center: to read and explain declarations from the revolutionary headquarters; to settle disputes between villagers; and to arrange talks by revolutionary lecturers. In short, it operated as a true peasant committee for all the political matters and everyday problems of peasant life—a distinction often difficult to draw. As long as these associations existed, they would constitute the Zapatist peasant political organization.

Its program, like all Zapatist policy after 1915, did not, of course, go beyond the horizon represented by Díaz Soto y Gama. However, the associations were important not for their policies but for the effort to build a political organization of the poor peasants. This is what they actually became in local village life.

The organization of village self-government was the other crucial aspect of the southern revolution at this time, firmly established in the decrees of the Tlaltizapán Zapatist headquarters. In reality, these decrees sprang from the villagers' own experience. Basing themselves on old traditions and the practice of collectively discussing community problems, the Zapatists created forms of organization and government not unlike the soviets the Russian Revolution was then reviving on the other side of the world.

In the law of March 1917 on the rights and obligations of villages and the Southern Liberation Army, the form of popular involvement in village administration was clearly laid down. Thus, the men of each village were to meet on the fifteenth of each month to discuss and decide on all the political affairs of the village. On the twentieth, delegates from such popular assemblies in each village of the municipal area would meet to take broader collective decisions, subsequently appointing delegates to a district meeting to be held on the first of the next month. This meeting would then deliberate and decide on all matters relating to the district as a whole. In counterposition to the system of secret elections and unmovable functionaries or deputies, this structure was a form of government completely different from that which the Convention had been intended to symbolize.

The law of March 1917 did no more than legalize, or give organic form to, a system the Morelos population had been operating ever since the southern revolution became the only power in the state.

Another decree, designed to check military abuses, established the rights of villages in relation to the commanders, officers, and soldiers of the Southern Liberation Army. Villages were to have the right not only to elect their local government bodies, but also to appoint people of their own choosing to the courts and the police force. Village authorities were empowered "to apprehend, disarm and deliver to headquarters" any commander, officer, or soldier who did not present his credentials from the appropriate commission. Army men were under an obligation to refrain from any interference in village political life or any personal levy of taxes. They had to respect the villagers' own distribution of the land, waters, and woodlands, and to obey the local customs and practices. Finally they were not allowed, on pain of court-martial, "to seize village or ex-hacienda land, since no armed individual, whether an officer or not, has a right to more than the land-area distributed to him."

The need for this legislation, nevertheless, was one of the many symptoms of those hard times: the villages were resisting, arms in hand if need be, the exactions of some out-of-control detachments of the Zapatist army.

Other decrees provided for the popular election of municipal functionaries and district presidents. The district was conceived as "a bond between the municipalities" which composed it. Villages were also to elect two unpaid, independent officials for a one-year term, with the function of representing and defending the village "in matters related to the land, woodlands and waters." These officials had to be residents of more than five years' standing, aged twenty-five years or more, and born in the village. One of their important tasks was to preserve the deeds and maps of communal land—those centuries-old documents which legally proved the existence of the village community as an entity with its own life and rights.

In early March, at a meeting of the Consultative Center in Tlaltizapán, it was agreed that no fictitious national authority would be created in place of the defunct Convention. Instead, the central Morelos government would be entrusted to the revolutionary headquarters, itself divided into departments of agriculture, war, education and justice, finance, and internal affairs. But the real government of the state remained with the local authorities, which continued to decide on the key questions of public works, the allocation of communal funds, relations with the Zapatist army, military contributions, education, and the distribution of land, woodlands, and waters.

While the nation was being shaken by tempestuous political and military upheavals, the Zapatists in Morelos had shattered the rule of the haciendas and transferred power to the villages throughout the territory of the state.

The Constitutionalist Army, however, was organizing its own power at the national level and surrounding the peasant state on all sides. In accordance with the Constitution of February 5, 1917, elections to Congress and the presidency took place on March 11. Apart from Morelos, where the Constitutionalists no longer held power, every state participated in the ballot. The duly elected president, Venustiano Carranza, assumed control of the war ministry on May 1, his predecessor, Alvaro Obregón, having temporarily withdrawn from public life and broken his links with Carranza. For his part, the unsuccessful "pacifier" of Morelos, Pablo González, resigned his command in July 1917 and took a temporary leave of absence.

Political isolation now began to do what González's army had been unable to achieve in Morelos. Although this was not directly expressed in daily village life, the pressure mounted every day on the political leadership of the movement. As the year progressed, the lack of perspective also sharpened the internal conflicts. Zapata himself left his secretaries to run affairs, writing a series of letters to prominent urban political figures in the illusory hope that the harsh encirclement of the state might be relieved. His ultimate objective was to reach an agreement that would preserve the conquests of the Morelos peasantry: land and village self-government. The Carranzist government, however, was concerned with dismantling precisely these gains. It might offer concessions—land for certain officers, an amnesty, political or military posts—but it could not leave standing the Zapatist land redistribution measures and the popular power that defended them.

In the internal struggle, Palafox continually lost ground to his ally, Díaz Soto y Gama; it was a far cry from his peak of power in late 1914 and early 1915, when he had promoted the agrarian commissions. By April 1917, everything indicated that he had entered a deep crisis of personal self-confidence and political perspective. Although he maintained a formal intransigence, this was no more than the reverse side of the crisis.

In May 1917, a Zapatist unit under Lorenzo Vázquez rebelled and tried to hold talks with Carranza. The revolt was quickly crushed by the Liberation Army and its leader hanged for treason. But other participants, now under arrest, accused Otilio Montaño of being the moving force behind the mutiny.

Some time before, Montaño had been removed from headquarters on account of intrigues and rivalry with Díaz Soto y Gama and Palafox. Even earlier, he had shown a conciliatory attitude in his reaction to the Huerta coup and in his close relations with Vázquez. Thus, although he loudly protested his innocence, he had lost his authority at headquarters and was unable to counter the testimony against him. The whole crisis of the Zapatist leadership burst forth in this incident.

It appears that Zapata was reluctant to have Montaño tried for treason and inevitably condemned to death. The former schoolmaster had, after all, been one of his first comrades-in-arms, and they had worked together on the Ayala Plan in 1911. Under pressure from the other secretaries, however, principally Díaz Soto y Gama and Palafox, he finally agreed to a trial. The court met on May 15, 1917, presided by Palafox. Zapata arranged to be away from Tlaltizapán, obviously so as not to have anything to do with the proceedings. Montaño continued to declare that he was the victim of a plot. But on May 18 the court sentenced him to death, and he was brought before a firing squad at midday.

A number of Zapatist officers continued to accept the government amnesty, some simply giving up the Liberation Army for a variety of business deals. The crisis even affected Zapata's brother, Eufemio, whose liking for alcohol had grown with the ebb of the revolutionary movement and fueled his irritability and lack of consideration toward both subordinates and fellow officers. One day in June 1917, in the middle of a drinking session, he suddenly exploded and hit the father of Sidronio Camacho, one of the leading officers under his command. Later, Camacho sought him out in the street, shot him to death, and then immediately passed over with his men to the Carranzists and accepted a government amnesty. Coming barely a month after the execution of Montaño, Eufemio's death in a street quarrel marked a new stage in the decline of the old Zapatist leadership.

The shooting of Montaño was also the end for Palafox. Unable to offer a new policy, he no longer even believed in the one he had previously advocated. Antonio Díaz Soto y Gama had not only displaced him as the dominant figure in the Zapatist leadership, but had increasingly pushed him aside in search of an alliance with Gildardo Magaña. From mid-1917 Magaña stepped up his efforts to negotiate a deal with the government and the opposition tendencies that would provide a bourgeois issue to the revolution. Palafox put up a last stand, denouncing the presence of "Carranzist spies" in Morelos. But he was not successful. Although some did not consciously realize it and others did not openly say it, everyone could see that the repression and shooting of "spies" would not prevent a rightward shift based on deep social causes. Indeed, such actions would merely worsen the climate of intrigue produced by political impasse and the disintegration of the political leadership of Zapatism.

The crisis even found expression in Zapata's own person. Womack quotes the testimony of one of his soldiers: "His natural taciturnity had changed into a somewhat neurasthenic sullenness, so that his guards were even afraid when he called them."

Magaña, who had received Zapata's approval for his attempts to negotiate, was naturally a rising influence in this situation. Acting from his political base in Tochimilco, he now initiated the first contacts with Carranzist leaders and with ex-Maderists like the Vázquez Gómez brothers, exiled in the United States. The political drift of these talks was revealed in a Zapatist declaration of early September 1917, which pushed the Ayala Plan into the background and called for the "integration" of all revolutionaries in the fight against the old *latifundistas*. At the same time, it clearly distanced itself from Félix Díaz's counterrevolutionary opposition which, with the financial support of old Porfirists, kept alive the Oaxaca rebellion in the name of the 1857 Constitution. However, the war did not stop for the negotiations. In November 1917, a fresh offensive brought Pablo González to the town of Cuautla.

In February 1918, Magaña went even further in his offer of talks. While maintaining contact with disaffected generals in many parts of the country, he sent an official note to the War Ministry, and hence to Carranza. In a nutshell, the memorandum proposed that if Zapatist authority were recognized in Morelos, the southern revolutionaries would accept Carranza's national government. Well aware that the Zapatists were in retreat, Carranza did not bother to answer. He could reach such deals with the bourgeois opposition, but no agreement was possible with the peasant revolution. For whatever the present situation, it might become a rallying center for the discontent then fueling Villa's guerrilla struggle in the north. Although Magaña's proposal contained no revolutionary demand and was in effect an act of submission to the government, Carranza was concerned not with the political ambitions of Magaña or other Zapatist leaders, but with the complete eradication of

all traces of the peasant revolution. What he wanted was unconditional surrender and the elimination of Emiliano Zapata; or, at the
very least, the disarming of the southern forces so that the national
army could restore property and order throughout the state of
Morelos. This was not what Magaña offered, and nor was it in his
power to do so. Everything suggests, however, that Carranza continued to hold open the possibility of negotiations and to feed
Magaña's hopes in other ways. Carranza was trying to gain time.
For time was on his side as the federal army completed its preparations for a fresh military offensive.

The official view was that the 1917 Constitution had secured
the victory of the revolution, and indeed many of Zapata's original
demands had been incorporated into the final text. Thus, whereas
the Morelos peasantry was essentially concerned with the land and
village self-government, the Constitution appeared to the petty-
bourgeois leaders of the movement as a permanent invitation to
join the "revolution-become-government," as it was then called.
The struggle for their remaining agrarian demands, which were
only formally the same as those of the peasantry, could then be
pursued within the legal limits of the official revolution.

In this situation, time also served to divide the Zapatist movement along class lines: on one side, the petty-bourgeois leaders and
a small layer of peasants either rich or in the process of enrichment; on the other side, the mass peasant base represented by
Emiliano Zapata and old-guard officers like General Genovevo de
la O. This division did not take the form of an open break or a
clear-cut internal struggle. Rather, the petty-bourgeois leaders mul-
tiplied their conciliationist letters, contacts, and declarations, while
the peasant leadership was unable to break the isolation of Morelos
by military means or to formulate a political alternative to such initiatives.

Like every national bourgeois government, Carranza played on
the isolation of the peasant movement. His military operations had
so far come unstuck against armed peasant resistance, or had
dissolved through contact with the revolutionary villages. But the

political offensive kept a steady pace, occasionally bolstered by fresh military action.

Palafox, already marginalized and politically defeated, underwent his final crisis in May 1918. The accusation was now flung in his face that past intransigence, of which he was the main symbol, had isolated Zapatism from the other currents of the revolution. In point of fact, his intransigence had not been a merely personal quality: it had reflected the rise of the peasant revolution, just as the crisis in 1918 reflected its decline. But whereas the peasantry faced adversity with guns, land, and village organization, Palafox's weakness, which in victory had expressed itself in arrogant behavior, now manifested itself in complete personal collapse. When, in the middle of it all, he was accused of being a homosexual, Zapata was so enraged that he very nearly had him shot. Only Gildardo Magaña eventually managed to restrain him, obviously fearing the scandal of such an incident a year after the shooting of Montaño. In the end, Palafox was removed from Zapatist headquarters in early May and sent to serve under Magaña at Tochimilco. A few months later, he deserted to Veracruz and placed himself under the command of General Manuel Peláez, a man in the pay of oil companies. His call for other Zapatist leaders to desert did not produce the slightest ripple, and his political ruination proved as total as the eclipse of his politics in an earlier period.[12]

Another symptom of the crisis of the southern revolution was the repeated clashes between Zapatist troops, mainly those commanded by fortuitous allies of Zapata, and the Morelos peasantry. In 1918 the villages grew reluctant to supply the contributions the officers demanded for their men, and on some occasions violence was used in support of these demands. At the same time, the disintegration of certain Southern Liberation Army units led to the appearance of roaming bandit groups. But the villagers, organized in militias and strengthened by the experience of self-government and the Associations for the Defense of Revolutionary Principles, put up armed resistance to the exactions and stubbornly defended their rights. In one typical case, a unit of Félix Díaz supporters was put to flight by militiamen from the village they had tried to tax. Although Zapata mediated in many conflicts and eventually upheld the villagers' right to armed self-defense, such incidents continued to undermine the solidity of the Zapatist camp.

In August, possibly on the advice of Díaz Soto y Gama, Zapata sent two letters to Obregón and urged him to rebel in order to defend "the conquests of the revolution" against "reaction." But although Obregón was then in opposition to Carranza, he sent no answer. In November, one month before Angeles rejoined Villa in Mexico, he also received a letter from Zapata at his Texas address. Further efforts were made to contact Pancho Villa in the North, and to seek support from Mexican politicians in exile or Carranzist dissidents inside the country. This whole policy assumed ever more unreal and desperate forms, carrying the preoccupations of the Zapatist political leadership ever further from the needs and urgent problems of the Morelos peasants. They wholeheartedly supported Zapata, but they had no interest or involvement in the political orientation of his secretaries. Yet Zapata continued to endorse this policy by signing letter after letter to the most diverse figures.

As Zapatism sank deeper into the mire, Zapata's physical existence became ever more of an obstacle to the deals his secretaries never tired of devising on his own authority. Although the precise form it would take was still open to question, Zapata's death was inexorably drawing nigh. The movement had forever lost its political radiance when its letters, notes, and public declarations dropped all reference to the Ayala Plan. An opportunity now had to be found for the removal of the living symbol of the peasants' revolutionary conquests.

Beyond its features as an armed peasant movement concentrating the aspirations of the whole Mexican Revolution, Zapatism expressed a will to raise itself to a national level and to become a form of people's power, at the same time seeking international support. This will appeared most clearly in Zapata's well-known letter drawing a parallel between the Mexican and Russian revolutions and envisioning a worker-peasant alliance.

Mexico's isolation was reinforced by the limitations of the world socialist movement. The Second International, whose influence and membership barely extended beyond the industrially developed countries, was not able to understand what was going on in Mexico. Even the Bolsheviks and the internationalist socialists did not pay any serious attention to the Mexican Revolution. Unlike the countries of the East or the Irish Easter Rising, for example, Mexico does not even appear in Lenin's writings.

Even in the United States, where Flores Magón had his center of ideological activity, the revolution had only a minor political impact on the workers' movement. This was the golden age of the struggles organized by the Industrial Workers of the World—the great Lawrence textile strike took place in 1912. But although the Wobblies influenced the Flores Magón brothers and the members of the Casa del Obrero Mundial, there does not seem to have been a flow in the opposite direction. In 1917, when the United States entered the world war, the one hundred thousand–strong IWW organization was decapitated by repression and thrown into a decline from which it would never recover.

The great exception was the lone figure of John Reed, whose revolutionary trail as a writer and reporter went from the Lawrence strike in 1912, to the Mexican Northern Division in 1914, to the Balkan wars in 1916 and the Russian Revolution in 1917–18.

The Mexican Revolution had its greatest echo in the rest of Latin America, where a common language and range of problems made it more accessible. Latin American radicals, workers' organizers, and left-nationalists looked with sympathy toward the Mexican Revolution and tried to find ways of expressing their solidarity. This was most apparent in the countries with a developed workers' movement: Argentina, Uruguay, and Chile. Right from the beginning, it was Zapatism that aroused the most interest and solidarity, particularly among the syndicalist and anarcho-syndicalist rank and file and the working-class socialists.

By contrast, the reformist socialist leaders and intellectuals took a reserved, even critical, attitude toward the Mexican Revolution, whose violence quite naturally repelled the devotees of social evolutionism and parliamentary socialism. *El Socialista*, journal of the Socialist Party of Uruguay, expressed this revulsion very well in an article of late 1911. "The backward Mexican people," it argued, "have no clear idea of society and history, are ignorant of their struggles and economic or political revolutions, and therefore do not know that, in the present historical phase, capitalism is at a peak of the expansion and domination of the international market."

The anarchists took a different position at the time. More inclined by their intellectual formation and methods to accept the violent, tumultuous forms of the Mexican Revolution, they had an ideological bridge to it in the work of Ricardo and Enrique Flores Magón and their journal *Regeneración*. In 1911 one of the editors of the Buenos Aires anarchist journal *La Protesta*, a nearly seventy-year-old doctor named Juan Creaghe, gave up his practice in Luján, Buenos Aires, sold enough to pay for his journey, and went off to join the Flores Magóns in California. From there he issued a manifesto that called on "the comrades of Argentina, Uruguay and the rest of the world" to give unconditional support to the Mexican Revolution, and in particular to the Zapatist cause.

The *Regeneración* group itself expressed this attraction of anarcho-syndicalists toward Zapatism. In a letter of August 1914 in which he tries to explain his lack of resources, Enrique Flores Magón tells a correspondent in Montevideo that the Magonists are a minority in Mexico. "The only people close to our own," he continues, "are the Zapata group which, though stronger, also cannot get money easily. The only way the 'Zapatist' and our own appeals can raise money is by catching rich men or monks and extracting the little they can. Yet this money is not enough to acquire more arms and, above all, more ammunition, which are so costly and hard to find in Mexico. All that can be expropriated are crops and livestock, plus whatever there is in the employers' shops. There's hardly any cash, since anything not banked in the big, well-garrisoned cities is sent abroad." This was not an exaggerated account. At the time in question, the southern revolutionaries did not even have enough money to cover their delegates' journey to the Aguascalientes Convention.

The three main factions of the revolution—Carranzism, Villism, and Zapatism—all had their own representatives abroad. But whereas the first two merely addressed themselves to the Mexican emigration, or concentrated on the establishment of diplomatic contacts with the American authorities or the purchase of arms and other war materiel, the Zapatist agents tried to spread the ideological influence of the revolution. For this was the only tendency with a program that could link it to the masses elsewhere in the world, the only tendency that had an interest in such links.

General Jenaro Amezcua, one of the signatories of the 1915 agrarian law, later established in Havana the most important foreign center for the diffusion of Zapatist ideas and activity. He kept up an abundant correspondence with working-class journals and militants, especially in the River Plate area and the United States. In 1918 he published in Havana a volume entitled *Revolutionary Mexico: To the Peoples of Europe and America, 1910–1918*. This book, which circulated in Latin America, included the Ayala Plan, the agrarian law and other Zapatist legislation, Zapata's public declarations, and texts by Antonio Díaz Soto y Gama and the *El Sur* editorial writers, as well as the Creaghe Manifesto and other Argentinian and Uruguayan documents in support of the Mexican Revolution. An article by the Uruguayan anarcho-syndicalist J. Vidal, for example, described the Mexican Revolution as "a great step in human progress towards genuine freedom" which would serve as the world starting point for the coming "historical movement of the human revolution" and "the triumph of our communist ideals." "The signal," he concluded, "will come from America."[13]

It was precisely to Amezcua that Zapata addressed his letter on the Russian Revolution. Dated February 14, 1918, Liberation Army Headquarters, Tlaltizapán, it was published in May in the Havana daily *El Mundo*. The main sections are as follows:

We, together with mankind and justice, would gain a great deal if all the peoples of America and all the nations of old Europe were to understand that the cause of the Mexican Revolution and Russia's cause are the cause of humanity, the supreme interests of all opressed peoples. . . .

Here as there we can see big lords, cruel, inhuman and avaricious, who from father to son have exploited and tortured the great mass of peasants. Here as there, slaves of work, men with a slumbering conscience, are beginning to wake up, to shake themselves, to move about, to inflict punishment.

Mr Wilson, president of the United States, was right when he recently paid homage to the Russian Revolution, describing it as a noble effort to attain liberties. It would be good, however, if he would remember this statement and bear in mind the clear analogy, the striking parallel, or rather the absolute equivalence between that movement and Mexico's agrarian revolution. Both are directed against what Tolstoy called "the great crime": the infamous usurpation of the land. For the land, which, like the water and air, belongs to everyone, has been monopolized by a few property-owners, supported by powerful armies and iniquitous laws.

It is no wonder, then, that the world proletariat cheers and admires the Russian Revolution, just as it will give its full commitment, sympathy and support to the Mexican Revolution when it realizes its precise aims. . . .

This is why your propaganda work in spreading the truth is so important. You should turn to all the workers' centers and formations in the world, so as to make them see the burning need to undertake and fulfil two tasks at once: training of the workers for struggle, and the development of peasant consciousness. It must not be forgotten that by virtue of proletarian solidarity, the worker's emancipation cannot be achieved if the peasant's freedom is not realized at the same time. Otherwise, the bourgeoisie will be able to set these two forces against each other, using, for example, the peasants' ignorance to combat and hold back the workers' righteous impulses, just as, if the opportunity arises, it will throw the less conscious workers against their fighting brothers.

This letter testifies that the Mexican Revolution, through its southern component, was striving to transcend its own nationalist or peasant limits and to link up with the revolutions of those times elsewhere. Already in the last stages of resistance, the Morelos Commune tried to make contact with the Soviet Republic. But the Russian Revolution, which was unable to prevent the defeat of the Hungarian Commune or the German Revolution in 1919, did not have the remotest chance of aiding the Morelos peasant commune. Indeed, it did not even know of its existence.

This was to be the last great flare of the Morelos Commune and its leader, Emiliano Zapata.

Toward the end of 1918, Pablo González launched a new drive to gain control of Morelos State. In November, the Spanish influenza epidemic reached Mexico on its journey round the world and caused ravages in Morelos. Zapatist civilians and soldiers, weakened by war and malnutrition, died in their thousands in December. Only a fraction of the population remained in Cuautla and Cuernavaca, and whole villages fled to more temperate parts after burying their dead.

Pablo González's army followed hard on the heels of the influenza virus. With eleven thousand soldiers, he occupied the main towns—Cuernavaca, Jojutla, Tlaltizapan, and others—and again compelled Zapata's scattered forces to take refuge in the highlands. In the middle of January, a journalist who had entered Cuernavaca with González in December described the completely forlorn state of the Morelos capital: "In almost every house, there is at least one fully decomposed corpse, and in some the whole family has succumbed to the terrible Spanish influenza." On December 13, González offered free passenger and freight transport to anyone who wished to move to Morelos, even placing whole railway wagons at the disposal of tradesmen.

In some areas, the federal advance drove the peasants to flight, and their cornfields reverted to the former landowners. Thus, according to a report by the daily *Excelsior*, by the end of December on the Penjamillo region of Michoacán, the advancing federal troops "found very fine cornfields which, having been grown by the rebels in alien land, now reverted to their owners."

This was the pattern throughout the country. On January 31, 1919, the same *Excelsior* reported: "In the Federal District, ninety-three persons have recovered property which had been under public control since the Constitutionalist victory. The number of returned properties is much higher in the states of the Republic. The devolution began in 1916." The paper then lists the beneficiaries, concluding from names such as Limantour, León de la Barra, Romero Rubio, García Pimentel, and Escandón that "all Porfirio's people are coming back into their property."[14]

In the first months of 1919, the situation of 1916 seemed to be repeating itself. All the towns of Morelos were occupied by federal troops, while Zapata and his principal leaders conducted a political campaign from their mountain hideouts. Yet the content and objectives of the campaign had undergone a profound transformation. Early in February, Zapata sent a letter to Vázquez Gómez in which he recognized this politician as the supreme leader of the revolution. He further accepted private enterprise in industry, commerce, oil, and all spheres of economic activity, and called for "small-scale property" in the countryside. Similar letters urged Villa and Peláez to recognize Vázquez Gómez and to endorse a proclamation of his new role.

All these letters and declarations came to be the political death certificate of the Zapatist movement. Zapata would remain the leader of the Morelos peasantry, but he had endorsed the policy of the wing that sought a rapprochement with Obregón. Magaña, who would later claim to be Zapata's heir, was thus inexorably drawing him into the fatal ambush. Meanwhile, the Zapatist peasant leaders, from Genovevo de la O to Francisco Mendoza, were paralyzed by the uncertain, hopeless prospects that faced their military activity.

★   ★   ★

When Emiliano was killed, his peasant Commune had already been destroyed. It is hard to identify the point at which it ceased to exist. As Womack says, "the fall of the original Morelos revolution was not a sudden collapse, but a confused, bitter and heart-rending process of decline." But we can be sure that the decisive change took place in the course of 1918. Rather than a cause, the disappearance of the Ayala Plan from the Zapatist documents was one effect of this decline.

The full-scale entry into bourgeois politics sounded the knell for Zapata. One has only to read the documents of early 1919, the letters to Vázquez Gómez and other politicians, in order to realize that they opened the gates to enemy infiltration and the consummation of treacherous activities of all kinds. Zapata's acceptance of this political reorientation could not fail to blunt the instinctive peasant wariness that had so far protected him from tricks and ambushes. The logic of negotiation and compromise made it just a matter of time before he fell into a more or less well-laid trap.

About March 1919, Magaña and Díaz Soto y Gama carried their policy of compromise to its logical conclusion: they suggested that Zapata temporarily give up military activity and go into hiding in order to facilitate the ripening of political negotiations. Although Zapata had signed many conciliationist documents prepared by his secretaries in previous months, his peasant base had not directly oriented themselves by these paper texts, but had looked above all to the attitude of their leader. Zapata now refused to accept Magaña's proposal, which would have involved the cessation of armed struggle with no victory in sight. Not only was he personally against the idea, but assent would have brought him into conflict with the peasant senior officers of the Southern Liberation Army, also weakening in the peasants' eyes the last center of authority at the disposal of the movement: Zapata himself.

This whole period, the most difficult in which Zapata had had to operate, is full of moving stories about the aid given by the rural and urban population of Morelos: warnings, information about troop movements, and many other forms of action that allowed the guerrillas to continue the struggle in the heart of enemy-held territory. It is also worthy of note that officers and soldiers who now accepted the government amnesty rarely joined the military campaign against Zapata. Most often, they would secretly return to their villages and remain as part of the unshakable Zapatist base, providing shelter, protection, and information to the guerrilla fighters.

For the broad masses, Zapata's physical existence was the crucial element focusing their struggle in the state. Zapata could agree to compromise on distant questions related to national politics. But he neither could nor would translate these into the language of local struggles. Nor would his people accept it.

Once Zapata had rejected the advice of his secretaries, his activity and existence clashed even more sharply with those of his political general staff. The line followed by these leaders now separated itself in practice from the life, interests, and thinking of the peasant base. It is of no use to speculate on the forms this conflict would have assumed. For it rapidly took the only definitive form possible at this stage: the physical elimination of Zapata. His death was the material expression of the final political retreat of revolutionary Zapatism, a movement whose possibilities were by then exhausted.

In March 1919, Zapata heard reports of a conflict between Pablo González and one of his subordinates, the cavalry colonel Jesús Guajardo. Although Guajardo was justly famous as a murderer, having organized veritable massacres in the zones occupied by his troops, Zapata sent a letter to him and suggested that he pass over to the Zapatist side with the men under his command. Guajardo and González took advantage of this letter to further their own plans. González advised the colonel to play along with Zapata by pretending to accept his proposal. The trap could then be sprung.

The rest is well known. Guajardo told Zapata that he would

change sides. They had a preliminary discussion. As a guarantee demanded by Zapata, Guajardo shot Zapatist deserters who were part of his troops. Then, they arranged to meet again at the Chinameca hacienda on April 10, 1919. Although Zapata seems to have heard rumors of a trap, his desperate search for allies led him to break with past practice and to reject all warnings. When Zapata and his guard entered Chinameca on April 10, they were greeted with a fusillade. Emiliano died on the spot. His body was taken to Cuautla, so that the people could see it and not have any doubt about his death. Thousands of peasants from nearby villages filed past. An *Excelsior* journalist present at the scene later recounted that "these humble folk trembled from head to foot" as they contemplated the remains of their leader.[15]

The southern peasants understood the full meaning of this event: the loss of their leader finally interrupted their revolution. New forces, new efforts, new struggles, and new organizational forms would be necessary to revive it in the future. Thrown back on their structures and relations of social life, on the conquests and the experience incorporated in their consciousness through ten years of revolution, they would nevertheless stubbornly defend their material gains with all the means at their command, preparing to unite in their villages to face the difficult era ahead. At the same time, they would patiently begin to weave in everyday life the social tissue of future revolutionary stages.

In its socioeconomic basis and its fundamental political forms, the Zapatist regime in Morelos had a different class character from the Convention government that Villists and Zapatists fleetingly installed in Mexico City. Although the peasant armies had taken the capital in December 1914, this government was really an extension of the bourgeois state, whose structure, apparatus, and laws remained intact. There was a change in the upper reaches—the president and his ministers; and the peasant army replaced the bourgeois army as their military support. But there was a continuity at the essential level of the state functionaries and decision-making bodies. It was therefore only a matter of weeks before the petty-bourgeois Conventionists turned this apparatus against the peasantry.

In Morelos, the bourgeois power apparatus had already been destroyed by the armed peasants. Its army and police were suppressed, along with the governor and the civil servants. Later, when the Convention moved to Cuernavaca for its last few months, it only formally appeared as a continuation of the December government. In reality it was a mere fiction superimposed on the rule of the Zapatist peasants. The ephemeral Conventionist government in Morelos was as if suspended in midair. Palafox's agrarian law was one of several attempts to bring the governmental form into line with the content of the peasant revolution. For reasons we have already seen, it was not successful.

The Zapatists did not confine themselves to destruction of the capitalist state apparatus in Morelos; they sought to use their own traditions as the basis for a new power governed by themselves. As always in a peasant-based revolution, the local authorities spontaneously recovered their character as organs of people's power.

Before the revolution, civil servants, even the governor, had been creatures of the real rulers in Morelos: the *hacendados*. Their power rested, in turn, on the national state and their ownership of the land and sugar complexes. The Zapatist revolution cut Morelos from the national state, driving out its functionaries and soldiers and repulsing them when they tried to return. It also suppressed, without compensation, all the big landed property in the region. The agrarian commissions fully implemented the Ayala Plan, although they did not spare the hacienda two-thirds which the plan vowed to leave untouched. They handed over all the land to the villages, nationalized the sugar mills, and effectively eliminated the capitalist and landowning class. All the capitalists and big landowners living in the state fled abroad or to the capital.

The nationalized mills were placed under the management of Zapatist officers. We do not have more precise information on the way in which they functioned. But since the old owners and their trusted employees disappeared from the state, it would seem evident that the technical and material aspects were left in the hands of workers from the Morelos villages. The 1915 sugar harvest, which went ahead in spite of all the war damage, proved that the industry could go on functioning perfectly well without the bosses. The only remaining private property was in the hands of petty traders and peasant smallholders. Palafox's agrarian law did no more than give juridical expression to this revolutionary transformation.

The village and municipal authorities were elected by the same peasants, small traders, and sugar workers—a government system that characterized the whole Zapatist period, but above all the years between 1913 and 1917. The old organs rooted in peasant tradition thus acquired a new function and content which nevertheless fused with that tradition. The local government decrees of early 1917, providing for monthly assemblies and recallable delegates, also legalized a structure whose basic element of village self-government had asserted itself from the moment when the landowners and their political agents were driven from the state.

The peasantry sought to endow its rule with the forms that best corresponded to its experience and therefore allowed the greatest degree of participation and decision making in all community problems. This Zapatist power structure, completely opposed to the bourgeois model in which state apparatuses are designed to impede popular involvement, is one of the crucial features defining the anticapitalist nature of the Morelos revolution.

At the same time, the main instrument defending private property—the federal army—was destroyed or expelled from Morelos. It was the Southern Liberation Army, mostly organized in territorial militias, which actually held the region. Its function was to safeguard village and peasant land ownership, revolutionary legality, and local self-government.

Already in 1913 and 1914, Zapatist decrees showed a concern that government should reside in the villages, and that their rights should be guaranteed vis-à-vis the Southern Liberation Army itself. Central power was invested not in the juridical fiction of the

Convention, which anyway ceased to exist even as a phantom in 1916, but in the military and political general staff headed by Zapata himself. So long as the Tlatizapán headquarters continued to function, it was the real seat of government in Morelos.

Although Zapata did, to be sure, pay heed to his team of secretaries, the central decision-making power was in his hands. And his decisions depended not only on the advice of his secretaries, but also on the relationship with the village authorities, with Zapatist leaders whose selection by the villagers and soldiers ultimately reflected opinion at the base, and with the political functioning of the villages at the level of everyday life and discussion. The same traditional structures through which Zapata had been elected leader of Anenecuilco allowed him to communicate with the entire peasantry of the region. In reality, then, a secretary's advice would be accepted if it more or less corresponded to the views and feelings of the villages. This explains why Zapata gave such weight to Palafox during the rise of the revolution, and why Palafox later fell into a deep crisis. And as the revolution began to ebb, involving a decline in rank-and-file intervention, Magaña's wing gained the ascendancy in Zapata's thinking and received his authorization for its political compromises. The change was not due to fickleness on Zapata's part, determination and tenacity being permanent features of his character. Rather, it was a change in the objective situation of the revolution and the state of mind of the population which reflected itself in the balance of forces within the political leadership.

The Zapatist government did not merely constitute itself as a military command, to be maintained until the triumph of the armed struggle, but sought to become a genuine government in all spheres of activity, to construct in Morelos a new state apparatus fused with village self-government, that would prefigure a similar structure throughout the country. It passed and applied a series of decrees on the land, education, supplies, finances, the police, and the army. After settling the crucial question of land distribution, it issued money, carried out public works, built schools, and so on.

It is a remarkable fact that the effective political leadership of the southern revolution was concentrated in the person of Emiliano Zapata. Many historians and commentators, like the Carranza government at the time, have tried to deny this by invoking one or another of his secretaries as the man really in charge. They find it inadmissible or intolerable that a peasant, rather than a "cultured" person, should be the main leader of a revolution. But the peasants of Morelos were never in any doubt about the true head of the movement. They saw themselves exercising power through Zapata, just as they exercised local power in the villages. It was this which gave Zapata, unlike the secretaries, an authority over the peasant officers and soldiers that was based on their complete trust.

Emiliano Zapata's role in the revolution was part of the confident, self-assertive drive of the Mexican peasantry to run their own lives and determine the country's fate. For this reason, his figure transcends the borders of Mexico and, alongside that of Pancho Villa, stands as a universal symbol of the agrarian revolution.

"*Jefe* Zapata" or just "Miliano"—the two names, alternating with each other according to the occasion, clearly express the relationship of authority and trust between the peasants and Zapata. Hardly ever did they give him the title "don," which, except as a mark of respect for the elderly, implies a social distance between the bestower and the recipient. More generally, the use of the familiar *tú* and other tokens of equality were the rule throughout revolutionary Morelos.

This brings us to the role played by the introduction of general socialist ideas: from Díaz Soto y Gama's early vague anarchism to Palafox's socialist-type projects. Whereas Díaz Soto y Gama's high-sounding talk ultimately served as a vehicle for liberal ideas, Palafox tried at his peak to build an elementary juridical framework that contained a number of socialist elements. The best example is his agrarian law, but his letters and other decrees provide further evidence.

No other current in the Mexican Revolution formulated such plans and programs. Not a few writers and politicians have therefore tried to obscure, erase, or minimize the role of his movement, naturally profiting from its own imprecision. Another contributory factor has been the weakness of Manuel Palafox himself, broken when he had to face the serious adversities of revolution.[16]

Without the Morelos Commune, however, there would have been no fight left in the Jacobin wing of the Querétaro Constituent Congress, and nor would any of the most advanced clauses have been incorporated into the 1917 Constitution.

The Morelos revolution, isolated though it would remain, transformed the economic, political, juridical, military, and, above all, social foundations of power in the region, establishing popular rule based on the armed poor peasantry and agricultural workers. François Chevalier named it "a peasant republic."

Yet this commune did not spring simply from the Morelos peasantry: it would not have existed without a nationwide popular revolution; and it was considerably influenced by more general socialist ideas originating in the city and coming, too, from former Mexican peasant upheavals in the nineteenth century. Moreover—and this is its essential feature—the southern revolution based itself on a unique combination between the agricultural and industrial proletariat of the sugar plantations and a peasant insurrection whose roots lay in traditional village organization, itself a product of the old agrarian commune.

When the revolution broke out in Morelos, there was a modern sugar industry with twenty-four established mills. The regional capitalists had made sizeable investments in both industrial machinery and cane-field irrigation, so that Morelos then accounted for a third of Mexico's sugar production. The 1910 Census listed twenty-four mills and forty plantations, in a state of 4,911 square kilometers with a total population of 180,000. These figures indicate a very high concentration of the sugar proletariat and the surrounding peasantry. The mills naturally recruited their workforce from the local peasantry, and many cane-cutters, in particular, were at once agricultural wage laborers and landless or poor peasants or workers on communal land kept from the clutches of the hacienda.

The *hacendados* were continually seizing more village land, not only for its own sake, but also in order to realize peasant labor and drive more and more families on to the plantation as permanent wage laborers. The pay was sixty-five centavos a day in the winter season and one peso during the spring harvest—considerably higher than the national average. But since the state economy increasingly turned upon large-scale production of sugar, rum, and rice, the high cost of imported staple items largely offset the difference.

Still, the concentration of labor in the hacienda did not proceed with the desired rapidity, and so wage laborers were attracted from other parts of the country. In both ways, the sugar workers that would be a crucial element in the revolution were very closely linked to the peasant villages. Already in early 1912, for example, Zapatist units began to demand wage-rises for plantation workers and even to impose them by force. As the revolution gained in strength and scale, the goals directly expanded to include the expropriation of the land and sugar mills.

The nine largest plantations, each between ten and forty thousand hectares, comprised 80 percent of the total hacienda land in Morelos. The population density in this small state was one of the highest in the country: 36.5 inhabitants per square kilometer, surpassed only by Tlaxcala and Mexico states, where Zapatist influence was also strong, and Guanajuato in Central Mexico. This great concentration of workers and peasants, within a tightly woven social fabric united by village life, constituted a social force that allowed one of the smallest and most exploited regions in the Republic to withstand enormous odds for a decade.

It is interesting to compare the 1910 Census figures for Morelos and for other states of the Republic, particularly Coahuila, Sonora, Chihuahua, and Durango, which were the home bases of the Carranzist, Obregonist, and Villist tendencies of the revolution

Table 8.1
Population Statistics for 1910

	Total area	Population	Peons %	Farmers %	Average life (yrs.)	Literacy %
Coahuila	165,219	362,092	72.3	27.6	40.1	30.63
Sonora	198,496	265,383	83.9	18.0	44.7	33.52
Chihuahua	233,214	405,707	73.7	26.2	38.0	28.16
Durango	109,495	483,175	86.8	13.2	37.6	18.29
Morelos	4,911	179,574	95.8	4.2	23.1	23.58
Tlaxcala	3,974	184,171	98.8	1.2	24.7	21.90
Mexican Republic	1,987,201	15,160,377	88.4	11.6	30.1	19.74

(see Table 8.1). The Federal District had 720,753 inhabitants. The category "farmers" generally comprises well-off small and medium landowners.

Coahuila and Sonora, the two states whose governors resisted Huerta and launched the armed insurgency in the North, laying the basis for the bourgeois wing of the revolution, were among the largest in the Republic. They had a powerful bourgeoisie with local roots and interests, a sizeable rural petty bourgeoisie, and a higher-than-average standard of living reflected in literacy and life expectancy.

Morelos, the base of its most radical tendency, not only had the highest proportion of wage laborers and landless peasants, but displayed many other signs of the exploitation of labor-power. These figures also indicate some of the great handicaps (illiteracy, lack of basic resources) the Zapatists had to overcome.

Under the Porfirio Díaz regime, the sugar mill and plantation workers were not able to form any kind of organization, and were subject both to direct hacienda repression and to the mercies of an entire police, judicial, and military state apparatus in the service of the *hacendados*. They also had to face exploitation in the employers' shops, as well as other forms of deduction from their wage.

In the southern revolution, however, traditional village structures were partially converted into a vehicle for the organization
and expression of the sugar workers, most of whom were either
themselves peasants from the village or related to it by multiple
family and social ties. But they brought with them the experience
of wage labor and the modern industrial organization of the sugar
mills.

If, by 1910, hacienda capitalism had already uprooted the traditional village structures, the sugar workers would have had to develop its own union organizations in order to embark upon
revolutionary struggle. If there had been no working class linked
to the peasantry in the Zapatist region, the traditional organization would not by itself have been able to generate forms of cen-
tralizing the struggle, and, above all, would not have had a social
base for the socialist ideas expressed in various measures taken by
the southern revolution. Many of the young leaders who formed
the original Zapatist nucleus provide evidence of this class aspect:
Genovevo de la O was a collier from the village of Santa María,
Felipe Neri a railway stoker from Chinameca hacienda, Fortino
Ayaquica a textile worker from Atlixco, Puebla, and Amador
Salazar a cowboy and peon from Yautepec. (Francisco Mendoza,
however, who was already forty years old at the outbreak of the
revolution, was a ranch hand and rustler from the Morelos–Puebla
border area.)

The social and structural combination of forces in Morelos
also gave concentrated expression to the broader insurrection of
the Mexican peasantry for land and self-rule. Their own feeling,
shaped in everyday life under Porfirian-style capitalism, was not
that capitalism should be "humanized" and stripped of its oppressive features, but that the capitalist mode of development did not
serve their interests. In Zapatist territory this idea acquired concrete expression; in other parts of the country, it manifested itself
in a more diffuse way. Yet it does account for the fact that the
southern peasants based themselves upon their own traditions and

leaders. Like the Paris communards, they "threw themselves into an assault on the heavens."

The Morelos Commune remains as one of the finest and most deeply rooted Mexican revolutionary traditions. It continues to come back time and again.

9

1920

The armed revolution finally came to an end in 1920. The dé-
nouement had already been heralded on April 10, 1919, by the
murder of Emiliano Zapata. The rest of this year and the first half
of the next were a period of political transition. Although the direct threat from the armed peasants had subsided, their resistance
impelled Alvaro Obregón to take advantage of the irreparable
damage they had inflicted upon the Carranzist regime. Obregón
regrouped his forces and eventually consummated his own rise to
power, thereby sealing the interruption of the revolution and
opening a period of stabilization and organization of the new
regime.

Zapata's death sparked a brief struggle for the leadership of the
ever more fragmented movement in Morelos. As one might have
expected from previous developments, this struggle ended with
the election of Magaña as Zapata's "successor" at a meeting of Zapatist leaders in Huautla on September 4, 1919. The changeover
summed up the whole decline of official Zapatism. Magaña had
opened the negotiations for it to become a prop of the new power,
drawing in return a number of concessions that mainly favored
himself and his fellow leaders.

In October and November 1919, a new crisis broke out between the Carranza government and the United States. Relieved
of the pressure of war and the immediate revolutionary aftermath
in Europe, Washington began a fresh diplomatic offensive "to protect the American interests threatened and violated in Mexico." It
was alleged that enemies of Carranza had kidnapped Consul Jenkins

in Puebla in order to demonstrate the government's incapacity to guarantee personal safety. But a week later Jenkins reappeared safe and sound, and the Mexican government held him for questioning on the suspicion that he had kidnapped himself. This brought the crisis to a head, and a U.S. Senate subcommittee chaired by Albert B. Fall demanded military intervention to protect U.S. investments.

As the crisis was raging, Magaña thought the time had come for a deal. General Lucio Blanco, who had recently been brought back into Carranza's army in the hope that he would serve as a counterweight to Obregón, agreed to mediate, and arranged a meeting between Carranza and Magaña for November 28, 1919. In the president's private office, Magaña recognized "the gravity of the international situation" and offered the surrender of Zapatist forces in return for guarantees of security. Carranza immediately accepted. Zapatist generals yielded one after another throughout the month of December. A few, like Genovevo de la O and Francisco Mendoza, though officially said to have surrendered, remained hidden in the mountains without undertaking any military activity. Yet given the lack of an alternative, the Zapatist army as a whole had no option but to observe Magaña's agreement.

The old landowners now launched a political drive to recover their plantations and mills. After the short experience of nationalization under Zapatist management, the mills were placed under the "control" of González's officers—poor soldiers and appalling managers, but excellent businessmen on their own behalf. This was only a temporary solution, however, which could last only as long as the military occupation of the state. Once the Zapatists had surrendered and Morelos had been organized and "pacified," the plantations could only be given to the peasantry or to the landowners. The decision was not hard to predict: no obstacle would delay any longer Carranza's policy of returning controlled property to the old Porfirian landowners. The army men left the mills; and between December 1919 and January 1920, the plantations and mills were delivered to their former masters. The more enterprising capitalists moved back to Morelos and restarted production. Thus, despite the halving of the Morelos population since 1910, the *hacendados* initiated a solid recovery of the private sugar industry in the midst of deep popular hostility.

In the North, the Villists had continued their guerrilla warfare after the departure of the U.S. punitive expedition. Although the towns were all under central government control, Villa's numerous military units would make lightning raids from the mountains, acquiring fresh supplies, punishing government agents and other enemies, and distributing food to the population. They would then quickly withdraw and disperse into small, undetectable groups. They did not have the Zapatists' organized village base, but they could count on popular sympathy and support.

The war in the North, possible because it expressed deep social dissatisfaction with the Carranzist regime, nevertheless lacked a precise series of objectives. Battles, skirmishes, storming of towns and villages, long marches, dispersal for work in the fields, regrouping for fresh actions—but for what purpose? "To bring down Carranza," they replied. But how, and to what end? Villa's lack of a program had never been so piercing as it was now in the guerrilla period of decline, when even the Carranza government fought the lingering peasant insurrection in the name of a reform program which, though not applied, had been solemnly proclaimed at Querétaro as the highest law of the nation.

Nellie Campobello has written a fine series of accounts of the Villist struggle in this period, seen through the eyes of a five- or six-year-old girl growing up amid the fighting, skirmishes, and gunfire of civil war.[1] She spent her childhood in the mining town of Parral, Chihuahua, then one of the centers of guerrilla activity. "Parral was Villa's favorite town," she recalls. "He often used to say: 'I love Parral even for dying there.'" Nellie Campobello reveals the tenacity of these popular guerrilla fighters and the extent to which the villages supported them. But she also brings out their lack of objectives. In another of her books, she recounts Villa's capture of the border town of Ojinaga in the early months of 1917. These few lines, written with passionate concern for the Villist cause, clearly express the situation in which the guerrillas found themselves:

> Villa's aim in attacking Ojinaga was to buy a few things which he and his boys [*muchachos*] needed. As they arrived, he seemed sad and pensive to his friends. So many of his boys had already died: Candelario Cervantes in Namiquipa, fighting the Americans in the last months of 1916; Pablito López, the one who set Columbus alight, brother of Martín, shot in Chihuahua; José Rodríguez, the cavalry commander; Fierro, loyal as a sheepdog; and so many more of his faithful and valiant warriors now so much missed. When he had bought the things he needed, he chatted for a while with Dona Magdalena, talking only of the boys who had died in Columbus: Ortiz, Castillo, Vargas and others. "But we can't give up," said General Villa. "Why should we? We'll carry on until Don Venus falls from the tree." He immediately turned and left, dragging his spurs along the ground.[2]

In this same year, a group of Mexican emigré politicians in New York founded the Mexican Liberal Alliance, whose declared aim was "to unite all revolutionaires opposed to the Carranza government." The Alliance members, some sympathetic to Villa, others not, included General Felipe Angeles, the lawyer Miguel Díaz Lombardo, and General Antonio I. Villareal, a founder of the Flores Magón Liberal Party, signatory of the Torreón Accords, and president of the Aguscalientes Convention. Others, like Angeles himself, declared their belief in "evolutionary socialism" and expressed their concern about a possible Yankee invasion at the end of the world war. The program of this group was distinctly to the right of the Querétaro Constitution. Its main demands were reintroduction of the 1857 Constitution, the overthrow of Carranza, and the disqualification of army men from standing for the presidency of the Republic. The reference to the 1857 Constitution was designed to provide a point of unity for men and factions whose common denominator was hostility to Carranza and absence from government. In rejecting the 1917 Constitution and harking back to the liberal past, however, they placed themselves to the right of Carranza, accepted him as the representative of the revolution, and identified him with the Obregón center and Jacobin left which had joined forces to impose the new constitution against his will. Above all, they took an open stand against the social reforms contained in the 1917 Constitution. The backward-looking program of the Liberal Alliance now fully merited the epithet "reactionary" which Obregón had used against Villa in 1915.

The lack of political objectives threw the Villist peasant leadership and its guerrilla campaign into crisis. For Pancho Villa accepted the Liberal Alliance program and persuaded his forces to do the same at a meeting in Río Florido, which lent it the name Río Florido Plan. He also accepted Angeles's argument that victory required the abandonment of the guerrilla tactic and the organization of a regular National Reconstruction Army. It was the same politico-military conception that Angeles had defended earlier, particularly after the entry into Mexico City in December 1914. But for a centralized army to become viable, it must base itself upon a centralized state and class organization. The Northern Division had been able to develop as such within the framework of Constitutionalism. But then it underwent that process of dispersion which gave rise to the conflicts between Villa and Angeles. As a peasant army, it could not go beyond the form of guerrilla warfare, which the Southern Liberation Army never fully overcame. The idea of building a National Reconstruction Army, with a liberal program written in New York, was a pure illusion dreamt up by exiled politicians. When the attempt was made to put it into practice, it inevitably began to clash with the peasant mentality and aspirations of the Villist guerrillas and their social base of support.

Felipe Angeles was the only man who, with a mixture of political naïveté and fatalism, actually faced all the risks and tried to make this illusion a reality. Since leaving Villa for exile in the United States, Angeles had moved through study toward a moderate, evolutionary socialism influenced by his experiences in the Mexican Civil War. His main political concern at this time was that the United States might, after the end of the world war, exploit the internal divisions in Mexico and Carranza's "provocative" foreign policy to invade and subjugate the country. His solution was a government of "national reconciliation" which, having discarded Carranza, would be able to negotiate an amicable return to good relations with the United States.

After establishing contact with Villa, Angeles crossed the frontier on December 11, 1918. While still in El Paso, Texas, he had expressed his view of the situation in a letter to a friend in New York:

> I'd have preferred not to be so alone: I'd have liked to be accompanied by some twenty patriots with a reputation in the Republic. But I did not find them. Perhaps many would have liked to join me, but their upbringing as refined, ultra-delicate people made it impossible. . . . Disgrace is in store for those Mexicans who do not tax all their resources to solve our problem, to prevent intervention by the United States. . . . You well know that I am aware of all the risks I am taking. I'm already old and cannot easily support a harsh open-air life, without food, without clothing, and dirty in the extreme. I'm going among people who commit crimes out of ignorance and savagery, and do not realize that those are crimes. And your good friend, the pious señor . . . will of course call me a bandit. Since Villa is one of the most important factors in the present struggle, I must force myself to change him from an element of anarchy into an element of order, and my enemies will certainly use this to discredit me in the eyes of the American government and people. Despite everything, I go with faith; for I shall be performing a duty, and I trust my good friends to help me succeed or to stand up for me if I fail.

Angeles joined Villa's forces in early 1919 at their Tosesihua camp in Chihuahua State. He set about organizing them militarily, on the principle that their guerrilla force should become the nucleus of a regular army and immediately begin to function as such. Villa had accepted this idea together with the Río Florido Plan. But as their small band of troops went through preparations in the Chihuahua Mountains, avoiding for the moment any major contact with the *federales*, military disagreements already began to sharpen between the two leaders. While Angeles proposed a formal war, involving the capture of strategically situated towns, Villa insisted that guerrilla raids should be continued as a way of gaining strength, even if this entailed fragmentation in the period between actions. Only later would it be possible to organize an army.

When Angeles objected that the army stage would never be reached through this method, Villa replied that the long years of war had depleted the resources of the region, and that it would not be easy to replace the material elements they had acquired. Angeles remained adamant: a regular campaign had to be fought for at least half a year, since the fragmentation following each guerrilla action would allow an enemy recovery and dissipate any beneficial effect. "Anyway, general," Angeles is said to have told Villa, "this roaming through the mountains seems quite worthy of a guerrilla leader, but not of the commander-in-chief of the National Reconstruction Army."

Although these may not have been his precise words, the military strategies, stemming from two conceptions of politics, were certainly at the root of an argument that revived their dispute of five years earlier. Now, however, they commanded a small, outlawed force, not the mighty Northern Division that had occupied the capital and driven Carranza and Obregón to the Veracruz seaboard. The military argument between Villa and Angeles did not reach a crescendo this time, yet it was shortly followed by another separation. When Angeles repeatedly expressed his admiration for the progress of civilization in the United States and voiced a hope that Mexico would advance along the same road, Villa finally exploded and said that he could take anything from Angeles except a drive to "gringoize" his people.

The other basic reason for the conflict had already been contained in Angeles's letter to his friend in New York. Guerrilla fighters, hunted by an army that took no prisoners, could not be made to respect the "rules of war" that formed part of Angeles's military training. In their failure to give quarter and their practice of shooting prisoners en masse, the Villist forces and the Carranzist army seemed to have much more in common with each other than with his model of an army. In reality, the conflict was insoluble. Angeles wanted to "regulate" the natural cruelty of war according to classical norms, while the peasants on both sides practiced it at an empirical level. It was not a conflict between "civilization" and "barbarism"—all war is barbaric; nor between cruelty and kindness— all war is cruel of necessity; but between two irreconcilable policies and worldviews.

For a time, however, Villa and Angeles continued to work together, and in April 1919 they waged a guerrilla campaign that involved the temporary occupation of large towns. Thus the Villists took Parral on April 18, withdrew a short time later, and moved to attack Ciudad Juárez at the end of the month. Angeles's plan for a formal military campaign may have been based in part on possession of this frontier town, but it certainly did not allow for the immediate and inevitable American intervention. When the young general Martín López, who would soon die in another action, had virtually captured Ciudad Juárez, hemming the government forces into a small area, American troops suddenly crossed the frontier and put the Villists to flight with the help of artillery fire from Fort Bliss. Angeles sent a letter to the military commander of El Paso demanding an explanation for this action. But the commander's verbal reply merely stated that as Washington had recognized the Carranza government, he owed no explanation to private individuals. Although the Americans had many quarrels with Carranza in these days, they had no interest in rekindling the peasant war in Mexico.

Angeles's hope of organizing an army began to seem ever more remote. In the months since he left the United States, he had not managed to attract a single person of note: no real "politician" saw Angeles as more than, at best, a well-intentioned dreamer who had thrown in his lot with a band of peasant outlaws. The conflict with Villa therefore became a crisis, barely five months after their reunion in Tosesihua. One day, Angeles offered to take a dozen men into the valley in order to find food and other supplies for the troops. Villa accepted. They took leave of each other in a cordial manner and agreed to meet at a fixed place within a month. But in the mind of each general was the idea that this might be their last separation. For unlike the golden period of the Northern Division, there were no victories that could dissolve or soften their differences. As the month came to an end, Villa received a message in which Angeles said that he would not return with his small group of men.

Angeles now remained virtually alone, leading a nomadic existence in the safety of the mountains. Finally, on November 15, 1919, a former Villist soldier who was sheltering him in a cave handed him over to government troops in return for a reward. At the time of his capture, Angeles had absolutely no men or resources; he was separated from Villa, the emigré opposition, and the Carranza government, without even the hopes that had animated him when he crossed the border eleven months before. In prison, he continued the book he had been reading in his mountain hideout: Ernest Renan's *Life of Jesus*. The prisoner was taken to Chihuahua, where a military court was convened on Carranza's personal orders. Clearly the president was not going to leave him alive.

The trial began in the Theatre of Heroes at 8 A.M. on November 24 and continued without a break until midnight of the next day. Hoping to gain time for his friends to wage an effective campaign in the capital, Angeles tried to draw out the proceedings by making long discourses on military art, the history of European armies, stories from the war, and his own political and philosophical ideas. But the end had to come, and the military court pronounced the death sentence already passed by Carranza. Felipe Angeles was shot at 6 A.M. on November 26, 1919. It was said at the time that Villa had appointed him provisional president of the Republic. Although Angeles denied this, his execution removed both a potential focus for the Maderist-liberal opposition and any chance of a national political perspective for Villa's guerrilla warfare.[3]

As the most important federal career officer to side with the revolution, Angeles had followed a trajectory that, though quite distinctive, was in its way symptomatic of the Mexican Revolution. He was born in 1869 into a partly Indian family, and his father had been a soldier in the Reform Wars. Felipe rose to some prominence through his distinguished record in the Porfirio Díaz army, particularly in the fields of mathematics, artillery, and ballistics. The outbreak of the revolution found him on an army mission in France, but he was recalled by Madero and appointed director of the Military College in January 1912. In August of the same year, when it became clear that General Juvencio Robles had failed in his terror campaign against the Morelos peasantry, Angeles was sent to replace him as head of anti-Zapatist operations. Angeles not only radically altered the methods of the campaign, but tried to combine military actions with a number of concessions to the peasantry. The first thing he did was to end the mass shootings and the seizure of villages and crops. Seeing at first hand the character of peasant life and the tenacity of their struggle, and seeing, too, the outrages committed by landowners, civil servants, and army officers, he now underwent a profound change and fell under the influence of the Morelos peasantry. During his exile in the United States, he later wrote some reminiscences of the Morelos campaign, justifying the struggle of Genovevo de la O and recognizing his military qualities.

When Angeles was sent from the Aguascalientes Convention to invite the Zapatists to take part, he was able to make the acquaintance of de la O in Cuernavaca. Genovevo told him that he had once been within range of a Zapatist ambush party: "We saw you pass, and we could have fought your troops and killed you. But why should we kill you? You'd been fair with us."

At the time of the Huerta coup, Angeles was captured in the National Palace and held with Madero and Pino Suárez during their last night on earth. He realized from the start that the two were going to be killed. According to an account given by the Cuban ambassador, Manuel Márquez Sterling, he said, "They're going to kill don Pancho." Huerta did not want to sharpen the conflict with the army, and so he simply left Angeles in prison and more or less banished him to Europe a few months later. But Angeles secretly returned to join the Constitutionalist revolution in October 1913, becoming undersecretary of war in Carranza's cabinet. He was also its highest-ranking and most experienced army man, since nearly all the career officers had smoothly made the transition from Díaz to Madero to Huerta within the federal army. He soon had his first quarrels with Carranza, while Obregón even reproached him for his past as a federal officer. Villa then asked for him to be attached to the Northern Division, and permission was immediately given at his own request. He fought Villa's whole campaign as second-in-command of the Northern Division.

This relationship between a onetime peasant outlaw and guerrilla leader, previously hunted by the *federales*, and a career officer in the landowners' army was one of the most striking features of the Mexican Revolution. Ever since that time, official historians and politicians have sought to present Angeles as "the reactionary brain" or the *eminence grise* behind Villa. Moreover, since the victors have defined the framework of the historical argument, even his supporters have been more concerned with justifying his actions than with arriving at a clear understanding of his role.

Obregón himself first invented the image of Villa as a puppet in Angeles's hands, much as he tried to deny the personality of the other peasant leader of the revolution, Zapata. For Obregón and all those who have followed him found it intolerable that a peasant, acting in the name of the peasantry, should have led elements originating in the so-called cultured classes. What is certain from all accounts of their collaboration is not only that Villa held the supreme command, but that the two men had a respect for each other that did not appear in other relationships. Given the differences in education, habits, and class background, Villa showed a fondness for

Angeles that he did not display toward anyone else not of peasant origin; and whereas the other petty-bourgeois Villist leaders wavered between feelings of fear and paternalism toward the peasant *jefe*, Angeles treated him with a genuine sense of respect.

Pancho Villa was a man who aroused feelings toward himself that really expressed feelings toward the peasant revolution in all its elemental force. (A pretty-bourgeois Northern Division general once complained that Villa sanctioned Rodolfo Fierro's excessive cruelty in shooting prisoners. Villa replied: "O.K., but when there are no more victories and the hard times begin, you will all desert me. Fierro will follow me to the end." And so it happened.)

In Angeles's relationship to Villa were expressed his own feelings toward the peasantry: there was no fear, but rather respect for those who had justice and right on their side. The revolutionary peasantry imposed its influence on Angeles the officer, and he placed himself at their service out of a sense of justice. Angeles, moreover, was of half-Indian ancestry, visible in his traits, which he never denied. The mixture of respect and paternalism expressed the unresolved contradiction, bending in one sense or the other according to the flow of the revolutionary tide.

The contradiction governed the relationship between Angeles and Villa, both in the 1913–15 period and in 1919. Yet it never shook the feeling of friendship which, more social than personal in character, explains their equal-footed collaboration, unmatched in this stage of the Mexican Revolution. When the Villist forces took the town of Parral in April 1919, Angeles addressed the population in the main square. "History will not have a single word to say about me," he insisted, "because I do not deserve one. I am a mere speck of dust which tomorrow's wind will blow away. But General Villa does have a right to the words of history." But, beyond the individual feelings and tactical discussions between Villa and Angeles, the former eventually returned to the defensive, guerrilla forms of peasant war, while the latter remained completely alone, isolated from the peasantry, which he would not win to his conception of struggle, and also from the bourgeoisie, which saw him as a military renegade linked to the stubborn, primitive fight of Villa's bands.

The peculiar essence of the Mexican Revolution also expressed itself in this individual case, impelling even an outstanding general of the federal army toward socialist ideas. When he was in the United States, Angeles studied a number of socialist and Marxist works and published several articles in support of such ideas. He argued that socialism was the goal of humanity, but that this had to be reached through the gradual progress of society. If an attempt was made to apply socialist laws to a backward country like Mexico— the intention, in his view, of the Jacobin wing of the Querétaro Constituent Congress—it would serve the interests of reaction rather than the country's advance. This way of thinking was current in the reformist wing of Russian socialism and the European socialist movement in general.

In an article published in 1917, Angeles wrote:

> The system of bourgeois society (free competition and unfettered private property) is rapidly passing away, thanks to the work of the utopians in the first half of the last century, of Marxist socialism in the second half of that enlightenment century, and of evolutionary socialism in the early years of the new century. . . . Socialists are returning from exile, or emerging from prison, in order to join governments; legislation is rapidly changing in every country, again under the influence of the socialist party. . . . The circle of ideas is extending in various ways: through books, on the platform of meetings, in the pulpit, in the press. But what makes the strongest impression on mass thinking is the power of example: *the Russian Revolution is worth more than a mountain of newspapers and propaganda leaflets. . . .* The present European war had been prophesied by all statesmen since the end of the first decade of this century. But the European cabinets did not clearly perceive that the war born of international rivalry would deliver countries to the action of the socialist tendency, which represents the aspirations of the world. In this way, the terrible war will yield the most precious fruits: freedom and justice.

It was in the name of these ideas, however, that Angeles rejoined the leader of the peasant war and counterposed a reactionary reform—reintroduction of the 1857 Constitution—to a Constitution whose main supporters, in a vehement yet similarly confused manner, also invoked the ideas of socialism. At the military court in the Theatre of Heroes, Angeles received public applause for the last defense of his beliefs:

> At this point, I would like to show how my thinking has evolved. In Aguascalientes, I was surprised that many people were socialists. Socialism is a general, world-wide movement of respectability, which cannot be vanquished. The world's progress points in the same direction as do the socialists. When I went to the United States, I began to study socialism, and I saw that it is essentially a movement of fraternity and love between men in different parts of the globe. Fraternity is a movement, it has been a movement which has driven society forward for very many centuries towards the well-being of the masses—the masses who fight in its struggles, the multitude which is a multitude in every part of the world. The poor are always at the bottom, and the rich care little or nothing for the needy. It is because of this inequality in the laws that the masses protest and struggle. An Austrian communist has shown that if everyone in the world were to work just three hours a day, there would be much more wealth. But the people who work are not the same as those who eat well.

Of all the figures of the Mexican Revolution, Felipe Angeles always seems to be in a solitary situation. He was a stranger in his time: a high-ranking officer in a caste army who was attracted by the peasant revolution and, at forty-five years of age, began to move toward the ideas of socialism. Placing his military knowledge at the service of the Northern Division, he helped to destroy the oppressor army in which he had been trained. Through a sense of justice, possibly his greatest merit, he was attracted to the peasant revolution first in the South and then in the North. Even if his military background may have prevented him from fully understanding Villa and his men, he learned to respect and value them. And they treated him as an equal, as they did no other officer alien to their class. It was for these reasons, and not only because of political miscalculation, that none of his New York friends could dissuade Angeles from putting his words into practice at the end of 1918. Despite all his contradictions, the final stage that ended in front of a Chihuahua firing squad reaffirmed his basic transformation in the 1912 Morelos campaign, his decision to join the Northern Division in 1913, and his political development in the Aguascalientes Convention of 1914.

The present-day Mexican Army took shape through the victory of the nationalist revolution, evolving in a two-sided manner that expressed the contradictory Bonapartist character of its founder, General Obregón. On the one hand, it had destroyed the old bourgeois-landowner caste army and resisted imperialist invasion and blackmail; on the other hand, it had fought and defeated the peasant armies of the revolution. Felipe Angeles, though officially ignored, represents the third, distinctive tradition of the career officers who sided with the revolution and joined Villa and his Northern Division.

By early 1920, Carranza had already assassinated Zapata, secured Magaña's surrender, and shot Felipe Angeles. He was facing up to U.S. pressure, particularly on the oil question. The sporadic Villist actions in the North were the last jolts of a civil war that, to a lesser or greater degree, had touched every part of the country.

Just as all opposition seemed to have been eliminated, Carranza's policy proved so unrepresentative of social forces in the country that it could no longer be sustained. The 1917 Constitution had been a real compromise, not just an imaginative exercise or a formal declaration. But Carranza represented only one part of this compromise, the socially weaker part, which nevertheless tried to base itself on the strength of the state. His government ran counter to the 1917 pact. Although the political figures of the revolutionary petty bourgeoisie had accepted or tolerated Carranza's policy as a crucial necessity to eliminate the unpleasant aftermath of peasant war, they had only agreed with that aspect which involved nationalist opposition to imperialism.

This situation was visible in the political withdrawal of Alvaro Obregón, the man who stood for the Querétaro compromise as such rather than either of the conflicting tendencies. In 1917 he retired to his Sonora lands and soon made them a thriving business. It would seem that Carranza's protection had something to do with this prosperity. For the president wished to keep his main opponent happy while he pursued the aim of the ruling faction: to develop a new bourgeois class intertwined with the old, using the state power to assist the enrichment of the military and political victors of the revolution.

More and more, however, its old thrust was to restore the old order, if not the old state power. In search of a social base for his policy, Carranza had to rely upon the old Porfirian landowning class from which he himself had originated. They began to recover possession of "controlled" property, and in Morelos, for example, even took back the haciendas from the hands of army officers.

The resistance to this policy manifested itself not only in the armed, if passive, support for Genovevo de la O and Francisco Mendoza after Magaña's official surrender of Morelos, or the continued activity of Villist guerrillas in the North and other groups elsewhere in the country, or the spate of workers' strikes and disputes in 1918 and 1919; but also through the opposition that young revolutionary officers began to present since 1917. This finally took the form of open conflict in the period before the 1920 presidential elections.

Carranza tried to impose as his successor Ignacio Bonillas, an engineer alien to the revolution, whereas a large part of the new officer stratum supported Obregón's candidacy, already announced in the middle of 1919. Obregón's program seemed moderate in character, its criticism being limited to the fact that norms of representative democracy had not been fulfilled. The *Excelsior* editorials were favorable: he displayed "not a single discordant note"; he presented "none of the Jacobin agitation that used to be ascribed to him," nor any of the "socialist tendencies which, in the past, terrified anyone who thought that he might one day take the path towards supreme office." Obregón offered guarantees to private property, capital, and foreign investment. Still, what was at issue was not representative democracy but Carranza's failure to keep the promises of the revolution. Presenting himself as the *caudillo* of the revolutionary army, Obregón seemed much closer to these promises than the designated "civilian" successor.

Obregón's candidacy became a pole of attraction for discontentment with the Carranzist regime. Early in 1920, the appointment of Ignacio Bonillas as the president's chosen candidate helped to tilt the army in favor of the general. In March, Bonillas began his election campaign, and the Constitutionalist movement divided into two irreconcilable wings. In the same month, Obregón concluded an alliance with Magaña that assured him of Zapatist support in the struggle against Carranza. Thus, when he was summoned to the Federal District in early April, supposedly to give testimony at a federal trial, he narrowly escaped arrest and perhaps assassination by journeying south through Morelos in a railwayman's disguise. From Guerrero, he then sent messages to his supporters throughout the country, and by mid-April the civilian and military authorities of Sonora, Sinaloa, Michoacán, and Zacatecas had withdrawn their recognition of Carranza. Other states would soon follow.

On April 23, 1920, Obregón issued his Agua Prieta Plan, which called for the removal of Carranza, the appointment of the Sonora State governor, Adolfo de la Huerta, as provisional president, and immediate elections for a new government. A flood of support placed virtually the whole army behind Obregón in the course of the following week. The social isolation of the Carranza regime was now brutally reflected in its political and military isolation. In the South, where Obregón had established his operational base, the old Zapatist leadership followed Magaña in supporting him against the hated Carranza, no doubt in return for a private promise that the land would be distributed to the peasantry and political posts given to the main leaders. By the end of April, the whole of Morelos had joined the Obregón rebellion, and the *hacendados* had once again fled the state. On May 2, together with the chief Zapatist leaders, Obregón addressed the population of Cuernavaca. He declared that the uprising would soon triumph and quash the Carranzist resistance in the Federal District.

On May 7, Carranza fled the capital by train in the hope of reaching Veracruz with his small escort of loyal troops and the contents of the national treasury. Two days later Obregón triumphantly entered Mexico City, riding alongside Genovevo de la O at the head of the southern forces. Carranza never reached Veracruz: under continuous attack from Obregonist and Zapatist units, he left the railway line and pushed deep into the Puebla Mountains. On May 21, 1920, some former members of his bodyguard killed him as he lay asleep in Tlaxcalaltongo encampment. Regardless of who inspired or ordered the assassination, it revealed the decomposition of the Carranza regime. Barely a year had passed since the treacherous murder of Zapata, only six months since the legal murder of Felipe Angeles.

The Congress had already supported Obregón before the fall of Carranza, and on May 24, 1920, it chose Adolfo de la Huerta as provisional president. On June 2, twenty thousand soldiers, including a number of Zapatists, marched past the National Palace in support of the new regime. On the balcony, alongside the president and General Obregón, were such disparate figures as Pablo González and Genovevo de la O. United under the banner of Obregonism, they already indicated the contradictory and even antagonistic social base on which Obregón and his successors would establish their power.

On May 10, just after the overthrow of Carranza, an American journalist interviewed Francisco Villa in Santa Cruz de Rosales, Chihuahua. Villa told him: "It's not clear that I'll decide to disband my men in the light of those changes. . . . Of course, I think that the present takeover is a step in the right direction. . . . I think the Obregonists will break for good with Carranza, but I'm not so sure they have the people's real interests at heart." He said that no talks had yet taken place, and that someone had already posed as a defector to lure him into the kind of trap in which Zapata died. "They'll never kill me like that," he added. "I have to be careful, because I'm the last hope for the Mexican people to improve its lot."

As soon as he was installed, de la Huerta sought to bring about Villa's surrender. Gildardo Magaña urged negotiations between the two sides and, claiming that the government was "very favorably disposed," called on Villa's supporters to enter talks. Early in July, a presidential envoy reached the guerrilla leader, who demanded, among other things, a hacienda in Chihuahua for him and his men, recognition of his rank as general, the right to maintain a government-paid bodyguard of his own choosing, and various safeguards and disbandment pay for all the men who would surrender with him. On July 9, the army and navy minister, General Plutarco Elías Calles, declared that there would be no deal with Villa and that he had to surrender unconditionally. "He is regarded not as a political factor but as a military problem," the minister stated. "If his conditions were accepted, the northern bandit would be given greater value and importance than he deserves." Calles, speaking on behalf of those who, like Obregón himself, were opposed to any agreement with Villa, thereby brought to an end the negotiations taking place in Saucillo, Chihuahua. Villa immediately struck camp and disappeared with his men, breaking off all contact with the government.

Troops set off in pursuit, but the guerrilla leader seemed to have vanished into thin air. Then he carried out his last military stroke. In a five-day forced march, he and his troops crossed the Mapimi Bulge—a large desert lying between Chihuahua and Coahuila in which there is not a drop of water for hundreds of kilometers. They then launched a surprise attack on Sabinas, in the heart of the Coahuila coal-mining district, and captured the town with its seventy-strong garrison on July 26, 1920. Seizing a few trains, they tore up the rails fifty kilometers to the north and south in order to avoid a counterattack.

No one expected Villa to be in the region, since it was considered impossible that any military unit, even the Villist knights, could so quickly cross the Mapimí Bulge under such conditions. Thus, when Villa cabled de la Huerta at 5 o'clock in the morning, announcing that he had taken Sabinas and wanted direct negotiations with the government, the president's first reaction was to disbelieve the whole story. Villa could not be there if he had been in Saucillo a few days before. Yet he was, and de la Huerta eventually agreed to appoint the Coahuila military commander as his representative in negotiations with Villa. Thus, the peasant leader had again successfully applied his favorite method of initiating talks: first he struck a lightning blow to improve the relationship of forces, and then he sat down to talk. It was what he had done six years earlier, on an incomparably greater scale, when he captured Zacatecas before imposing the Torreón Accords on Carranza.

The federal general duly arrived with a small escort, and an agreement putting an end to the Villist rebellion was signed on July 28, 1920, at Sabinas, Coahuila. The terms were as follows:

1. General Villa shall lay down arms and retire to private life. 2. The Executive of the Mexican Union shall transfer to General Villa the full legal ownership of the Canutillo hacienda, located in the state of Durango, and shall hand over the deeds to the property. 3. In the aforementioned place, General Villa shall keep an escort of fifty trusted men chosen by himself, which shall come under the army and navy ministry and be paid a corresponding salary. The said escort may not be removed or distracted from its sole function: to watch over General Villa's personal safety. 4. The government shall pay a year's salary, corresponding to current rank, to all other persons who presently form part of Villa's forces both in this town and in various places to which they have been assigned by General Villa. Those concerned shall also be given the ownership of land in the

place they indicate, so that they may dedicate themselves to work. 5. Those who wish to continue a military career shall be incorporated into the national army.

In making his way to Tlahualillo, the agreed point at which his thousand well-equipped guerrillas were to hand in their arms, Francisco Villa made a wide detour through various pueblos in the North and received an enthusiastic welcome from the poorer inhabitants. Although the government had offered him trains, he chose to ride on horseback not only as a precaution against a trap, but also in order to demonstrate the popular support he still attracted in the North.

Guarded by his *dorados*, Villa spent three years working his farmland at Canutillo. He used modern machinery, and established a primary school named after Felipe Angeles for children of the hacienda and of the region. Although he took no part in politics, neither was he any help to the government of Obregón, as Gildardo Magaña and Antonio Díaz Soto y Gama were. His negotiated surrender left free an ongoing threat to the regime: the very figure of Villa.

Pancho Villa frequently traveled from Canutillo to Parral. On June 20, 1923, he was in his car with five of his men. On a city street, a group of ambushers took them by surprise, and more than one hundred bullets ended Villa's life, along with the lives of his companions, without giving them time to even reach for their guns. Many years later what everyone then suspected was confirmed: the order had come from the government of the Republic.

Five years later, in the middle of June 1928, when he had just been elected for a second presidential term, Alvaro Obregón, the last of the five great *caudillos* of the Revolution, was also—like Madero, Zapata, Carranza, and Villa before him—cut down by bullets.

The Carranza experience had been the third attempt to process the social gains of the revolution into a mere personnel change and a political restructuring of bourgeois domination.

The first attempt was the Ciudad Juárez Accords and the Madero regime. The second attempt was the Huerta regime, which turned to naked repression in place of Madero's mixture of conciliation and repression. But the basic goal was the same: to end the revolutionary stage, and to establish a successor to the Díaz regime without undergoing major social upheavals or economic changes. This time, it was not struggle at the top but a national insurrection driven by the peasant masses that brought the plans to ruin.

The third attempt, though weakened by the revolutionary upsurge and the violent overthrow of Huerta, could take advantage of the later downturn in the revolution and, to some extent, cloak itself with the Querétaro program. Like Madero's regime, it was brought to an end by a revolt within its own apparatus. This time, however, the blow came from the left, and was designed not to stifle the masses through repression, but to contain them through a policy of concessions that no longer jeopardized the whole system of private property.

As we have seen, Obregón played a decisive role in the defeat of the Villist army and the ratification of the Querétaro Constitution, took part in the negotiations over the departure of the U.S. punitive expedition, and held talks with the workers' leaders while the 1916 general strike was being repressed. But then he withdrew from both the government and the struggle against the Carranza regime, leaving it strengthened as a result of his military and political activity. Indeed, Carranza was even able to use the 1917 Constitution as a cover for his policy.

Obregón retired to Sonora to cultivate his estates. The peasantry, however, had no estates to cultivate and never gave up resistance. Although the ebb of the revolution made conditions much more difficult, they continued the struggle in 1916, 1917, and 1918 and maintained their independence of the national authorities. This constant activity wore down the Carranzist army, reached out for international contacts, and, above all, stimulated the revival of the workers' movement after the defeat of the general strike.

Another important factor in this revival, particularly intense in

1919 and 1920, was the European revolutionary upsurge impelled by the victory of the Russian Revolution. Strikes and wage demands were continually growing in the railways, the oil industry, textiles, electricity, the Tampico and Veracruz docks, and a number of other sectors. The workers also fought for social demands: application of the conquests enshrined in the Constitution and, above all, the right to trade-union organization. In May 1918, a national labor congress in Saltillo set up the Mexican Regional Workers Federation (CROM), the first national workers' organization in the country. This wave of mobilizations reached an even higher level with the fall of Carranza and the interim presidency of Adolfo de la Huerta.

In the North, the government armies proved unable to suppress the Villist guerrillas, or even to prevent the steady stream of defeats suffered at their hands.

The growing isolation of Carranza highlighted the inflexibility of his policy of restoring the land to its former proprietors and reviving the influence of the old ruling class. At the same time, this very quest for support among the old landowners heightened still further the isolation of his regime.

Despite its clashes with Carranza's nationalist policy, and despite its constant pressure to capitalize on the regime's difficulties, the U.S. government did not make any fundamental mistakes in its analysis of the Mexican situation. Already in 1915 Washington recognized Carranza as the lesser evil; and it increasingly saw him as the party of order, bent on ending the revolution, who should be supported against any tendency to breathe new life into the revolution or to drive the regime politically and socially to the left. The military commander of El Paso made the U.S. positions clear in 1919: we have recognized a government in Mexico, and we will not talk with rebels. Gone were the quite recent times when Washington sent agents to each of the warring factions. Washington acted accordingly, trying to force concessions out of Carranza, yet backing him against any force that might open the gates to any comeback of revolutionary forces. It had no sympathy for the rise of Obregón, however moderate his election campaign.

The revolutionary-nationalist wing of the army clearly perceived Carranza's failure to fulfill the Querétaro promises: it resisted the measures to restore the position of the old landowners; it condemned the rapacious activity of the nouveaux riches officers; it recoiled from the mass repression and the murder of Zapata.[4] And yet, it was held in check by Carranza's nationalist policy vis-à-vis the Americans. The role of anti-imperialist officers finally expressed itself in the great army turnaround and the Agua Prieta Plan. For many generals and officers, however, the main fear was that a "civilian" administration under Bonillas would take away the power and privileges they had acquired through their military functions.

The president's appointment of Bonillas as his successor was not merely a crude personal response to the situation. The aim was to liquidate from above all the social conquests; to convert ten years of revolution into a mere change of political personnel; to "modernize" the old regime.

This enterprise died in Tlaxcalaltongo with Carranza. In ten years of combat, the popular energies had suffered enormous attrition. Yet, as Pancho Villa said, the people did not give in: they managed to link their tenacity to the new epoch and, through indirect representatives, made a supreme effort to bring down Carranza and his reactionary faction. This put an end to the last attempt of that period to establish a regime that would not have to depend on the support of the people. It is therefore not surprising that the figure of Carranza, rooted in the Porfirian past, has a higher place on the altar of the Mexican bourgeoisie than the figure of Obregón, rooted in the provincial petty bourgeoisie.

When Pancho Villa laid down arms in July 1920, he was not merely giving way to weariness or lack of prospects. Rather dimly, it is true, the Villists saw that the overthrow of Carranza had accomplished the objective then within reach. They had no confidence in the new victors: "It looks to me like the same bull that's just been touched up," Villa told an American journalist. Yet they expressed the conclusion that any further advance would require more strength than they then possessed. Villa did not follow Magaña along the road of capitulation; nor was his action like that of Angeles in 1915 and 1919. "We'll carry on until Don Venus falls from the tree," Villa had said the previous year. And now "Don Venus" Carranza had indeed breathed his last. Villa's peasant tenacity had never involved mere obstinacy. When he said to Angeles in 1919 that Chihuahua was "no longer any good for making revolutions," he was referring not only to the material resources in the region, but also, indirectly, to the exhaustion of the peasants themselves. At that point, he could do nothing other than break off the struggle. Villa's surrender of arms symbolized not the defeat or the final conclusion of the revolution, but its interruption until the development of a more favorable stage.

Obregón came forward to establish national power on a new political basis. Consistent with his whole trajectory during the revolution, he understood that the development of a new bourgeoisie required certain concessions to the masses within a tightly controlled framework. At the same time, it would be necessary to lean on them in order to confront both imperialism and the forces of restoration, as well as the possible alliance between the two.

Although the old landowners did not forfeit most of their property, remaining—at least until the Cárdenas period—the economically strongest sector of the bourgeoisie, they were definitively excluded from power. For its part, the industrial bourgeoisie was then a weak force, torn between the mass of foreign investment and state-controlled holdings. At the political level, it seemed completely tied to the old, prerevolutionary regime.

This accounts for the peculiar character of Obregón's Bonapartism, which rested politically on the instrument of the Mexican Army, and socially on union organizations under the control of a bureaucracy tied to the state apparatus.[5]

In August 1919, at the start of his election campaign, Obregón signed an agreement with the Mexican Regional Workers Federation

(CROM). Its leader, Luis N. Morones, would later be one of the strongest pillars of the Obregón regime and make his fortune as a government minister. He was the prototype of those labor bureaucrats who, while enriching themselves and providing political personnel for the bourgeoisie, eventually come to rely upon armed gangsters to crush any attempt at rank-and-file opposition. In December, CROM and Morones founded the Labor Party and declared their support for Obregón's candidacy. At the beginning of 1920, Obregón reached a further pact with Magaña and Díaz Soto y Gama. Antonio Díaz Soto y Gama subsequently formed the Agrarian Party as another of the political foundations of the Obregón regime.

These two pacts, together with the support of the army, gave Obregón all the prerequisites for his coup d'état. By suppressing the most odious features of Carranzism and granting certain concessions to his left, he used the trade-union and Zapatist leaderships to channel the nationwide resistance of the workers and peasants; and by associating these leaderships with the state apparatus, he ensured that he would keep a hold over them. This very structure further allowed him to control the military factions, and to exploit the army as a political force. The nationalist sentiments of the army, as of the population itself, could also be used in the process of confrontation and negotiation with Washington.

This complex balancing game was the only political and social basis that could have permitted the economic development of a bourgeoisie, without provoking a direct clash with the peasants and urban workers or political abdication to the alliance of the old oligarchy and imperialism.

The new bourgeoisie that emerged from the revolution through scandalous state-organized plunder encouraged the involvement of the old bourgeoisie in a subordinate position. But neither Obregón nor his successors would allow the existence of a traditional oligarchic or bourgeois political party to challenge the legitimacy of the revolution or the regime that issued from it. When the Church, by force of circumstance, was impelled to fill this vacuum and to operate as a de facto political party of reaction, Obregón and then Calles mobilized against it the whole accumulated weight of the liberal, anticlerical tradition of the Mexican revolutions. Similarly, Obregón and Calles mercilessly crushed attempts to organize an opposition within the army. Between 1920 and 1928 (the year of Obregón's assassination), dozens of officers who had served in the Constitutionalist Army, including Obregón's closest collaborators in the campaigns against Huerta and Villa, were brought before a firing squad or otherwise liquidated.

Nevertheless, the regime would remain a prisoner of the revolution and its working-class and peasant base: its weakness from birth prevented it from developing an independent class base, which could only have been attained through an alliance with representatives of the old regime. The play of bourgeois parliamentary parties, characteristic of capitalist democracy, vanished in Mexico; and although a parliament continued to exist in name, it did not play any role in national politics. The extreme concentration of presidential power was not a sign of strength, but an indication that the regime cannot sustain legal, parliamentary struggles between rival bourgeois sectors and parties. It had to place itself completely in the hands of a supreme presidential arbiter: that is the essence of the Bonapartist form of government.

The U.S. government continued to put pressure on Obregón in order to keep the 1917 Constitution, and particularly article 27, as far as possible from its own holdings in the country. However moderate Obregón's declarations, Washington could see that the class base of the new regime would not allow the consolidation of a firm bourgeois power; that it would not be possible to avoid a nationalist policy on the part of the Mexican government; and that, ultimately, the danger of renewed popular movements was still present. Initially, therefore, it withheld from de la Huerta and Obregón the official recognition it had given Carranza in 1915. Diplomatic links were restored only in July 1923, a few days after the murder of Pancho Villa, which was a kind of token, and after the Mexican government had undertaken, through the Bucareli Accords, to respect the property rights of Americans in the country. The next year, however, in his typically Bonapartist style, Obregón made Mexico the first country on the American continent, and one of the first in the world, to recognize the Soviet Union.

The officers of Carranza's army had enriched themselves by buying up the best lands of the old Porfirian oligarchy at knockdown prices, while the agrarian redistribution for which the peasants had fought the revolution barely went further than the parchment of the Constitution. Under Obregón, this system of capitalist class formation reached quite scandalous proportions, and state-organized plunder became a veritable national institution through such forms as economic concessions, handouts, public contracts, and even more brazen diversion of public funds. The postrevolutionary bourgeoisie developed through this peculiar system of "primitive accumulation" (already tested in Europe centuries before), then invested its gain in banking, industrial, and commercial concerns and went on enriching itself by the normal mechanisms of capital accumulation. Forces newly attached to the state political apparatus then took their turn to become capitalists through the plunder of state funds. Many years before, when he was still fighting Huerta, Obregón had anticipated such a future in a conversation with Lucio Blanco. Pouring scorn on those who concerned themselves with land redistribution, he said with a smile, "We'll be the *científicos* of tomorrow."[6]

This system played an indispensable role by making the trade-union bureaucracy a partner in the use of the state apparatus for private gain. Together with the firing squad and the assassin's pistol, it also served to maintain control over the military factions which, given the preponderant role of the army in establishing and maintaining the regime, were constantly incited to fresh conspiracies. Obregón again summed it up well: "No general can withstand a 50,000-peso cannon-shot." Obregón created the model to which subsequent Mexican governments have clung. The old principle of transformation of power into property became the golden rule of the Mexican postrevolutionary political regime.

The presidential elections of September 5, 1920, formally confirmed what had already been resolved by nonelectoral means. On December 1, Alvaro Obregón legally assumed office as president of the Republic.

10

Epilogue

The 1910–20 Revolution was a crucial juncture in the history of Mexico: all the previously active customs, traditions, conquests, upheavals, and dreams poured into the great flux; the tendencies and determinations of all subsequent years flowed away from it along countless channels. None of the dramatic events that have occurred since then have left such a powerful and lasting mark on contemporary Mexico.

There has been much debate on the character and results of the ten-year period. Some writers deny that a revolution actually took place, while others, at the opposite extreme, argue that the revolution has continued ever since in an unbroken line. We cannot now enter into that dispute. We may, however, close our account of the Mexican Revolution by reviewing its social, economic, and political consequences.

In 1917, Vladimir Ilyich Lenin, soon to become the leader and theoretician of the first socialist revolution in history, made the following pertinent distinction:

> If we take the revolutions of the twentieth century as examples we shall, of course, have to admit that the Portuguese and Turkish revolutions are both bourgeois revolutions. Neither of them, however, is a "people's" revolution, inasmuch as in neither does the mass of the people, its enormous majority, come out actively, independently, with its own economic and political demands to any noticeable degree. By contrast, although the Russian bourgeois revolution of 1905–07 displayed no such "brilliant" successes as at times fell to the

lot of the Portuguese and Turkish revolutions, it was undoubtedly a
"real people's" revolution. For the mass of the people, its majority,
the very lowest social strata, crushed by oppression and exploitation,
rose independently and placed on the entire course of the revolution the impress of *their own* demands, *their* attempts to build in their
own way a new society in the place of the old society that was being destroyed.[1]

Some years later, another leader of the Revolution, and its historian, wrote, "The history of a revolution is for us first of all a history
of the forcible entry of the masses into the realm of sovereignty over
their own destiny."[2]

For both Lenin and Trotsky, then, a revolution is essentially defined by the manifold intervention of the masses to decide the
whole fate of society. The program, leadership, and outcome are
naturally important, as is the idea its actors form of the events. But
the key is the irruption into history of the broadest masses, the
most exploited, oppressed, and muted in times of calm and stability.

If we use the yardstick of mass intervention and mobilization,
weighing up their spatial and temporal extent and the changes in
the life, habits, and mentality of millions of men and women, then
the Mexican Revolution was unquestionably one of the most profound in Latin America and one of the greatest anywhere in a century so rich in revolutions. This criterion allows us to plot what
we may call the *social curve* of the revolution. The peak will not be
the ratification of the 1917 Constitution, as it is for the institutional,
state-centered optic of official histories, but the point when the
strength and mobilization of the armed peasant masses culminated
in the occupation of Mexico City. It will be the victory of December 1914.

We may thus distinguish four phases of the revolution: (1) the
period up to Madero's triumph over Porfirio Díaz, when two tendencies of the bourgeoisie were locked in a struggle for power; (2)
the Maderist regime and the continuing struggle against the Zapatist insurgency in the South; (3) the sequel to Huerta's coup and

the assassination of Madero, again dominated by a clash between bourgeois tendencies, Federalist and Constitutionalist, only this time with mass participation in the armed struggle; and (4) the period following Huerta's defeat in 1914, when the new victors divided along clearer class lines between the Constitutionalist Army of Carranza and Obregón and the peasant armies of Zapata and Villa. The revolution grew ever more radical up to the occupation of Mexico City by the Northern Division and the Southern Liberation Army, continually drawing in new fighters and spreading through the territory of the Republic. In the first and third phases, the bourgeois tendency which led and invoked the revolution generally bandied the land question in order to mobilize a mass peasant base. In the second and fourth phases, the same wing of the bourgeoisie turned to repress those peasants who sought to continue the revolution and the struggle for land. Not once—as in all the classical bourgeois revolutions—but *twice* did the victorious bourgeois leadership move against the extreme wing of the revolution in order to hold the movement within the confines of capitalist property.

The first time, the Madero leadership was able to maintain the continuity of the old Porfirian state, symbolized in the federal army and the letter and the institutions of the 1857 Constitution. The second time, however, the revolution completely destroyed the military backbone of the old state: the ensuing regime established itself upon a new army, a new constitution, and a new state, still bourgeois in character and largely drawn from the administrative personnel of the old state, yet involving different relations with, and a new mode of domination over, the Mexican people.

The fourth phase of the revolution continued the previous rise in December 1914 and January 1915, but then entered a long, grim downturn full of incident, which stretched from the advance of Obregón's Operational Army on Mexico City and the defeat and dissolution of the Northern Division in 1915, through the defeat of the workers' movement in 1916, to the reorganization of the state in the 1917 Constitution and the large-scale drive to annihilate the stubborn resistance of the Morelos villages in the South, the Villist units in the North, and the peasantry in every part of the country.

The whole curve embraces a period of ten years. During that time, the peasant masses—that is, the people of Mexico, 85 percent of whom lived in the countryside in 1910—underwent the most dramatic experiences: they took up arms, forced their way into a history that had previously unfolded above their heads, marched across the country in every direction, shattered the army of their oppressors at Zacatecas, occupied the national capital, raised Villa and Zapata (two peasants like themselves) to the summit of the insurrection, issued a series of laws, and embarked on a systematic attempt at self-government in the South, creating elementary decision-making bodies and a new juridical structure. In other words, they "rose independently and placed on the entire course of the revolution the impress of *their own* demands, *their* attempts to build in their own way a new society in the place of the old society that was being destroyed." In their last momentous experience, the painful ebb of the revolution, they and their leaders continued to fight in defense of positions already won, with a tenacity that is one of the revolution's most precious bequests to the collective consciousness. Even after they had lost their leader and suffered defeat in the South, they made a last great effort to tip the scales in the victorious faction against Carranza's right-wing policies.

In its objectives and outcome, the national uprising was a bourgeois revolution. At the same time, however, it was a peasant war for land in which the most radical wing, grouped around the Ayala Plan, made proposals and took measures of an anticapitalist character. As in every bourgeois revolution, the plebeian left wing went beyond the limits of capitalism and pointed toward a social revolution. Its ideas and aspirations could not emerge triumphant, any more than Munzer could in Germany's Peasant War, the *enragés* in the Great French Revolution, or the Paris workers in the Revolution of 1848. The meeting point and center of gravity for the various participants in the Mexican Revolution were the demands and proposals inscribed in the 1917 Constitution. Still, without the tenacious armed intervention of the peasants and their most advanced programs, that center of gravity would have been much further to the right—for example, in the positions of Madero, Vázquez Gomez, or Venustiano Carranza and his Guadalupe Plan. Only at isolated times and places, particularly in Zapatist territory, were the peasants able to transcend the globally bourgeois character of the revolution. Yet their activity ensured that it was not *another* kind of revolution, equally bloody but much more limited and conservative in its results. Thus, it would be wrong merely to say that they were defeated, just as the official version is wrong in saying that they were victorious.

During the ups and downs of a ten-year armed struggle, the Zapatists were the only tendency that never laid down arms. The revolution was officially brought to an end after Madero's victory and again after Carranza's pronunciamento. What kept it *alive* was the southern insurrection, which sustained the deepest currents of the revolution until they returned to cover the whole country.

The Zapatist movement had four essential features: it *always* refused to hand over its guns; it developed a program of its own in the Ayala Plan, whose juridical bases, though rudimentary, were incompatible with bourgeois legality; it created a form of popular self-government still unique in Mexican history; and it issued radical legislation which, as in the case of Palafox's agrarian law, partly went beyond the juridical limits of capitalism.

All this did not, of course, amount to a socialist revolution, but neither was it merely a bourgeois revolution. It is true that every bourgeois revolution has a left wing that breaks its bounds at the climactic moment and is then smashed by the victorious center. In Mexico, however, this wing not only embodied the continuity of the whole revolutionary cycle, but for a whole period of time— longer than the Paris Commune of 1871 or the Berlin and Hungarian communes of 1919—evolved a form of popular power that has been ignored in all the official histories. This experience of mass self-organization, like the military exploits of the Northern Division, set a hidden mark on the whole future development of people's consciousness. Pancho Villa, in Chihuahua, also received support from the working population and took measures in their favor. But the Zapatist power in Morelos was qualitatively distinct, both in its juridical basis and in the real, though rudimentary, character of peasant self-government.

Clearly peasant support for the southern revolution, as well as certain aspects of the Zapatist program itself, rested upon the millenary vision of a "golden age" that looked backward to its roots in precapitalist conditions. While always pursuing these utopian objectives, however, peasant wars have been the basis of both bourgeois and socialist revolutions. Wherein lies the difference? In the epoch of the rise of the bourgeoisie, the peasant risings of Munzer in Germany or Winstanley's Diggers in England eventually succumbed to fierce repression without leaving any trace in the new order. In the epoch of imperialism, when world reality has already posed, if not resolved, the question of socialism as a nonutopian possibility, a peasant war may either merge with this perspective or, in its extreme forms, herald its emergence. Thus, although Zapata's armed struggle and "utopian" Commune were defeated, they left their mark on the emergent Republic, so that the Mexican peasants could never be disregarded in its political and social life.

There were a number of reasons why the working class played only a secondary role in the Mexican Revolution—its previous history, its relatively small numerical weight, and the very disposition of the central conflict. Some of its struggles were important, and its class organization moved forward, but its policy and leadership did not attain independence of the state and the leading bourgeois tendencies of the revolution.

Ultimately the decisive tendency was the so-called Sonora dynasty, leaders of the capitalist petty bourgeoisie from Sonora State who were equipped with a program for national development. But although they finally prevailed over Carranza's landowner tendency, more directly linked to Madero's class tradition, they also grouped around them the whole new bourgeoisie which, by means of the revolutionary movement, had made headway against the state of the landowners and *cientificos*. This new force comprised Constitutionalist Army officers from the provincial urban petty bourgeoisie; members of the liberal professions recruited to the state administration; owners of large or medium-size industrial and mining concerns; landowners who had managed to save or recover their property in the midst of the revolutionary turmoil and resurfaced alongside the victors in 1917 and 1918; and a host of careerists of diverse origin, not very different from those whom Napoleon I, and later Louis Bonaparte, assembled after the French revolutions.

The axis of the new power bloc was unquestionably the state apparatus itself, which later played a key role in the formation and growth of the Mexican bourgeoisie. The class of big landowners was excluded from the state and lost its political power for ever, although the main transfer of agrarian property would only take place in the Cárdenas era. In the course of the revolution, the new bourgeoisie (the "revolutionary bourgeoisie" or "revolutionary family," as it would come to be known) gained considerable experience in relating to the masses and developing characteristic methods of domination. Similarly, the fact that its leaders participated in the armed struggle secured a certain popular legitimacy both for themselves and for the post-1920 state.

The urban petty bourgeoisie did not assume an independent role in the revolution, even though its representatives fought in both the Constitutionalist and Villist armies and, to a limited, highly selective degree, in the Zapatist movement. However, just as it provided some of the leaders of the new bourgeoisie, so it produced the representatives of the "Jacobin," radical-democratic wing of Constitutionalism. These men, with their socialist-type ideas, were among the most eminent figures at the 1917 Constituent Congress, and the current would again burst forth in the Cárdenas period.

The population of Mexico fell by nearly a million, from 15.2 to 14.3 million, in the ten years of the revolution. Apart from the actual fighting, other important factors were the declining birthrate, the flight northward from the effects of the civil war, and the influenza epidemic that lashed the country in 1918–19 and struck with particular severity in the sectors and regions (Morelos, for example) most weakened by the war.[3]

The economy underwent violent changes, above all where the military conflict was at its sharpest. There was never a general collapse, however, and some sectors like henequen profited from the especially favorable world market conditions before and after the outbreak of world war. Oil exports soared from 200,000 pesos in 1910–11 to 516,800,000 in 1920, while the oil contribution to gross domestic product climbed by a yearly average of 43 percent, from 33 million 1950-pesos in 1910 to 1,733 million in 1921. Both oil and henequen came from Constitutionalist-held territory, the Gulf of Mexico and Yucatán, providing the financial mainstay for the struggle against Villa and Zapata. This also explains why Felipe Angeles was eager to concentrate his forces in the North and to occupy the Tampico region and port, whereas Villa accepted battle on Obregón's chosen ground, the agrarian regions of the Bajío.

War destruction mainly hit the agriculture of the Laguna district and central Mexico, while the Morelos sugar industry, one of the country's main export sectors just before 1910, produced only for local consumption. However, the resulting decline in global agricultural production did encourage the development of certain crops in less affected regions: in the Northwest, for example, cotton exports filled the gap left by the La Laguna. Similar processes were apparent in the mining industry. Small and medium-size mines suffered a major downturn, but many of the larger, foreign-owned mines were able to maintain production. Total output in this sector fell from 1,039 million 1950-pesos in 1910 to 620 million in 1921 and only regained the 1910 level in 1923.

Although information about the course of the economy during these years is scarce and unreliable, everyone agrees that the bottom was reached at the height of the revolutionary curve in 1914–15.

Thus between 1910 and 1915, gold production fell from 41,420 to 7,358 kilograms and silver from 2,417 to 1,231 tonnes. Lead production plummeted from 124.3 to 5.7 tonnes, but gradually recovered after 1916 in the high-demand conditions of world war.

The revolution seriously disorganized the railway network, turning the trains to civil war requirements and destroying a great deal of track and rolling stock. This, of course, created further obstacles to production. But since various goods were unable to reach distant markets, local producers often stepped in to fill the gap in their own area. Craft production and craft labor therefore tended to shift from one part of the country to another. It should also be borne in mind that much of this local production, like nearly all agricultural output for local or subsistence consumption, does not figure in the statistics for market-oriented production. As is always the case in an overwhelmingly peasant country, the real figures diverged all the more from official statistics to the extent that wartime disorganization forced a return to precapitalist forms and relations of production and exchange. There can be no doubt that, during the ten years of revolution, Mexico was able to make ample use of these means of survival offered by a not-so-distant past; and that, particularly for the key 1914–15 period, the real fall in agricultural, artisanal, and mining production is somewhat exaggerated by the inevitable statistical focus on *market sectors*.

At the level of the economy as a whole, gross domestic product declined from 11,650 million 1950-pesos in 1910 to 11,273 million in 1921. Although the fantastic leap in oil production served to offset the decline in other areas, the contribution of manufacturing output only fell from 1,836 million 1950-pesos in 1910 to 1,669 million in 1921. This indicates a certain continuity in the activity of major industries, situated as they were in towns and regions relatively unscathed by the vicissitudes of war. By contrast, the share of agriculture in GDP fell from 2,609 million 1950-pesos in 1910 to 1,441 million in 1921, only regaining its prerevolutionary level in 1925. The livestock figures show a no less dramatic drop from 1,501 million pesos in 1910 to 905 million in 1921, the earlier level only being recovered in 1925.

Even in the absence of other data, the growth rate in various sectors of the economy indicates not only that Mexico and the Mexican Revolution were of an essentially peasant character, but that industry and the working class played a marginal role in the course of the civil war. Table 10.1, which provides data from the last fifteen years of the old regime through 1967, sets out this evidence.[4]

The turmoil in the credit and banking system also reached a peak in 1914–15, when contending military factions precipitated military disorder by uncontrolled issues of currency.

As regards Mexico's integration into the world economy, the course of events during this period merely reinforced and made irreversible a trend that was already apparent by the end of the Porfirio Díaz regime. Womack puts it well: "After the promulgation of the new Constitution, together with United States intervention in the world war, the Mexican economy began a recovery more dependent than ever upon developments in the United States."

Lastly, we should consider the crucial question of the revolution, the land. The relationship of peon dependence upon the hacienda virtually disappeared throughout the country. The same was not true, however, of the haciendas themselves. There was a regionally uneven transfer of land ownership; but with the exception of Morelos and some south-central regions, the great concentrations changed hands without undergoing any reduction in size. This is another argument, if one is necessary, explaining the profound vitality of the Zapatist movement.

According to Womack's calculations, the communal holdings (*ejidos*) covered 1.6 percent of the total in 1910; holdings between 0.1 and 1,000 hectares accounted for 26.6 percent; and haciendas over 1,000 hectares for 71.8 percent. In 1923 the three corresponding figures were 2.6, 19.6, and 77.9 percent, respectively. Although other writers have given different estimates, they have not significantly altered the broad proportional breakdown. We may therefore conclude that the key question of the revolution did not

Table 10.1
Average Annual Growth Rate (in percent)

Years	Total	Agriculture	Live-stock	Forestry	Fisheries	Mining	Oil	Manufac-turing	Building	Electrical Energy	Transport	State Administration	Trade	Others
1895–1900	4.9	3.4	1.3	3.9	n.a	4.2	n.a	8.9	5.7	20.0	3.1	4.5	7.7	4.6
1901–1910	3.5	4.8	1.2	6.5	n.a	6.6	54.0[1]	3.1	6.8	17.9	2.2	1.3	3.4	3.1
1911–1921	–0.3	–5.2	–4.6	0.2	n.a	4.6	43.0	–0.9	2.2	0.7	3.1	1.3	0.2	0.7
1922–1935	3.4	5.3	5.7	7.0	8.2	4.4	–7.1	3.8	6.8	12.1	3.7	4.1	4.3	2.9
1936–1956	5.8	4.9	2.9	4.0	9.6	4.2	4.7	7.5	8.7	6.5	7.0	6.5	6.3	5.9
1957–1962	6.2	3.8	4.2	4.4	4.9	1.6	7.6	8.0	7.4	9.4	3.6	5.4	6.3	6.5
1895–1910	3.6	2.3	1.2	5.7	n.a	5.9	n.a	4.9	6.3	18.7	2.5	2.3	4.8	3.6
1921–1967	5.2	4.7	4.1	4.2	8.0	2.3	1.7	6.5	7.8	8.9	5.2	5.5	5.7	5.2

Sources: Bank of Mexico, Department of Economic Studies, *Producto Nacional Bruto: Revisión de las estimaciones para los años 1919–1949*, December 17, 1964; *Estatísticas de Produción Nacional 1950–1966*, February 22, 1967.

(1) Figure for the period 1903–1910.

receive an answer, and that the concentration of agrarian property was not changed. Only in 1940 would a markedly different structure emerge: 22.5 percent for the *ejidos,* 15.9 percent for holdings under 1,000 hectares, and 61.6 percent for haciendas over 1,000 hectares. As we can see, Cardenism changed the terms but did not remove the land question. But had there been no revolution, there would not even have been Mexican agrarian reform and Cardenism.[5]

If history were just a matter of economic statistics, it would not be far from the truth to say that virtually nothing changed in the course of the Mexican Revolution, and that, all things considered, there was no revolution. Some people have actually argued this point, which logically ought to be applied to the French, English, and many other revolutions. If accepted, it would certainly thin out the history of revolutions and strengthen the argument that they are a useless endeavor.

The Mexican Revolution, some may argue, did not even open the road to capitalist development, since the irreversible drive in this direction took place under Porfirio Díaz or, to be more specific, between the years 1885 and 1905. Indeed, if there had been no civil war between 1910 and 1920, such development would have been able to profit from the world war (as happened in Argentina, Brazil, and Chile) and the landowning class would gradually have transformed itself into an industrial bourgeoisie, no doubt through inner class conflicts but within the constitutional limits of the existing state. The same three countries show that this was a real possibility. (In Argentina, the crucial political change occurred in 1912, when President Roca, representing the landed oligarchy, decreed the law on secret and universal suffrage that allowed Hipolito Yrigoyen, representing the interests of the nascent industrial bourgeoisie, to take over as president in 1916.) Francisco I. Madero was set on the same course when, through "sheer bad luck," the subaltern classes escaped both his and everyone else's control.

The type of capitalist development established in the late nineteenth century was, it is true, pointing toward the transformation of the landowning class into a bourgeois class through a process of imbrication. This trend, however, combining with the solid implantation of foreign capital in specific sectors of the economy and a distinctive mode of integration into the world division of labor, was cut short and sharply deflected by the violent irruption of the revolutionary movement. This was, in turn, encouraged or permitted by the exacerbation of intra-bourgeois conflict, due to the explosive accumulation of contradictions at the heart of such capitalist development.

The irruption, lasting for roughly ten years, brought to power another section of the bourgeoisie that later swelled through its control of the new state apparatus and established *new relations of domination* with the masses.

As a result of the social, political, and economic contradictions peculiar to capitalist development in Mexico, the Mexican people underwent a hitherto unprecedented experience. Feeling themselves to be the subject, and no longer the mere object of history, they stored up a wealth of experience and consciousness that altered the whole country as it is *lived* by its inhabitants.

It was impossible to ignore or depreciate this change in the eventful century that followed, up to the Zapatista Indian armed rebellion in Chiapas in 1994, and after. In this specific sense, we can rightly say that the Mexican Revolution not only changed Mexico and had a deep and long-lasting influence all over Latin America, but also set the stage for the anti-colonial and socialist uprisings that spanned the twentieth century and still reverberate in the many movements for justice and freedom today.

NOTES

CHAPTER 1

1. In one of his studies on the development of capitalism in Porfirian
Mexico, Fernando Rosenzweig writes:

> The material basis of the Mexico that took the road of modernization
> in 1867 was, bar a few new features, the same as that of the Mexico
> which had found such a path blocked sixty years earlier; and with only
> incidental differences, the solution that had once been blocked was the
> solution that could be implemented the second time. As in the last years
> of colonial rule, so at the dawn of modern Mexico economic activities
> were tied to local, particularist forms, only rarely transcending artisan
> structures, subsistence agriculture or food production for nearby mar-
> kets. In a landscape dominated by mountains, and at a time when mules
> were virtually the sole means of transport, distances tended to isolate
> centers of production and consumption and to keep them small except
> in the expanding cities. Although trains already ran between Mexico
> City and Veracruz at the beginning of the Díaz era, the only connec-
> tions for freight and passengers alike were pack-animals or stage-
> coaches. Internal markets were generally of a closed, self-sufficient
> character, ill designed, except in one or two places, to handle the out-
> ward flow of such specialized agricultural products as sugar and veg-
> etable dyes, or the inward flow of implements, raw materials and
> consumption goods. The national economy, too, was little short of be-
> ing a closed structure, and foreign trade preserved its colonial pattern
> almost intact. Thus precious metals made up the great bulk of exports
> alongside one agricultural product or another. (Henequen still occu-
> pied a major place, but cochineal and dye wood were making an ap-
> pearance and sugar was continuing its first steps.) The main imports

were consumer goods for the well-off urban minorities and various appliances or materials for the mining and manufacturing sectors. Both in internal and external trade, the system of duties and tariffs represented a decisive obstacle. (F. Rosenzweig, "El desarrollo económico de México: 1877 a 1911," *El Trimestre Económicos* 23 [July–September 1965]: 405–54)

2. "Men have often made man himself into the primitive material of money, in the shape of the slave, but they have never done this with the land and soil. Such an idea could only arise in a bourgeois society, and one which was already well developed. It dates from the last third of the seventeenth century, and the first attempt to implement the idea on a national scale was made a century later, during the French bourgeois revolution." K. Marx, *Capital,* Vol. 1 (Harmondsworth, 1976), p. 183.

3. "The creole and mestizo towns provided both labor for employment and, in a wider area around the urban center, social demand that required satisfaction. Manufacturing was generally dispersed among small workshops, but the factory system had already made its mark in such industries as textiles. The equipment of the English Industrial Revolution, which could already be glimpsed in the final years of the colonial period, was brought into use, however narrowly, in the fourth decade of the century thanks to the pioneering efforts of Antunaño. In the early part of the Díaz era, however, steam engines and mechanical looms alternated with manual processes or machines driven by animal or human power." Rosenzweig, "El desarrollo económico," p. 407.

4. "With regard to the division of powers, the parliamentary regime enshrined in the 1857 Constitution was effectively replaced by the rule of an Executive with various extraordinary, discretional and dictatorial powers. The conflict between the executive and legislative powers, so intense during the Juárez and Lerdo administrations, was yet another symptom of the contradiction inherent in the liberal-oligarchic state. Represented in Congress were the interests of the regional and local oligarchies, which reaped profits from speculation, smuggling and trade monopolies. The Executive embodied the national interests and functions of the state, so that the conflict between the two was resolved through the strengthening of the Executive in response to demands for the consolidation of a national state." Juan Felipe Leal and

José Woldenberg, *Del Estado liberal a los inicios de la dictadura porfirista* (Mexico City, 1980, pp. 257–8).

5. "The victory of the Reform movement in 1867 opened the way to a fairly dynamic development of Mexico's economy. At the political level, the defeat of French intervention and the restoration of the liberal Republic created a government worthy of the respect of foreign powers, at a time when European imperialism, shortly followed by the United States, was preparing to absorb the undeveloped parts of the planet and to convert them into colonies or protectorates. Inside the country, the 1857 Constitution was finally established through the ratification of human and civil rights, the formal eradication of privileges and legal exemptions, and the assertion of the principle of a federal, representative and democratic government—the goals for which Mexican liberals had fought since independence. The appropriate structures were being established for the formation of capital, the circulation of wealth and the smooth functioning of a rising capitalist economy. In this new political reality, the forces that would change the landscape of a national economy still burdened with feudal characteristics were already advancing from two securely held points. One of these was the towns, where internal capital sought to break its localist fetters, diversify its activity and gain advantages from economies of scale and technological innovation. The other was the industrial heartlands themselves, whose capitalist development was tending to spread its roots to countries that produced primary products. Economic life was thus cohering at the level of a national market, which was in turn very broadly linked to the great international markets of the time." Rosenzweig, "El desarrollo económico," pp. 412–3.

6. Marx records the complaints made by Russian landowners concerning the emancipation of the serfs in 1861. The first was that they did not have enough money to pay the wages of their recently emancipated laborers.

> The second complaint is more typical, namely that, even when they have money, the labour-power to be bought is not available in sufficient quantity and at the right time. This is because the Russian agricultural worker, owing to the common ownership of the soil by the village community, is not yet fully separated from his means of production, and is thus still not a "free wage-labourer" in the full sense of the term. But

the presence of such "free wage-labourers" throughout society is the indispensable condition without which *M-C,* the transformation of money into commodities, cannot take the form of the transformation of money capital into productive capital. (*Capital,* Vol. 2 [Harmondsworth, 1978], p. 117).

7. John Kenneth Turner stated in 1910 that a conscripted worker's life expectancy was no more than one year. It was cheaper for the boss to kill him through overwork and hunger than to maintain the labor-power in better living and working conditions. See Turner, *Barbarous Mexico* (London: Austin, 1969).

8. "Land-ownership, ranching and commercial agriculture also drew major capital investment from the United States. Conditions were especially favorable in the Yaqui and Sonora river valleys in the southern half of Sonora State. Here, for example, the Richardson brothers divided up more than a hundred thousand acres of land and fifty miles of canals among California farmers, profiting from the extension of the Sonora railroad and the expulsion of the Yaquis from their ancestral lands. Both in the south and in the Sonora valley around Hermosillo, tomatoes and green vegetables were grown for the California market. By about 1902, North American corporations owned more than a million hectares in Sonora and even more in the neighbouring state of Sinaloa." Barry Carr, "The Peculiarities of the Mexican North, 1880–1928: An Essay in Interpretation," University of Chicago, Latin American Center, n.d.

9. Héctor Aguilar Camín offers the following interpretation:

Yaqui history from 1876 to 1930 should probably be written as if the Mexican Revolution had never taken place. Whether Porfirian or revolutionary, the anti-Yaqui repression in Sonora followed the same historical impulse and shared the same social context. The conclusion therefore belongs to a single, terrifying story.

In this unified process, Civilization wrenched the most fertile lands of Sonora from the Yaquis and overcame their resistance through a pitiless war that peaked in campaigns of *eradication* and *extermination*. In 1908 the Porfirian general Lorenzo Torres summed things up as follows: "According to the reports given by General Luis Torres, Vice-President Ramón Corral and the War Department, Sonora should be cleared of all Indians. . . . I shall remove both rebellious and peaceful

Indians, with no distinction as to class." In 1917 the revolutionary general Plutarco Elías Calles decided to wage "a final energetic and, if necessary terrible campaign" against that "relatively insignificant group of individuals who are resistant to any civilizing influence." The local congress backed him and agreed that the only "quick and efficient" way to solve the Yaqui problem was "the total extermination of the tribe, however painful it might be; for we are faced with the terrible dilemma of to be or not to be, to submit or to perish. ("Los jefes sonorenses de la Revolucion Mexicana," in *Saldos de la revolución* [Mexico City, 1982], p. 18)

10. Nor were Mexico's sugar plantations a model of modern labor relations. "In 1914," writes Friedrich Katz, "John Lind, the special representative of Woodrow Wilson in Mexico, and Admiral Fletcher of the US fleet in Veracruz were invited to visit a sugar-cane plantation owned by a US citizen Emery Sloane that employed only contract labor. Lind later reported:

> The workers sent here by the government were virtual prisoners. Admiral Fletcher and I saw an uncommon sight for the twentieth century: groups of eight to ten men scattered throughout the plantation were accompanied by an overseer-chief, a tall, robust coastal Indian with a pair of pistols in his belt and an eight-to-ten-foot whip in his hand. He closely followed the group as it went about digging, while on the other side of the field a man watched over them with a sawn-off shotgun. In the morning they were marched off to work by these overseers, and at night they were locked up in a huge shed. Both Admiral Fletcher and I were astounded that such a situation could exist, but it did. (Katz, *La servidumbre agraria en México en la época porfiriana* [Mexico City, 1976], pp. 31–32)

11. See Gastón García Cantú, *El socialismo en México: Siglo XIX* (Mexico City, 1969); Jean Meyer, *Problemas campesinos y revueltas agrarias, 1821–1910* (Mexico City, 1973); John M. Hart, *El anarquismo y la clase obrera mexicana, 1860–1931* (Mexico City, 1980); Leticia Reina, *Las rebeliónes campesinas en México, 1819–1906* (Mexico City, 1981).

12. Leal and Woldenberg note:

> With all its limits, the state that arose out of the liberal revolution was a capitalist state, whereas the same cannot be said of the instances of political domination that existed in Mexico between 1821 and 1854.

In reality, the liberal–oligarchic state is a public power clearly and legally distinct from particular powers; it expresses a separation between society and state from which it derives its relative autonomy. Thus, the attack on corporations and obstacles to internal trade, the dispossession of the direct producers, the organization of public finances, the creation of a distinctive army and bureaucracy, the provision of funds for railways and harbors—all these functions can only be successfully fulfilled by a capitalist type of state.

Nevertheless, the primary function of the liberal–oligarchic state was not initially to operate within the limits of an extensive capitalist system, but to *produce* capitalist relations of production and to liquidate or subordinate to the new requirements all the earlier forms of production. . . .

Thus from about 1867 to 1880 democratic freedoms were widely practiced in Mexico, although, of course, only by the very small urban section of the population. After 1880 these freedoms were gradually restricted as the authoritarian features of the state began to develop. As we shall see, this new situation corresponded to the explosive spread of the strictly capitalist conditions of production. (Del Estado liberal, pp. 258–59)

13. A clear account of this world process may be found in chapter 2 of Ernest Mandel, *Late Capitalism* (London, 1975). For a succinct historical analysis of the downward pressure on wages exerted by the industrial reserve army in Mexico, see Jeff Bortz, "La determinación del salario en México," *Coyoacán* No. 13 (1981).

14. It is worth quoting once again The Questions from a Worker Who Reads (Bertolt Brecht, *Poems 1929–1938* [London, 1976]):

Who built Thebes of the seven gates?
In the books you will find the names of kings.
Did the kings haul up the lumps of rock?
And Babylon, many times demolished,
Who raised it up so many times? In what houses
Of gold-glittering Lima did the builders live?
Where, the evening that the Wall of China was finished
Did the masons go? Great Rome
Is full of triumphal arches. Who erected them?

15. Although different estimates have been given, all authors agree on the

apocalyptic magnitude. Woodrow Borah (*New Spain's Century of Depression* [Los Angeles, 1952], pp. 2–3) notes the general concurrence of views that "at time of the Conquest there was a relatively dense aboriginal population in central Mexico." Basing his estimates on studies by S.F. Cook and L.B. Simpson, he sets a figure of 11 million for 1519, descending to 1.5 million at the critical point of the mid-seventeenth century in the whole of central Mexico.

> By then mixed-bloods, Negroes and whites were elements of demographic importance, numbering together perhaps 300,000. The Indian population *ca.* 1650 was thus approximately 1,200,000. Demographic recovery began toward the end of the seventeenth century. It meant at first a slow and then a relatively rapid rise in numbers. By 1793 the total population of central Mexico was perhaps 3,700,000, approximately two-and-one-half times the value for *ca.* 1650 but only four-fifths of the Indian population in 1565 [some 4.4 million].

Only in the late nineteenth or early twentieth century would the population density of the early sixteenth century be restored, albeit with a quite different ethnic composition.

16. "The necessary conditions for the conquistador economy (the Republic of Spaniards) came from exploitation of the indigenous community. Since the Spanish brought neither capital nor means of production, the only available source was the labour and surplus product of this community. The historical role of the *encomienda* system was precisely to transfer the surplus to the farms, haciendas, manufactories, mines, plantations, and so on. . . . The indigenous community and the economy of the Republic of Spaniards were woven together in a highly elaborate series of local combinations of various forms and levels of development. In the north, for example, mining and ranching were predominant and agrarian communities virtually non-existent; in the centre, developed agrarian communities coexisted with major Spanish farms; and in the south, the traditional community prevailed in an often isolated form, while new settlements were rare and the Spanish minority was not much in evidence." Semo, pp. 29–30.

17. "The *only* branch of production that gave the metropolis some comfort in its colonies was the extraction of precious metals. Silver production made it possible to pump out the surplus from even the most

backward sectors of the economy, by means of the marketing of produce. But it only slightly affected the means of production prevalent
in the other sectors." Ibid., pp. 31–32.

18. "The history of work in the land and cattle sector lends support to a
still valid hypothesis: namely, the rise of the big historical enterprise,
from the modest slave-based sugar plantation of the sixteenth century to the almost boundless hacienda of the Díaz era, proved a
success because it could attract, utilize, secure and exploit peasant
labor-power without absorbing all the costs of subsistence and reproduction. The coexistence of free, proletarianized labor with autonomous peasant labor on small plots and various forms of forced
labor based on debt or 'joint ownership,' is neither an anomaly nor a
historical aberration but a secular constant that has still not disappeared." Arturo Warman, Preface to Roberto Melville, *Crecimiento y
rebelión: El desarrollo económico de las haciendas azucareras en Morelos
(1880–1910)* (Mexico City, 1979).

19. For a more detailed account, see Katz, *La servidumbre agraria*.

20. History presents even more extreme examples. In a report to the
Fourth Congress of the Communist International, Trotsky noted:

> We observe more than once in history, the development of economic
> phenomena, new in principle, within the old integuments, and more-
> over this occurs by means of the most diverse combinations. When
> industry took root in Russia, still under the laws of feudalism, in the
> days of Peter the Great and thereafter, the factories and plants, while
> patterned after the European models of those times, were nevertheless
> built upon feudal beginnings, that is, serfs were attached to them in the
> capacity of the labor force. (These factories were called manorial fac-
> tories.) ("Report on NEP" [November 1922], in *The First Five Years of
> the Comintern,* vol. 2 [New York, 1953], pp. 247–48).

21. Katz makes the following observations:

> In the haciendas of central Mexico, only a small middle group of
> labour contractors, foremen and well-off tenant-farmers had the pos-
> sibility of upward mobility. The great mass of hacienda labourers,
> occasional workers, tenant-farmers and co-partners were not only
> unable to save anything but saw their means of life continually re-
> duced. However, at the point when the communal villages were suf-
> fering a sharp decline of their traditional way of life and a general loss

of security, the hacienda peons were in a comparatively much better situation. For loyalty to the master would often be rewarded with advancement to a privileged position of trust. (*La servidumbre agraria,* p. 54)

22. "From the 1860s on, each and every Mexican government anxiously strove to foster the development of the railways, offering generous subsidies and inducements to any Mexican or foreign group that presented reasonable plans for completion of this task. Such efforts only bore fruit after the installation of the first government capable of inspiring minimum confidence that the subsidies would be paid and the concessions granted. During the thirty-four years of the *Pax Porfiriana,* the railway network was rapidly completed under the hegemony of foreign, mainly US, capital." John H. Coatsworth, *El impacto económico de los ferrocarriles en el porfiriato,* vol. 2 (Mexico City, 1976), p. 77.

23. "Contemporary commentators, including officials of the Díaz regime, saw the railways as the main driving-force of export-led economic growth. The growth of state control in the 1890s, and the Mexicanization of the bulk of railway lines between 1902 and 1910, reflected the regime's determination to ensure that the new transport system would continue to play this role. The principal beneficiaries of railway 'Mexicanization' were the mostly foreign holders of Mexican railway bonds and the exporting sector of the economy, itself also largely in foreign hands. Foreign bondholders gained from the fact that the Mexican government bailed out companies on the verge of bankruptcy. Foreign mine-owners could reduce costs and avoid the breaks in service which, in the United States, for example, accompanied the manipulation of the railways by North American finance groups. It was US capitalists who benefited most from Limantour's efforts to prevent the Mexican railway system from falling into the hands of an American monopoly." Ibid., pp. 77–78.

24. In 1879 Marx wrote a letter to Danielson concerning railway development in capitalist countries. He says, among other things:

The appearance of the railway system in the leading states of capitalism allowed, and even forced, states where capitalism was confined to a few summits of society, to suddenly create and enlarge their capitalistic *superstructure* in dimensions altogether disproportionate to the bulk of the social body, carrying on the great work of production in the traditional modes. There is, therefore, not the least doubt that in those states the railway creation has accelerated the social and political disintegration, as in the more advanced states it hastened the final development, and therefore the final change, of capitalistic production. In all states, except England, the governments enriched and fostered the railway companies at the expense of the public Exchequer. In the United States to their profit a great deal of the public land they received as a present, not only the land necessary for the construction of the lines, but many miles of land along both sides of the lines, covered with forests, etc. They became the greatest landlords, the small immigrating farmers preferring of course lands so situated as to ensure their produce ready means of transport. . . . Generally, the railways gave of course an immense impulse to the development of Foreign Commerce, but the commerce in countries which export principally *raw materials* increased the misery of the masses. Not only that the new indebtedness, contracted by the governments on account of the railways, increased the *bulk of imposts* weighing upon them, but from the moment every local production could be converted into cosmopolitan gold, many articles *formerly cheap,* became unsaleable to a great degree, such as fruit, wine, fish, deer, etc., became *dear* and were withdrawn from the consumption of the people, while, on the other hand, *the production itself,* I mean the special *sort of produce,* was changed according to its *greater or lesser suitableness for exportation,* while formerly it was principally adapted to its consumption *in loco.* Thus in Schleswig-Holstein agricultural land was converted into pasture, because the export of cattle was more profitable, but, at the same time, the agricultural population was driven away. All the changes were very useful indeed for the great landed proprietor, the usurer, the merchant, the railways, the bankers and so forth, but very dismal for the real producer. (Marx-Engels, *Selected Correspondence* [Moscow, 1975], pp. 298–99)

In Mexico, too, railway development was accompanied with a marked rise in the price of basic necessities.

In 1910, Mexico, with a population of density of 7.7 inhabitants per square kilometer, had one kilometer of railway for each hundred kilometers of territory and thirteen kilometers of railway for every ten thousand inhabitants. The figures varied from double to one-half the national average according to the region in question. On the eve of

World War I, Trotsky notes, "Russia had 0.4 kilometres of railway for every one hundred square kilometres of land, Germany 11.7, Austria-Hungary 7.0." Leon Trotsky, *History of the Russian Revolution*, p. 27.

25. "From 1877, a growing number of reports on peasant movements, protests, manifestos, petitions and rebellions appeared in the Mexico City press. If we examine these newspapers and a variety of secondary sources, we find information about some 55 serious conflicts between indigenous villages and nearby haciendas in the years between 1877 and 1884. Most of the incidents were triggered by an illegal usurpation of land by the *hacendados,* and nearly all involved some form of active peasant resistance (prolonged litigation, petitions to officials, violent protests or armed rebellions). A series of maps have been drawn up to locate these incidents in relation to existing or projected railway lines. The results are impressive. Of the 55 recorded incidents, only five (9.1 percent) took place at a distance of more than forty kilometers from a railway line or from the route of a line for which a government concession already existed. Thirty-two cases (or about sixty percent of the total) occurred less than twenty kilometers from an existing or projected railway line." Coatsworth, *El impacto económico,* pp. 54–55.

26. Almost all of the figures used in this section are taken from Rosenzweig, "El desarrollo económica."

27. In this period world exports of raw materials grew by only two and a half times, at an annual rate of 3.6 percent; while world imports of raw materials grew by 3.3 percent a year and imports of manufactured goods by 3 percent.

28. Rosenzweig, "El desarrollo económico," p. 430. With regard to technological innovations, Rosenzweig adds:

> New capitalist activities could depend upon a plentiful surplus of cheap labor-power, drawn above all from the flow of peasants to the towns and of unemployed artisans to the factories. In the early part of the Díaz era, industry was able to boost its profits and accumulate resources for wider investment by applying a greater quantity of labor to a constant plant capacity. In later years, the increased productivity of the more efficient and better equipped factories, responding to higher internal demand in conditions of virtual wage stagnation, raised profit margins to a level that encouraged the formation of capital.

At another point (p. 422) Rosenzweig argues: "External demand was a determining factor of growth and modernization in mining and metallurgy, and of the development of an agricultural sector. Such activities in turn created a demand for labor and nationally produced materials that strengthened the internal market for light industrial goods and allowed the development of new branches of production."

29. Rosenzweig (ibid., p. 434) gives the following breakdown of foreign capital by area of investment:

	European investment (in percentages)	U.S. investment (in percentages)
Railways	28.2	41.4
Extractive industries	18.1	41.8
Public debt	20.8	4.6
Commerce and banking	11.6	3.3
Electricity and public services	10.7	1.0
Land, cattle and forestry activity	5.4	6.3
Processing industries	5.2	1.6
Total	100.0	100.0

José Luis Ceceña has calculated the foreign stake in each branch of the economy: *railways,* 61.8 percent of all investment in this branch (18.4 percent British, 9 percent American through U.S.-controlled companies, and 34.4 percent American through Ferrocarriles Nacionales de Mexico); *mining,* 97.5 percent (81 percent North American, 14.5 percent British, 2 percent French); *banking,* 76.7 percent (45.7 percent French, 11.4 percent British, 18.3 percent American, 1.3 percent German); *oil,* 100 percent (60.8 percent British, 39.2 percent American); *industry,* 85 percent (53.2 percent French, 12.8 percent British, 15.3 percent American, 3.7 percent German); *electricity,* 87.2 percent (78.2 percent British, 8 percent American, 1 percent French). Ceceña, "La penetración extranjera y los grupos de poder en México, 1870–1910," *Problemas del desarrollo* No. 1 (October–December 1969).

30. In connection with the *partido* system, one of the first labor disputes in Mexico's history broke out in 1766 between the Real del Monte miners and the mine owner, Pedro Romero de Terreros.

31. "The total number of spinners and weavers declined from 60 to 52 thousand between 1895 and 1900, artisan employment falling from 41 to 26 thousand and the number of factory jobs rising from 19 to 26 thousand. In the first decade of the twentieth century, the factories expanded their workforce to 32 thousand, while the artisans saw their number reduced to a mere eight thousand. In other words, the total of employed textile workers fell by eight thousand between 1895 and 1900 and a further twelve thousand in the following ten years: the entire loss was borne by the artisan sector. Similar processes were at work in tobacco, chemicals, pelts and other branches of industry. . . . This tendency seemed to become more pronounced after the turn of the century, when the slower impetus of national manufacturing development heightened the problems affecting artisan activities." Rosenzweig, "El desarrollo económico," p. 444. The dramatic collapse of artisan production was also expressed in the location of many textile concerns in regions that provided access to the old artisan tradition of peasant weavers as well as hydraulic energy for the new machinery.

32. In these years foreign, mainly U.S., capital bought up abandoned or inefficient mines and made them profitable through the injection of new capital and technology. In this way, as well as through the purchase of concessions linked to the railway, U.S. capital investment in Mexican mines rose from $3 million in 1888 to $55 million in 1892.

33. In 1910 the labor force totalled 5,272,100 out of a national population of 15,160,400. The land and cattle sector accounted for 3,592,100 (68.1 percent); the extractive, processing, construction, transport, fuel, and energy industries for another 850,500 (16.1 percent); and the private and public services (commerce, technicians, professional workers, white-collar employees, servants, and the armed forces) for a further 15.8 percent. The largest sector of industrial workers (606,000 or 11.5 percent of the labor force) was to be found in the processing industry. This was followed by the extractive industry (104,100 or 2 percent), construction (74,700 or 1.4 percent), transport (55,100 or 1 percent), and fuel and electricity (10,600 or 0.2 percent). See Rosenzweig, "El desarrollo económico," p. 438, although we have transferred transport workers from the service to the industrial sector.

34. See the figures produced by the Mexico Modern History Seminar and quoted in ibid., p. 447:

Minimum daily wage in cenlavos, 1877–1911

Year	Total Current prices	1900 prices	Agriculture Current prices	1900 prices	Manufacturing Current prices	1900 prices	Mining Current prices	1900 prices
1877	22	32	22	32	22	32	22	32
1885	23	29	22	27	28	34	27	31
1892	30	28	29	26	36	26	33	30
1898	34	39	31	37	39	50	40	47
1902	37	33	35	32	41	36	46	43
1911	49	30	44	27	59	36	118	72

While noting the disparity between different estimates—González
Roa and Tannenbaum calculate that real wages fell 30 percent during
the Díaz era—Friedrich Katz concludes: "Light has been thrown on
two of the many profound changes that took place during the Díaz
era: the expropriation of communal village land, and the decline in the
real wages earned by hacienda workers. According to available statistics, more than ninety-five percent of village communities had lost
their land by the end of the *porfiriato*. The purchasing-power of an
agricultural laborer's daily wage declined enormously between 1876
and 1910" (*La servidumbre agraria*, p. 15).

35. "Small independent producers, in both town and country, made a
crucial contribution to the liberal revolution, not only during the actual fighting but also in the construction of the resulting state and
society. . . . One thinks, for example, of the short-lived liberal dream of
a society of small, independent agricultural producers, or the unsuccessful attempts to abolish debt-peonage, or the mystique of the
workshop and free municipality. Sooner or later, Jacobin liberalism
would be displaced within and outside the state, and would prove
incapable of meeting the demands of urban artisan layers. As the
twilight of liberalism descended, these artisans became receptive to
new currents of thought: utopian socialism and anarchism. But the
perspective remained that of the petty commodity producer." Leal
and Woldenberg, *Del Estado liberal*, p. 157. The same authors argue
that the doctrines of Ricardo Flores Magón, which formed a distinctive and developing whole between the turn of the century and the

outbreak of revolution, should ultimately be traced back to these roots.

36. The fire the Commune lit in Mexico continued to smolder beneath the surface, covered but not extinguished by defeat and the *Pax Porfiriana*. Thus Octavio Jahn, a veteran of the Paris Commune, later took part in the Mexican Revolution. Indeed, everyone who had kept alive the memory of the Commune would join the revolution in its early stages. When I was in Lecumberri Prison, I met Fernando Cortés Granados, born in 1910, who joined the Communist Party in 1930 and had been arrested in 1968. One night, he told me the following story in his cell:

> Although I was still very young, my mother began to talk to me about revolution. In 1875, when barely four years old, she had seen her father hold a meeting with other craftsmen in their home, and had heard them discuss the experience of the Paris Commune. My grandfather and mother later joined Flores Magón's Liberal Party. In 1914, while they were planning a pro-revolutionary uprising in Tapachula, my grandfather and his comrades were discovered, arrested and shot. Shortly afterwards, my mother separated from my father, because he had thrown the concealed weapons into the river when he heard about my grandfather's arrest. From then on, she alone educated us children. She always used to say with pride: "I'm from the year of the Commune," having been born in 1871. In 1930, when I was already a union organizer for the Soconusco Regional Workers and Peasants Federation, she gave me some Communist underground papers and suggested that I join the Communist Party. "That's the workers' and peasants' party," she said. "It'd be a different story today if we'd had something like that during the Porfirio Díaz dictatorship. Join, and you will only leave it when you die." My mother died a Communist in Chalpas, at 94 years of age.

37. Here, perhaps, we can hear an echo of the debate on the relationship between capital and labor, wages and strikes. Thus, on the occasion of the 1875 hatworkers' strike, Guillermo Prieto had written in *El Socialista*: "Everyone agrees that labor is a commodity offered by the worker and solicited by the capitalist; that both have a right freely to set the value of the exchange between labor and money; and that the worker's only recourse—a legitimate one at that—is to withdraw his commodity from the market if the price is not right."

38. Gastón García Cantú, from whose work we have extracted much of our information on the workers' movement under Porfirio Díaz, writes that "the workers shot at Pinos Altos were the first victims suffered by the labor movement in the Americas. Their shooting took place three years before the execution of the Chicago strikers."

39. In a letter to Engels dated October 8, 1858, Marx wrote a paragraph that confirms the early Marxist origins of the theory of permanent revolution:

> We cannot deny that bourgeois society has experienced its sixteenth century a second time—a sixteenth century which will, I hope, sound the death-knell of bourgeois society just as the first one thrust it into existence. The specific task of bourgeois society is the establishment of a world market, at least in outline, and of production based on this world market. As the world is round, this seems to have been completed by the colonization of California and Australia and the opening up of China and Japan. The difficult question for us is this: on the Continent the revolution is imminent and will moreover immediately assume a socialist character. Is it not bound to be crushed in this little corner, considering that in a far greater territory the movement of bourgeois society is still in the ascendant? (Marx-Engels, *Selected Correspondence*, pp. 103–4)

40. *Científicos* (literally, "scientists") was the popular nickname for the group of leading positivist politicans and "modernizers" of the time.

CHAPTER 2

1. These figures are taken from Frank Tannenbaum, *Peace by Revolution* (New York, 1933). He says there (pp. 194–95):

> One other point should be noted in the description of rural Mexico before the Revolution. The plantation communities were generally smaller than the remaining free villages. The 56,825 plantation communities had an average population of 97, the 12,724 free villages had an average size of 541. In other words, the plantation in destroying the free village tended to reduce it in size, to scatter its population into smaller groups, to subject it to more direct control, and to make it both economically and politically, a less independent and capable group.
>
> We may summarize by saying that at the end of the Díaz regime

there were fewer than 13,000 free villages in Mexico as against nearly
57,000 plantation communities; that the plantation community was
less than one fifth the size of the free village; that the free village had
best survived in mountainous regions surrounding Mexico City; that
the plantation communities were more frequently found in the less
mountainous states; that this system of reducing village to plantation
had gone on for four hundred years; that under the Díaz regime it was
being pushed with greater energy than ever before; and that it was
against the villages in states surrounding the Valley of Mexico where
the free community had best survived that the attack was most evident.

2. See "Co-operation," chapter 13 of *Capital,* vol. 1. In vol. 3, chapter
20, he says:

> The obstacles that the internal solidity and articulation of pre-capitalist
> national modes of production oppose to the solvent effect of trade are
> strikingly apparent in the English commerce with India and China.
> There the broad basis of the mode of production is formed by the union
> between small-scale agriculture and domestic industry, on top of which
> we have in the Indian case the form of village communities based on
> common property in the soil, which was also the original form in China.
> In India, moreover, the English applied their direct political and eco-
> nomic power, as masters and landlords, to destroying these small eco-
> nomic communities. In so far as English trade has had a revolutionary
> effect on the mode of production in India, this is simply to the extent that
> it has destroyed spinning and weaving, which form an age-old and inte-
> gral part of industrial and agricultural production, through the low price
> of English commodities. In this way it has torn the community to pieces.
> Even here, their work of dissolution is succeeding only very gradually.
> These effects are felt still less in China, where no assistance is provided by
> direct political force. The great economy and saving of time that results
> from the direct connection of agriculture and manufacture presents a
> very stubborn resistance here to the products of large-scale industry,
> whose prices include the *faux frais* of the circulation process with which
> they are everywhere perforated. In contrast to English trade, Russian
> trade leaves the economic basis of Asiatic production quite untouched.

Marx adds in a footnote: "More than that of any other nation, the history of English economic management in India is a history of futile
and actually stupid (in practice, infamous) economic experiments. In

Bengal they created a caricature of English large-scale landed property; in the south-east they created a caricature of peasant smallholdings. In the north-west they did all they could to transform the Indian economic community with common property in the soil into a caricature of itself." Engels adds a later footnote on Russian trade: "Since Russia has been making the most frantic attempts to develop a capitalist production of its own, one that is exclusively directed towards its home market and the adjacent Asiatic one, this is beginning to change." *Capital,* vol. 3, pp. 451–52.

3. "Co-operation in the labour process, such as we find it at the beginning of human civilization, among hunting peoples or, say, as a predominant feature of the agriculture of Indian communities, is based on the one hand on the common ownership of the conditions of production, and on the other hand on the fact that in those cases the individual has as little torn himself free from the umbilical cord of his tribe or community as a bee has from his hive. Both of these characteristics distinguish this form of co-operation from capitalist co-operation." *Capital,* vol. 1, p. 452.

4. In Asia the Vietnamese revolution has conclusively demonstrated these potentialities.

5. Reproduced in T. Shanin, *Marx and the Russian Road* (London, 1982). Eleven years later, Engels gave a more definitive answer on that particular case, more distant than the latter Marx from the sensibilities of Russian populists. But *in historical terms* he, too, posed the possibility of a leap from communal ownership to the communist form of collective ownership:

> You yourself admit that "the social conditions in Russia after the Crimean War were not favourable to the development of the form of production inherited by us from our past history." I would go further and say, that no more in Russia than anywhere else would it have been possible to develop a higher social form out of primitive agrarian communism unless—that higher form was *already in existence* in another country, so as to serve as a model. That higher form being, wherever it is historically possible, the necessary consequence of the capitalistic form of production and of the social dualistic anatagonism created by it, it could not be developed directly out of the agrarian commune, unless in imitation of an example already in existence somewhere else. Had the West of Europe

been ripe, 1860–1870, for such a transformation, had that transformation then been taken in hand in England, France etc., then the Russians would have been called upon to show what could have been made out of their Commune, which was then more or less intact. But the West remained stagnant, no such transformation was attempted, and capitalism was more and more rapidly developed. And as Russia had no choice but this: either to develop the Commune into a form of production from which it was separated by a number of historical stages, and for which not even in the West the conditions were then ripe—evidently an impossible task—or else to develop into capitalism, what remained to her but the latter chance?

As to the Commune, it is only possible so long as the differences of wealth among its members are but trifling. As soon as these differences become great, as soon as some of its members become the debt-slaves of the richer members, it can no longer live. The kulaks and *miroed* (village exploiters) of Athens, before Solon, destroyed the Athenian *gens* with the same implacability with which those of your country destroy the Commune. I am afraid that institution is doomed. But on the other hand, capitalism opens out new views and new hopes. Look at what it has done and is doing in the West. A great nation like yours outlives every crisis. There is no great historical crisis without a compensating historical progress. Only the *modus operandi* is changed. *Que les destinées s'accomplissent!* ("Letter to Danielson," October 17, 1893, *Selected Correspondence,* pp. 438–39).

6. On June 27, 1905, in Chicago, Western Federation of Miners leader Bill Haywood opened the founding congress of the Industrial Workers of the World with the following words:

We are here to confederate the workers of this country into a working-class movement that shall have for its purpose the emancipation of the working class from the slave bondage of capitalism. . . . The aims and objects of this organization should be to put the working class in possession of the economic power, the means of life, in control of the machinery of production and distribution, without regard to capitalist masters. The American Federation of Labor, which presumes to be the labor movement of this country, is not a working-class movement. It does not represent the working class. . . . This organization will be formed, based and founded on the class struggle, having in view no compromise and no surrender, and but one object and one purpose and that is to bring the workers of this country into the possession of the full value of the product of their toil. (Quoted in Melvyn Dubobski, *We Shall Be All* [New York: Guadress, 1973], p. 81)

7. In preparing this action, Ricardo Flores Magón wrote a letter to his brother Enrique that sums up his insurrectional conceptions, close to those of Russian populism, and curiously similar to the *foquismo* so widespread in Latin America more than half a century later. The letter, dated June 7, 1908, contains these two paragraphs:

> I think Orizaba can fall to the revolution if the following plan, which I have sent to Olivares for his on-the-spot consideration, is actually put into practice. There must be at least 1,500 men in Orizaba, and the only way to move against them is to dynamite their barracks. At the same time, a small group will be sent to destroy the Necaxa plant, which produces energy for the Rio Blanco, Nogales, Cocolapan, El Yute and other factories in this important region. Then the mass of workers will descend like an avalanche from Orizaba, whose barracks will be exploding at that very moment, and the town will fall into the hands of the revolution. Orizaba is a very wealthy city, from which several million pesos can be removed, along with a great quantity of arms and ammunition.

> I'll say something here about the uprisings. A number of groups will be fully prepared—that is, as well armed as both they and we would like. If we were to wait until every group is fully prepared, no revolution would ever take place: time would pass as one postponement followed another, and the foremost groups, already fully prepared, would grow discouraged; they would have to be revisited in an attempt to raise their spirits, and in the meantime the unprepared groups that slowed down the movement and held back the combat-ready groups would themselves grow discouraged . . . so that the action would be postponed until I know not when. We must therefore stop hoping that we shall ever have a perfect organization of fully prepared groups. In our view, we should get each group to give a "solemn promise" that it will rise up on the appointed day, whatever state it is in. If a half or even a third keep their promise, the revolution will be assured. This will be so even if it begins with poorly armed groups; for since there will be several rebel groups in the large territory of the Republic, the slaves of the dictatorship will not be able to crush them in one day. And every day that a group

survives, it will increase its size, increase its stock of weapons and acquire resources of every kind. Brave people in every area will find encouragement and launch fresh risings, thereby assisting the valiant one who lit the fuse. There is reason to hope that things will happen in this way. (Quoted in Armando Bartra's Introduction to *Regeneración, 1900–1918* [Mexico City, 1977], pp. 26–27)

8. The U.S. ambassador in Mexico sent a report to the State Department about the events in Cananea. "In an interview I had today with President Díaz," he wrote, "he informed me that the movement in Cananea was a revolutionary movement designed to overthrow his government. It was led by some twenty revolutionaries—all of Mexican nationality, he thought—and directed from St. Louis, Missouri." Quoted in Ciro F.S. Cardoso, Francisco G. Hermosillo, and Salvador Hernández, *De la dictadura a los tiempos libertarios,* Vol. 3 of *La clase obrera en la historia de México* (Mexico City, 1980), p. 138.

Despite its obviously false and exaggerated character, the report to the U.S. ambassador reveals the consternation of the ruling class at these events of unprecedented magnitude.

9. In November 1910 Ricardo Flores Magón wrote in *Regeneración*:

The Mexican people are in a very special situation. Now working against the authorities are the poor people, represented by the Liberal Party, and the bourgeoisie, represented by the Democratic Nationalist Party and the National Anti-Re-election Party. This situation must inevitably be resolved in armed conflict. The bourgeoisie is looking for deals that the *científicos* will not grant. The proletariat is seeking economic well-being and social dignity by means of land-seizures and union organization, which are opposed by both the government and the bourgeois parties.

10. From the beginning of 1911, Ricardo Flores Magón and his *Regeneración* comrades spoke out against this path of liquidating the revolution. "What need is there to delay the expropriation of the land until a new government has been established?" asked Flores Magón on January 28.

In the present uprising, when the movement is in full flood and the Liberal Party is establishing the necessary preponderance—that is, when the Party's strength can guarantee the success of expropriation—then is the time for village land-seizures to be carried out. For the aspirations of the disinherited masses can then no longer be brushed aside.

Comrades! During the Reform revolution, Benito Juárez was urged not to take away the clergy's property until peace had been made. But Benito Juárez could see far enough to realize that if the clergy's property were expropriated after peace had been made, the clergy would again break the peace and the country would be caught up in another revolt. In order to avoid bloodshed, he replied: "It's better to do in one revolution what would otherwise take two." And that is what happened. We liberals should do the same. In a single uprising, we should leave the seizure of the land as an accomplished fact.

In a programmatic manifesto dated September 23, 1911, Los Angeles, California, the Liberal Party declared:

Every day the hard times are returning. Maderists, Vazquists, Reyists, *cientificos,* de la Barra supporters—all are calling on you, Mexicans, to support their washed-out banners that defend the privileges of the capitalist class. Don't listen to the sweet songs of these sirens! They want to use your sacrifices to set up a government—another dog that will defend the interests of the rich. Rise up, one and all, but in order to expropriate the property held by the rich!

Expropriation should be carried out by blood and fire during this great movement, just as our brothers have done and are doing in Morelos, southern Puebla, Michoacán, Guerrero, Veracruz, northern Tamaulipas, Durango, Sonora, Sinaloa, Jalisco, Chihuahua, Oaxaca, Yucatán, Quintana Roo and parts of other states. Even the Mexico City bourgeois press has had to admit that the proletarians have here taken over the land without waiting for a paternalist government to deign to make them happy. They know that nothing good can be expected from governments, and that "the emancipation of the workers must be the act of the workers themselves."

These first acts of expropriation were crowned with the most joyful success. But it is not enough to seize the land and the agricultural implements: all industries should be resolutely taken over by their own workers, so that the land, the mines, factories, workshops and foundries, the carriages, railways and boats, the stores and warehouses of every kind, the houses should remain in the hands of each and every inhabitant of Mexico, without distinction of sex. . . .

If, immediately after expropriation, production is organized on a
new basis, free of masters and according to the people's needs in each
area, then no one will go short of anything in spite of the armed uprising. And once the uprising comes to an end with the disappearance of
the last bourgeois and the last authority or agent of authority, once the
law that upholds privilege has been shattered and everything has been
handed over to the toilers, we shall hold one another in a fraternal embrace and greet with cries of jubilation a system that will guarantee
bread and freedom for every human being.

It should be underscored, however, that Flores Magón's anarchist
propaganda did not engage the consciousness of the great majority
of the Mexican people. Although an unsuccessful attempt was made
to put it into practice through a rebellion in Baja California between January and July 1911, other paths would be found to assure
the continuation of the revolution that Madero had declared to be
at an end.

CHAPTER 3

1. For a further account of this meeting, see Jesús Sotelo Inclán, *Raíz y
   razón de Zapata,* and above all the preface to John Womack, *Zapata and
   the Mexican Revolution* (London, 1969).
2. Many years later, in 1973, one of the peasant signatories of the plan,
   Zapata's adjutant Francisco Mercado, recalled these days during which
   Emiliano discussed his ideas with Montaño: "Every time the teacher
   Montaño talked with him, *jefe* Zapata argued that there should be a
   plan, since we were being treated as mere bandits and rustlers and mur-
   derers and as if we were not fighting under a banner. And so, don Emiliano wanted to have this Plan as our banner." Rosalind Rosoff and
   Anita Aguilar, *Así firmaron el Plan de Ayala* (Mexico City: Sepsetentas,
   1976).
3. After mentioning that Zapata and Montaño had spent three days discussing and drafting the plan in the Sierra de Ayoxustla, Gildardo Magaña gives this picture of the council meeting:

   > All the Zapatist leaders operating in the region received orders to go at
   > once to the Ayoxustla mountains. On 28 November Ayoxustla, a lonely
   > spot in the mountains, became a revolutionary encampment. Scores of

men, with cartridge-belts across their chest and horny brown hands holding carabines still smelling of gunpowder, formed a motley crowd which stood commenting on recent events and pondering the purpose of this evidently important gathering.

Inside the tent they had used for shelter, General Zapata and the schoolteacher Montaño were involved in a discussion which, for all their curiosity, the men outside were unable to hear. Eventually Zapata appeared, standing in the warmth of the tent-entrance, and said with an air of gravity combined with amicability: "Those who aren't afraid, come and sign!"

Montaño, standing by a small country log-table, which the people of Ayoxustla still keep as a historical relic, immediately proceeded to read out the Ayala Plan in his gruff voice marked with the accents of a village schoolteacher. Everyone present greeted the document with wild enthusiasm, and the leaders and officers signed it in a spirit of emotion.

4. Some of these plans appear in Jesús Reyes Heroles, *Mexican Liberalism* (Mexico City: Fondo de Cultura Económica, Francois Chevalier, notes).

The Zapatista uprising is not the isolated, extraordinary or unique phenomenon presented to us by some historians of the Mexican Revolution. It appears like an explosion in the most critical area of this deep social discontent whose most evident manifestations had been banditry (endemic in the state of Morelos in the nineteenth century), and above all the almost uninterrupted succession of insurrections of Indigenous people and campesinos motivated essentially by agrarian questions.

Zapata's movement is the last link on a long chain that includes the northwest with its Yaqui Indian uprisings in 1825, 1885 and 1890, as well as the southeast with the terrible insurrection of Yucatan that began in 1847, and across all the territory of Mexico: like the uprising of Lozada, the old peon of Nayarit who promoted agrarian rights; that of 1859, precisely of the peons of Morelos; that of 1878 in the state of Puebla, which attempted to redistribute the haciendas; that which took place the following year among the Indigenous and mestizo peons of Querétero and Guanajuato, who demanded liberty; those of the state of Veracruz (Acayuca and Papantla) in 1883 and 1891, et cetera. . . .

Finally, we cite the 1879 rebellion in the Huasteca, in the east, that took for its rallying cry "municipal government and agrarian law," (Tamazunchale), or the other one led by the priest of Valle de Maíz, who preached an agrarian policy that favored the campesinos with no land.

5. Right from the first moment, Zapata was well aware of the historical importance of his plan and the perspectives of his struggle. Thus in his communication to Gildardo Magaña of December 6, 1911, he enclosed the following letter:

> Dear friend, I have great pleasure in sending you the Villa de Ayala Plan, which will serve as our banner in the fight against the new dictator Madero. You should therefore suspend all dealings with the Maderists and ensure that this important document is printed and made known to everyone. As you will see from the text, my men and I are prepared to continue the work that Madero mutilated in Ciudad Juárez; we shall not bargain with anyone about anything until our most fervent desire, the consolidation of the revolution, has been made a reality. We do not care that the mercenary press revile us as bandits—they did the same to Madero when he was thought to be a revolutionary. But as soon as he sided with the rich and powerful, placing himself in the service of their interests, they stopped calling him a bandit and began praising him to the skies. . . . There is no integrity or sincerity, no firm intention to carry out the promises of the revolution; since I still have a few men under arms, who are doing no harm to anyone, they are out to kill me and thus to finish off the group that has dared to demand the return of the usurped lands; the prisons of the Republic are crammed with worthy, virile revolutionaries who acted like men in protesting Madero's botched piece of work. How, then, could I be so naive as to offer myself to be sacrificed for the satisfaction of the Revolution's enemies? Is not the case of Abraham Martínez eloquent testimony—cast into jail for capturing some Porfirist plotters against the life of the then Head of the Revolution? Or Candido Navarro and so many others who have been unjustly thrown as criminals into the dungeons of the metropolis? Is that to be called a victorious revolution?
>
> Since I am no politician, I do not understand those half-victories or victories in which the losers are the winners; nor for victories in which, as in my case, I am being asked or required to leave both

my home state and my native country, after the revolution is said to have triumphed. . . . I am determined to fight everything and everybody, with no other weapon than the trust, love and support of my people.

6. Sometimes, whole villages joined a Zapatist unit in combating the federal troops. In February 1912, government forces located a column led by Zapata and prepared to attack it the following day. That night, however, the encamped federal troops woke to find themselves surrounded by a circle of fire, which scattered both men and horses and prevented any military action. The local peasantry had teamed up to set fire to the hay. Afterwards, the retreating army could not find anyone: some had joined the guerrillas, while the majority had simply emptied the villages at the approach of the *federales*.

A few years later, the Soviet state adopted these old methods of peasant warfare as a complement to the regular actions of the Red Army. Thus, a military proclamation signed by Trotsky in August 1919 issued the following call to struggle against the Whites:

The workers and peasant masses, led by their soviets and the Communist organizations, must rise up as one man against the white raiders. The landlords' mercenaries must be made to feel that they are in the land of the workers and peasants, that is, a land that is hostile to them. Danger must lie in ambush for the white bandits at every corner, behind every hillock, in every gully. . . . Intelligence must be flawlessly organized. Information must be collected about every enemy patrol, which must be tracked down, taken by surprise, and either annihilated or made prisoner. Wherever the Whites think of spending the night, they must be awakened by fires. Their horses must run against barbed wire where, the day before, there was an open, unencumbered road. (Trotsky, *Military Speeches and Writings,* vol. 2 [London, 1981], pp. 391–92).

7. The Tacubaya Plan, the first anti-Maderist program, sprang from the urban radical wing of the movement, upon which Madero had foisted José María Pino Suárez as vice presidential candidate instead of its own leader, Emilio Vázquez Gómez. Issued on October 31, 1911, a month or so before the Ayala Plan, it is a protest against the Ciudad Juárez Accords and the alliance between Maderism and the old Díaz oligarchy. Madero, it charges, "has paved his own way to the presidency, fighting

or jailing every opponent; he has poured scorn on his own promises, imposed governors despite the repeated protests of the governed, re-installed local chieftains and excluded the revolutionary leaders . . . outlawed revolutionaries who demand legality and justice." With regard to the provisions of the San Luis Potosí Plan, Madero declares that "if the people want land, then they must buy it, and if they want freedom, then they have to work for it"—a clear challenge to the proletarian class that raised him to power. "While insurgents are being excluded, humiliated, imprisoned or killed," it continues, "the third men and servants of don Porfirio . . . are regrouping around the leader and his brotherhood and devouring the fruits of the revolution. Madero is not concerned with freedom: the people mean nothing to him, accustomed as he is to exploiting them on his haciendas." After these accusations, the Plan merely promises that the (unspecified) "solutions to the agrarian problem" will be applied "as soon as victory is assured." It declares Madero's election null and void, and calls for him to be overthrown and replaced as president by Vázquez Gómez.

The San Luis Potosí Plan did not have much impact in its birthplace, Mexico City, receiving the support only of a small nucleus soon to be dissolved by repression. (One of its signatories, the journalist Paulino Martínez, later joined Zapata's movement.) However, it encouraged the appearance of the Ayala Plan in the South and of Orozco's Empacadora Plan in the North. It also showed that resistance to Madero's deal with the old oligarchy had a base not only in the peasantry, but in a section of the urban petty bourgeoisie.

8. On February 27, 1913, Zapata wrote to Genovevo de la O: "I have news that the current illegal government is trying to enter into treaties with the revolutionary chiefs by way of the famous conferences, which are nothing more than ambushes to trap and shoot them. So take your precautions in the future and attack *the enemy as often as he makes his presence known* and don't lose any opportunity to beat him back because it is the only way of *getting rid of them*." Emiliano Zapata, *Cartas* (Mexcio City: Ediciones Antorcha, 1987).

9. Cabrera referred to these communal traditions in support of his proposal.

It will be said: "The administration of communal land would become a real jungle!" But no, what seems most difficult to cultured minds in a new economic situation is, in reality, the most simple. Our villages display a profound fervor to preserve traditional customs. We deputies did not take part in any elections for thirty-five years. But the Indians of the Puebla mountains have never stopped electing people for thirty-five years. The Indians of the Puebla mountains, for example, had no problem whatsoever when it came to electing deputies. Why? Because, acting against the law, outside the law, and in spite of the law, they religiously continued to appoint people with clearly defined duties. In the same way, I can guarantee that our rural classes have not lost the habit of administering their communal property.

If one were to deepen this extraordinary comparison between the system of bourgeois-liberal right and the traditional social organization of the peasant communities, one would begin to explain the superimposition and interpenetration of the two systems within the consciousness and political life of the broad masses. The secret of single-party regimes is that, being unacceptable to those who feel the need for independent mass organization, they strive to appear less oppressive than liberal regimes in the eyes of the masses. The single party is able to exploit in a distorting manner the traditions which have partially molded popular consciousness, whereas the liberal regime has to destroy them in order to assert its rule.

It is important to study the full text of Cabrera's speech (*Problemas Agrarios e Industriales de México* 4, no. 2 [1952]). For he very clearly expresses the position of the national bourgeois tendency which was prepared to grant major concessions to the masses in order to further the development of capitalism, provided, of course, that the revolution was ended and juridical continuity maintained. Its aim was not to eliminate the latifundia, but, on the contrary, to reconstitute communal land as a complement to the haciendas that would fix the cheap labor-power required for certain months of the year.

Cabrera not only remained Carranza's ideologue even after his downfall. At a later stage, he denounced as "communist" Cárdenas's agrarian measures (see *Un ensayo comunista en México* and other writings), although they were formally similar to many of his own proposals in 1912 on the reconstitution of communal land. In fact, the essence of his position, maintained over more than twenty years, was basically at odds with Cárdenas's agrarianism.

CHAPTER 4

1. Friedrich Katz, notes:

> There was only one major leader of the revolutionary movement in Chihuahua who can be said to have sprung from the ranks of the peasantry: Francisco "Pancho" Villa. To be sure, his link to, or descent from, this group is by no means clear. His background was extremely varied—hacienda peon, miner, bandit, merchant—and much of it is shrouded in legend. The story of his becoming a bandit because he killed a *hacendado* who raped his sister is still disputed, but his record as a cattle rustler is not. Rustling was not considered a disreputable activity among a large segment of Chihuahua's pre-revolutionary population for, until 1885, everyone had access to large herds of unclaimed cattle that grazed on the state's immense public lands. After that year, when the Apache wars ceased and railroads linked this northern state to the United States and to the rest of Mexico, the *hacendados* began exporting cattle and appropriating public lands. The traditional right of the people to dispose of such "wild" cattle was abolished, but in the eyes of many Chihuahua peasants Villa was simply reinstating a privilege that [had] once been theirs. (Katz, *The Secret War in Mexico* [Chicago, 1981])

2. The fullest study of Sonora's crucial contribution to the revolution is Héctor Aguilar Camin, *La frontera nomada: Sonora y la revolución mexicana* (Mexico City, 1977).

3. Michael C. Meyer has made a noteworthy contribution to our understanding of this historical figure with his study, *Huerta: A Political Biography*. In a general evaluation of the Huerta dictatorship, he writes:

> Politically, to be sure, the Huerta regime represents a counterrevolution as it manifested a reaction against the government which resulted from the overthrow of Díaz. But Huerta and his advisors both realized that the days of Díaz were gone forever and the advisors recognized the need for reform. They did not attempt to stem the new energies and forces unleashed in 1910; rather they attempted to moderate them. Except for the obvious and censurable abuses of political power,

there is simply no evidence to support the contention, repeated in study after study, that the Huerta regime represents an attempted reincarnation of the Age of Díaz.

That Mexico desperately needed a fundamental social transformation is scarcely at issue. While new scholarship may yet show that there was more opportunity in Porfirian Mexico than is commonly supposed, nevertheless, society was predominantly stagnant. The possibility of social mobility was nonexistent except for the select few. What is at issue is precisely when and how that social transformation was spawned. The answer is embodied in an analysis of the universal historical problem of continuity and change. The orthodox representation of the early Revolution is that the change came with Madero, that the Huerta regime embodied a belated attempt at reestablishing Porfirian continuity, and that Carranza methodically began to sow the revolutionary seeds first thrown into the winds by Madero. But one can embrace this interpretation only if he does not allow the historical data to get in his way. What clearly emerges is an undulating line of progression from the late Díaz period to the Madero presidency, through the Huerta regime to Venustiano Carranza and the Constitution of 1917. And even more inescapable is the fact that the downward undulations are not more prominent from 1913 to 1914 than in any other period circumscribed by the fall of Díaz and the promulgation of the new constitution. (P. 231)

Although we may disagree with some of Meyer's formulations, it is impossible to deny the solidity of his arguments against demoniacal views of Huerta.

4. *The Eighteenth Brumaire,* p. 244.

5. John Reed, *Insurgent Mexico*

6. In November 1920, in a speech on the organization of the Red Army, Trotsky said:

> Every viable army has a moral idea as its basis. How does this assert itself? For Kudinich (the prototype of Suvorov's Tsarist soldier), the religious idea illuminates the idea of Tsarist power, giving light to his peasant existence and fulfilling, albeit in a primitive manner, the role of a moral idea. At the critical moment, when his age-old faith was shaken, and he found nothing with which to replace it, Kudinich surrendered. Modification of the moral idea provoked the disintegration

of the army. Only a fundamentally new idea could allow a revolutionary army to be built. This does not mean, however, that each soldier knows for what he is fighting. It would be a lie to suggest that it does. It is said that when a social-revolutionary who had taken refuge in the south was asked about the causes of the Red Army victories, he replied that the Red Army knew in whose name it was fighting. Still, this does not mean that every red soldier knew. But as we have a high percentage of conscious individuals who know in whose name we are fighting, we do have a moral idea that can produce victory.

7. Katz, *Secret War,* is the main source concerning U.S. intervention in the revolution and the rivalry among U.S., British, and German imperialism over Mexico.

CHAPTER 5

1. All emphases and capital letters are in the original text, quoted here from Gildardo Magaña, *Emiliano Zapata y el agrarismo en México.*
2. Ibid. Emphasis in the original.

CHAPTER 6

1. The Spanish word *silla* means both "chair" and "saddle" (Translator's note).
2. Quoted in Jesús Silva Herzog, *Breve historia de la revolución mexicana* (Mexico City, 1966).
3. Francisco J. Grajales, "The Campaigns of General Obregón," prologue to Alvaro Obregón, *Eight Thousand Kilometers in Campaign* (Medico City: Fondo de Cultura Económica, 1970).
4. Tannenbaum, *Peace by Revolution,* p. 162.

CHAPTER 7

1. Some ex-COM leaders, such as Antonio Díaz Soto y Gama, had already joined the ranks of the Zapatists.
2. C. von Clausewitz, *On War* (Harmondsworth, 1968), pp. 140–41.
3. See Miguel Gutiérrez Reynoso, "El ocaso de la división del Norte," *Excelsior,* June 17–25, 1969.

4. See Alperovich and Rudenko, *La Revolución mexicana de 1910–1917 y la política de los Estados Unidos* (Mexico City, 1960).
5. Reed, *Insurgent Mexico,* p. 276.
6. Alperovich and Rudenko, *La Revolución Mexicana.*
7. Concerning the attitude of the various imperialist powers toward the Mexican revolution, Katz writes in the last chapter of *The Secret War:*

> Between the fall of Madero and the end of World War I, three powers attempted to influence events in Mexico on a massive scale: Great Britain, Germany and the United States. Britain's policies had the most important repercussions in Mexico in 1913–14 and those of Germany from 1915 to 1919. United States policy was of decisive importance for events in Mexico during the whole course of the revolution.
>
> The interventions of Britain and Germany in Mexican affairs were largely indirect and covert, those of the United States were direct and overt. Britain and Germany managed to maintain consistently good relations with the factions they supported (Britain with Huerta throughout his regime, the Germans with Carranza from mid-1916 until his overthrow), but the Americans did not. For short periods of time, the Europeans exercised considerable influence on the factions they favored. In the long run, however, only the United States decisively influenced the course of the Mexican Revolution.
>
> Among the great powers, Britain pursued the most consistent policy in Mexico between 1910 and 1920. Not even remotely considering the option of sending a Lawrence to influence the Mexican revolutionaries, it opposed every revolutionary faction in those ten years and consistently supported counter-revolutionary groups. The conviction expressed by the British envoy Thurstan that what Mexico needed was "a government of white men," was shared by most responsible officials in the British Foreign Office. Racism, however, was not the main determinant of Britain's policies. The close relationship of British interests with Porfirian forces as well as the fluctuating alliances of the revolutionaries with both the United States and Germany strongly influenced the British role. On the whole, the consistency of British policy was matched by its ineffectiveness. . . .
>
> Among all the great powers the policies of the United States toward the Mexican Revolution seemed the most contradictory. Every victorious faction in Mexico between 1910 and 1919 enjoyed the sympathy,

and in most cases the direct support of US authorities in its struggle for power. In each case, the administration in Washington soon turned on its new friends with the same vehemence it had initially expressed in supporting them.

The Taft administration at first viewed the Madero revolution with great sympathy. Some historians maintain that Taft even gave it covert support. One year later that same administration sharply reversed its stand concerning Madero and in February 1913 Ambassador Henry Lane Wilson played a decisive role in the coup that toppled Madero and brought Huerta to power.

Woodrow Wilson took even more energetic measures and interfered even more drastically in Mexico's affairs in order to force Huerta from the office to which H. Lane Wilson had aided in elevating him. In the process of fighting Huerta, Woodrow Wilson threw his support to both Pancho Villa and Venustiano Carranza. A short time later he turned against Villa and helped Carranza to inflict a decisive defeat upon the latter. Subsequently he nearly went to war with Carranza.

This consistent American inconsistency had one common denominator: the fact that every Mexican faction, once it assumed power, carried out policies considered detrimental by both the administration in Washington and US business interests.

8. Pancho Villa met the punitive expedition with classical guerrilla tactics. Katz writes:

> He soon became a master at the art of guerrilla warfare and the Americans proved virtually impotent to do anything against him. This fact was registered with great bitterness by the officers of the punitive expedition. "I feel just a bit like a man looking for a needle in a haystack," Pershing wrote, and he went on to urge the United States government to agree to the occupation of the whole of the state of Chihuahua by American troops. A short time later he went a step further and advocated the occupation of all of Mexico. These views were enthusiastically shared by one of his lieutenants, George S. Patton. "Intervention will be useless; we must take the country and keep it," he wrote to his father in September 1916. The basis for his opinion was expressed in another letter by Patton: "you have no idea of the utter degradation of the inhabitants. One must be a fool indeed to think that people half savage and wholly ignorant will ever

form a republic. It is a joke. A despot is all they know or want." (*Se-cret War*, p. 309)

9. The letter is one of a number of documents found among the belongings of a Villist who died in Columbus. It was first published in 1975, having been discovered in United States archives. See Friedrich Katz, "Pancho Villa and the Attack on Columbus, New Mexico," *American Historical Review* 83 (February 1978).

10. For a detailed analysis see Katz, *Secret War*.

11. On August 29, 1916, the radical Constitutionalist General Múgica sent an interesting letter from Teapa, Tabasco, to General Salvador Alvarado, commander of the Southeast Army Corps based in Mérida, Yucatán. The letter begins:

> Dear General, It seems proper to tell you of my immediate impressions, since I know that I am talking to a pure blood-comrade, not to one of the countless last-minute supporters or converts. . . . I do not agree with the general policy: it is not only misdirected and ill-defined, but has many conciliationist features. You are well aware that the great ideal of this revolution is the land question, in connection with which only a single clear, semi-liberal (though unsettled) law has been issued: the law of 6 January.

It goes on to say that the application of this law has been paralyzed, and that "the press—that is, the voice of officialdom—emphatically declares that with the national lands the problem is solved." "Here in Tabasco," Múgica complains, "I received orders from the Chief to return the El Chimal Island lands to the Tabasco Agricultural Company, Ltd. (composed of Spaniards and Yankees)—lands robbed from the children of Jonutla which I had restored to them as communal land on the basis of the only agrarian law issued by the Revolution."

He then refers to the violation and plunder of Michoacán Indian woodland perpetrated by officials of the revolution, Porfirists, Huertists, and Yankees, and says that similar actions are taking place throughout the Republic.

> When I was in Mexico City in February and March, I saw more rancor towards the Villists, Zapatists and Conventionists than towards the Huertists. Dr Miguel Silva was being remorselessly persecuted, while the lawyer Olaguibel went unpunished. The journalists of the revolution (apart from Novelo and Martinez) are men from the dictatorship

and the coup d'etat. They are 80 percent Huertists in the ministry of finance, and though they are a minority in other ministries, there are enough of them.

Mugica next recounts the history of some ex-Huertist governors and their various abuses, mentions the revival of old-regime courts, and denounces the administrative chaos of most ministerial departments, full of individuals whom "revolutionary opinion rejects as intriguers or careerists."

Without even mentioning the other major source of friction, the repression of the general strike a few weeks earlier, the final paragraph reaches a pitch of indignation and bitterness that indicates the high tension then existing between Constitutionalist tendencies:

Where will all this lead us, dear general? Send me some encouragement, because I feel truly sad and disillusioned at the sight of so many wasted lives, so many orphans, so much national wealth and energy sacrificed to achieve a mere half of what we wanted for the fatherland. Just think that in those days it was decided to rearrange the state churches so that public schools could be put in them, since there are no suitably owned buildings in the region. But my overwhelming eagerness, which seems suited to the present situation, was shattered by an order from the commander-in-chief. For although there are currently no services, holy pictures or priests in these buildings—the revolution having destroyed everything—the "ladies and gentlemen" from various parts of the region pleaded for them to be placed in their charge. I confess that this blow deeply affected my faith as a convinced rebel. I now see that any force alien to the revolution can do more than its fervent supporters; I see that influence is again rearing its head, and I can foresee that the fatherland will still have to pay in blood for its redemption, progress and advance. But if this is my view, you will say in fright, why remain within the Constitutionalist movement? Why not leave, why not split away? Because I still have faith in Carranza the leader, because I still think the ideal can be saved, because I love the cause with a fervent, blinding impulse. This is the reason which must keep you fighting against the central ideas and policy, different from your own, which have in the end been imposed on you. . . . I do not think I am mistaken: my principles are the same as yours, and you must feel the same as I do. Remember now and again the property tax, re-

member now and again the agrarian law, and remember everything unknown to me which they have destroyed or threatened. But you have
not left that behind, just as I will not do unless I completely renounce
my self-denial and conviction, pushing aside truth and constancy. So I
repeat, my dear general, send me some encouragement, because I want
to go on working for our ideal, and I need to believe that our efforts will
not be wasted and we will not remain for ever at a standstill.

It should be noted in passing that this letter gives a rapid idea of the
innumerable motives still driving forward Villa's peasant war.

12. Tannenbaum, *Peace by Revolution*, pp. 166–67.

13. A clear example is the redistribution of land. By the end of 1919, the
Carranza government had transferred communal lands to only 148
villages, while many of the army-controlled haciendas had been returned to their old Porfirian owners. By 1926, fewer than 5 percent
of the rural population had received a total land area amounting to
less than 3 percent of the territory of the Republic. At the other extreme, in 1923 half the rural area of the country was concentrated in
holdings of five thousand hectares and owned by fewer than twenty-
seven hundred proprietors. Nearly a quarter of this total (22.9 percent) belonged to just 114 latifundia, each more than hundred
thousand hectares in size.

14. The author's study on the Cardenist period is Adolfo Gilly, *El
cardenismo—Una utopía mexicana* (Mexico City: Cal y Arena, 1994;
Ediciones Era, 2001).

CHAPTER 8

1. Basing his work on an exhaustive study of mainly Zapatist archives,
John Womack has given a detailed account of this period in *Zapata
and the Mexican Revolution*. Womack's book has been the main source
material for this chapter.

2. Womack (pp. 229–30) gives this description of Palafox at that time:

The revolution in land tenure in Morelos in 1915 was an orderly process, largely because of Manuel Palafox. His ambition brought himself
and other *agraristas* into the Conventionist government, and his
peremptory conduct there assured official ratification of local reforms. This seemed only the beginning of a historic career. When

the Zapatistas had occupied Mexico City, Palafox had entered the precincts of glory and stateliness, the classic forum of the heroes of his country. He was then a mere twenty-nine years old. What this meticulous, cunning, intense little man conceived his destiny to be is still unknown, his private archives supposedly having burned, his associates mostly having died or learned to vilify him, his few surviving confidants secretive and in doubt about him; but it seems likely that he imagined himself another great reforming figure in the line that went back through the immortals of the mid-nineteenth century, Benito Juárez and Melchor Ocampo, back to the enlightened founding fathers of the Republic. During his stay in the capital he behaved as if by design to lay claim to historians' attention. Bold and ingenious in his programme, determined, arrogant, incredibly busy, Palafox sprang into action at the first opportunity. Leaving a reliable aide, Santiago Orozco, to run the southern headquarters, he set up another Zapatista headquarters in Mexico City after the Xochimilco conference. And from his office in the Hotel Cosmos—"The Leading International Hotel in Mexico City, San Juan de Letrán 12, with two telephones"—he manoeuvred strenuously to advance the *agrarista* cause.

Within days, Palafox became secretary of agriculture in the Conventionist cabinet, the ranking Zapatista in the government. And to the reporter who asked him on the day of his appointment if he meant now, like officials before him, "to study the agrarian question," he replied, "No, señor, I'll not dedicate myself to that. The agrarian question I've got amply studied. I'll dedicate myself to carrying [the reform] into the field of practice."

3. The Executive Council is described in the preamble as "the supreme authority of the Revolution while the Sovereign Revolutionary Convention is not sitting." Zapatism, which in the Ayala Plan invoked Benito Juárez, refers here to the communal rights that preceded the laws of Juárez, and the preexisting titles that protect those rights. In the name of those rights and titles, the campesino communities that supported the 1869 rebellion of Julio Chávez had arisen against Benito Juárez.

4. A number of other radical figures and currents joined Palafox in drafting the agrarian law, and four of the five signatories are particularly significant. Díaz Soto y Gama and the Magañas do not appear on the list.

But it does include, after Palafox himself, Otilio Montaño, Zapata's collaborator on the Ayala Plan; Jenaro Amezcua, who would later represent the Zapatist movement abroad, directing its revolutionary propaganda from a base in Havana; and Miguel Mendoza L. Schwerdtfegert.

Schwerdtfegert was one of the members of the Casa del Obrero Mundial who joined the Zapatists in mid-1914 and helped to give their socialist tendencies a more precise outline. Others were Díaz Soto y Gama, then a semi-anarchist; Rafael Pérez Taylor, a socialist; Luis Méndez, in whose house the ephemeral Workers Socialist Party was founded in 1911; and Octavio Jahn, a French syndicalist and self-declared veteran of the Paris Commune. In 1914 Schwerdtfegert published a study under the title *Free Land!*, setting forth his opposition to smallholder redistribution and arguing for nationalization and collective farming of the land. These views were possibly influenced by the American disciples of Henry George. At any event, although Schwerdtfegert later rallied to Obregón, his ideas of the time influenced the agrarian law which he signed and helped to elaborate. In *Free Land!* he writes:

We should not let ourselves be lulled into false expectations: the landowners' proposal to subdivide landed property will merely tend to swell the number of privileged people, increasing their protection but not affording the just distribution of wealth we so ardently desire. Ownership is extremely divided in France, while in England the land is concentrated in the hands of thirty thousand farmers. Yet the French and the English people suffer the same misery and degradation, and the land monopoly ensures that the condition of the proletariat is the same in both cases.

Division of the land will undoubtedly augment the well-off class of the population, but without improving the condition of the laboring class. The booty will be more widely distributed, but those who are robbed will suffer the same privation. As now, the proletarians will not have the least stake in the land, and will in no way be better off.

Moreover, division of the land tends to diminish the production of wealth. Everyone who observes the course of industries knows that they tend toward ever greater concentration in order to produce on a large scale and to avoid the losses of small-scale production. Workshops have thus given way to big factories, low-load transport to railways and steamships, and peasant-owned plots to plantations. The cultivation of large fields is more productive of wealth than small-scale farming, for modern, costly machinery makes it efficient and less laborious for the cultivators.

Thus division of the land is in no way advantageous to the laborer's condition or to the production of wealth. It will tend to block all paths to the abolition of private land-ownership, benefiting the majority of those who defend this institution. It should therefore be absolutely rejected by the wealth-producing classes. (Quoted in Diego G. López Rosado, *Historia y pensamiento económico de México,* pp. 235–36)

5. Womack calls it "a radical agrarian law that gave the secretary of agriculture immense authority over urban and rural property and national resources." "By this remarkable law," he adds, "the Department of Agriculture would be the central agency of *a stupendous nationalizing reformation of Mexico*" (*Zapata,* p. 246; emphasis added).

6. Marte R. Gómez recounts an incident witnessed by one of his Agrarian Commission colleagues in Amecameca:

He met a couple in the vicinity of the station: a señor, who stood out for miles as a city-man and, to cap it all, was dressed like a Plateros trickster in the last days of the Porfirio Díaz era; and a finely constumed señora, who was wearing a hat on her head and a fur around her neck. Our comrade was surprised that this pair of *catrines* dared to walk in such clothes to the zone controlled by southern troops, but at the time he did not think much more about it. Nor did he a few minutes later, when he heard people shouting and running in a crowd. But as he returned along the Sacromonte road, he shuddered at the sight of the two passers-by dangling from a conifer tree. The revolutionaries had punished them as an effigy of their wealthy class enemies, acting with a drama that Posada himself did not manage to capture. (Gómez, p. 102)

7. Womack, p. 242.

8. Womack (pp. 254, 258) quotes an anonymous account of the evacuation at the small village of Tehuztla, near Jojutla, in May 1916. Tehuztla

presented the look of a fair, but a fair of pain and rage. People's faces were furious. They would barely mumble out a few words, but everyone had a violent remark for the Constitutionalists on the tip of his tongue. In conversations, comments on the news alternated with reports which emigrants asked of each other about roads, villages, little settlements stuck up in the steepest part of the mountains, inaccessible, unheard of places—so they could go there to leave their families. . . . It seemed that a single family had reunited there. Everybody talked to everybody else with complete confidence. People lent each other help, and men and women who had never seen each other talked as intimately as old friends.

The witness adds that once they had deposited their family in some "inaccessible" place, the majority returned to dispute the land with the enemy. Their decision, surprising to the Constitutionalist officers, lies behind the resurgence of Zapatist resistance in the following months.

9. Womack (p. 268) quotes a letter written by a Zapatist a few months earlier:

Never did anyone believe that there would be ruffians who surpassed Huerta's . . . come and see . . . pueblos completely burned down, timbered levelled, cattle stolen, crops that were cultivated with labor's sweat harvested by the enemy . . . to fill the boxcars of their long trains and be sold in the capital. . . . Robles, damned a thousand times, is little in comparison. . . . This business of seeing three or four men pulling a plough, taking the place of the beasts they owned but which the Carrancistas stole from them—this is a revolting thing.

10. Womack.
11. Womack, pp. 275–78.
12. "A revolutionary epoch quickly exhausts people," Trotsky wrote in 1929. "People spend themselves, their nerves fail, consciousness gets worn out and falls apart. This fact can always be observed in a revolutionary struggle." "Tenacity, Tenacity, Tenacity!" in Leon Trotsty, *Writings 1929* (New York, 1975), p. 163.
13. See Carlos Rama, *Historia social latinoamericana*. In his novel *The Birth of Our Strength,* written in Leningrad between 1929 and 1930—memoirs of his participation as a typesetter in the revolution of Barcelona in the year 1917—Victor Serge recalls a Mexican sailor, El Chorro, who spoke "with admiration of the legendary Emiliano Zapata who founded in the mountains of Morelos, with revolutionary campesinos, descendents of the ancient copper-colored races, a social

republic, the first of modern times," the Mexican proudly affirmed.

14. The return of the haciendas became a general, uninterrupted process after 1915. The new bourgeoisie emerging from the Constitutionalist movement thereby showed its understanding of the fact that the revolution was on the decline; and that its hands were becoming free to restore full land ownership rights, now including its own, and to forge alliances with the old property-owning classes on the basis of its privileged position within the state apparatus. Katz remarks:

> In his proclamations Carranza had repeatedly underlined the necessity for radical agrarian reform, which was to expropriate the large landholdings of the old Porfirian *hacendados,* but, as in the case of Madero, he took few practical steps in this direction. In fact, his actual policy went in the opposite direction. From 1915 on, he ordered the return of the confiscated haciendas to their former owners. By 1917 he was in a position to inform the Constituent Assembly of the successful implementation of such measures in most of the parts of Mexico under his control. There were a few notable exceptions, such as Tlaxcala, where a former Zapata ally, Domingo Arenas, had joined with Carranza. In return, the First Chief allowed some of his peasant followers to keep lands they had occupied. In Sonora, some generals became owners of haciendas they had confiscated from Porfirian landowners. Unfortunately the development and causes of this massive return of land, which distinguishes the Mexican Revolution from other great social revolutions, have never been studied. It is therefore not easy to analyze the modes of action and the reactions of those affected by it and those who carried it out. Carranza's own motivations are relatively easy to explain, since his actions were quite in keeping with his conservative ideology; in addition, however, economic and political factors played an important role. (*Secret War,* pp. 256–57)

15. As is typical for a peasant hero, Zapata's legend has remained in countless ballads that still circulate in Morelos and testify to the vitality of the revolution. Here is one example from this period: "But if my luck runs out / Or I fall on the field of war / I shall die firmly shouting / Viva the southern army! Viva Zapata!"

In an essay published in 1970, Carlos Fuentes mentions a strange example of the revolutionary function this legend continues to serve.

As he and an American writer were passing through the Valley of Morelos, they "stopped at a village with no name, forgotten by the route-maps and road-signs." "We asked a peasant what the village was called," Fuentes continues. "The answer was: 'Garduño in time of peace, Zapata in time of war.'" Fuentes does not point out, however, that the peasant spoke thus to two strangers from the city, one of them with gringo features, possibly hostile and certainly alien to the peasantry. Without renouncing the traditional cordiality toward travelers, he gave them a special kind of warning. "Zapata, if you're looking for war," he meant to say. And yet, he phrased it as a general statement, so that if the strangers proved friendly, they would understand it in a different way: "The times of the revolutionary war will return, and the day is not far off when all the villages of Morelos will be called Zapata." The peasant's thinking was not a static nostalgia for the past, but a dynamic preparation for the future.

16. The southern revolution, and even Zapata, underwent a number of socialist and anarchist influences, of which the most important, spread among various tendencies, came from the Flores Magón brothers. More than thirty years later, in his book *La revolución agraria del sur y Emiliano Zapata, su caudillo,* Antonio Díaz Soto y Gama persisted in downplaying these influences. The following account may nevertheless be considered accurate, since in a characteristic confusion of ideas, the author proves the exact opposite of what he had wanted to demonstrate:

In 1916 or 1917 another Zapatist leader, Colonel Prudencio R. Casals, a man of very advanced views, gave General Zapata a book which expounded the anarchist theories—I do not recall its title—and asked him to read it.

We saw Zapata tell the chief of his guard to keep the book in his horse's "case" or saddle-bag, so that he could read it later with the necessary calm.

After he had done this, he summoned Casals and said: "I have carefully acquainted myself with the contents of the book you lent me, and I tell you frankly that although I have nothing at all against its ideas, I realize how many years will have to pass before they can be put into practice. As to whether I should alter or expand the Ayala Plan in any way so as to make room for these ideas, I assure you I won't do any such

thing. For I'm convinced that if the Plan's proposals are fully implemented, they will lead to happiness for the Mexican people. So I won't
get involved in the profundities you are putting before me."
Díaz Soto y Gama adds a similar account that Serafin Robles, Zapata's
secretary at the time, gave in a 1947 interview. According to Robles,
Zapata replied:

> I have read the books you gave me with great attention, and I've lis-
> tened with great interest to your explanation of communism. These
> ideas seem fine and human to me, but I must tell you that it's not our
> job to carry them into practice. That will be up to future generations,
> and who knows how many years will be required for them to take
> root. . . . That's my opinion, and I won't add or subtract a single
> comma from the Ayala Plan. When what it says is fulfilled, I'm sure it
> will bring happiness to the people.

CHAPTER 9

1. N. Campobello, *Cartucho: Relatos de la lucha en el norte de México.*
2. N. Campobello, *Apuntas sobre la vida militar de Francisco Villa.*
3. The detachment that seems to have marked Angeles's solitary figure
   even appears in the irony of an incident from his final days. Being an
   atheist, the general refused to receive the priest who wanted to hear his
   last confession. In *Cartucho,* Nellie Campobello recalls how, as a young
   girl, she sneaked into Angeles's trial, only to be found and sent away by
   her mother on the grounds that "Villa may come at any minute to free
   Angeles, and then there'll be a lot of bloodshed." Angeles "had already
   been shot," she wrote later.

> I went with Mother to see him: he was not in the coffin, he was wear-
> ing a black suit and had some cotton-wool in his ears, his eyes were
> firmly closed. He looked as if he were tired from the days he had spent
> talking at the military court—three days I think it was. Pepita Chacón
> was chatting with Mother, and I did not miss a word. She had been to
> see him the previous night. He was eating chicken for supper and was
> very pleased to see her come in: they had known each other for years.
> When he saw the black suit left on a chair, he asked: "Who sent that?"
> "The Revilla family," someone replied. "Why should they bother?
> They are in a very bad situation themselves. I can be buried with the

suit that I am wearing," he said, slowly, sipping his coffee. As they were saying farewell, he asked: "Pepita, what became of that lady you introduced me to one day in your house?" "She's dead, general, she's in heaven. Say hello from me." Pepita assured Mother that he answered with a graceful smile: "Yes, I'll be very glad to say hello."

Similarly, the sense of fatalism that had accompanied Angeles since he crossed the border is inadvertently recorded in the ballad of his execution: "I'm not such a coward / To walk in fear of death / Death kills no one at all / 'Tis fate that strikes us down." [Yo no soy de los cobardes / que le temen a la muerte. / La muerte no mata a nadie, / la matadora es la suerte:]

4. Womack describes the reaction of these officials to reports of Guajardo's treacherous assassination of Zapata:

In private the affair irked many established revolutionaries. Army officers especially resented the promotions coming to Guajardo and his partners in the plot. Some even complained to the President, and leaked their gripes to the press. Other more generous revolutionaries plunged into the gloom of divided loyalties. A young aide in the government's General Supply Office, Jesús Romero Flores, later remembered the morning he read the reports. He and his superior, General Francisco Múgica, considered themselves on "the extreme left." As delegates to the 1916–17 Constitutional Convention, both had advocated radical articles on land, labor and education; in swinging the votes to drive the reforms into the charter, Múgica had been the key figure in the key committee. Although in the early days in 1911 Múgica had once volunteered to fight Zapata, he had come through the years to admire his long and constant struggle. Besides, he could not dent his childhood friendship with the Magaña brothers—whose father had helped him through the Zamora seminary and later as an oppositionist newspaperman. Romero Flores also sympathized with the southern agraristas, and he too, another Michoacano, knew the Magañas. On learning of the assassination he thought the times were "black." He and Mugica spent that Friday morning at their office "deeply moved, almost without speaking." This new death reminded him of the past winter's terrible flu epidemic, when "a feeling of sadness and fear seemed to envelop everything." When he read the government's boast of treachery, his depression burst into indignation against "the mob of wheeler-dealers" in power.

5. "The Bonapartist regime," Trotsky wrote in 1932,

> can attain a comparatively stable and durable character only in the event that it brings a revolutionary epoch to a close; when the relationship of forces has already been tested in battles; when the revolutionary classes are already spent but the possessing classes have not yet freed themselves from the fear: will not tomorrow bring new convulsions? Without this basic condition, that is, without a preceding exhaustion of the mass energies in battles, the Bonapartist regime is in no position to develop. ("The Only Road," p. 265)

6. Carranza had put a complete stop to the redistribution of land to the peasantry, leaving article 27 of the Constitution and his own law of January 1915 a dead letter. Figures show that Obregón's concessions in this field remained very limited. During Carranza's rule between 1915 and 1919, only 148 villages received communal land, 66 of them in the final year. A further 95 villages were endowed with such land in the transitional year, 1920. The figure for 1921, the first year of the Obregón regime, already climbed to 396, and the total was 1,981 for the period between 1921 and 1924.

At the same time, however, estates of more than five thousand hectares made up 50.1 percent of the rural area in 1923, belonging to 2,682 owners or less than 1 percent of all rural proprietors. The 114 *latifundistas* who each owned more than hundred thousand hectares accounted for nearly a quarter (22.9 percent) of all privately owned land. By 1926, a mere 4.3 percent of the peasant population had received any communal land, the area in question being 2.64 percent of the total in the Republic. The limited character of the land redistribution is even more apparent if we take regional disparities into account. In Morelos, the old Zapatist stronghold, 25 percent of the population had received an area of land amounting to 33 percent of the state total. In Yucatán 22 percent of the rural population had received some land, in Campeche 14 percent. In Puebla and San Luis Potosí, 9 to 10 percent of the land area had passed into the hands of the villages. In the rest of the country the figures were minute. Tannenbaum, *The Mexican Agrarian Revolution,* (New York, 1939.)

CHAPTER 10

1. V.I. Lenin, *State and Revolution* (Moscow, 1970), p. 46.
2. Trotsky, *History of the Russian Revolution,* p. 15.
3. See Leopoldo Solis, *La realidad económica mexicana: retrovisión y perspectivas* (Mexico City, 1970); and J.R. Womack, "The Mexican Economy During the Revolution," *Marxist Perspectives* No. 4 (Winter 1978), which has provided the basis for some of my arguments.
4. Solis, *La realidad económica,* pp. 92–93.
5. "As far as land redistribution under the Cárdenas regime is concerned, 10,651 *ejidos* were formed through the distribution of 20,136,935 hectares to 775,845 peasants. Together with the redistribution measures taken by previous governments, this gave a total of 13,091 *ejidos* with 31,158,332 hectares distributed to 1,723,371 peasants. The major regions of land redistribution under Cárdenas were: Comarca Lagunera, the Yaqui zone, Los Mochis, Yucatán, Lombardia and Nueva Italia, El Mante, Mexicali and Soconusco." (Gerrit Huizer, *La lucha campesina en México.*) In *La tenencia de la tierra en México,* one of the most serious surveys of the land question, Carlos Tello argues that in 1940 there were still 308 latifundia with an average of more than 100,000 hectares, and 1,179 between 10,000 and 40,000 hectares covering a total land area of more than 54 million hectares.

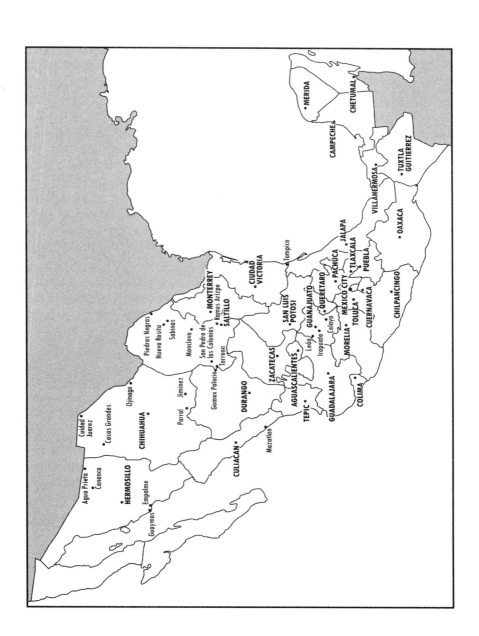

INDEX